DATE DUE

SEP 28 2017		
12-5-17		

DEMCO 38-296

BLOOM'S PERIOD STUDIES

Elizabethan Drama
The American Renaissance
Literature of the Holocaust
The Victorian Novel
The Harlem Renaissance
English Romantic Poetry

BLOOM'S PERIOD STUDIES

The Harlem Renaissance

Edited and with an introduction by
Harold Bloom
Sterling Professor of the Humanities
Yale University

CHELSEA HOUSE
PUBLISHERS
An imprint of Infobase Publishing

Bloom's Period Studies: The Harlem Renaissance

Copyright © 2004 by Infobase Publishing
Introduction © 2004 by Harold Bloom

Chelsea House
An imprint of Infobase Publishing
132 West 31st Street
New York NY 10001

ISBN-10: 0-7910-7679-2
ISBN-13: 978-0-7910-7679-8

Library of Congress Cataloging-in-Publication Data

The Harlem Renaissance / edited and with an introduction by Harold Bloom.
    p. cm. — (Bloom's Period Studies)
Includes bibliographical references and index.
    ISBN 0-7910-7679-2 (hardcover) — ISBN 0-7910-7986-4 (pbk.) 1. American literature—African American authors—History and criticism. 2. American literature—20th century—History and criticism. 3. Harlem (New York, N.Y.)—Intellectual life—20th century. 4. African Americans—Intellectual life—20th century. 5. African Americans in literature. 6. Harlem Renaissance. I. Bloom, Harold. II. Series.
    PS153.N5H225 2003
    810.9'896073—dc22   2003016873

You can find Chelsea House on the World Wide Web at
http://www.chelseahouse.com

Contributing Editor: Aimee LaBrie
Cover designed by Keith Trego

Printed in the United States of America

Bang EJB 10 9 8 7 6 5 4 3 2

This book is printed on acid-free paper.

Contents

Editor's Note   vii

Introduction   1
Harold Bloom

Harlem Renaissance Re-examined   5
Warrington Hudlin

Shape and Shapers of the Movement   13
Margaret Perry

Black-White Symbiosis: Another Look
at the Literary History of the 1920s   23
Amritjit Singh

Langston Hughes: Evolution of the Poetic Persona   35
Raymond Smith

"Refined Racism": White Patronage
in the Harlem Renaissance   53
Bruce Kellner

Color, Sex, and Poetry in the Harlem Renaissance   67
Akasha Gloria Hull

Black Autobiography and the Comic Vision   99
Richard K. Barksdale

Harlem and the First Black Renaissance   113
Eva Lennox Birch

Reading the Harlem Renaissance   123
David Levering Lewis

Black Manhattan   149
James Weldon Johnson

The New Negro   161
Alain Locke

The Negro Renaissance and Its Significance   167
    Charles S. Johnson

The Pulse of the Negro World   179
    Amy Helene Kirschke

The Negro Author and His Publisher   195
    Sterling A. Brown

Aspects of Identity in Nella Larsen's Novels   207
    Cheryl A. Wall

Survival and Song: Women Poets   223
of the Harlem Renaissance
    Maureen Honey

Iconography of the Harlem Renaissance   243
    Patti Capel Swartz

Toomer's *Cane* and the Harlem Renaissance   255
    Geneviève Fabre

The Syncopated African   275
    Michel Feith

Chronology   295

Contributors   301

Bibliography   305

Acknowledgments   315

Index   319

Editor's Note

My Introduction first ponders Zora Neale Hurston's short story "Sweat," a fierce celebration of life feeding upon death. In briefly considering some of the poets of the Harlem Renaissance, I stress the refreshing freedom from Eliot—Pound High Modernism in the Keatsian mode of the best poems of Claude McKay, Countee Cullen, and the earlier Sterling Brown, as well as the *Cane* (1933) of Jean Toomer.

Warrington Hudlin, Margaret Perry, and Amritjit Singh all give useful overviews of the movement, while Raymond Smith charts the development of Langston Hughes.

White Patronage is patronized by Bruce Kellner, after which Akasha Gloria Hull examines gender issues.

Comedy in African-American autobiography is considered by Richard K. Barskdale, while Eva Lennox Birch reflects upon Harlem as literary context.

David Levering Lewis attempts a general introduction to reading the movement, after which James Weldon Johnson, poet of the eloquent *God's Trombones*, perceives complex elements in the Harlem context.

Alain Locke argues for a radical newness in the Renaissance of blackness while Charles S. Johnson and Amy Helene Kirschke offer contrasting views of the movement.

The poet Sterling A. Brown muses with gentle irony on the relationship between black author and publisher, after which Cheryl A. Wall considers the tragic mulatto woman character in the fiction of Nella Larsen.

Anne Spencer and other women poets of the Renaissance are studied by Maureen Honey while Patti Capel Swartz identifies jazz performers as the leading icons of the movement.

Jean Toomer's *Cane* is analyzed by Geneviève Fabre, after which Michel Feith concludes this volume by bringing together aspects of music and a visual art with the literature of the Harlem Renaissance.

Introduction

I

As a narrative fiction, Zora Neale Hurston's *Their Eyes Were Watching God* (1937) evidently was an attempt at exorcism, written in seven weeks or so after the end of an intense love affair. It seems now to owe at least part of its fame to a more general exorcism, one that the fiercely individualistic Hurston might have scorned, since she was ideologue, whether of race or of gender. Her vitalism allies her art to D.H. Lawrence's; like him she yields only to visionary politics, and like him also she celebrates a rare sexual fulfillment as an image of finality. The madness of the later Lawrence of *The Plumed Serpeant* might have amused her, yet I think of Lawrence at times when I reread *Their Eyes Were Watching God* or "Sweat," the most memorable of her short stories. Delia Jones the washwoman, the protagonist of "Sweat," suffers the brutality of her husband, Sykes, who after fifteen years of marriage sees her only as an obstacle to his happiness. The story begins with Sykes maliciously frightening her by letting his bullwhip fall upon her from behind, so that she believes a snake is attacking her. At the story's conclusion, an actual rattlesnake, introduced into the house by Sykes, rids Delia of her oppressor forever.

> She saw him on his hands and knees as soon as she reached the door. He crept an inch or two towards her—all that he was able, and she saw his horribly swollen neck and his one open eye shining with hope. A surge of pity too strong for support bore her away from that eye that must, could not, fail to see the tubs. He would see the lamp. Orlando with its doctors was too far. She could scarcely reach the Chinaberry Tree, where she waited in the growing heat while inside she knew the cold river was creeping up and up to extinguish that eye which must know by now that she knew.

1

The dispassionate vitality of this terror is free of animus; we are nowhere in the neighborhood of any of our contemporary versions of the spirit of revenge in the defensive war of some African-American women writers against African-American men. What marks the passage, and so much else of Hurston's work, is its power, in the sense of Delia's thwarted potential for more life. The thwarting, in the broadest sense, brings death to Sykes, but brings no trite reflections of morality or of sexual politics, whether to Hurston or to her reader. What is given instead is vision of an eye shining with the desperate hope of survival until it approaches the extinction of a knowledge that destroys. Terror dominates Delia, but she experiences also a realization almost too subtle to convey, a mingling of compassion and of freedom. The triple repetition of that "one open eye" culminates a litany of destructions that have guaranteed Sykes's doom. Earlier in the story when Delia begs Sykes to have mercy and remove the rattlesnake from the house, his reply is prophetic: "Ah aint gut tuh do nuthin'uh de kin'—fact is ah aint got tuh do nuthin' but die." In Hurston, freedom is always an image of pathos, and never a political metaphor. But Hurston, in literature as in life, was High Romantic, and for her the pathos of freedom always bordered upon death. Sykes dies so that Delia can live and be free; passion, in Hurston, as in Lawrence, feeds upon life. It hardly matters that Delia, who once loved Sykes, now hates him, while Janie Crawford still loves Tea Cake when she is compelled to kill him. In Hurston, the drive is always that of the heroic vitalist, a drive that seeks the freedom of more life, of the blessing. It was appropriate, even inevitable, that Hurston's hero should have an African Moses, who as man of the mountain ascended to bring back the only power that mattered, the blessings of more life for his people.

II

Countee Cullen, introducing his anthology, *Caroling Dusk* (1927), said of the African-American poets of the Twenties that "theirs is also the heritage of the English language." "Rhymed polemics," he added, did not typify his poets, who went back to Paul Laurence Dunbar (1872-1906) and then included James Weldon Johnson, Claude McKay, Sterling Brown, Langston Hughes, Cullen himself, and Jean Toomer, the principal poets now generally assigned to the Harlem Renaissance. McKay, Brown, Hughes, Cullen, and Toomer hardly constituted a school, though they help to mark off an era. Except for Toomer, these poets had more in common with John Keats than with Ezra Pound and T.S. Eliot: their blackness insulated them against literary

Modernism, which may have been all to the good. Langston Hughes, on internal evidence, was stimulated by Carl Sandburg, now forgotten as a poet but useful in helping to focus Hughes's polemic on behalf of his people. Like his fellow poets of the Harlem Renaissance, Hughes shrewdly found his models in poets a little remote from him in time and place. Only in the generation prefigured by Melvin B. Tolson, and culminating in Robert Hayden and in Gwendolyn Brooks, is there much of a direct influx of the High Modernism of Eliot and of Hart Crane, and by then enough of a black poetic tradition had been forged so that the influence could be accommodated, most brilliantly by the Hayden of the "Middle Passage," "Runagate Runagate," and such ballads as those of "Remembrance" and "Nat Turner."

There are powerfully shaped poems in Claude McKay's work, where the mode of insulation is heightened by culture, and by the penitence of his turn to Roman Catholicism. His devotional sonnets seem to me stronger than most critics now acknowledge, and are scarcely fashionable, yet their highly wrought baroque intensity will preserve them into a time more receptive to formal control than our own. Countee Cullen already seems undervalued, as does Edwin Arlington Robinson, who meditated Keats for Cullen (on the basis again of internal evidence). Like Robinson, Cullen tones down his cadences to a perpetually dying fall, perfectly expressive not only of a sense of belatedness, as in Robinson, but also of a disciplined sensibility attempting an impossible balance between moral outrage and the realization that such outrage in itself cannot constitute a poem. Like Oscar Wilde, and like E. A. Robinson, Cullen knew that all bad poetry is sincere, and he had a passionate conviction that he must not add to the mass of bad poetry. He saw himself not as a black Keats but as a black poet who identified Keats both with nature and with poetry. At our confused moment, Keats is held by many to be irrelevant to an African-American poet, but Cullen prophesied against such a limitation in his "To Certain Critics":

> No radical option narrows grief,
> Pain is no patriot,
> And sorrow plaits her dismal leaf
> For all as lief as not.

The play on "leaf" and "lief," a melancholy poetic pun, is characteristic of Cullen, whose wry nobility of stance rarely faltered. Like McKay, Cullen may return in favor. Impressive as Langston Hughes's exemplary career was, his actual poems rarely go beyond the rough populism of Sandburg's *The People, Yes*. Few poets have been more consistently sincere in their poems than Hughes, and his selfless love for his people is morally powerful. But— unlike McKay and Cullen at their best—Hughes gave all his heart to prophesy, and little of his care to working out an adequate form. Sterling Brown wavered between the Milton-Keats mode of McKay and Cullen and the Sandburgian rhetoric of Hughes, finally evolving into more of the latter. It may be that Jean Toomer's *Cane* (1923) will be seen eventually as the poetic masterpiece of the Harlem Renaissance. Anything but an ideologue, Toomer is a strange, later flowering of what needs to be called black pastoral, and his friend Hart Crane. The best poem in Cullen's *Caroling Dusk* seems to me Toomer's "November Cotton Flower," with its magical vision of a time of natural epiphany:

> ... the branch, so pinched and slow
> Failed in its function as the autumn rake;
> Drouth fighting soil had caused the soil to take
> All water from the streams; dead birds were found
> In wells a hundred feet below the ground—
> Such was the season when the flower bloomed.

Toomer is the official link between Dunbar and the African-American poets of highest achievement: Robert Hayden and Jay Wright, Rita Dove and Thylias Moss. Protest and politics will wane as economic justice gains; someday perhaps black poets will be free for purely poetic struggles.

WARRINGTON HUDLIN

Harlem Renaissance Re-examined

The Harlem artists did not constitute a "school" of literature in the traditional sense. These individuals (Langston Hughes, Arna Bontemps, Zora Hurston, Rudolph Fisher, Wallace Thurman, Eric Walrond, Jean Toomer, among others) were drawn primarily by the metropolitan charisma of New York City and word that "something" was happening. For writers the atmosphere of New York was quite attractive. The major publishing houses were located there, the theaters on Broadway, in Greenwich Village, and of course, Harlem. It is not simplistic to say Harlem became the black cultural center, because New York City was the white one. These individuals, young, talented, began to think of themselves as a group, as the result of their association with scholars such as Alain Locke and Charles S. Johnson. There was no single literary philosophy guiding them, nor even a uniform perception of what phenomenon was taking place around them. They were linked together, however, by a common black experience. It is necessary, therefore, to keep in mind, when one refers to the ideas and attitude of the Harlem artist, that there will automatically be both exceptions and contradictions.

The foundation of the Renaissance was laid in the dialectical development of social and political thought during the turn of the century. The previous twenty years had been referred to as the "Age of Washington." This was a time when Booker T. Washington and the "men of Tuskegee"

From *The Harlem Renaissance Remembered*, edited by Arna Bontemps. © 1972 by Arna Bontemps.

waged their campaign for self-help and race pride. Washington's program centered on economic nationalism. He argued that the "beggar demands" of social and political equality be abandoned in favor of an interdependence relationship with whites. Black and white Americans were to remain "separate as the fingers but united as the fist." In keeping with the self-help orientation, technical skills replaced higher education as a priority. White America found his presentation, if not his program, palpable. The philosophy, while it served as a basis for much positive self-improvement for blacks, did not constitute any confrontation or demand of white America. W.E.B. Du Bois was to constitute his opposition.

W.E.B. Du Bois was appalled by Washington's accommodation. He embraced the notion of "group economy," but felt far too much of Washington's position had implications of black inferiority. Du Bois instead proposed the utilization of the "talented tenth," educated blacks who could not only work in the group interest but serve as living examples of blacks fitness for equality. He avowed political and social equality as goals to be obtained through protest and agitation.

It was on the note of agitation, however, that Du Bois and a good number of the middle class parted. Many of the black middle class rejected the thought of confronting, even annoying, for the fear that they might jeopardize their chance for assimilation. Du Bois was considered a radical. Their mentality is comparable to that of many free blacks during the slavery era. They feared the antislavery agitation might return them to servitude.

This same middle class had a presence in Harlem during the Renaissance. Their demand of the Harlem artist was that he write "uplift literature." The Harlem artist, however, had transcended the propaganda criteria. (Du Bois also shared the demand for propaganda.) The Renaissance, however, owed its existence to this middle class. The Harlem artist was indebted to the middle class on the most basic level; without a middle class (leisure class) there can be no literature, which is precisely the reason why there is no literature written by field slaves during slavery times—when would they write? Clearly the financial status of the middle class afforded the time to produce what comprises the Afro-American literature of the 1800s. In the case of the Renaissance there was an additional development. The Harlem writers constituted an intelligentsia rather than a middle class, the distinction being that the intelligentsia are individuals who have broken with their middle-class backgrounds to form a community of free intellectuals. (There were, however, middle-class writers in Harlem.)

There also was a debt by the definition of the Renaissance as a point in the Afro-American literary tradition. The assimilationist goals and literature of the middle class provided the Harlem artists with a focus from which to "bounce off," or more specifically a factor in the dialectical process. Most of the literature was written in the Romanticist tradition, saturated with Victorian ideals, and consisted of appeals to white America to consider them equal or at least better than the common blacks. Their black experience was considered a plague from which they wished to escape. Having ignored the depth of their own experience, they wrote escapist literature that was usually shallow and artificial.

These were the roots of the Renaissance which synthesized all these forces. The assimilation was rejected, the separation was rejected, the accommodation, the agitation were all discarded, or rather transcended, for a new perspective of themselves and their relationship to the rest of society, hence a "New Negro." Having dealt with the assimilationist-separationist dichotomy, the political philosophy of the Harlem artist was what one might best call "conditional integration." Whites were neither all bad nor all good, they were the people with whom you had to deal. The relationship would be based on their behavior, for the moral advantage was the black man's. There was a commitment for a better understanding and adjustment. (This is a key factor in the eventual collaboration with the white artist and the larger white society.) Alain Locke spoke of "rehabilitating the race in world esteem,"[1] and the reevaluation of the race due to cultural recognition, which he felt would "precede or accompany any considerable further betterment of race relationships."[2] Locke did not labor under any illusion that "if the Negro was better known he would be better liked or better treated"; he merely felt that mutual understanding is the basis for any subsequent cooperation and adjustment.[3]

A new appraisal of black Americans would neither be "fixed" nor at any price. "The Negro today wishes to be known for what he is, even in his faults and shortcomings, and scorns a craven and precarious survival at the price of seeming to be what he is not."[4] Thus an approach, qualitatively different from its propagandist forebears.

Race pride was the number one avowal. Folklore and the black African heritage were revered (Garvey's shadow on the Renaissance) again in contrast to their black literary predecessors. The sense of cultural nationalism of the Harlem artist was tempered by the sense of "cultural dualism." He recognizes both Africa and America. Locke confirms: "The racialism of the Negro is no limitation or reservation with respect to American; it is only a constructive effort to build the obstructions in the stream of his progress into an efficient dam of social energy and power."[5] The goals of the new Negro are "happily already well and finally formulated, for they are none other than the ideals of American institutions and democracy."[6]

The forces that created the Renaissance were not created in an ethnic vacuum. Certain developments in white society and even world economics played an essential part in the emergence of the black cultural Renaissance. Synchronization of the literary and social revolt in the United States with the economic upswing that followed World War I brought about the mood necessary for a cultural Renaissance. The ingredients, a weakening of old ideas and values, a sense of adventure and rebellion among the intellectuals and tolerance among the status quo (all of which were facilitated by the economic upswing) created "the Roaring Twenties."

The literary avant-guarde became established, and there was a refocus on naturalism. Exoticism became the craze of Europe. The victims of its colonies throughout the world became subjects of concern and empathy. The intellectuals sought identification with the outcasts of society. A parallel development occurred in the United States. The plight of the American Indian became a topical concern for many intellectuals. Blacks constituted the logical extension.

The Renaissance can be divided into two parts; Arna Bontemps calls them Phase I and Phase II. Chronologically, it denotes the period of Primary Black Propaganda (1921–24) to the eventual additional impetus of white society (1924–31). The entrance of a new directional force marked the beginning of the second phase of the Renaissance. If this new force had a personified manifestation it would be the white literator, Carl Van Vechten. He did as much as, if not more than, anyone to bring the Renaissance into the public (*i.e.* white) eye.

During the first phase, however, the most outstanding supporters of the movement were *The Crisis* and *Opportunity* magazines. *The Crisis* was the official organ of the National Association for the Advancement of Colored People. W.E.B. Du Bois, its founder, served as editor. *Opportunity: A Journal of Negro Life* served a similar function for the Urban League. Charles S. Johnson was its editor. These two publications not only devoted space to exhibition and review of the work of the Harlem artist, but also held literary contests with cash prizes. The Charles Chesnutt Honorarium, offered through *The Crisis*, was a considerable distinction during this period. Their efforts did much to create literary interest in the Harlem community. They clearly destroyed the barrier that forced black writers in the past to feel as lepers, barred from print or relegated to some obscure publishing house, many times at their own expense. It was not unusual for a writer to resort to presenting his work anonymously.

The Harlem artists, themselves, also responded to the need to develop interest in the Harlem community. Countee Cullen and Langston Hughes offered a special edition of their poetry at a drastically reduced price to come within reach of the common man's budget. This move was of considerable importance, since paperback books were not printed in the United States during this era and hard-bound books were quite expensive.

In 1924, Charles S. Johnson gave a "coming out" party for the Harlem artists. Prominent white artists, publishers, and wealthy patrons attended. The meeting was a fateful one. Several of the writers obtained patrons, who supported them while they devoted time to their work. The stipends received were modest but allowed them to live comfortably. On occasion a patron would attempt to dictate to his protege, which would result in a break between the two. Langston Hughes was involved in such a situation. The patron/advisor relationship with several prominent whites in no way meant the Harlem artists would submit to paternalism.

The Harlem writers had a twofold reason for establishing this type of relationship with the white intelligentsia. First, the white intelligentsia had access to publishing mechanisms that were essential to the young artist. Their greater experience and literary training must have also attracted the Harlem artists. There was, too, the sense of contributing to a better social understanding, as well as being understood. Alain Locke qualifies the reasoning, ... the desire to be understood would never in itself have been sufficient to have opened so completely the protectively closed portals of the thinking Negro's mind. There was still too much possibility of being snubbed or patronized for that. It was rather the necessity for fuller, truer self-expression, the realization of the unwisdom of allowing social discrimination to segregate him mentally, and a counterattitude to cramp and fetter his own living—and so the "spite wall" that the intellectuals built over the color line has happily been taken down.[7]

The white intelligentsia seem to have had a different motivation. Their involvement with the black artist appears to have been merely a part of their fascination with the exotic. Blacks represented the uninhibited man that they idealized. He was the noble savage, the carefree child of nature. These were the days of the "Roaring Twenties" with their sexual revolution, bathtub gin, and jazz. The Harlem writers and their art would be the new fad for white society. This was not true of all the whites professing interest, but it was true of far too many. The Harlem writers were not oblivious to this development and felt betrayed and bitter. Langston Hughes remarked in *Fighting Words*, "Here are our problems; in the first place, Negro books are considered by editors and publishers as exotic. Negro materials are placed, like Chinese materials or Bali materials into certain classifications. Magazine editors tell you, 'we can use but so many Negro stories a year.' (That 'so many' meaning very few). Publishers will say, 'We already have one Negro novel on our list this fall.' When we cease to be exotic, we do not sell well."

The stage was set. Carl Van Vechten's *Nigger Heaven* depicted Harlem and its residents as exotic, so many blacks capitulated. Not all blacks took whites' intentions seriously. Zora Neale Hurston suspected the interest was a fad and decided to play it for whatever it was worth. It is difficult to say to what extent the Harlem writer internalized the sense of exoticism. Claude McKay in his novel *Home to Harlem*, outdid Van Vechten.

The Harlem Renaissance with its black cultural revival and goal of a greater social understanding was abdicated for a vogue. The new Negro became merely a new stereotype. The Harlem artist could only try to raise his voice higher than the vogue rumblings and salvage what he could.

Meanwhile, whites flocked to Harlem; some were sincere, with real appreciation of black folk-culture; others were merely curiosity seekers; still others were simply slumming. The Harlem community observed this odd procession and the hustlers in the group made some extra money.

In 1929 the stock market crashed. The effects were not immediately felt in Harlem. By 1931, however, the depression had taken its toll. One by one the artists began to leave Harlem. America had resolved to tighten its belt, leaving no room for the Harlem writers. The "good times" were over; a new environment was created that would produce a new writer in a new tradition. Many of the Harlem writers would continue to produce works, often excelling their Harlem contributions.

The legacy of the Harlem Renaissance is its art, its artists, and its idea. The reactions they encountered are for our education. The Harlem writers did not leave any "stone and mortar" institutions, but rather lived on as "living institutions." What better institution than Arna Bontemps? While the essence of the Renaissance was captured in the literature, what all this meant was concretized in the manifestos. Alain Locke's *New Negro*, Langston Hughes's "The Negro Artist and the Racial Mountain," contemporary issues of *The Crisis* and *Opportunity* magazines, all speak to the phenomenon that was occurring in Harlem.

The activity in Harlem should be considered political, even though this opposes the usual appraisals. The political quality of the Renaissance is the result of its having synthesized the dialectical forces that had polarized the black intellectual community in the previous decade. The Renaissance's political philosophy, that of "conditional intergration," is no less a political philosophy than separation, assimilation, Pan-Africanism, or any other. The philosophy in essence rested on a single axiom: It will be necessary for blacks to change their perspective of their selves before whites will change their image of them. The Harlem artists were neither didatic nor dogmatic about their belief. In fact, there seemed to be an air of transcendence about its acceptance. "We Negro artists who create now intend to express our individual dark skinned selves without fear or shame. If white people are pleased, we are glad. If they are not, it doesn't matter. We know we are beautiful and ugly too. If colored are pleased, we are glad. If they are not, their displeasure doesn't matter either. We build our temples for tomorrow, strong as we know how, and we stand on top of the mountain, free within ourselves."[8]

It is difficult to write about the Renaissance without reaction to criticism leveled against it. There have been analyses of this era in which the Harlem artists were viciously indicted, as if they were superhuman architects, consciously constituting the period, rather than ordinary human beings in the grip of a series of events that would have remarkable historical significance. The hindrance of close historical proximity is never considered. Still, what occurred in Harlem needs neither apology nor qualification. The situation, the alternatives were all created by the forces of the period, just as the environment of the next decade would, with its repressive forces, create black protest writing. There is a certain naïveté in much of the criticism. How does one expect mass participation in the art of the Harlem writers when literature by definition is bourgeois? The Harlem writers did not have any illusions about this. Langston Hughes wrote: " ... there were mostly intellectuals doing the thinking. The ordinary Negroes hadn't heard of the Negro Renaissance, and if they had, it hadn't raised their wages any." Who but intellectuals have time to think?[9]

The Harlem Renaissance is a point in the evolution of Afro-American literature. It is ludicrous to criticize beginnings; rather they should be placed in perspective to compute its significance. It "opened the door" for the black writing of today. The Renaissance will aways be remembered for this reason. It will be valued for its merits. It will come again to importance because of its idea.

NOTES

1. Alain Locke, *New Negro* (New York, Atheneum, 1969), p. 14.
2. *Ibid.*, pp. 8–9.
3. *Ibid.*, p. 15.

4. *Ibid.*, p. 11.

5. *Ibid.*, p. 12.

6. *Ibid.*, p. 10.

7. *Ibid.*, p. 9.

8. Langston Hughes, "The Negro Artist and the Racial Mountain," *The Nation*, Vol. 122, (1926) pp. 692–94.

9. *Ibid.*, pp. 692–94.

MARGARET PERRY

The Shape and Shapers
of the Movement

The Harlem Renaissance was self-proclaimed and, in the end, it was self-denounced. Alain Locke, who helped to reveal the black talent burgeoning in Harlem by editing *The New Negro* (1925), wrote in 1931: "Has the afflatus of Negro self-expression died down? Are we outliving the Negro fad?"[1] The spiral of literary talent among blacks, then, was brief, but it was an important period in the history of the black American writer. It was an important time for all blacks because it provided the genesis for the search back to a national past. This journey of self-discovery manifested itself variously in the novels and poetry of the Renaissance writers, but the essential element was a questing spirit. That is why some of the black writers of the 1920s—Marita Bonner, Angelina Grimké, and James D. Corrothers, for example—cannot be included among the writers of the Renaissance. The spirit that pervaded the writing of the major and minor writers of the Harlem Renaissance was missing from the works of these writers. There were others who simply ignored the spirit of the times, and some who, after publishing an insignificant poem or story, sensibly gave up writing entirely. A few, notably Arna Bontemps and Zora Neale Hurston, were of the period in time and in spirit but developed and matured artistically later and produced the bulk of their work after the true time of the Harlem Renaissance. In a graphic manner, the Harlem Renaissance might be charted as a smooth curve that

From *Silence to the Drums: A Survey of the Literature of the Harlem Renaissance*. © 1976 by Margaret Perry.

begins in 1919, reaches its peak in the years 1925 to 1928, and tapers off in 1932. (A chronology appears in the appendix of this book.)

When Carl Van Vechten's *Nigger Heaven* appeared in 1926, it was merely a link in the chain of events that made the Negro more real to the white world. *Nigger Heaven* helped the Renaissance to get some recognition, but did not—as some would have it—create the movement that made the world see the black man as a creative force in the artistic life of America. Van Vechten, Alain Locke, and James Weldon Johnson formed a spiritual triumvirate dedicated to exposing black artists to the world, and each in his special way was important in nurturing this creative moment in black history. All three men knew one another; Johnson and Van Vechten were especially close friends.

Langston Hughes, who gives a quick but interesting picture of the Renaissance period in his autobiography, *The Big Sea*, presents this view of Alain Locke: "He [Rudolph Fisher] and Alain Locke together were great for intellectual wise-cracking. The two would fling big and witty words about with such swift and punning innuendo that an ordinary mortal just sat and looked wary for fear of being caught in a net of witticisms beyond his cultural ken."[2] Locke, indeed, was a formidable personality on the surface: a graduate of Harvard, the first black Rhodes Scholar to Oxford, and a student at the University of Berlin. As an encourager of young black artists, Locke was supreme. He did not tell them how to write or prod them to write in one particular mold; he simply encouraged them to express themselves and gave them advice that was practical and needed at a time when exposure to the reading public (mostly white) was difficult for the Negro writer. In a manner of the spectacular, Alain Locke edited a special edition of *Survey Graphic* (March 1925) in which the writings of young Negro artists were exposed to a highly literate and sophisticated audience. The issue was a smashing success. A striking portrait by Winold Weiss of the young Roland Hayes staring dreamily into some unknown world faced the opening page which announced, quite simply, HARLEM. Alain Locke went on to explain:

> The Negro today wishes to be known for what he is, even in his faults and shortcomings.... The pulse of the Negro world has begun to beat in Harlem.... Our greatest rehabilitation may possibly come through such channels, but for the present, more immediate hope rests in the revaluation by white and black alike of the Negro in terms of his artistic endowments and cultural contributions, not only in his folk-art, music especially, which has always found appreciation, but in larger, though humbler and less

acknowledged ways.... A second crop of the Negro's gifts promises still more largely. He now becomes a conscious contributor and lays aside the status of a beneficiary and ward for that of a collaborator and participant in American civilization. The great social gain in this is the releasing of our talented group from the arid fields of controversy and debate to the productive fields of creative expression.[3]

For Locke, then, the path to understanding between the races might develop as a result of this flowering of talent among young Negro artists. Some of these writers would soon express a mild contempt for such a notion, as Langston Hughes did so splendidly in his now-famous "The Negro Artist and the Racial Mountain," but Locke was neither chided nor discredited nor rebuked for intoning this sentiment at a time when presenting such a special issue was a novelty in itself. Those young black writers knew the depth of Locke's commitment to the Negro artist and his art. For instance, Locke was an avid collector of and writer about African art, and he emphasized the manner in which these artistic creations proved to white and black alike "that the Negro is not a cultural foundling without an inheritance."[4]

Later in 1925, this special issue was expanded and printed into a book called *The New Negro*. Although Locke continued to aid and encourage Negro artists, writers, and intellectuals, for the purpose of understanding his significance in relation to the Harlem Renaissance one need only read through *The New Negro* to sense the tremendous role he played. The writers would have produced their works even without the encouragement of Locke, but with his spiritual and intellectual backing the movement was given a concrete and meaningful boost.

James Weldon Johnson was quite literally a giant personality in the black world during the first three decades of the twentieth century. He was a man who accomplished much in his personal life, because of the variety of his work, the barriers he overcame, and the breadth of his interests and involvement in literature, music, politics, and social justice. He was a significant figure in the Harlem Renaissance, a man whose role was that of precursor, participant, inspirer, and historian. Johnson has been called a Renaissance man, and it is significant that one of the most fruitful periods of his life should have occurred during the Harlem Renaissance era.

A little over one hundred years ago, on 17 June 1871, James Weldon Johnson was born in Jacksonville, Florida, of parents who had spent many years in the British colony of Nassau. Johnson had a happy childhood, as his reminiscences of his mother, in particular, reveal: "She belonged to the type of mothers whose love completely surrounds their children and is all-pervading; mothers for whom sacrifice for the child means only an extension of love.... The childhood memories that cluster round my mother are still intensely vivid to me; many of them are poignantly tender."[5] Both of his parents possessed exceptional intelligence and culture, although his father was self-educated. Their combined incomes—Mrs. Johnson was a teacher, Mr. Johnson a head waiter—provided a healthy enough income to send Johnson to Atlanta University. He graduated in 1894 and then went to Stanton School in Jacksonville where he taught and later became the principal. One of Johnson's first accomplishments was to study law and to become the first Negro since Reconstruction to be admitted to the bar in Florida through open examinations. Johnson turned to the law after a short-lived side career as editor of a Negro newspaper, the *Daily American*. His newspaper venture lasted eight months before he and his partner were forced to suspend publication because "the colored people of Jacksonville ... were not able to support the kind of newspaper I sought to provide for them."[6] Johnson's next profession, however, brought him fame and fortune: he collaborated with his brother, J. Rosamond, and Bob Cole, in the writing of songs for Tin Pan Alley. At one period in his life, Johnson was still at the Stanton School, practicing law, though not too strenuously, and writing songs in partnership with his brother and Bob Cole. Johnson gave up teaching and the law and concentrated on his successful career in the show business world—a career that ended, while still at great heights, in 1907. At that time, Johnson, who had been actively involved in politics, accepted a consular appointment at Puerto Cabello, Venezuela. He later served as consul at Corinto, Nicaragua, but left the consular service when Woodrow Wilson was elected president in 1913.

Important qualities that Johnson shared with Locke and Carl Van Vechten were his ability to perceive talent in young writers and his willingness to aid and encourage them. Johnson, like many of these writers, understood and loved Harlem and felt in the marrow of his bones that this one place was the spiritual and cultural milieu of black Americans. Yet he also saw a certain uniqueness in the temper of life lived by the Negroes in this black metropolis. The "immigrants" to this new land soon shed many of their old ways (or adapted them to city living, as in the case of the rent party) and became New Yorkers. The influence of Harlem was pervasive; a seductive air wafted over its quarters. The Harlem Renaissance writers shared with the ordinary black the realization that this was no ordinary place, no ordinary amalgamation of streets and flats and churches and clubs: here was home. In the words of Claude McKay, each black person, in one sense or another, came "home to Harlem." No one understood this better than Johnson, although he deplored exploitation of Harlem by blacks and whites and cautioned them about it. He wrote a book about Harlem in 1930, *Black Manhattan*, in which he gave a brief description of the Harlem Renaissance as he saw and participated in it.

In *Black Manhattan*, Johnson gives this assessment of the artistic movement in progress:

> The most outstanding phase of the development of the Negro in the United States during the past decade had been the recent literary and artistic emergence of the individual creative artist; and New York has been, almost exclusively, the place where that emergence has taken place. The thing that has happened has been so marked that it does not have the appearance of a development; it seems rather like a sudden awakening, like an instantaneous change.[7]

If anyone understood the Harlem Renaissance, could see it forming, encourage it, analyze it, help to explain it to the world, it was James Weldon Johnson. As both a forerunner and a member of the movement, he presented a living example of the artist-humanist triumphant in a society that sought to disinherit him. He would not be defeated, and he inspired others to feel the same and to express the sentiments of being black in American society.

It was said by many, both black and white, that Carl Van Vechten used Harlem and made a cult of its exotic and more colorfully exciting sections. James Weldon Johnson believed that this was a false view of his friend, and Arna Bontemps agreed with Johnson's judgment of the one white man who literally soaked up black culture during an extensive portion of his life. One of the objections to Van Vechten was his novel, *Nigger Heaven*, published in 1926. Johnson's opinion was that "most of the Negroes who condemned *Nigger Heaven* did not read it; they were stopped by the title."[8] It is a fact, in any case, that Van Vechten did introduce the publishers Alfred and Blanche Knopf to several Negro writers—James Weldon Johnson, for one, and also Rudolph Fisher. According to one of Van Vechten's biographers, "Alfred Knopf often relied on Van Vechten's judgment entirely in decisions about manuscripts [from Negro writers]".[9]

In his time, Van Vechten was famous for his parties where persons of all races met, although at times there were almost more black faces to be seen than white. Despite his own understanding and encouragement of the expression of black culture, Van Vechten still deferred to the judgments of James Weldon Johnson and Rudolph Fisher before publishing *Nigger Heaven*; he wanted to be sure his portrayal of the character traits and the language of blacks (especially the "private Negroese") was true to black life. If one were to put *Nigger Heaven* beside a novel written by a black during the same period, it is doubtful that one would judge it to have been composed by a white man. The novel sounds authentically Negro, even though it is not a particularly good book—not good perhaps for the reasons his biographer happily rattles off: "*Nigger Heaven* is part sociological tract, part intellectual history, part aesthetic anthropology, but it is all novel."[10]

Even though *Nigger Heaven* fits into the genre of literature for this period in Harlem, the importance of its author goes beyond the book and beyond the age. During the 1920s, Van Vechten helped to bring attention to black artists—writers, performers, and musicians. He brought the white and black worlds together frequently and was a very influential catalyst in the mixed brew of artistry bubbling over in Gotham City. Van Vechten was famous and he was rich. He was a writer, a critic, a photographer, and, by nature, a cosmopolite. His enthusiasm for Harlem and for black life and culture was not the result of a sudden conversion; he had been interested in blacks since his early life, and he developed this even further when, as a college student, he attended performances by Negro musicians and singers. But his "addiction," as he himself termed it, for the darker citizens of the United States grew more pronounced in the early 1920s. Van Vechten was a serious gadabout in the clubs, theatres, shops, and homes of Harlem. He savored every moment he spent in what was, for most whites, a purlieu not only of Manhattan but of civilization itself. Van Vechten, however, didn't stop with going to Harlem: he also brought Harlem to his elegant home in mid-Manhattan:

> After his marriage to the Russian actress, Fania Marinoff, he developed his own fabulous reputation as a genial, imaginative host drawing to the Van Vechten apartments the high and the low, the exotic and the plain, the dark and the light, the intellectual and the emotional representatives of literature, society, and the arts. All together, his social exploits qualify him as a ringmaster worthy of star billing in the Circus Maximus of the Twenties.[11]

Part of the Van Vechten charm was his unabashed enthusiasm for the new and the interesting. He judged each person, each act, each artistic production on its own merits. His interest in Walter White's novel, *Fire in the Flint* (1924), led him to contact the author; years later, Van Vechten reminisced, "'Walter and I got on like a house afire.'"[12] It was the beginning of a deeper immersion into black life and the black world that spread like black ink from 110th Street northward, away from the chic midtown towers where the Van Vechtens lived. Even though the Harlem Renaissance was forming and rising at this time, even though it would have become a reality without Carl Van Vechten, it owes a debt to him for popularizing and supporting it. Without white support the Harlem Renaissance would have suffered from a lack of money and readers, and Carl Van Vechten was a prime mover in securing this patronage.

There is a note to Carl Van Vechten from Countee Cullen in the Cullen file at Yale in which the poet briefly discusses the donation of an original manuscript to Van Vechten. To establish a collection of Negro literature at the Yale University Library had been a dream of Van Vechten's since the late 1940s. Through gifts of his writer friends and others, through gifts of his own (including some of his justifiably highly praised photographs), Van Vechten was finally able to realize his dream when the James Weldon Johnson Memorial Collection of Negro Arts and Letters was dedicated officially on 7 January 1950. This contribution to the black arts is enough to enshrine the name of Carl Van Vechten as one of those who valued the black man's contribution to America's artistic tradition.

There were many others who championed the writers of the Harlem Renaissance—Fannie Hurst, Zona Gale, and Jessie Fauset, for instance—but two men, in particular, should be mentioned: W.E.B. DuBois and Charles S. Johnson.

DuBois's relationship to the Harlem Renaissance is a bit curious and distant. He abhorred the portrayals of low life, such as in the novels of Claude McKay, yet he recognized the genuine talent of Langston Hughes. The concern, however, that formed the nexus between this thorough New Englander and the new men of the Harlem Renaissance was "the race." Racial pride was forceful in DuBois; it was the sort of pride that had faith in at least a portion of the black race. He called upon the "talented tenth," of whom the writers were a part, to show to the world the Negro's beauty and strength. The fear DuBois voiced from time to time was a fear that the black writer would forget his duty to uplift the race and to elevate the rest of the world's opinion about his black brethren. In his review of *The New Negro* DuBois wrote:

If Mr. Locke's thesis is insisted on too much it is going to turn the Negro renaissance into decadence. It is the fight for Life and Liberty that is giving birth to Negro literature and art today and when, turning from this fight or ignoring it, the young Negro tries to do pretty things or things that catch the passing fancy of the really unimportant critics and publishers about him, he will find that he has killed the soul of Beauty in his Art.[13]

The interest DuBois had in the movement was not ignored—indeed, as the editor-in-chief of *The Crisis* he was an obvious influence—but it was one that remained on an intellectual rather than a personal plane. In his articles and various discussions, he attempted to define and, through definition, to direct the unifying elements in this whole artistic movement. DuBois's main weakness was his inability to realize that his predilection for propagandizing for the race through art was a flaw that all the rhetoric in the world could not cure.

Charles S. Johnson is not as well known as DuBois, Locke, or James Weldon Johnson but is, nevertheless, praised by Langston Hughes as one who "did more to encourage and develop Negro writers during the 1920's than anyone else in America."[14] Johnson was a sociologist, the first black president of Fisk University, and also the editor of *Opportunity* for five and a half years. Johnson's initiation of the *Opportunity* contests gave the reading public and literary critics exposure to a variety of talented Negro writers, such as Hughes, Arthur H. Fauset, John Matheus, and Bontemps, and gave much-needed encouragement (and some money) to the young writers. Recently it has been noted that

it was in the *Opportunity* contests and dinners, however, that Charles S. Johnson was most successful as an entrepreneur in promoting the new awakening of black culture. Johnson recognized the creative genius of the many black artists of the 1920's. But this genius was of limited value until the racial barriers of publishers were removed. Johnson, along with Urban League official William H. Baldwin, moved deliberately to bring the white publishers and the black writers together.[15]

It is in this context, then, that Charles S. Johnson effected his greatest influence upon the fledgling black writers of this period. His intelligence, his selflessness in the cause of these beginning artists, and his ceaseless encouragement of them in practical, remunerative manners earn him a high place among the primary patrons of Harlem Renaissance writers.

By 1924 there was little question that a movement was stirring. *Cane*, the most remarkable piece of literature to emerge from the Harlem Renaissance, had been published during the previous year; poets like Countee Cullen, Langston Hughes, and Claude McKay were mentioned with frequency and with praise. This rash of folk expression, touching upon the very nature of the black soul, strengthened and matured quickly during the quixotic twenties, shaping itself and growing, in part, through the encouragement of these deans of black intellectual life in America. Locke and DuBois believed keenly in the idea of the "talented tenth"; James Weldon Johnson, in his own way, also believed that a demonstration of intellectual stamina and talent among Negro creators would change the world's view of the black man. Carl Van Vechten recognized a spawning of talent that could not be denied and should not go unrewarded, and he aided in basically practical ways. Van Vechten also helped to advance the cause of the black artist by his genuine acceptance of the contribution of blacks to American arts and letters. Last, in his role as a real friend to the Negro, Van Vechten was able to bring about what DuBois and James Weldon Johnson had lamented seldom occurred—social, cultural, and intellectual intercourse between the leaders, the "aristocracy," of both races.

From 1924 until the end, or at least the ebb of the movement, there was a series of hosannas and praise and benediction. The few shrill cries of dissent were vociferously countered by more paeans from the literary gods. There was an exhilaration that was captured in many earnest efforts. Although individual works often suffered under close critical scrutiny, praise was routinely given to some part of nearly every work penned by a black author. The works which were produced attempted to dramatize the resentment the black man held against racial prejudice or the illogical or foolish aspects of such prejudice. Of course, there were the folksy and the bizarre and the exotic tales. Finally, whatever the special quality of a particular offering, there was always the pride of race, the search for roots, the belief that black writers and artists possessed sparks of genius that would set the nation aflame.

NOTES

1. Alain Locke, "This Year of Grace," *Opportunity* 9 (February 1931): 48.

2. Langston Hughes, *The Big Sea* (New York: Hill and Wang, 1940), pp. 240–241.

3. *Survey Graphic* 53 (March 1925): 632, 633, 634.

4. Ibid., 673.

5. James Weldon Johnson, *Along This Way* (New York: Viking, 1933), p. 11.

6. Ibid., p. 140.

7. James Weldon Johnson, *Black Manhattan* (New York: Knopf, 1940, c. 1930), p. 260.

8. Johnson, *Along This Way*, p. 382.

9. Edward Lueders, *Carl Van Vechten and the Twenties* (Albuquerque: University of New Mexico Press, 1955), p. 65.

10. Ibid., p. 87.

11. Ibid., p. 24.

12. Bruce Kellner, *Carl Van Vechten and the Irreverent Decades* (Norman: University of Oklahoma Press, 1968), p. 197.

13. *The Crisis* 31 (1926): 141.

14. Hughes, *The Big Sea*, p. 218.

15. Patrick J. Gilpin, "Charles S. Johnson: Entrepreneur of the Harlem Renaissance." In Arna Bontemps, editor, *The Harlem Renaissance Remembered* (New York: Dodd, 1972), p. 224.

AMRITJIT SINGH

Black-White Symbiosis: Another Look at the Literary History of the 1920s

In *Harlem Renaissance* (1971), Nathan Irvin Huggins describes the white–black relationship in America as symbiotic: "Blacks have been essential to white identity (and whites to black)." Huggins's use of this biological concept bears heavily on the main thesis of his book which argues that the black American's confusions over identity are uniquely American: "White Americans and white American culture have no more claim to self-confidence than black." Huggins's approach is valuable because in focusing on the role of black–white interdependence (conscious and unconscious) in shaping American character and culture, it allows us to gain perspective on the overrated issues surrounding assimilationism versus nationalism in black American life.[1] However, what makes Huggins's thesis controversial is the absoluteness with which he views the black American's dilemmas in self-definition on equal terms with the white American's. The term "symbiosis" in its original sense is more to the point here; symbiosis is defined as "the relationship of two or more different organisms in a close association that may be but *is not necessarily of benefit to each*"[2] (Italics added). Time and again in American history, the one-sided and unequal relationship between blacks and whites has obliged blacks to serve as eternal footmen holding the identity coats for whites.

On the literary scene of the twenties, this symbiosis is measured best by the nature of white writing on black life and by the quality of exchanges, real

From *The Harlem Renaissance Re-examined*, edited by Victor A. Kramer. © 1987 by AMS Press, Inc.

23

and potential, between black and white writers and intellectuals. In retrospect, it seems that these literary efforts failed, with one or two partial exceptions, to rise above the major stereotype—the Negro as a primitive—that so strongly dominated the public mind in those years. Although the image of the Negro as primitive was not entirely new on the American scene, it caught the American imagination in a big way for the first time in the twenties. A number of factors combined to turn the Negro, as Langston Hughes would put it later, into a vogue. Historically, commercialism and standardization that followed industrialism led to increasing nostalgia for the simple, forceful and unmechanized existence that the Negro came for various reasons to represent. In the Jazz Age it had become fashionable to defy prohibition and to find joy and abandon in exotic music and dance. In such an atmosphere, "the Negro had obvious uses: he represented the unspoiled child of nature, the noble savage—carefree, spontaneous and sexually uninhibited."[3] European artists Pablo Picasso and George Braque found insight and inspiration in African sculpture to develop their interest in cubism. The exotic curiosity of a few in African art forms was matched by the romantic interest of the many in primitive life and culture, an interest that made little distinction between Africans and Afro-Americans. A popular misinterpretation of Freudian theory contributed to the promotion of primitivism in Europe and North America. Freud was seen as the champion of instinct over intellect in a revolt against the Puritan spirit. In his *Civilization and its Discontents,* Freud had contended that civilization was based upon the renunciation of "powerful instinctual urgencies," and that the privation of instinctual gratification demanded by the cultural ideal was a major source of neurosis. No wonder, then, that popularized Freudianism became "the rationalization of sex primitivism," and gave the "cult of the primitive ... an extraordinary foothold on this continent."[4]

On the plus side, this Negro fad of the twenties in the United States led to an unprecedented artistic activity that focused on the depiction of the Negro in fiction, drama, poetry, painting and sculpture. More white writers in the South as well as the North wrote about the Negro and in sheer quantity the record remains unmatched to this day. One group of writers and intellectuals, centered at the University of North Carolina, Chapel Hill, devoted their careers almost entirely to Negro-related writing.[5] Known generally as writers of the Southern Renaissance, the group included Paul Green, Julia Peterkin, DuBose Heyward, T. S. Stribling, Elizabeth Lay Green, and Edward Sheldon. Friederich Koch, the director of the University's little theater group, the Carolina Playmakers, and former student of George Pierce Baker, particularly encouraged plays that made an artistic use of Negro themes. Under the leadership of Harry Woodburn Chase, the Massachusetts-born president of the University, liberal Southern social scientists such as Frank Graham and Howard Odum published many important studies of the Negro and in 1927, 1928 and 1929, the *Carolina Magazine* devoted one number entirely to work by Negro contributors. In the North, many white writers such as Eugene O'Neill, Sherwood Anderson, and e. e. cummings followed the trend already set by Gertrude Stein's "Melanctha" (1909) and Vachel Lindsay's *The Congo* (1914) in presenting the alleged primitivism of the Negro as a bulwark against increasing standardization. Besides, anthropologists like Franz Boas and Melville Herskovits published many pioneering studies of the Negro.

The most significant result of the Negro vogue was the encouragement that black musicians, writers, and other artists received from white audiences and important white individuals. Jazz and blues thrived and defined the mood of the period. Black musicians—Roland Hayes, Duke Ellington, Louis Armstrong, Bessie Smith, among others—came to public attention. In 1921, *Shuffle Along*, produced by Flourney Miller and Aubrey Lyles, ran for so long at the 63rd Street Theatre that it came to symbolize black New York. It was followed on Broadway by the moderate success of many other revues of the same variety. Black actors and actresses like Josephine Baker, Charles Gilpin, Paul Robeson, and Florence Mills gave spectacular performances in plays by black and white dramatists. In painting and sculpture, black artists such as Aaron Douglas, Hale Woodruff, Richard Barthe, and others moved away from the academic realism of Henry O. Tanner to experiment in a variety of styles and to attempt a more objective and effective self-portrayal.

But it is in literature that we see the most impressive results of this new and open mood. There were more books published by blacks in the twenties than ever before and it would not be until the sixties that Afro-American literary activity would again exhibit equal or greater vitality. The collective literary product of the period is indicated today by the term "Harlem Renaissance" or "Negro Renaissance." The young writers of the period were guided and encouraged not only by their black seniors such as Alain Locke, James Weldon Johnson, Charles S. Johnson, Walter White, W.E.B. Du Bois and Jessie Fauset but also by many sympathetic whites including Waldo Frank, Carl Van Vechten, Victor F. Calverton, and others.

It is not my purpose here to attempt a detailed history of the Harlem Renaissance as a movement. It has been done elsewhere.[6] It is agreed that the phenomenon identified generally as Harlem Renaissance appeared on the American scene during the closing years of World War I, was publicly recognized by men such as Alain Locke and Charles S. Johnson in 1924 or

1925, and had begun declining about the time of the stock market crash in 1929. While the Afro-American creative writing of this brief period often years or so is duly credited for its abundance and variety, it is felt that the black writers of the period failed to achieve their potential as writers and did not fully grapple with the implications of Alain Locke's elaborate effort to develop a conscious "local color" movement of Afro-American arts. The stock market crash had no doubt severely hampered white America's ability to sustain and enjoy the Negro fad. Perhaps, as Ralph Ellison has pointed out, the black writer of the twenties "had wanted to be fashionable and this insured, even more effectively than the approaching Depression, the failure of the 'New Negro' movement."[7] Black writers had "climbed aboard the bandwagon" of exoticism and decadence signalled by Carl Van Vechten's *Nigger Heaven* and enjoyed the era when the Negro was in vogue. By the mid-thirties, exotic and genteel novels were no longer popular with the publishers and were attacked by a new breed of black writers and critics. In 1934, Eugene Saxton, who had handled Claude McKay's work at Harper and Brothers, bluntly informed him that his popularity had been part of a passing fad.[8] In 1940, Langston Hughes spoke for many when he said, "I had a swell time while it [the Negro Renaissance] lasted. But I thought it wouldn't last long.... For how could a large number of people be crazy about Negroes forever?"[9]

Although Carl Van Vechten's *Nigger Heaven* (1926) was not the first or the only work by a white writer to exploit the exotic-primitive stereotype in relation to the Negro, it was certainly the most influential novel in establishing this image in the minds of the reading public in the twenties. The book ran into several editions and sold over 100,000 copies; it fanned an unprecedented nationwide interest in the Negro and clearly demonstrated the commercial value of books written in the primitivistic framework. A few months before the publication of this book, as a participant in the symposium on "The Negro in Art—How Shall He be Portrayed?" initiated by Du Bois in the pages of *The Crisis*, Carl Van Vechten had made a statement most revealing of his attitude to the subject. He had said:

> The squalor of Negro life, the vice of Negro life, offer a wealth of novel, exotic, picturesque material to the artist. On the other hand, there is very little difference if any between the life of a wealthy or cultured Negro and that of a white man of the same class. The question is: are Negro writers going to write about this exotic material while it is still fresh or will they continue to make a free gift of it to white authors who will exploit it until not a drop of vitality remains?[10]

Nigger Heaven thus represented a real threat of preemption to young black writers if the latter refused to heed Van Vechten's advice and exploit a market ripe and eager for exotic versions of black life.

Described by a contemporary as an "archeologist of the exotic," Carl Van Vechten was interested in the Negro long before he published *Nigger Heaven*. Born and brought up in Cedar Rapids, Iowa, he came to New York in 1906 after studying at the University of Chicago and working a short stint as journalist for the *Chicago American*. He was among the first to take jazz seriously as an art form and had become interested in the Negro by way of jazz and Gertrude Stein. In 1913 he saw a Negro vaudeville show, *Darktown Follies*. "How the darkies danced, sang, and cavorted," Van Vechten recalled later in his *In The Garrett*. "Real nigger stuff this, done with spontaneity and joy in the doing." By this time, he was promoting interracial gatherings by entertaining blacks at his home. During the early twenties, he came to know many black writers and leaders such as Walter White, James Weldon Johnson, Countee Cullen, Langston Hughes, Zora Neale Hurston, Rudolph Fisher, and Eric Walrond. Soon he was a regular visitor in Harlem, and according to Ethel Waters, came to know more about New York's black belt than any other white person with the exception of the captain of Harlem's police station.[11]

Even before publishing his own book, Van Vechten was influential as a friend and adviser to black writers. He was in fact their major contact with white journals and white publishers. He was also responsible for many contacts between white and black artists. Through his interracial parties and gatherings in Harlem and in the Village, he made it smart to be interracial. Ethel Waters recalled meeting Eugene O'Neill, Sinclair Lewis, Dorothy Thompson, Alfred Knopf, George Jean Nathan, Alexander Woolcott, Heywood Broun, Cole Porter, Noel Coward, and Somerset Maugham at the Van Vechten apartment.[12] Paul Robeson's singing at an interracial gathering at Van Vechten's place led directly to his first New York concert. Van Vechten was instrumental in getting Langston Hughes's first two volumes of poetry, *The Weary Blues* (1926) and *Fine Clothes to a Jew* (1927), accepted for publication by Alfred Knopf. Through Van Vechten again, Hughes found his way to the pages of *Vanity Fair*. He also persuaded Alfred Knopf to publish James Weldon Johnson, Nella Larsen, Rudolph Fisher, and Chester Himes.

Although a detailed analysis of *Nigger Heaven* may not be pertinent here, it is necessary to indicate the influence Van Vechten and his book had on the milieu and literary careers of the Harlem Renaissance writers. *Nigger Heaven* is the story of Mary Love, a prim and pretty Harlem librarian, who falls in love with Byron Karson, a struggling young writer. Byron, a recent

graduate of the University of Pennsylvania, has been told that he has
promise, which he interprets to mean: "pretty good for a colored man." Mary
Love cannot take sex and love lightly. Randolph Pettijohn, the numbers king,
desires her and offers her marriage. "Ah ain't got no education lak you, but
Ah got money, plenty of et, an' Ah got love," he tells her. Byron meanwhile
fails to find a job compatible with his level of education and refuses to accept
a menial job. The exotic and primitive aspects of Harlem life surround
Byron's orgiastic affair with Lasca Sartoris, "a gorgeous brown Messalina of
Seventh Avenue." Lasca, however, deserts Byron for Pettijohn. Byron
avenges himself by impulsively firing two bullets into the prostrate body of
Pettijohn, who has already been killed by Scarlet Creeper. At the end, Byron
surrenders helplessly to the police.

The spectre of *Nigger Heaven* lurks behind most book reviews written
after 1926. Benjamin Brawley, Allison Davis, and W.E.B. Du Bois asserted
that some younger black writers and many white writers were misguided by
Nigger Heaven, and they argued that the emphasis on the exotic and the
primitive, the sensual and the bawdy in the depiction of the Negro was
detrimental to the black's political future in the United States.

If the fad of primitivism cannot be blamed entirely on Van Vechten or
on the group of whites who wrote about the Negro in the twenties, it is
reasonable to conclude that the book seems to have had a crippling effect on
the self-expression of many black writers by either making it easier to gain
success riding the bandwagon of primitivism, or by making it difficult to
publish novels that did not fit the profile of the commercial success formula
adopted by most publishers for black writers. The unusual success of *Nigger
Heaven* and later of McKay's *Home to Harlem* clearly indicated an eagerness
for works exalting the exotic, the sensual, and the primitive. This interest had
"no minor effect on the certain members of the Harlem *literati* whose work
was just what the Jazz Age ordered." Thus, black writers who were willing to
describe the exotic scene "had no trouble finding sponsors, publishers and
immediate popularity."[13] In his autobiography, *The Big Sea* (1940), Langston
Hughes recalled the pessimistic judgment of Wallace Thurman, who
thought that the Negro had made the Harlem Renaissance writers "too
conscious of ourselves, had flattered and spoiled us, and had provided too
many easy opportunities for some of us to drink gin and more gin."[14]

So the decade of the twenties was replete with black literary activity
which for the most part took its cue from and satisfied the deep psychological
needs of the white majority. Out of weakness or necessity, many black writers
felt obliged not to offend the white readers' (and whose else were there in the
twenties?) preconceptions of what the Negro was. A consideration of literary

works by black authors highlights two dominant trends that form a revealing pattern of near-obsessive concern with the major white stereotype of Afro-American existence. The first trend is defined by such black writing which, like much writing on the subject by white contemporaries (although with significant minor variations), presents black life as exotic and primitivistic. One thinks, for example, of novels such as Arna Bontemps's *God Sends Sunday* (1931), Claude McKay's *Home to Harlem* (1928) and *Banjo* (1929) and poems such as Countee Cullen's "Heritage" and Waring Cuney's "No Images." On the other hand were works by writers who with equal force and terror attempted to show that the black American was different from his white counterpart only in the shade of his skin. These writers found it expedient to plead their case by presenting black middle-class characters and situations in their fictional works in order to demolish the prevailing stereotype. Among such works one may mention the novels by Jessie Fauset, Walter White, Nella Larsen and W.E.B. Du Bois. However, the primitivistic mode had such wide and deep appeal among their readership that white publishers often hesitated to publish their works. Zora Gale, for example, had to come to Jessie Fauset's rescue with a preface to *The Chinaberry Tree* (1931) because the publisher said "White readers just don't expect Negroes to be like this."[15] But it was important for these black writers to be published by major publishers and to reach the white audiences at whom their works were primarily aimed. When H. L. Mencken suggested that Walter White seek a Negro publisher for his unrelentingly propagandist novel *Fire in the Flint* (1924), White replied; "It is not the colored reader at whom I am shooting but the white man and woman ... who believes that every lynching, is for rape, who believes that ex-confederates are right when they use every means, fair or foul, to keep the nigger in his place."[16]

This evidence is corroborated even by statements by such writers who had, consciously or unconsciously, dispensed the white stereotypes in their own works, or else had striven to remain independent in their views on race and art. When in 1930, Arna Bontemps submitted for publication his first novel "with autobiographical overtones about a sensitive black boy in a nostalgic setting," many editors suggested that he rewrite the novel into a sensual-primitivistic story centered around a minor character.[17] The result was published the following year as *God Sends Sunday*. Even Claude McKay, whose *Home to Harlem* had successfully tapped the market fed a few years before by *Nigger Heaven*, resented and rejected the suggestion from some quarters that he should "make a trip to Africa and write about Negro life in pure state." He complained that white critics approached his work "as if he were primitive and altogether stranger to civilization. *Perhaps I myself unconsciously gave that impression*"[18] (Italics added). Jean Toomer, the mystical poet-observer of *Cane* (1923), complained to Waldo Frank that his friendship with Sherwood Anderson could not develop because the latter "limits me to Negro." "As an approach," Toomer added, "as a constant element (part of the larger whole) of interest, Negro is good. But to try to tie me to one of my parts is surely to lose me. My own letters have taken Negro as a point, and from there have circled out. Sherwood, for the most part, ignores the circles."[19]

Some of the writers, especially Hughes, experienced white patronage of a different kind. Langston Hughes, Zora Neale Hurston, Louise Thompson, and some other young black artists had a rich white patron who wanted them to express their "primitive" instincts in their work for the generous support offered. Later in his career, Hughes was never able to recall his experience with this patron without getting sick in the stomach, but in the early thirties he found courage to leave the relationship because, to quote Hughes, "I did not feel the rhythms of the primitive surging through me, and so I could not live and write as though I did. I was only an American Negro—who had loved the surface of Africa and the rhythms of Africa—but I was not Africa. I was Chicago and Kansas City and Broadway and Harlem."[20] Hughes, in fact, asserted his artistic independence by promising to steer clear as much of the white readers' stereotypes as of the black middle-class readers' taboos. He expressed his views strongly in a *Nation* article entitled "The Negro Artist and The Racial Mountain" (1926), which remains the clearest statement on the subject to come from the period. Late in the thirties, Hughes also summed up the Negro writer's difficulties with white publishers. First of all, he complained, Negro books are considered by editors and publishers as exotic and placed in a special category like Chinese or East Indian material. His more serious charge was that books by black writers cannot sell unless they "make our black ghetto in the big cities seem very happy places indeed, and our plantations in the deep south idyllic in their pastoral loveliness.... When we cease to be exotic, we cease to sell."[21]

If among black writers Hughes was one of the few exceptions to the bandwagon influence of the white stereotype, there were some exceptions on the other side too. The most significant man among the whites, who supported and encouraged black writing in the twenties without capitulating to the primitivistic view of black life, was an intellectual rather than a creative writer. V. F. Calverton, who edited the first *Anthology of American Negro Literature* (1929) for the Modern Library, encouraged black writers, intellectuals, and journalists in the pages of his journal, *The Modern Quarterly*. Born George Goetz (1900–1940), Calverton was a literary radical whose interests were as diverse as literature, anthropology, sociology, Marxism and hypnosis.[22] As an independent-minded Marxist, he tried to look at American life and literature and Afro-American contributions to them in socio-economic terms. His sharp sense of the Negro's economic status in American life would allow little scope in his vision for the exotic-primitive type. In grappling with the socio-economic and literary issues of his time, Calverton became fully sensitive to the rigidity of the American color caste. In an essay on the Negro, written for Harold E. Stern's *America Now* (1938), he said:

> Being a Negro in the U.S. today is like being a prisoner in a jail which has several corridors and squares, in which it is possible occasionally to see the sun and walk amid the flowers and fields that belong to the unimprisoned elements of humanity. Beyond the contours of that circumscribed world there is little territory, economic or physical, in which he can have that freedom necessary for individual advance and social progress.[23]

Calverton's deep understanding of the Negro's status in a segregated limiting world did not make him blind—as it did many latter-day white sociologists—to other elements in the life of black Americans. He traced the origin of blues, spirituals and labor songs to the peculiar socio-economic conditions of slavery and extolled these art forms as "America's chief claim to originality in cultural history."[24]

Although close to the Communist Party in the twenties, Calverton broke away from it in 1933 and remained an unorthodox Marxist, to the end expressing independent views as a social and cultural critic. He urged the Party to see the futility of attempting to transplant the Russian experiment in the United States where unique conditions existed because of widespread industrialization. Calverton also tried unsuccessfully to interest black Marxists and intellectuals in his thesis called "Cultural Compulsive." According to him, the compulsive nature of social thought explained the limited character of a people's point of view. It assumed that it was impossible for any mind to achieve objectivity in its evaluation of social phenomena. The awareness of this inescapable subjectivity, he thought, would allow for more care and flexibility in criticism "within the radius of the cultural compulsive itself." Black Americans could, thus, use this "cultural compulsive" thesis as a basis for functional social theory in their struggle for social and cultural rights. Regardless of whether one agrees or not with Calverton's views, one cannot but marvel at his ability to have remained untouched by the pervasive stereotype of his time, especially when one considers the depth and sincerity of his interest in black American life. Looking back, Calverton's independent commitment to the racial situation in the United States seems all the more impressive, in view of the facile involvement of many blacks in the thirties and forties with the rhetoric of the American Communist Party.

However, the exceptional independence of white stereotypes that Calverton showed underscores only the general failure of black and white authors to escape the influence of the commercial success formula represented by certain works about blacks by white writers. Also, while a certain combination of factors dramatized the white–black symbiosis on the literary scene of the twenties, its relevance to other periods of American history is well expressed in the following words of Saunders Redding:

> *The Negro, and especially later, the Negro writer, has always known who he is.... Certainly he has not had to seek it. Quite the contrary, he has tried to lose it*; ... The Negro's identity was locked into the white man's fantasy construct of the slave, and Emancipation did not free him. The fantasy construct (perpetuated as an historical fiction), as Alain Locke pointed out forty years ago, was the image of the Negro that none but the negro himself wanted to reject. And in order to do this, he had first to suppress the knowledge and deprive himself of the redemptive use of his true identity.... The [slave] identity was still useful to the [white] conscience, for it justified the social abuses practised against their freedom, and since the identity of the Negro was locked into this, he could not rid himself of the one without ridding himself of the other. And this, strange and aberrant though it may be, is what he did, or tried to—in fact, in fiction, and in verse.[25]

Too long have black writers either succumbed to white stereotypes or else been obliged simply to try to fight these stereotypes to an early death. The burden has been heavy and generally debilitating, as evidenced in many Afro-American literary works. The exceptions are so few that they only prove the rule. Not until very recently have blacks been able to publish works that are not partially or wholly determined by the peculiar preconception at any given time of white audiences, white editors and white publishers. One is beginning to observe the impact of growing black audiences, the presence of black publishers and the traumatic changes that America experienced in the sixties. The true meeting of the minds between black and white artists is symbolized best by the meetings that never took place between Jean Toomer and Allen Tate, both of the South and both proponents of new ideas and experiments in literature. They corresponded and planned twice to meet at a small Louisiana railroad station. They never met. One can only hope that genuine attempts at the portrayal of the Negro may come from both black and white writers with the conviction, to borrow Ellison's words, that "it is important to explore the full range of American Negro humanity and to affirm those qualities which are of value beyond any question of segregation, economics or previous condition of servitude. The obligation was always there and there is much to affirm."[26]

NOTES

1. Huggins, *Harlem Renaissance* (New York: Oxford University Press, 1971), pp. 12, 84, 305.

2. *The American Heritage Dictionary* (1969).

3. Robert Bone, *The Negro Novel in America*, rev. ed. (New Haven: Yale University Press, 1965), p. 59.

4. Oscar Cargill, *Intellectual America* (New York: Macmillan, 1941), p. 608.

5. This brief résumé of this group of writers is based on Trudie Engel, "The Harlem Renaissance" (Master's thesis, University of Wisconsin Madison, 1959), pp. 72–81.

6. See relevant sections in Huggins, *Harlem Renaissance*; Arna Bontemps, *Harlem Renaissance Remembered* (New York: Dodd Mead, 1972); Amritjit Singh, *The Novels of the Harlem Renaissance: Twelve Black Writers*, 1923–33 (Pennsylvania State University Press, 1976).

7. James Thompson, Lennox Raphael, and Steven Canyon, "A Very Stern Discipline: An Interview with Ralph Ellison," *Harper's*, March 1967, p. 79.

8. Wayne Cooper, ed. *The Passion of Claude McKay: Selected Poetry and Prose, 1912–1948* (New York: Schocken, 1973), p. 36.

9. Langston Hughes, *The Big Sea* (New York: Hill and Wang, 1940), p. 228.

10. *The Crisis*, 31 (March 1926), p. 219.

11. Ethel Waters, *His Eye Is on the Sparrow* (New York: Doubleday, 1951), p. 195.

12. Waters, p. 196.

13. Faith Berry, "Voice for the Jazz Age, Great Migration or Black Bourgeoisie," *Black World*, 20 (November 1970), p. 12.

14. Hughes, *The Big Sea*, p. 238.

15. Based on Marion L. Starkey, "Jessie Fauset," *Southern Workman*, 62 (May 1932), pp. 217–20.

16. Letter from Walter White to H. L. Mencken, 17 October 1923, NAACP

papers, Manuscripts Division, Library of Congress. Quoted in Charles F. Cooney, "Walter White and the Harlem Renaissance," *Journal of Negro History*, 57 (July 1972), p. 232.

17. Bontemps, "The Awakening: A Memoir" in *Harlem Renaissance Remembered*, pp. 25–6.

18. "A Negro to His Critics," *New York Herald Tribune Books*, 6 (March 1932).

19. Jean Toomer to Waldo Frank (c. 1922–3). Quoted in Mark Helbling, "Sherwood Anderson and Jean Toomer," Negro *American Literature Forum*, 9 (Summer 1975), p. 36.

20. *The Big Sea*, p. 325.

21. Quoted in Donald Ogden Stewart, *Fighting Words* (New York: Harcourt Brace & World, 1940), pp. 58–9.

22. For a detailed analysis of Calverton's interest and involvement with Black Americans, see Haim Genizi, "V. F. Calverton: a Racial Magazinist for Black Intellectuals, 1920–1940," *Journal of Negro History*, 57 (July 1972), pp. 241–53.

23. "The Negro" in Stearns, *America Now* (New York: The Literary Guild of America, 1938), p. 485.

24. Calverton, "The Growth of Negro Literature," *Anthology of American Negro Literature* (New York: The Modern Library, 1929), p. 3.

25. Saunders Redding, "The Problems of the Negro Writer," *Massachusetts Review*, 6 (1964–5), pp. 58–9. See also the two seminal essays on white portrayal of Negro character by Sterling Brown; "Negro Character as Seen by White Authors," *Journal of Negro Education*, 2 (January 1933), pp. 180–201; "A Century of Negro Portraiture in American Literature," *Massachusetts Review*, 7 (1966), pp. 73–96; and Edward Margolies, "The Image of Primitive in Black Letters," *Midcontinent American Studies Journal* (Fall 1970), pp. 70–76.

26. Ellison, *Shadow and Act* (New York: Random House, 1964), p. 17.

This article is a revised version of an article which appeared in a book printed in India and permission has been granted by The Oxford University Press-India to reprint.

RAYMOND SMITH

Langston Hughes: Evolution
of the Poetic Persona

Langston Hughes's career as a poet began with the publication of "The Negro Speaks of Rivers" in the June, 1921 issue of *The Crisis*. By 1926, before the poet had reached the age of twenty-five, he had published his first volume of poems, *The Weary Blues*. Of this volume Alain Locke, the leading exponent of "The New Negro," announced that the black masses had found their voice: "A true people's poet has their balladry in his veins; and to me many of these poems seem based on rhythms as seasoned as folksongs and on moods as deep-seated as folk-ballads. Dunbar is supposed to have expressed the peasant heart of the people. But Dunbar was the showman of the Negro masses; here is their spokesman."[1] With the publication of his second volume of poems, *Fine Clothes to the Jew* (1927), Hughes was being referred to as the "Poet Laureate of the American Negro." During a visit to Haiti in 1932, he was introduced to the noted Haitian poet Jacques Roumain, who referred to Hughes as "the greatest Negro poet who had ever come to honor Haitian soil."[2] When the noted Senegalese poet and exponent of African negritude, Léopold Senghor, was asked in a 1967 interview "In which poems of our, American, literature [do] you find evidence of Negritude?" his reply was "Ah, in Langston Hughes; Langston Hughes is the most spontaneous as a poet and the blackest in expression!"[3] Before his death in 1967, Hughes had published more than a dozen volumes of poetry, in addition to a great

From *The Harlem Renaissance Re-examined*, edited by Victor A. Kramer. © 1987 by AMS Press, Inc.

35

number of anthologies, translations, short stories, essays, novels, plays, and histories dealing with the spectrum of Afro-American life.

Of the major black writers who first made their appearance during the exciting period of the 1920s commonly referred to as "the Harlem Renaissance," Langston Hughes was the most prolific and the most successful. As the Harlem Renaissance gave way to the Depression, Hughes determined to sustain his career as a poet by bringing his poetry to the people. At the suggestion of Mary McLeod Bethune, he launched his career as a public speaker by embarking on an extensive lecture tour of the South. As he wrote in his autobiography: "Propelled by the backwash of the 'Harlem Renaissance' of the early 'twenties, I had been drifting along pleasantly on the delightful rewards of my poems which seemed to please the fancy of kindhearted New York ladies with money to help young writers.... There was one other dilemma—how to make a living from *the kind of writing I wanted to do*.... I wanted to write seriously and as well as I knew how about the Negro people, and make *that* kind of writing earn me a *living*."[4] The Depression forced Hughes to reconsider the relation between his poetry and his people: "I wanted to continue to be a poet. Yet sometimes I wondered if I was barking up the wrong tree. I determined to find out by taking poetry, *my* poetry, to *my* people. After all, I wrote about Negroes, and primarily *for* Negroes. Would they have me? Did they want me?"[5]

Though much of the poetry Hughes was to write in the thirties and afterward was to differ markedly in terms of social content from the poetry he was producing in the twenties, a careful examination of his early work will reveal, in germinal form, the basic themes which were to preoccupy him throughout his career. These themes, pertaining to certain attitudes towards American and vis-à-vis his own blackness, had in fact been in the process of formulation since childhood. Hughes's evolution as a poet cannot be seen apart from the circumstances of his life which thrust him into the role of poet. Indeed, it was Hughes's awareness of what he personally regarded as a rather unique childhood which determined him in his drive to express, through poetry, the feelings of the black masses. Hughes's decision to embark on the lecture tour of Southern colleges in the 1930s is not to be taken as a rejection of his earlier work; it was merely a redirection of energies towards the purpose of reaching his audience. Hughes regarded his poetry written during the height of the Harlem Renaissance as a valid statement on Negro life in America. The heavily marked volumes of *The Weary Blues, Fine Clothes to the Jew*, and *The Dream Keeper* (published in 1932 but consisting largely of selections from the two earlier volumes) used by Hughes for poetry readings during the thirties and forties and now in the James Weldon Johnson

Collection at Yale University, indicate that Hughes relied heavily on this early work and in no way rejected it as socially irrelevant.

Hughes's efforts to create a poetry that truly evoked the spirit of Black America involved a resolution of conflicts centering around the problem of identity. For Hughes, like W.E.B. Du Bois, saw the black man's situation in America as a question of dual consciousness. As Du Bois wrote in his *Souls of Black Folk* (1903): "It is a peculiar sensation, this double-consciousness, this sense of always looking at oneself through the eyes of others, of measuring one's soul by the tape of a world that looks on in amused contempt and pity. One ever feels his twoness,—an American, a Negro; two souls, two thoughts, two unreconciled strivings; two warring ideals in one body, whose dogged strength alone keeps it from being torn asunder."[6] Hughes was to speak of this same dilemma in his famous essay, published in 1927, concerning the problems of the black writer in America, "The Negro Artist and the Racial Mountain": "But this is the mountain standing in the way of any true Negro art in America—this urge within the race toward whiteness, the desire to pour racial individuality into the mold of American standardization, and to be as little Negro and as much American as possible."[7] In *The Weary Blues* (New York: Alfred Knopf, 1926), Hughes presented the problem of dual consciousness quite cleverly by placing two parenthetical statements of identity as the opening and closing poems, and titling them "Proem" and "Epilogue." Their opening lines suggest the polarities of consciousness between which the poet located his own persona: "I Am a Negro" and "I, Too, Sing America." Within each of these poems, Hughes suggests the interrelatedness of the two identities: the line "I am a Negro" is echoed as "I am the darker brother" in the closing poem. Between the American and the Negro, a third identity is suggested: that of the poet or "singer." It is this latter persona which Hughes had assumed for himself in his attempt to resolve the dilemma of divided consciousness. Thus, within the confines of these two poems revolving around identity, Hughes is presenting his poetry as a kind of salvation. If one looks more closely at Hughes's organization of poems in the book, one finds that his true opening and closing poems are concerned not with identity but with patterns of cyclical time. "The Weary Blues" (the first poem) is about a black piano man who plays deep into the night until at last he falls into sleep "like a rock or a man that's dead." The last poem, on the other hand, suggests a rebirth, an awakening, after the long night of weary blues: "We have tomorrow/Bright before us/Like a flame."[8] This pattern of cyclical time was adopted in the opening and closing poems of *Fine Clothes to the Jew*, which begins in sunset and ends in sunrise. Again, it is the blues singer (or poet) who recites the song: "Sun's a risin',/This is gonna be ma song."[9] The poet's song, then, is Hughes's resolution to the problem of double consciousness, of being an American and being black.

Hughes viewed the poet's role as one of responsibility: the poet must strive to maintain his objectivity and artistic distance, while at the same time speaking with passion through the medium he has selected for himself. In a speech given before the American society of African Culture in 1960, Hughes urged his fellow black writers to cultivate objectivity in dealing with blackness: "Advice to Negro writers: Step *outside yourself*, then look back— and you will see how human, yet how beautiful and black you are. How very black—even when you're integrated."[10] In another part of the speech, Hughes stressed art over race: "In the great sense of the word, anytime, any place, good art transcends land, race, or nationality, and color drops away. If you are a good writer, in the end neither blackness nor whiteness makes a difference to readers." This philosophy of artistic distance was integral to Hughes's argument in the much earlier essay "The Negro Artist and the Racial Mountain," which became a rallying call to young black writers of the twenties concerned with reconciling artistic freedom with racial expression: "It is the duty of the younger Negro artist if he accepts any duties at all from outsiders, to change through the force of his art that old whispering 'I want to be white' hidden in the aspirations of his people, to 'Why should I want to be white? I am a Negro—and beautiful!'"[11] Hughes urged other black writers to express freely, without regard to the displeasure of whites *or* blacks, their "individual dark-skinned selves." "If white people are glad, we are glad. If they are not, it doesn't matter. We know we are beautiful. And ugly too. If colored people are pleased we are glad. If they are not, their displeasure doesn't matter either. We build temples for tomorrow, strong as we know how, and we stand on top of the mountain, free within ourselves" (p. 694). In this carefully thought-out manifesto, Hughes attempted to integrate the two facets of double consciousness (the American and the Negro) into a single vision—that of the poet. His poetry had reflected this idea from the beginning, when he published "The Negro Speaks of Rivers" at the age of nineteen. Arna Bontemps, in a retrospective glance at the Harlem Renaissance from the distance of almost fifty years, was referring to "The Negro Speaks of Rivers" when he commented: "And almost the first utterance of the revival struck a note that *disturbed* poetic tradition."[12] (Italics mine)

In Hughes's poetry, the central element of importance is the affirmation of blackness. Everything that distinguished Hughes's poetry from the white avant-garde poets of the twenties revolved around this important affirmation. Musical idioms, jazz rhythms, Hughes's special brand of "black-white" irony, and dialect were all dependent on the priority of black selfhood:

> I am a Negro
> Black as the night is black
> Black like the depths of my Africa.[13]

Like Walt Whitman, Hughes began his career as a poet confident of his power. Unlike Whitman, however, who celebrated particular self ("Walt Whitman, the Cosmos"), Hughes celebrated racial, rather than individual, self. Hughes tended to suppress the personal element in his poetry, appropriating the first person singular as the fitting epitome of universal human tendencies embodied in race. "The Negro Speaks of Rivers" seems almost mystical in comparison to Whitman's physicality:

> I've known rivers:
> Ancient, dusky rivers.
> My soul has grown deep like the rivers.[14]

One could venture too far in this comparison; of course, Whitman declared himself the poet of the soul as well as the body. Few would deny he had mystical tendencies.

In Hughes, however, there is little hint of the egotism in which Whitman so frequently indulged. Indeed, Hughes was hesitant to introduce the element of the personal into his poetry. In an essay published in the journal *Phylon* in 1947 on his "adventures" as a social poet, Hughes remarked that his "earliest poems were social poems in that they were about people's problems–whole groups of people's problems—rather than my own personal difficulties."[15] Hughes's autobiographical account of the writing of "The Negro Speaks of Rivers" confirms this point, and sheds light on the process by which Hughes transformed personal experiences into archetypal racial memories. The poem had evolved out of personal difficulties with his father, who had emigrated to Mexico when Langston was a child, and had not seen his son in over a decade. Hughes had been summoned unexpectedly by his father to join him in the summer of 1919, hoping to persuade the son to enter into the business world. The elder Hughes felt nothing but contempt for the country and the race he had left behind. The following conversation, recorded in Hughes's autobiography *The Big Sea*, suggests the irreconcilable differences between the two:

> "What do you want to be?"
> "I don't know. But I think a writer."
> "A writer?" my father said. "A writer?

Do you think they make money? ... Learn something you can
make a living from anywhere in the world, in Europe or South
America, and don't stay in the States, where you have to live like
a nigger with niggers."
"But I like Negroes," I said.[16]

The following summer, on a train trip to Mexico, Hughes's dread of the
eventual confrontation with his father over his future vocation led to the
writing of the poem: "All day on the train I had been thinking about my
father, and his strange dislike of his own people. I didn't understand it,
because I was Negro, and I liked Negroes very much."[17] Despite Hughes's
severe emotional state, the poem itself displays little hint of the personal
anxiety that led to its creation.

Perhaps the closest Hughes ever came to incorporating his personal
anxiety into a poem was his "As I Grew Older," published initially in 1925,
and later included in *The Weary Blues*. The poem is almost reduced to
abstractions; it is a landscape of nightmare, a bleak and existential
examination of blackness. The poet begins by recalling his "dream," once
"bright like a sun," but now only a memory. A wall which separates the poet
from his dream suddenly appears, causing him severe anxiety. It is at this
point that the poet is thrust back upon himself and forced to seek an
explanation for his dilemma:

Shadow.
I am black.

These two lines appearing at the center of the poem provide the key to his
despair and to his salvation. As he begins to realize that his blackness is the
cause of his being separated from his dream, he simultaneously realizes that
blackness is central to his ontology. It is as much a physical reality as it is a
metaphysical state of mind. In order for the dream to be restored, the
spiritual and the physical blackness must be reintegrated. As the poet
examines his hands, which are black, he discovers the source of his
regeneration as a full person:

My hands!
My dark hands!
Break through the wall!
Find my dream!
Help me to shatter this darkness,

To smash this night,
To break this shadow
Into a thousand lights of sun,
Into a thousand whirling dreams
Of sun![18]

In order for the poet to transcend his temporal despair, he must accept the condition of his blackness completely and unequivocally. The poem thus ends, not in despair, but rather in a quest for self-liberation, dependent on the affirmation "I am black!"

The words had been used much earlier by another poet, W.E.B. Du Bois, far better known as the founder of the NAACP, editor of *The Crisis*, and lifelong champion of black pride. His poem "The Song of the Smoke," published in the magazine *Horizon* in 1899, opened with the words:

I am the smoke king,
I am black.

Later in the poem, Du Bois wrote these ringing lines:

I will be black as blackness can,
The blacker the mantle the mightier the man,
My purpl'ing midnights no day may ban.

I am carving God in night,
I am painting hell in white.
I am the smoke king.
I am black.[19]

The poem, published when Hughes was five years old, prefigures the point in time, fifteen years later, when the careers of the two—Du Bois and Hughes—would converge, with the publication of Hughes' poem "The Negro Speaks of Rivers," in Du Bois's journal *The Crisis*, with the poem's dedication also going to Du Bois.

This early connection between Hughes and Du Bois is important, for it was Du Bois who was calling for a renaissance of black culture as early as 1913, in an essay on "The Negro in Literature and Art": "Never in the world has a richer mass of material been accumulated by a people than that which the Negroes possess today and are becoming conscious of. Slowly but surely they are developing artists of technic who will be able to use this material."[20]

By 1920, Du Bois was actually using the word "renaissance" in referring to the new awakening of black creativity in the arts: "A renaissance of Negro literature is due; the material about us in the strange, heartrending race tangle is rich beyond dream and only we can tell the tale and sing the song from the heart."[21] This editorial in *The Crisis*, almost certainly read by Hughes, must have encouraged him to submit the poem for publication. In his autobiography, Hughes credited Du Bois and *The Crisis* for publishing his first poems and thus giving his literary career its first official boost: "For the next few years my poems appeared often (and solely) in *The Crisis*. And to that magazine, certainly, I owe my literary beginnings, insofar as publication is concerned."[22]

While Hughes certainly owed Du Bois a debt of gratitude for his official entrance upon the literary scene, it seems that Hughes's very special sensitivity as a budding young poet developed organically from his experiences as child. Though he did credit Dunbar and Sandburg among his influences, these literary mentors pale in light of what Hughes had to say about his method of poem-writing: "Generally, the first two or three lines come to me from something I'm thinking about, or looking at, or doing, and the rest of the poem (if there is to be a poem) flows from those first few lines, usually right away" (p. 56). This spontaneity of approach worked both for and against Hughes. Many of his poems, written in hasty response to some event reported in yesterday's newspaper, for example, have badly dated. The spontaneity that resulted in his best poetry came from the depths of his own experiences as a black man in America, though these personal experiences often were disguised as archetypal ones.

The tension between his awareness of growing up black and his acceptance of the "dream" of America, however tenuously defined, provided the dynamic for his poetry. From an early age, Hughes developed the distinction between the social versus the physical implications of black identity in America: "You see, unfortunately, I am not black. There are lots of different kinds of blood in our family. But here in the United States, the word 'Negro' is used to mean anyone who has *any* Negro blood at all in his veins. In Africa, the word is more pure. It means *all* Negro, therefore *black*" (p. 11). During a trip to Africa as a merchant seaman in 1922, he discovered that the Africans who "looked at me ... would not believe I was a Negro" (p. 11). The semantic confusion was of American origin. Whatever the semantic distinctions, Hughes desired to be accepted as Negro by the Africans, and was disappointed with their reaction to him.

Hughes's middle-American background (he grew up in Lawrence, Kansas) sheltered him from some of the more blatant forms of racial prejudice toward Negroes in other regions of the country. When he lived in Topeka, he attended a white school, his mother having successfully challenged the school board to have him admitted. Most of his teachers were pleasant, but there was one "who sometimes used to make remarks about my being colored. And after such remarks, occasionally the kids would grab stones and tin cans out of the alley and chase me home" (p. 14). For a while he lived with his maternal grandmother, from whom he heard "beautiful stories about people who wanted to make the Negroes free, and how her father had had apprenticed to him many slaves ... so that they could work out their freedom.... Through my grandmother's stories always life moved, moved heroically toward an end.... Something about my grandmother's stories ... taught me the uselessness of crying about anything" (p. 17). Hughes's poem "Aunt Sue's Stories," published in *The Crisis* in July of 1921, furnishes an example of how Hughes transformed such memories into poetry. His childhood was not a happy one in Lawrence, as he related in his autobiography, and he turned to books for solace (p. 16). Parallels between his childhood experiences and later poems abound. Many of his poems focused on unhappy or wrongly treated children, for whom the American dream had no relevance. This empathy with wronged children had its origins in Hughes's own unhappiness as a child.

Many of his poems about black laborers originated out of his difficulties in finding work while in school. A job he had in a hotel, cleaning toilets and spitoons, while only in the seventh grade, was to result in one of his more well-known poems, "Brass Spitoons," included in his second volume of poetry *Fine Clothes to the Jew* (1927). Four decades after a local theatre owner put up a sign "NO COLORED ADMITTED" in Lawrence, Kansas, Hughes would recall the event in *ASK YOUR MAMA*:

IN THE QUARTER OF THE NEGROES
WHERE THE RAILROAD AND THE RIVER
HAVE DOORS THAT FACE EACH WAY
AND THE ENTRANCE TO THE MOVIE'S
UP AN ALLEY UP THE SIDE[23]

A beating administered by a group of white toughs in Chicago the summer before the Chicago riots would be transformed into "The White Ones" seven years later:

I do not hate you,
For your faces are beautiful, too.

I do not hate you,
Your faces are whirling lights of loveliness and splendor, too.
Yet why do you torture me,
O, white strong ones,
Why do you torture me? [24]

These parallels between Hughes's early life and his later poetry indicate that he had formulated certain attitudes towards his race and towards white America before he had ever considered the idea of becoming a poet.

It was only by accident that he became a poet. He was elected to the position of class poet at Cleveland's Central High because, as he humorously recalled, he was a Negro, and Negroes were supposed to have "rhythm." "In America most white people think, of course, that *all* Negroes can sing and dance, and have a sense of rhythm. So my classmates, knowing that a poem had to have rhythm, elected me unanimously—thinking, no doubt, that I had some, being a Negro.... It had never occurred to me to be a poet before, or indeed a writer of any kind."[25] Thus the role of poet was thrust upon Hughes by accident, or perhaps, by design, because he was Negro in a white society. It was the social implications of his blackness, however, that fitted him for the role. The incidents of his childhood and youth had marked Langston Hughes as a black man, and his poetry would affirm his acceptance of the mission, to be a spokesman for the black masses.

At the same time, Hughes could not deny the double nature, the dual-consciousness of being an American as well as a black. The very fact that he had been chosen by his classmates as class poet *because* he was Negro only accentuated his separateness from them. By the same token, he had never been completely exposed to the full brunt of prejudice, American-style, during his youth. Up until the time of his Southern lecture tour of 1931, his acquaintance with Southern mores had been merely peripheral. Indeed, he often began these programs by explaining how truly "American" his upbringing had been: "I began my programs by telling where I was born in Missouri, that I grew up in Kansas in the geographical heart of the country, and was, therefore very American."[26] His audiences, which consisted largely of Southern Negroes, must have found his initial declaration of Americanism rather disorienting. As Hughes himself explained in his autobiography, this first-hand encounter with racial prejudice in the South provided an introduction to an important aspect of racial heritage to which he had never been fully exposed: "I found a great social and cultural gulf between the races in the South, astonishing to one who, like myself, from the North, had never known such uncompromising prejudices."[27]

In a poem published in *The Crisis* in 1922, Hughes outlined his ambivalence towards the region in rather chilling imagery:

> The child-minded South
> Scratching in the dead fire's ashes
> For a Negro's bones.

He indicated in the poem's conclusion that the South had a strong attraction, but that he was more comfortable in resisting, its allure:

> And I, who am black, would love her
> But she spits in my face
> And I, who am black,
> Would give her many rare gifts
> But she turns her back upon me.[28]

In the same year that Hughes published "The South," Jean Toomer published *Cane*. One of the poems in *Cane*, "Georgia Dusk," evoked similar imagery:

> A feast of moon and men and barking hounds,
> An orgy for some genius of the South
> With blood-hot eyes and cane-lipped scented mouth,
> Surprised in making folk-songs from soul sounds.[29]

Where Toomer's *Cane* was the product of direct experience (a six-month sojourn in Georgia as a rural schoolteacher), Hughes's South was an imaginatively evoked nightmare. The last lines of Hughes's poem suggest that he was not yet ready to embrace the Southern experience as Toomer had done. Hughes's Gothic South was a far cry from Toomer's seductive lines in "Carma":

> Wind is in the cane. Come along.
> Cane leaves swaying, rusty with talk,
> Scratching choruses above the guinea's squawk,
> Wind is in the cane. Come along.[30]

If Hughes feared the direct Southern confrontation during the twenties, he found much to admire in those Southern blacks who came to settle in the teeming cities of the North, and from them he derived material for his poetry. In seeking communal identity through them, Hughes overemphasized the exotic, as this passage from *The Big Sea* indicates: "I never tired of hearing them talk, listening to the thunderclaps of their laughter, to their troubles, to their discussions of the war and the men who had gone to Europe from the Jim Crow South.... They seemed to me like the gayest and the bravest people possible—these Negroes from the Southern ghettoes—facing tremendous odds, working and laughing and trying to get somewhere in the world" (pp. 54–55). The passage suggests the attitude of a sympathetic observer rather than that of an engaged participant. In some ways, Hughes's attitude towards Southern Negroes was directly counter to that of his father's. According to Langston, the elder Hughes "hated Negroes. I think he hated himself, too, for being a Negro. He disliked all of his family because they were Negroes and remained in the United States" (p. 40). Hughes, on the other hand, proudly affirmed his racial heritage. Where his father rejected both race and country, Hughes could reject neither.

At the end of his lecture programs in the South, Hughes would recite his poem "I, Too, Sing America." As often as he invoked this poem, he would be reaffirming his faith in the American dream. Some of Hughes's earliest poems reveal an almost childlike faith in the American ideal, as in the opening lines of the following first published in 1925:

> American is seeking the starts,
> America is seeking tomorrow,
> You are America,
> I am America
> America—the dream,
> America—the vision.
> America—the star-seeking I.

The same poem affirmed the unity of black and white America:

> You of the blue eyes
> And the blond hair,
> I of the dark eyes
> And the crinkly hair,
> You and I
> Offering hands ... [31]

This affirmation of racial unity had a direct relation to Hughes's experience with racial integration at Cleveland's Central high, where he was often elected to important class positions because of his acceptability to various white ethnic factions: "Since it was during the war, and Americanism was being stressed, many of our students, including myself, were then called down to the principal's office and questioned about our belief in Americanism.... After that, the principal organized an Americanism Club in our school, and ... I was elected President" (*The Big Sea*, p. 31). While this experience might serve to strengthen his faith in an ideal America, it also, paradoxically, reinforced his sense of separateness as a Negro. His race was clearly an advantage in terms of popularity among his peers; still, it was his color which marked him as different.

At the same time, Hughes's experience in racial integration set him apart from the experience of those Negroes from the South whose lifestyle he so admired. Hughes must have realized that his experience vis-à-vis that of most black Americans was rather unique. Though he claimed at times to have had a typical Negro upbringing, it was nevertheless different, as he pointed out in this passage from *The Big Sea*: "Mine was not a typical Negro family. My grandmother never took in washing or worked in service or went to church. She had lived in Oberlin and spoke perfect English, without a trace of dialect. She looked like an Indian. My mother was a newspaper woman and a stenographer then. My father lived in Mexico City. My grandfather had been a congressman" (p. 303). In addition, Hughes harbored no grudges against white society: "I learned early in life not to hate *all* white people. And ever since, it has seemed to me that *most* people are generally good, in every race and in every country where I have been" (p. 14).

Hughes often sought to dispel the distinction between American and Negro by affirming his nationality in no uncertain terms. The following incident from his autobiography illustrates this point. He had been teaching English to Mexicans during his final summer in Mexico with his father. The teacher who was to replace him was a white American woman who found it incredible that a Negro could be capable of teaching anything:

> When she was introduced to me, her mouth fell open, and she said:
> "Why, Ah-Ah thought you was an American."
> I said, : "I am American!"
> She said: "Oh, Ah mean a white American."
> Her voice had a Southern drawl.
> I grinned. (p. 78)

Another incident from his autobiography concerns his refusal to deny his race. On the return trip to the United States from Mexico after his first

summer there, Hughes attempted to purchase an ice cream soda in St. Louis.
The following exchange took place:

> The clerk said: "Are you a Mexican or a Negro?"
> I said: "Why?"
> "Because if you're a Mexican, I'll serve you," he said. "If you're
> colored, I won't."
> "I'm colored," I replied. The clerk turned to wait on someone
> else. I knew I was home in the U. S. A. (p. 51).

These incidents were to have their counterparts in his poetry, where he
could affirm with equal assurance his two credos of identity: "I am a Negro"
and "I, Too, Sing America." But while affirming these polar commitments,
Hughes was alienated from both of them. As a black man, he was aware that
his race had never been granted full participation in the American dream.
His exposure to the possibilities of that dream, however, through his
experience with racial integration, and his relative innocence (this was to
disappear, of course) in matters of Southern mores, would distinguish his
circumstances from the lot of the black masses, with whom he sought to
identify to the extent of becoming their spokesman. This peculiar set of
conditions allowed Hughes to assume a degree of sophistication in racial
matters quite unusual among his contemporaries, white or black. This
sophistication, coupled with his insistence on maintaining the necessary
aesthetic distance of the artist, provided the stimulus for his poetry and
endowed the poet with a sense of mission. He was absolutely confident of his
self-imposed mission as a poet of the black masses. His familiarity with white
Bohemian intellectual circles in New York during the twenties provided him
with the additional stimulus of communicating his message across racial
lines. Thus two kinds of poetry emerged in the twenties: the black vernacular
poetry, utilizing dialect, jazz talk, and everyday subject matter; and "message"
poetry, which concentrated on the position of the black man in white
America. *The Weary Blues*, Hughes's first book, contained much of this
message poetry, besides some experiments in jazz poetry ("The Cat and the
Saxophone," "Blues Fantasy," "Negro Dancers"), and additional non-racial
lyrics. The second book, *Fine Clothes to the Jew*, concentrated almost entirely
on the vernacular subject matter, and contained many poems written in blues
dialect. These two tendencies in Hughes's early work were to predominate
throughout his career.

Shakespeare in Harlem (1942), for example, may be considered a sequel
to *Fine Clothes*, while *Montage of a Dream Deferred* (1951) integrated the

vernacular subject matter with the thematic concerns introduced in *The Weary Blues*. *Montage*, along with *ASK YOUR MAMA* (1961), will probably remain Hughes's most important achievements in poetry since his work of the twenties. *ASK YOUR MAMA*, permeated with humor, irony, and exciting imagery, contains echoes of "The Negro Speaks of Rivers," "As I Grew Older," and "The Cat and the Saxophone." As in these earlier poems, Hughes transforms personal experiences and observations into distillations of the Black American condition.

Hughes wrote in his autobiography: "My best poems were all written when I felt the worst. When I was happy, I didn't write anything" (p. 54). When he first began writing poetry, he felt his lyrics were too personal to reveal to others: "Poems came to me now spontaneously, from somewhere inside.... I put the poems down quickly on anything I had a hand when they came into my head, and later I copied them into a notebook. But I began to be afraid to show my poems to anybody, because they had become very serious and very much a part of me. And I was afraid other people might not like them or understand them" (p. 34). These two statements regarding his poetry suggest deep underlying emotional tensions as being the source of his creativity. And yet the personal element in Hughes's poetry is almost entirely submerged beneath the persona of the "Negro Poet Laureate." If, as Hughes suggested, personal unhappiness was the cornerstone of his best work, it then follows that, in order to maintain the singleness of purpose and devotion to his art, he would be required to sacrifice some degree of emotional stability. Thus poetry became a kind of therapy, masking deeper emotional tensions. We know from his autobiography that Hughes experienced two severe emotional breakdowns. The first one had to do with a break with his father over the course of his vocation: the second followed upon a break with his wealthy white patroness in the late twenties over the kind of poetry he was writing. Both of these emotional traumas were directly related to his decision to become a poet of his people.

The persona of the poet was the role Hughes adopted in his very first published poem, as *the Negro* in "The Negro Speaks of Rivers." It was a persona to which he would remain faithful throughout his lengthy career. The link between his personal experiences and his poetry has been suggested in this paper. It cannot be defined because it seems clear that Hughes suppressed the more frightening excursions into his own personal void. Poetry was an outlet as well as a salvation. Only occasionally, as in the poem "As I Grow Older," does Hughes provide a window upon his inner anxieties, and even in this poem the real root of these anxieties is hidden, and the poem becomes an allegory of the black man's alienation in white America.

Hughes's early attempts in the twenties to fill the role of Poet Laureate of the Negro led him to create a body of work that was organic in nature. The traditional literary sources of inspiration were for the most part bypassed. The source of his poetry was to be found in the anonymous, unheard black masses: their rhythms, their dialect, their life styles. Hughes sought to incorporate this untapped resource of black folk language into a new kind of poetry. His personal experiences, as related in his autobiography, combined with this folk material to provide thematic dimension to his work. The basic themes regarding the American dream and its possibilities for the black man were always present in his poetry. The tension between the unrealized dream and the realities of the black experience in American provided the dynamic. This tension between material and theme laid the groundwork for the irony which characterized Hughes's work at its best.

NOTES

1. "The Weary Blues" (Review), *Palms*, 4, No. 1 (October 1926), 25.

2. Langston Hughes, *I Wonder As I Wander* (1956; rpt. New York: Hill and Want, 1964), p. 31.

3. Quoted in Arthur P. Davis, "Langston Hughes: Cool Poet," in *Langston Hughes: Black Genius: A Critical Evaluation*, ed. Therman B. O'Daniel (New York: William & Morrow & Company, 1971), p. 25.

4. *I Wonder As I Wander*, pp. 4–5.

5. *I Wonder As I Wander*, pp. 41–42.

6. *The Souls of Black Folk*, rpt. Greenwich, Conn.: Fawcett Publications, 1961), pp. 16–17.

7. *Nation*, 122 (June 23, 1926), 692.

8. *The Weary Blues*, p. 109.

9. Langston Hughes, *Fine Clothes to the Jew* (New York: Alfred A. Knopf, 1927) pp. 17–89.

10. "Writers: Black and White," in *The American Negro Writer and his Roots* (New York: American Society of African Culture, 1960), p. 44.

11. "Negro Artist and Racial Mountain," *p.* 694.

12. "Negro Poets, Then and Now," in *Black Expression: Essays by and about Black Americans in the Creative Arts*, ed. Addison Gayle, Jr. (New York: Weybright and Talley, 1969), p. 83.

13. Hughes, *The Weary Blues*, p. 108.

14. *The Weary Blues*, p. 22.

15. "My Adventures as a Social Poet," *Phylon*, 8 (Fall 1947), 205.

16. *The Big Sea* (1940); rpt. New York: Hill and Wang, 1963), pp. 61–62.

17. *The Big Sea*, p. 54.

18. *Weary Blues*, pp. 55–56.

19. W.E.B. Du Bois, "The Song of the Smoke," (1899) rpt. in *Dark Symphony: Negro Literature in America*, ed. James A. Emanuel and Theodore L. Gross (New York: Free Press, 1968), p. 44.

20. *The Seventh Son: The Thought and Writings of W.E.B. Du Bois*, ed. Julius Lester (New York: Random House, 1971), I, 451.

21. *The Emerging Thought of W.E.B. Du Bois: Essays and Editorials from The Crisis*, ed. Henry Lee Moon (New York: Simon and Schuster, 1972) p. 354.

22. *The Big Sea*, p. 72. Subsequent references to *The Big Sea* will appear parenthetically in the text.

23. Langston Hughes, *ASK YOUR MAMA: 12 MOODS FOR JAZZ* (New York: Alfred Knopf, 161). p. 5.

24. *Weary Blues*, p. 106.

25. *The Big Sea*, p. 24.

26. *I Wonder As I Wander*, p. 57.

27. *I Wonder As I Wander*, p. 52.

28. *Weary Blues*, p. 54.

29. *Cane* (1923); rpt. New York: University Place Press, 1967), p. 22.

30. *Cane*, p. 16.

31. "America," *Opportunity*, 3 (June 1925), 175.

BRUCE KELLNER

"Refined Racism": White Patronage in the Harlem Renaissance

Despite their good intentions, white intellectuals and philanthropists bestowed mixed blessings in support of black artists and writers during the Harlem Renaissance. Their involvement contributed indirectly to the Black Arts Movement of the 1960s, yet the cost to the 1920s is undeniable. The black writer both thrived and suffered, torn between well-meant encouragement from the white race to preserve his racial identity (usually described as "primitivism") and a misguided encouragement from his own race to emulate the white one. Madame C.J. Walker's products, designed to straighten hair, and surely those of her competitors, designed to lighten skin, as well as the regular practice of black comedians wearing blackface makeup, are extreme examples at opposite ends of this appalling scale. Nevertheless, at the time of the Harlem Renaissance, that "renaissance" would never have progressed beyond Harlem without the intervention and support of white patrons. Inevitably, such support manifested itself in action which in retrospect seems patronizing, but to deny its positive aspects is intellectually indefensible. White patronage, for good as well as ill, was merely an unavoidable element in getting from the past to the present, and the roles of people like Albert C. Barnes, for example, Charlotte Mason, all the Spingarns—Joel and Amy and Arthur—and Carl Van Vechten, make a strong supporting cast. Some were bad actors; some were better.

From *The Harlem Renaissance Re-examined*, edited by Victor A. Kramer. © 1987 by AMS Press, Inc.

Alphabetical order is a reasonable approach to such a list; coincidentally, it is an order leading from the weakest to the strongest involvement with the Harlem Renaissance, although quantity and quality are rarely equal.

I

Albert C. Barnes—"the terrible tempered Barnes" as Carl McCardle called him[1]—might begin either list. This brash and opinionated Philadelphia millionaire began to collect impressionist and post-impressionist art around 1907, and fifteen years later he founded the Barnes Foundation in Merion, Pennsylvania, with what was then the most important collection of work by Henri Matisse in America, along with substantial representations of Renoir, Dégas, Picasso, Cézanne, and dozens of other celebrated painters. During the years Barnes was amassing these holdings, he rescued African art from ethnology, "stripping [art] of the emotional bunk," he declared, "[with] which the long-haired phonies and that fading class of egoists, the art patrons, have encumbered it."[2] He extolled the aesthetics of African art, even though he could only define it in abstract terms, unable to get far beyond vague references to color and line and space. But he saw himself with the "emotional intensity of a moral reformer, ... as one of the few true friends of black Americans, ... beleaguered by misinformed and even racist others," as historian Mark Helbling put it.[3] In 1923 when Barnes was trying to write an essay called "Contribution to the Study of Negro Art in America," he called on the influential black educator Alain Locke for assistance. Locke, in turn, sensing possibilities for financial as well as emotional support for young black artists, encouraged a friendship by introducing Barnes to several figures who would shortly become active in the Harlem Renaissance, among them Walter White, already a powerful gadfly in the NAACP. White himself was trying to do an article about black art in America just then and sought help from Barnes; but White had cited several of those "long-haired phonies" as his authorities, and not surprisingly Barnes damned it. Then, when white editor H.L. Mencken turned down Barnes's article to consider White's for publication in *The American Mercury*, the "terrible tempered Barnes" began to court the Urban League's Charles S. Johnson, hoping that an issue of the organization's magazine *Opportunity* might be devoted to African art, featuring his own article of course, and offering his Foundation as bait since it exhibited black and classical Greek and Egyptian sculpture side by side. Like Locke, Johnson welcomed Barnes's knowledge, his own decorum able to hold in check his reactions to the paranoid outbursts that emanated regularly from Merion, Pennsylvania. *Opportunity* did run a special issue on African art, with Barnes's essay, but his impact was not felt fully until the following year when the white periodical *Survey Graphic* gave over its March 1925 issue to "The New Negro." That title was used for Locke's impressive anthology eight months later, with Barnes's article expanded, and reproductions of various works of African art in the Barnes Foundation.

Albert C. Barnes was an important voice in attempting to give to both races a sense of what negligence had lost, but he tried to focus the reconciliation of a primitive African art and a new cultural spirit among the emerging black intellectuals of the Harlem Renaissance, and Alain Locke was dissatisfied with his questionable analysis. Actually, Locke had hoped to engage Carl Van Vechten to write an article about black American art, but at that time Van Vechten was contributing almost monthly essays on various black subjects to the posh white magazine *Vanity Fair* and begged off, leaving Locke with Barnes's "kindly but vague assertions" that white Americans were devitalized because of their comfortable culture.[4] Of white Americans, Barnes wrote in *The New Negro:* "Many centuries of civilization have attenuated his original gifts and have made his mind dominate his spirit. He has wandered too far from the elementary human needs and their easy means of natural satisfaction. The deep and satisfying harmony which the soul requires no longer arises from the incidents of daily life." The imagination of the black American, on the other hand, he contended, had been intensified by the existence of racism. The "daily habit of thought, speech, and movements of Afro-Americans," he continued, "are flavored with the picturesque, the rhythmic, the euphonious." As for African art, Barnes was only able to say that the "renascence of Negro art" was as "characteristically Negro as are the primitive African sculptures."[5] What that "characteristic" was, however, Barnes could never make clear, so it is not surprising that Alain Locke wrote an essay of his own on the subject for *The New Negro*, even though his argument was similar—that African art was at the root of Afro-American artistic expression. Fifty years later, Nathan Irvin Huggins, in his pioneering study of the Harlem Renaissance, suggested that such a conviction was a measure of our distance from our true identity: "America and Americans were provincials. That was the problem. Black men as well as white men were forced through condition and education to look elsewhere for the springs of civilization and culture.... So black men yearned as American provincials, to find meaning and identity in Africa; their frustration was a measure of their Americanization."[6]

By 1925, Albert C. Barnes's emphasis on form and abstract content in

African art and his innocent physical descriptions of what he had squirrelled away in Merion, Pennsylvania, do not really come to terms with the influence of primitivism at all. His concern with the cultural identity of black Americans, however, the African collection in the Barnes Foundation, and certainly his money, speak to that cultural awakening during the twenties.

II

Money seems to be the only matter contributed to the movement by Mrs. Rufus Osgood Mason, born Charlotte Louise Vandevere Quick, and called "godmother" by her protégés when she could get her way. She got it most of the time, because the purse strings she controlled were like tentacles. They gave rein to young black writers; they could strangle. As Agatha Cramp in Rudolph Fisher's *The Walls of Jericho*, as Dora Ellsworth in Langston Hughes's *The Ways of White Folks*, and indeed as Godmother in Zora Neale Hurston's *Dust Tracks on a Road*, Charlotte Mason has been immortalized, but with marked ambivalence.

Widowed at fifty-one when her physician husband died at seventy-three, Mrs. Mason first used her vast wealth in some preliminary anthropological studies of American Indians, even making some field trips at the turn of the century. She was interested as well in psychology and psychic phenomena, through her husband's influence, but by the twenties her interests had shifted to the primitive and therefore innocent elements (or so she judged them) in Afro-American arts and letters.

From her regal penthouse on Park Avenue, surrounded by Indian and African artifacts, minor though respectable European paintings, eighteenth-century French furniture, a staff of servants, and a retinue of white toadies, this old dowager ruled over a stable of young Afro-American artists and writers. At one time or another during the Harlem Renaissance, she considered as her personal property both Hughes and Hurston, as well as Aaron Douglas, Richmond Barthé, Hall Johnson, Claude McKay, Louise Thompson, and especially Alain Locke. None of them was permitted to divulge her identity as the source of their good fortune, even though one or another of them served as escort on several occasions. Langston Hughes remembered her white chauffeur driving him home to Harlem after these outings to the theater, and Louise Thompson remembered similar discomfort. When Godmother wished to communicate with her godchildren by mail, she employed the services—without pay presumably—of white sometime poet Katherine Garrison Chapin and her sister, sometime sculptor

Cornelia, members of an artistic circle that included muralist George Biddle and his wife Helene Sardeau. To young and inexperienced black writers, the power of that white world, not to speak of its glamour, must have been somewhat intimidating, but they were privy to it so long as they fulfilled Charlotte Mason's expectations. They were to live in Harlem; they were to emphasize in their work what she identified as folk culture or primitivism, and they were to eschew subjects she judged as didactic or smacking of social reform. Plenty of those letters the Chapin sisters were obliged to write for her to Alain Locke, after all, expressed her open hostility toward organizations designed to improve relations between the races.

She paid Langston Hughes's living expenses while he was writing his first novel, *Not Without Laughter*. She underwrote the single performance on Broadway of Zora Neale Hurston's musical drama, *The Great Day*. She picked up the monthly rental for Richmond Barthé's Greenwich Village studio so he could devote all his time to sculpture. She financed research trips, college tuition, rehearsal time in concert halls; she doled out pocket money for shoes, winter coats, bus fares; and she called each of her protégés "my child." She invested today's equivalent of about half a million dollars in young black artists and writers, but she broke off the alliances when her charges proved disloyal by abandoning what she considered the purity in their work, its "primitivism." Because she believed in "primitivism" with cult fervor and disapproved of social protest, the breaks were frequent and the value of the support, as Nathan Irvin Huggins suggested, was questionable: "Whatever other burdens Negro artists carried, this arrangement stigmatized Negro poetry and prose of the 1920s as being an artistic effort that was trying to be like something other than itself."[7]

Langston Hughes was still a Lincoln University student when Alain Locke took him to Mrs. Mason's apartment. As was her wont, she sat on a dais at one end of the drawing room *in* rather than *on* a chair best described as a throne, and before Hughes left she slipped him a fifty dollar bill. To Zora Neale Hurston, Mrs. Mason delivered a monthly $200 stipend for two years. At today's rate of exchange that pushes $30,000. Both rewarded her in their autobiographies: Hurston claimed that she and her godmother were mystically tied together, pagans spiritually joined; Hughes wrote in awe of her power that he didn't "know why or how she still found time" for him, since she moved in circles far removed from his own.[8] Both broke with her when their work was less than what she considered "beautiful" which is to say "primitive." By that time, however, the stock market had fallen, and Harlem's plight replaced its popularity. Hughes's poems began to reflect a world in which Mrs. Mason had no interest, and he asked to be released, to remain a friend but without the onus of financial obligation. In turn, in venom apparently, she berated his talent and his character. It was not a reaction that surprised Hughes's friend Louise Thompson, a young teacher who had been brought to the Mason apartment by black painter Aaron Douglas, and who escaped from it when she realized its power to corrupt.

One of the most fascinating figures of the Harlem Renaissance, Louise Thompson deserves a biography of her own, and it is not untoward to include its outlines here, since the role of the white patron is perhaps more clearly defined through her than through the better known Hughes and Hurston. Louise Thompson brought to the movement an awareness of racism in its various disguises that strongly influenced her later life as well as the lives of many of the young black artists and writers with whom she came in contact.

Reared in several states as her rover stepfather moved from job to job, Louise Thompson was often the only black child in a town, so that first exposure to racism was an awareness of isolation. Then at Berkeley, she encountered it in the form of indifference from her fellow students, white of course, until, awakened to her own potential when W.E.B. Du Bois lectured there, she took a teaching job in Arkansas. Her students were barely able to read, in a community where isolation and indifference were too easily replaced by racial violence, and her memories of its terrors were still clear sixty years later. In the mid-twenties, she went on to the Hampton Institute to teach business administration and there encountered another form of racism, somehow more invidious. A "refined racism," as she later called it, hid comfortably behind the mask of white patronage.

At the height of the Harlem Renaissance, she was denied the right to any social exchange with her students; black and white faculty members could neither publicly nor privately fraternize; and the predominately white administration demanded strict enforcement of social rules from another age. At a time when on white campuses F. Scott Fitzgerald coeds rouged their knees and their male counterparts carried hip flasks, Hampton's black students were not allowed to date. Even weekend movies in the college chapel required a faculty member as chaperone for every four students. At that juncture, Louise Thompson accepted a National Urban League scholarship in New York and began to come in contact with many young black intellectuals, among them Wallace Thurman, editor of the notorious *Fire!!*, spokesman for the movement, and scandalous *bon vivant*. They married after a brief courtship and separated six months later. It was at that time that she came under the influence of Charlotte Mason who employed her as secretary to Hughes and Hurston. Long afterward, Louise Thompson said she might have known on her first visit what lay ahead when, nervous and trying to please, she exclaimed at the extravagant bouquet of flowers on the dining table. "Which color do you prefer, my child?" she remembered Mrs. Mason asking. When she said she thought the red ones were especially pretty, Mrs. Mason withered her with a smile: "Yes, of course, you *would* prefer red...."[9] Godmother, who tried to disguise her suffocating hold on young black writers with largesse, only convinced Thompson to break her ties, and, she later declared, she convinced Langston Hughes to do the same. But Hughes was a long time in recovering his emotional equilibrium, while Thompson was not. To complete this capsule biography of an extraordinary woman, she went on to conduct seminars all over the South for the Congregational Education Society; she organized that group of young black intellectuals who went to Russia to make a movie in Moscow about life in America (which never got made, incidentally); she was deeply involved in the Scottsboro Case and the National Committee for Political Prisoners; and she served for fifteen years in the International Workers Order. Wallace Thurman died in 1934, and in 1940 she married William Patterson who had been lawyer for the Scottsboro boys. But Charlotte Mason had left permanent scars, as she had on many of her protégés, and Louise Thompson's bitterness over the disturbing contradiction in patronage that could so subtly transform itself into patronizing left her with some disturbing suspicions about the role of the white supporter. The weight of evidence was strong.

As for the eccentric Charlotte Mason, with her strong biases about what Negro art was supposed to be, she remains a shadowy figure, denied by accident or intention an obituary in *The New York Times* when she finally died, at the age of ninety-two, and, in the work of her own protégés given only cautious attention. Without her support, would we have had Richmond Barthé's *Feral Benga?* Langston Hughes's *Not Without Laughter?* Zora Neale Hurston's anthropological studies? Perhaps.

III

The most selfless of these white philanthropists were surely the Spingarn brothers, Arthur and Joel. They devoted their lives to racial equality as the leading twentieth-century abolitionists and constant supporters of the National Association for the Advancement of Colored People and its interests, motivated by the indifference of the white race, the despair of the black race, and the driving need they felt for integration. Both were involved in the founding of the NAACP, and as early as 1914 both were touring at their own expense to picket in the South against Jim Crow laws. Arthur was the NAACP's lawyer from its beginnings, its vice-president from 1911, and its president from 1940 until his retirement in 1966, as well as its unpaid legal counsel until his death in 1971. His first of several legal successes for the race came in 1927, when the Supreme Court upheld his challenge to the all-white Democratic primary election in Texas, and that one was succeeded by many others. At the beginning of his career, Arthur Spingarn's law practice suffered because of his racial sympathies, but he believed in later years that his racial sympathies actually increased it. Like his brother, he believed unquestioningly in the theory of the "talented tenth," sharing with W.E.B. Du Bois and many others the idea that within any group there would be ten percent capable of extraordinary achievement, gifted by the gods or by circumstances to speak for the rest. If white America could be awakened to that "talented tenth" in black America, they reasoned, segregation would diminish, conditions would improve, and in time prejudice would disappear. Hindsight tells us that the theory was too firmly grounded in idealism ever to survive the dream. The advocates of art as well as its practioners do not, alas, populate the "untalented ninetieth" in either race.

Arthur Spingarn's brother Joel, three years his elder, began his career as a professor of comparative literature at Columbia University with a formidable reputation as a scholar—he was an authority on the Italian philosopher and art critic Benedetto Croce—but that lasted less than a decade. A colleague had been dismissed because of a breach-of-promise suit against him; when Joel Spingarn rose in defense of academics being allowed their private lives, he was fired too, although he seems not to have mourned long. Twenty-five years later he celebrated the anniversary with a cocktail party for his friends, many of them, perhaps most, Afro-Americans.

Long before he left Columbia, Joel Spingarn had been deeply involved with the race. Already, he had dismissed politics, failing in a bid for a congressional seat in 1908 and resigning from the Republican party in 1912 because it had no black delegates. By that time, from his family home, Troutbeck, New York, he was editing his suffragist newspaper *The Amenia Times* and was deeply committed to the NAACP. He served as its chairman of the board until 1919, its treasurer until 1930, and its president until his death. His wife Amy completed his final term of office. Joel Spingarn's long tenure was not entirely smooth. Black newspapers like the New York *Age* regularly complained because of too many whites in influential positions in the NAACP, and W.E.B. Du Bois, who respected Spingarn's commitment as well as his intellect, inevitably and understandably resented what was at that time a practical necessity. At the same time, he recognized Joel Spingarn's contributions and paid them strong tribute. In 1914, as I observed earlier, the Spingarn brothers barnstormed to protest segregation practices. In 1915, Joel Spingarn attempted to stop showings of D.W. Griffith's racist film epic *The Birth of a Nation*. In 1916, he organized the first Amenia Conference, with many influential blacks in attendance, to formulate official policy combatting racial inequities. In 1917, he drafted the first deferral anti-lynching legislation. In 1918, as a major in the army, he laid aside his anti-separatist stand long enough to force the establishment of a black officers' training school.

Independently wealthy after 1919, he devoted the majority of his time to the NAACP, and he was in part responsible for its 300 branches by 1921. Both Joel Spingarn and his wife Amy regularly contributed funds to the NAACP throughout their lives and spent a good deal of time soliciting funds from others for its various causes. In 1925, when the literary contests in *The Crisis* and *Opportunity* were at their height, Amy Spingarn established financial awards of her own, voted by a committee to Rudolph Fisher for fiction, Marita Bonner for drama, and Countee Cullen for poetry (Frank Horne and Langston Hughes placing second and third in the latter category). Joel Spingarn himself had long before established the most prestigious award for the race, the Spingarn Medal, and he insured its continuance by setting up a trust fund in his will. The gold medal was to be awarded annually for "the highest and noblest achievement of an American Negro during the preceding year or years." The cover of the June 1914 issue of *The Crisis* carried a drawing of the medal's design.

For the record, it went first, in 1915, to Ernest E. Just, a professor of physiology at Howard University, and next, to Lieutenant Colonel Charles Young in the United States Army. In subsequent years, through the period of the Harlem Renaissance, the Spingarn Medal was awarded to critic/poet William Stanley Braithwaite; lawyer Archibald Grimké; W.E.B. Du Bois; actor Charles Gilpin; sociologist Mary Burnett Talbert; educator George Washington Carver; James Weldon Johnson; singer Roland Hayes; historian Carter G. Woodson, who founded the *Journal of Negro History*; Anthony Overton, who was president of the Victory Life Insurance Company; novelist Charles W. Chesnutt; Howard University president Mordecai Johnson; Fort Valley, Georgia, Industrial School president H.A. Hunt; Tuskegee's Robert Russa Moton; Max Yergan, who directed the YMCA in Africa; Tuskegee's William T. B. Williams; educator Mary McLeod Bethune. Later recipients also active during the Harlem Renaissance included Walter White; labor leader A. Philip Randolph; Paul Robeson; and Langston Hughes. Now that list has little to do with white patronage, but it is certainly an impressive one, and it speaks well for Joel Spingarn, a ruthless and single-minded integrationist whose belief in the "talented tenth" never seemed to waver. We may know that the roots of such a theory can never be more than an ideal in purely practical terms, but the names of the recipients of the Spingarn Medal must surely give pause for hope.

IV

The last white patron in this brief catalog, Carl Van Vechten, is probably the most controversial, the one about whom white as well as black scholars feel strong prejudice. Nathan Irvin Huggins's conclusions in his book on the period of the Harlem Renaissance do not underestimate Van Vechten's contributions but, he contends, "it is open to question how well, or in what way, Van Vechten served Harlem and the Negro" and equally important to question how well they "served him."[10] In *When Harlem Was in Vogue*, David Levering Lewis allows that Van Vechten "praised everything artistically good or promising with enthusiastic good sense, balanced by sympathetic dismissal of whatever Harlem produced that was clearly mediocre,"[11] but he allows for the possibility "that Van Vechten was a literary voyeur, exploiting his Harlem connections in order to make himself even richer."[12] On the other hand, James Weldon Johnson said Van Vechten was "one of the most vital forces in bringing about the artistic emergence of the Negro in America,"[13] and the assessments of Van Vechten's contemporary biographers reinforce that judgment.

By the time Carl Van Vechten had become addicted to black arts and letters during the twenties, he was already well established as a music critic of considerable perception and, on the strength of four highly popular novels, a successful writer hardly in need of being "served," not financially at least. But he certainly seems to have discovered the potential for artistic excellence in the race before the race had fully realized that for itself, and he announced it with the same enthusiasm he had brought to any number of other matters labelled *avant-garde* in their own time. It is not difficult, however, to understand why others—white as well as black—might misinterpret Van Vechten's motives, assuming, on the basis of his reputation as a dandy, a dilettante, that he was not only self-serving but slumming.

His interest was of long standing, however. At the turn of the century, Van Vechten had fallen under the spell of ragtime and, before the first war, of jazz, about which he wrote in *Red* (from the mid-twenties), it "may not be the last hope of American music, nor yet the best hope, but at present, I am convinced, it is its only hope."[14] Even before he had praised the music of Igor Stravinsky, Erik Satie and George Gershwin, the operas of Richard Strauss, the dancing of Isadora Duncan and Anna Pavlova, the writings of Gertrude Stein—all in advance of anybody else in America—he had begun his campaign. In 1914, he was advocating in print the formation of a Negro theater organization, with black actors and black playwrights.

In the mid-twenties he met Walter White through their mutual publisher and, through him, he came to know the entire set of Harlem literati, including his greatest friend, James Weldon Johnson. If Van Vechten needed a catalyst for his growing enthusiasm for black arts and letters, he found it in that remarkable figure. He met the young poets Langston Hughes and Countee Cullen, and eventually Eric Walrond, Wallace Thurman, and Zora Neale Hurston—the latter responsible for having coined the term "niggerati" to describe the young black intellectuals of the period, and for having dubbed Carl Van Vechten the first "Negrotarian." Shortly, he had arranged for the work of Cullen and Hughes to appear in the pages of the prestigious *Vanity Fair*, and through his instigation Alfred Knopf published Hughes's first collection of poems *The Weary Blues* as well as novels by Nella Larsen and Rudolph Fisher. For *Vanity Fair*—as popular and influential in the twenties, apparently, as any magazine in recent history— Van Vechten wrote several articles himself: about the spirituals, about the blues, about blues singers Bessie Smith and Ethel Waters, about black theater. He wrote dozens of reviews of books by black writers; he financed Paul Robeson's first recitals of spirituals in New York; and he became, in Nathan Irvin Huggins's apt phrase, "the undisputed downtown authority on uptown life."[15] Although he devoted an inordinate amount of time to shabby pursuits—getting regularly drunk in speakeasies, collecting handsome Harlem sycophants about him, unconsciously propagating stereotypes through his own delight in Harlem's exotic elements—there is nothing in any of his work to suggest that his respect and admiration were not genuine, and it is clear that his desire to share his discoveries resulted in a cultural interchange unique at the time. In their glamorous apartment, Van Vechten and his wife, the Russian actress Fania Marinoff, entertained frequently and lavishly, always with fully integrated guest lists. The parties were eventually reported as a matter of course in some of the black newspapers of the city, and Walter White called their West 55th Street address "the mid-town office of the NAACP."[16]

And then Carl Van Vechten wrote *Nigger Heaven*. The title alone guaranteed controversy, but readers were violently split in their reactions to

the content, and despite the support of several influential black writers, there
was widespread feeling that he had used his Harlem acquaintances badly.
Nigger Heaven is no great novel, but it certainly created a large white
readership for black literature, and it popularized Harlem and brought
plenty of money into the cabarets north of 125th Street. Whether those two
influences are close enough in value to be mentioned in the same sentence is
open to question. *Nigger Heaven* is usually criticized because of its
preoccupation with Harlem's seamy side, although only about a third takes
place in speakeasies and bedrooms. Those passages surely are rough and
erotic, and blacks espousing the theory of a "talented tenth," eager to put a
best foot forward in Harlem, did not enjoy seeing it depicted as frequently
engaged in the Charleston, or otherwise tangled up in the bedsheets of pimps
and courtesans. The other two-thirds of the novel is about Harlem's black
intelligentsia, with a pedantic heroine and a feeble hero locked in a pathetic
little romance that ends in melodramatic violence more appropriate for the
silent movies of the period. W.E.B. Du Bois wanted to burn the book, but
Wallace Thurman suggested that a statue of the author be erected in
Harlem. The real problem with *Nigger Heaven* is not a question of either its
sincerity or its scandal-mongering, but the fact that it is consciously didactic,
a deliberate attempt to educate Van Vechten's already large white reading
public by presenting Harlem as a complex society fractured and united by
individual and social groups of diverse interests, talents, and values. The
scandalous drinking and sleeping around in *Nigger Heaven* goes on in all of
Van Vechten's novels; such vagaries are hardly limited to the white race. In
his afterword to a subsequent paperback edition of *Nigger Heaven*, Van
Vechten declared, "Negroes are treated by me exactly as if I were depicting
white characters, for the very excellent reason that I do not believe there is
much psychological difference between the races."[17] As a consequence—
though it is probably true that this only proves itself to somebody willing to
read Van Vechten's other novels—*Nigger Heaven* is best understood as the
one of his books which has characters who happen to be black. But who
could have known that, or have even cared to, faced with a title like *Nigger
Heaven*?

Whatever its limitations, the novel strengthened Van Vechten's ties
with the race—certainly he lost no friends because of it—and increased his
loyalty. Through the rest of his long career, he devoted his time and
substantial funds from his million-plus inheritance beginning in 1927, to a
wider recognition of black achievement, first, by making documentary
photographs of virtually every celebrated black person. The list is staggering,
in quality as well as quantity, and especially in the number of people

photographed before their talents were generally recognized; but Van Vechten's eye and ear had been fairly unerring since the turn of the century, so it is not surprising to discover Shirley Verett at 24, Leontyne Price at 23, Lena Horne at 22, Diahann Carroll at 18, and about thirty years ago such subjects as James Baldwin, Alvin Ailey, Harry Belafonte, James Earle Jones, Chester Himes, LeRoi Jones, and Arthur Mitchell. Second, Van Vechten established the James Weldon Johnson Memorial Collection of Negro Arts and Letters at Yale University, surely one of the greatest repositories for black studies, and he specified in his will that any money ever realized from reprints of his own books and photographs be donated to the collection's endowment fund. It is difficult to conceive of the books written since Van Vechten's death, on various black figures and subjects, without the materials he amassed and collected and supported.

None of the preceding discussion addresses itself to the subtle distinction between patronage and patronizing. From the vantage point of the 1980s, it is difficult to embrace without strong reservation the naiveté and paternalism of the twenties as faultless when sincere, or forgiveable when devious. It is doubtless easy for the one to become the other, but it may be almost as easy for the one to *seem* to become the other—blanket judgments are always dangerous—because of black dismay over the circumstances that led to white patronage in the first place.

NOTES

1. Carl McCardle, "The Terrible Tempered Barnes," *Saturday Evening Post*, 21 (March 1942), p. 93.

2. Quoted in McCardle, p. 93.

3. See Mark Helbling, "African Art: Albert C. Barnes and Alain Locke," *Phylon*, (March 1982), p. 6.

4. Alain Locke, "The Legacy of the Ancestral Arts," *The New Negro* (New York: Atheneum, 1969), p. 254.

5. Albert C. Barnes, "Negro Art in America," *The New Negro* (New York: Atheneum, 1969), p. 20.

6. Nathan Irvin Huggins, *Harlem Renaissance* (New York: Oxford University Press, 1971), pp. 82–83.

7. Huggins, p. 129.

8. Langston Hughes, *The Big Sea* (New York: Alfred A. Knopf, 1940), p. 324.

9. Louise Thompson Patterson, interview with the author, November 1983.

10. Huggins, p. 93.

11. David Levering Lewis, *When Harlem Was in Vogue* (New York: Alfred A. Knopf, 1981), pp. 182–83.

12. Lewis, p. 181.

13. Quoted in Bruce Kellner, *Carl Van Vechten and the Irreverent Decades* (Norman: University of Oklahoma Press, 1968), p. 233.

14. Carl Van Vechten, *Red* (New York: Alfred A. Knopf, 1925), p. xv.

15. Huggins, p. 100.

16. Quoted in Bruce Kellner, *"Keep A-Inchin' Along": Selected Writings of Carl Van Vechten About Black Arts and Letters* (Westport, Connecticut: Greenwood Press, 1979), p. 8.

17. Carl Van Vechten, *Nigger Heaven* (New York: Avon Publishing Company, 1951), p. 189.

AKASHA GLORIA HULL

Color, Sex, and Poetry
in the Harlem Renaissance

The year is 1927:

Alice Dunbar-Nelson is writing lively, informative columns in the Washington, D.C., *Eagle* about musical and literary prizes being offered to black artists, the black-and-tan cabarets of Harlem, James Weldon Johnson's *God's Trombones*, the Pan-African Congress, and the musical shows "Rang Tang" and "Africana." Her poem "April Is on the Way" wins honorable mention at the annual *Opportunity* awards dinner and is published that same year in *Ebony and Topaz*.[1]

Angelina Weld Grimké receives a friendly note from Langston Hughes on May 8, 1927, and is enjoying the distinction of having more of her poems included in Countee Cullen's landmark 1927 collection, *Caroling Dusk: An Anthology of Verse by Negro Poets*, than any other woman writer.[2]

Georgia Douglas Johnson, already renowned as a poet, receives first place in the 1927 *Opportunity* competition for her folk drama *Plumes*. Five months later, she is featured by society writer Geraldyn Dismond in the October 29, 1927, "Through the Lorgnette" column of the Pittsburgh *Courier*.

Georgia Douglas Johnson's Saturday Nighters salon at her Washington, D.C., home is especially brilliant this year. Grimké was, in Gwendolyn Bennett's words, a "particularly pleasing" component of a "charming medley" of participants on June 4, 1927, while Dunbar-Nelson

From *Color, Sex, and Poetry: Three Women Writers of the Harlem Renaissance.* © 1987 by Akasha Gloria Hull.

was the guest of honor at a July 23, 1927, evening, where there was "much poetry and discussion and salad and wine and tea."[3]

In this wide range of ways at the height of the Harlem Renaissance, these three women writers—Alice Dunbar-Nelson, Angelina Weld Grimké, and Georgia Douglas Johnson—are contributing to the brightness of the period. Their varied backgrounds and experiences both accord with and diverge from the flow of the movement. Yet, because of sheer timing, they were swept fortuitously into the New Negro cultural awakening of the 1920s.

Viewed from one angle, the Harlem Renaissance was what Nathan Huggins has called it, "a channeling of energy from political and social criticism into poetry, fiction, music, and art."[4] A historical cause that helped to generate it was the founding of such organizations as the National Association for the Advancement of Colored People, the National Urban League, and the Association for the Study of Negro Life and History, which fostered a growing mood of racial confidence, assertiveness, and protest. W.E.B. DuBois's Talented Tenth became the New Negro shedding old, demeaning stereotypes and assuming a bold new face. The Great Migration of blacks from South to North brought more money and freedom, along with an air of excitement, opportunity, and drama. World War I had introduced black soldiers to a wider world of tolerance, thus intensifying their abhorrence of American racial prejudice. In general, United States blacks added their voices to the international outcry of black self-assertion. As seen most clearly in Garveyism, this attitude involved race solidarity and pride and a conscious connection with the African homeland. All of these moods and ideas emerged as newly articulated themes in the art and literature of the period.

Although the designation *Harlem* Renaissance discounts other geographical activity, the development of that black metropolis as a race capital located within the cultural capital of the country made it the acknowledged locus of the movement. In particular, the proximity to the publishing world was crucial. It facilitated opportunities for mainstream outlets that augmented those provided by race magazines such as *Opportunity*, *Crisis*, and, to a lesser extent, the *Messenger*. In the same way, white patronage from downtown was worth more than the prizes awarded in the *Opportunity* and *Crisis* annual contests. White participation in the Renaissance is a reminder that the 1920s were also the time of the Jazz Age and the Lost Generation, and of experimentation with black themes by white writers like Eugene O'Neill, DuBose Heyward, and Julia Peterkin. Freudian-influenced whites were fascinated with the potential naturalness and exoticism of blacks and with these manifestations in all forms ranging from Harlem street life to the singing and dancing of black musicals such as *Shuffle Along* (1921) and *Running Wild* (1923). Fresh developments in music were paralleled by the rise of fine artists like Aaron Douglas, Sargent Johnson, Augusta Savage, and Richmond Barthé, who likewise mined the racial dimensions of their talent.

In literature, names from an earlier era continued to be called—Fenton Johnson, Alice Dunbar-Nelson, W.E.B. Dubois, James Weldon Johnson, and others. Many new writers surfaced—notably, Claude McKay, Jean Toomer, Countee Cullen, Jessie Fauset, Langston Hughes, Nella Larsen, Eric Walrond, Rudolph Fisher, Gwendolyn Bennett, Arna Bontemps, Willis Richardson, Helene Johnson, and Zora Neale Hurston. Utilizing the major genres of poetry, short stories, novels, and plays, these writers produced a remarkable and diverse body of work. Timeless subject matter in traditional modes competed with more daring topics, approaches, and techniques. This juxtaposition of generations and concepts of art led to a critical debate between what are most often designated as the genteel and the bohemian schools. Alice Dunbar-Nelson pictured it as conflict between "those to whom literature is a beautiful dignified mistress" and those to whom it is "a strident, dishevelled gutter-snipe."[5] True it was that jazz, free verse, primitivism, and sensationalism attracted more attention than conventional verse and mannered depictions of Afro-American life. History and folklore (both rural and urban), satire, issues of identity and power all found expression in this Harlem Renaissance work, which, on the whole, came more assuredly from an ethnic center.

As one commentator put it, any investigation of the Harlem Renaissance must recognize its "emotive and symbolic character."[6] Ever since the period, those writing about it have done so with their various analytic methodologies glazed by their own subjective biases, needs, and imaginations. Historians have de-emphasized the magic of the era by reconstructing its social and political causation. Many participants and onlookers have cast highly flavored memoirs. Textual scrutiny has revealed the thematic and linguistic strategies of the writers. During the 1970s, a black-is-beautiful generation saw itself adumbrated by the earlier age, while some harsher critics viewed it as another baleful lesson in racial co-optation. The social historians' picture of a glittering interracial assemblage of the avant-garde home, a forum for meetings, people, and ideas. In fact, Regina Anderson and Gwendolyn Bennett gave Charles Johnson the suggestion for his celebrated 1924 Civic Club dinner, where black writers of all generations were brought into contact with sympathetic white writers and publishers.[11]

In Washington, D.C., Georgia Douglas Johnson extended the list of black women who were hostesses to the Renaissance:

> In the living room of her S Street house behind the flourishing rose bushes, a freewheeling jumble of the gifted, famous, and odd came together on Saturday nights. There were the poets Waring Cuney, Mae Miller, Sterling Brown, Angelina Grimké, and Albert Rice. There were the artists Richard Bruce Nugent and Mae Howard Jackson. Writers like Jean Toomer and Alice Dunbar-Nelson (former wife of Paul Laurence Dunbar), and philosopher-critic Locke came regularly to enjoy the train of famous and to-be-famous visitors. Langston Hughes used to bring Vachel Lindsay; Edna St. Vincent Millay and Waldo Frank came because of Toomer; James Weldon Johnson and W.E.B. DuBois enjoyed their senior sage role there; occasionally, Countee Cullen and, more often, the suave Eric Walrond accompanied Locke. Rebecca West came once to encourage Georgia Johnson's poetry. H. G. Wells went away from one of the Saturday nights saddened by so much talent straining to burst out of the ghetto of American arts and letters.[12]

Johnson's role as cultural sponsor was all the more important because she played it outside of Harlem, New York, thus becoming a nexus for the intercity connections that helped to make the movement a truly national one.

Even in as unlikely a place as Lynchburg, Virginia, another female poet, Anne Spencer, was helping to "unpretentiously initiate a cultural and intellectual awakening."[13] James Weldon Johnson had discovered Spencer shortly before the 1920s and first published her poems in his *Book of American Negro Poetry* (1922). She had also established a local chapter of the NAACP in her southern city. Brought thus into the political and artistic ferment of the age, Spencer's home at 1313 Pierce Street became a popular stopover point for black leaders and artists traveling between the North and South, as well as a Renaissance focus for the state. Drawn to her doors were the likes of Roland Hayes, Marian Anderson, W.E.B. DuBois, Walter White, Mary McLeod Bethune, and Georgia Douglas Johnson.

Of course, from a feminist perspective, it is ironic that one of the notable ways women contributed to the period was through hostelrying-hostessing-salon keeping, refinements of their traditional domestic roles extended into the artistic and cultural arena. Most notably, A'Lelia Walker used her late mother's fortune to give large parties where famous guests of all classes and callings from home and abroad rubbed shoulders with one another. She and Carl Van Vechten were the fete-givers supreme of this party-mad era. And Geraldyn Dismond reported them in the *Inter-State Tattler*.

In other areas, too, women made their presence felt. There were the chorines whose unkempt (Afro-Americans say "rusty") knees Dunbar-Nelson execrated in one of her columns. There were also Garveyite daughters, actresses like Nora Holt and Rose McLendon, and singers such as Bessie Smith, Ethel Waters, and Billie Holiday. Most importantly, black women augmented the rich outpouring of literature. Major talents like Jessie Fauset, Georgia Douglas Johnson, Gwendolyn Bennett, and Zora Neale Hurston made their mark across a range of genres. Some, like Nella Larsen, Anne Spencer, and Helene Johnson, excelled in one specific form. Still others, especially poets such as Clarissa Scott Delaney and Lucy Ariel Williams, flashed briefly and less brightly.

Yet, despite what appears to be full participation of women in the Harlem Renaissance, one can discern broad social factors and patterns of exclusion. One of the most basic is how male attitudes toward women impinged upon them, how men's so-called personal biases were translated into something larger that had deleterious effects. This became especially invidious when such men were in influential and critical positions. They then made blatant the antifemale prejudice inherent in the whole of society. An excellent, though upsetting, case in point is Alain Leroy Locke, who was such an indispensable personage that Langston Hughes said he helped to "mid-wife" the Renaissance into being.[14] A Harvard-trained Ph.D., Rhodes scholar, and Howard University philosophy professor, Locke gave definitive shape to "the New Negro" in his 1925 anthology of that name. More importantly, his smooth, learned manner inspired patrons to make of him a conduit for their largesse to black artists. Thus, Locke dispensed not only money but also advice, support, and vital aid to many needful young writers. His handling of his role was controversial, but no one denied its centrality.

The problem with Locke, however, is that he behaved misogynistically and actively favored men. From the standpoint of the 1980s his unequal treatment of women makes his position all the more controversial. A "certified misogynist," he customarily "dismissed female students on the first class day with the promise of an automatic grade of C."[15] Owen Dodson explains: "He [Locke] didn't believe in women's lib for instance. If women enrolled in his classes as seniors, he'd say, 'You come here at your own risk.'"[16] This contempt for women and disparagement of their intellect inevitably carried over into his judgments and actions, with precious few exceptions. One of these was Zora Neale Hurston, whom, for some reason, Locke liked and recommended. Yet, there was still something in his attitude that caused her to label him "a malicious, spiteful little snot," who "lends out his patronage.... And God help you if you get on without letting him represent you."[17]

Locke's behavior becomes even more problematic because of his obvious partiality toward young males, to whom he was sexually attracted. Locke, in fact, functioned within a homosexual coterie of friendship and patronage that suggests that literary events were, in more than a few instances, tied to "bedroom politics" and "sexual croneyism"—as they no doubt may have been in the heterosexual world also. The point here, though, is that women were definitely excluded from Locke's beneficence and this particular sphere of favoritism. One story is illustrative. Cullen, whose homosexuality was openly tittered about, once described to Hughes a weekend he had spent with Locke: "Hughes crackled with curiosity, wanting to know about Howard, the city, and Locke. 'Is Mr. Locke married?' he wondered." Locke had begun a correspondence with Hughes after reading his early poems in the *Crisis*. Finally Hughes decided to "take Locke up on his repeated offers of a special relationship," perhaps with Cullen's urging. Eventually, in the summer of 1924, Locke came to see Hughes in Paris, "promising to bring him details of a possible Howard scholarship, offering to introduce him to famous Parisians." There, they had a "glorious time" and also met again in Venice. It was Locke who introduced Hughes to the wealthy, eccentric patron Mrs. Charlotte Osgood Mason (affectionately known as "Godmother") and "secured what amounted to a blank check" for him.[18]

The operation of a circle is further, and interestingly, revealed in this passage about Richard Bruce Nugent, a handsome, "self-conscious decadent who had shortened his name to Richard Bruce to allay maternal embarrassment about his homosexuality":

Georgia Douglas Johnson believed in Nugent's promise and mothered his neuroses when he returned to Washington in 1924. Alain Locke pursued him, offering Godmother's largesse if the young man would discipline his talents. But it was meeting Hughes at Georgia Johnson's one winter evening in 1925, and walking each other home "back and forth all night," that was the turning point in Nugent's life. He followed Hughes to New York, met Van Vechten, and fashioned his personality ... after Van Vechten's libertine [character] Peter Whiffle.... [19]

Carl Van Vechten, photographer, writer, columnist, and critic, was notorious for his lifestyle and his novel *Nigger Heaven*. He frequented the "transvestite floor shows, sex circuses, and marijuana parlors along 140th Street,"[20] and his lavish parties were said to resemble a "speakeasy deluxe peopled by literary figures, stage and screen celebrities, prizefighters, dancers, elegant homosexuals, and Lorelei Lee gold diggers."[21]

> Yet this was the figure whose assistance to the growth of the Harlem Renaissance ... was probably greater than that of any other white American. It was Van Vechten who talked Frank Crowninshield, the editor of *Vanity Fair*, into publishing some of the first poems of Countee Cullen and Langston Hughes, and who encouraged Alfred Knopf to bring out Hughes' first collection [*The Weary Blues*, 1925]. Among other editors and publishers of his acquaintance, he tirelessly promoted the work and the careers of the young Harlem writers.

This personality-patronage issue broadens into general revelations about the customary male circles of power and friendship, which during the period crossed racial lines. In his autobiography *The Big Sea*, Hughes recalls that Alfred A. Knopf, Jr., James Weldon Johnson, and Carl Van Vechten annually celebrated their common birthday together. In 1928, Charles Chesnutt, Afro-American fiction writer of an earlier generation, asked Johnson to assist him in bringing out a new edition of his novel *The House Behind the Cedars*. Johnson graciously responded: "I shall make some preliminary inquiries among publishers that I know well, and when you come to New York it will be a great pleasure to me to introduce you to these publishers."[22] Johnson also wrote the following to Edwin R. Embree, president of the Rosenwald Fund on August 22, 1931: "I got in touch with Langston Hughes and he tells me that he has written you about a scholarship. I need not say that I hope he will get it."[23]

Hughes was particularly fortunate. In Depression-stricken 1933, he returned from Russia to the United States as the guest of Noel Sullivan, "a rugged, shy bachelor whose family was one of San Francisco's oldest and richest." He was met at the dock by a "liveried chauffeur" and given a Carmel cottage in which to write.[24] Even Claude McKay, whose personality was difficult, had incredible "luck." During 1924, he was penning second-rate poetry and receiving money from Walter White and radical philanthropist Louise Bryant, and fifty-dollar monthly grants arranged by James Weldon Johnson and Walter White from the Garland Fund—all to write an execrable novel, "Color Scheme," which even Knopf rejected and left to die "of its own considerable defects."[25]

After its failure, he reworked similar material into an equally flawed second novel and wrote a few short stories. In France, disillusioned and broke in 1926, he asked Schomburg for money, then subsequently obtained greater assistance from Bryant. She persuaded her husband, diplomat William Bullit, to edit McKay's stories, and Bullit also got for him a $500 advance from Alfred Harcourt of Harcourt, Brace. Meanwhile, Bryant herself "was in New York with McKay's stories, charging through publishers' offices like an evangelist, preaching McKay's genius and showering desks with manuscript...." She retained for him a prestigious agent who negotiated a contract with Harper's to expand one of the stories into a novel. "With an advance and expense money from Bryant to pump him up," McKay was able to finish *Home to Harlem* in 1927.

Manna such as this was never showered upon the women writers of the period. Locke secured Mrs. Mason's backing for Hurston, Van Vechten helped Gwendolyn Bennett, Walter White volunteered to have his secretary type Larsen's *Quicksand*, and women received a good word or a small favor here and there. Yet the Renaissance, despite its veneer of equal opportunity, was a time when not only Harlem and the Negro, but men as usual were "in vogue." In a world that values and caters more to males, they enjoyed the lion's share of all the available goods and, in the field of literature, were more apt to be seriously encouraged as professional writers. This was not solely a matter of merit. For example, in 1926, McKay's reputation rested on *Harlem Shadows*, a volume of poetry published in 1922. He had been writing badly since (and was continuing to do so). Nevertheless, Bryant, White, Johnson, and others generously aided him. His novel that resulted, *Home to Harlem*, benefited not only from all this moral and material support (with which he should have produced something creditable) but from its exploitation of popular Harlem low-life themes.

The issue here is not whether friends—male or female, homosexual or heterosexual—should help one another. However, when the persons are men with power and position who almost exclusively benefit their male friends, then women suffer. In addition, all of this happens while the fiction of pure individual worth is maintained. It is telling that when James Weldon Johnson was assisting Chesnutt, Dunbar-Nelson was complaining about the "curious selfishness" she found in his crowd,[26] and in 1931, when Johnson was unofficially endorsing Hughes to the Rosenwald Fund, she and Georgia Douglas Johnson were desperately applying for jobs and grants. At no point during their lives did anyone ever provide them with leisure to write. The need for this creative space preoccupied Johnson. A 1928 newspaper article revealed that her "great fear" was that she would not be able to accomplish her artistic goals, for, "although she works incessantly, her time is too much taken up with making a living to give very much of it to literary work."[27]

True, quieter, less-visible female support networks existed, and women were sometimes able to serve their sisters. Nevertheless, because of women's less-advantaged status, these networks could often only amount to consolation circles for the disfranchised. Even when female spheres of patronage and aid were possible, they did not always realize their potential because of women's interests, positions, or socialization. An interesting case in point from the period is provided by hair-straightening heiress A'Lelia Walker. She spent freely on "the circle of handsome women attending her," "the effete men ... who organized her socials" (she was "especially fond of homosexuals"), and "her retinue of domestics." Her lavish parties made her "Harlem's principal salon-keeper, doing for the Renaissance what Mabel Dodge had done before the war for the artists and intellectuals of Greenwich Village": "But to the intellectuals and artists of Harlem she opened her houses and almost never her purse."[28]

Class (not in the sense of money) and caste differences operating on both sides prevented someone like Dunbar-Nelson from gaining some sort of place within Walker's circle of handsome women, which included French princess Violette Murat, who had come to the United States with Harold Jackman, Cullen's lifelong intimate, and was "perhaps too fond of women for some Harlemites."[29] It would have been difficult, but not impossible, for them to move past their superficial differences. Though not an intellectual, A'Lelia was not unintelligent; and Dunbar-Nelson, for her part, loved eating, drinking, and playing bridge as much as A'Lelia, although she generally cloaked her bohemian self with proper manners and social squeamishness. Had A'Lelia Walker been made to see that aiding other women (albeit artistic and intellectual New Negro ones, whom she probably mistrusted as a type) was a good project, many could have benefited. She was feminist enough to specify in her will that the Walker Manufacturing Company be perpetually headed by a female.[30]

Clearly, where the personality-patronage issue is concerned, individuals are most strongly drawn to their type. This observation raises the question of Harlem Renaissance fraternization and its relation to female role expectations. True to the upbeat flavor of the era (and to masculine behavioral norms), a great deal of this professionally vital male socializing occurred after hours in bars and over bottles. For example, after Walter White had enlisted writer Sinclair Lewis to help McKay, Lewis kept his promise by "spending two nights drinking and talking about writing with McKay at Harry's Bar, and taking a careful look at the unfinished novel."[31] At this time, even women's smoking was appalling. Ethel Ray Nance recounts being shocked when she first saw Jessie Fauset sitting at a table in the Civic Club with DuBois and smoking: "but she was very graceful about it.... And as I sat there, I thought, when I write home to my father, I guess I just won't mention this part of it."[32] Despite the fact that women did "go out," most of them—unlike the notorious actress Nora Holt—were not liberated enough to drink and/or talk about writing all night in a bar. Respectable, conscious black women were especially careful to counter negative stereotypes of themselves as low and sluttish. Female socialization can also be seen in women's relative reluctance to promote themselves confidently and boldly. Doing so helped to make Hurston a scandalous topic.

In the same way that women could not blithely "hang out" in bars or hop freighters to France and North Africa, they all could not, at the drop of the Renaissance, come flocking to New York City. They were much more likely to be tied to place via husbands, children, familial responsibilities, parental prohibitions, lack of fresh opportunities or the spirit of adventure, and so on. Although Jessie Fauset, Gwendolyn Bennett, and Helene Johnson were in Harlem during its heyday, Georgia Douglas Johnson and Angelina Grimké lived in Washington, D.C., while Alice Dunbar-Nelson orbited between Philadelphia and Wilmington, Delaware. Certainly, they were adversely affected by geographical immobility and being located away from the New York social and literary scene.

It is also instructive that, in this revolutionary movement that officially proclaimed its youthfulness, older men seem to have fared better than older women. Dunbar-Nelson, Grimké, Johnson, Anne Spencer, and Jessie Fauset were, like James Weldon Johnson and Claude McKay, born before 1890, and not after the turn of the century as were younger figures such as Hughes, Cullen, and Bennett. This means that quite a number of the women writers who were discovered or who received first-time prominence during the period did not fit the brash, youthful model. This was evident in the view and treatment of them that tended to make them passé rather than venerable. Recognizing this fact, women as unlike each other as Georgia Johnson and Zora Neale Hurston used false birthdates that represented them as being younger than they really were. In Hurston's case very recent scholarship has revealed that she was actually an additional decade older than her already corrected birthdate of 1901 indicates.[33] The new date of 1891 edges her into this older generation of women born in the late nineteenth century. Between 1927 and 1930, when Johnson applied to the Harmon Foundation, she cited her birthdate as 1888, an untruth that added two more years to the six by which she customarily shortened her life. She rightly suspected that, in this instance, it was better to be thirty-nine rather than forty-one or forty-seven. Obviously, Time "brushing cold fingers through [one's] hair" (in Johnson's poetic words) was a liability for women in more areas than romance.[34]

Other specifically literary factors further illuminate the status of women writers in the Harlem Renaissance. A principal one is the issue of poetry as a genre. During the period, it was, in a real sense, the preeminent form—based on its universality, accessibility for would-be writers, suitability for magazine publication, and classical heritage as the highest expression of cultured, lyric sensibility. The big three writers of the era—McKay, Cullen, and Hughes—made their reputations as poets. And most of the notable women writers of the period were poets, with only Larsen and Hurston not essaying verse. In addition to Johnson, Dunbar-Nelson, and Grimké, six others produced significant work—Anne Spencer, Jessie Fauset, Effie Lee Newsome, Gwendolyn Bennett, Helene Johnson, and the lesser-known Gladys Mae Casely Hayford.

Anne Spencer is an arresting poet because of the originality of her material and approach. Working in forms that are an eccentric mixture of free verse and rhymed, iambic-based lines, she treated subjects as varied as her titles: "Before the Feast of Shushan," "At the Carnival," "The Wife-Woman," "Dunbar," "Letter to My Sister," "Lines to a Nasturtium," "Neighbors," and "Creed." She is most modern in her predilection for casting herself into roles, her sense of woman-self and female identity, and her style, which is characterized by terseness, apt or unusual diction, and vivid images and metaphors. Known best as a novelist, Fauset is usually represented in anthologies by her love poems. Some of them are distinguished by the French titles she gave them and by her sometimes humorous and ironic cast of mind. Effie Lee Newsome primarily wrote children's verse based on nature lore.

Gwendolyn Bennett and Helene Johnson are the stellar poets of the younger generation. Bennett's poetry can be quite impressive. She was, by occupation, an artist, and consequently in her work she envisions scenes, paints still lifes, and expresses herself especially well in color. Of all the women poets, Helene Johnson's work most reflects the qualities commonly designated as characteristic of the Renaissance. She took "the 'racial' bull by the horns" (as James Weldon Johnson put it),[35] and also wrote poems in the new colloquial-folk-slang style popular during that time. Although the bulk of her poems are traditional romance and nature lyrics, her "Sonnet to a Negro in Harlem" is pro-black and militant. In her frequently reprinted

"Poem," she waxes ecstatic over the "Little brown boy / Slim, dark, big-eyed," who croons love songs to his banjo down at the Lafayette Theater.

Gladys Mae Hayford's distinctions are being born in Africa and having two of her poems—"Nativity" (in which the Christ Child is black) and "The Serving Girl"—published in the *Atlantic Monthly*. A Fanti, she committed herself to imbuing "our own people with the idea of their own beauty, superiority and individuality." Because Africa for her was a very real place, her poems have a concrete specificity not usually found in some other Harlem Renaissance works on that theme. She talks about blue lappah, frangipani blossoms, and the brass ankle bells that guard "Brown Baby Cobina." Her regularly accented couplets also employ various lyric personae and speak naturally about love and sex (particularly "Rainy Season Love Song"). "The Serving Girl" catches her themes and style:

> The calabash wherein she served my food,
> Was smooth and polished as sandalwood:
> Fish, as white as the foam of the sea,
> Peppered, and golden fried for me.
> She brought palm wine that carelessly slips
> From the sleeping palm tree's honeyed lips.
> But who can guess, or even surmise
> The countless things she served with her eyes?

Lyric poetry has long been considered the proper genre for women, defining them as surely in literature as the home has defined them in society. Yet, despite poetry's historical, across-the-board respectability, when women write it, it somehow becomes a lesser form than when it is handled by men. Furthermore, during the 1920s as in other periods, there was always professional pressure to create a novel. In 1924, when Walter White was succoring McKay, what White wanted him to do was generate "book-length fiction that would be snapped up by the public rather than critically acclaimed but barely read poetry."[36] It is not surprising then that many of the female poets tried their hand at imaginative prose although, during the Renaissance proper, only Fauset, Larsen, Bennett, and Hurston published fiction. Women both kept themselves and were kept in their lyric sphere.

The three women who are the focus of this study—Dunbar-Nelson, Grimké, and Georgia Douglas Johnson—have been granted the niche they occupy in literary history because of their poetry. Their names are rarely called unless that is the topic. This narrow treatment reduces their status as writers, and seeing them solely as poets is one of the first misconceptions that a close scrutiny rectifies. Beginning with her very first publication, Dunbar-Nelson wrote short stories and continued to do so until the end of her life, even though most of them were published before the 1920s. Essays, journalism, a diary, and an occasional play received more of her attention than did verse. Grimké was both a poet and a dramatist, who could also write a creditable piece of short fiction. Johnson, too, worked in these three forms, adding to them some now-lost unpublished essays and longer fiction. If poetry does remain a convenient and useful entrée to these women's literary output, that avenue must be widened to accommodate their other interests. Investigating them through their total writings, in conjunction with their color and race, and their gender, yields a much more accurate picture of them (and often, by extension, of their cohorts) as earlier twentieth-century black women writers. Their lives and their works are of dual importance. Not nearly enough has been known about them; thus, biographical information—interesting in itself—is also necessary for giving them personal and literary substantiation and for the practice of a holistic scholarship.

Even though some particularities keep these three women writers individually and collectively unique, they constitute a coherent and representative trio to study. They are similar, yet different enough to give requisite breadth and variety (thus making understanding and generalization even more valid and persuasive). As mentioned earlier, they were not based in New York City, and they belonged to the same older generation, having been born in 1875 and 1880. Consequently, they already had achievements to their credit when they were "picked up," as it were, in the 1920s. Given the dynamics of the black cultural elite, it is also not surprising that they associated with one another personally and professionally. For instance: Dunbar-Nelson wrote a Harmon Foundation recommendation for Johnson and reviewed her books; Johnson gave Grimké warm and friendly care. There is no record of direct interaction between Dunbar-Nelson and Grimké (although they surely knew each other), but Johnson was demonstrably close to the two of them.

All three writers had considerable contemporary reputations. The only female poet to publish not just one, but three, volumes of her work during the period, Johnson was hailed as the foremost woman poet of the age. Her plays also won Renaissance prizes, and her role as nexus gave her extensive recognition. Grimké was known for her family name and the notoriety of her 1916-20 problem drama *Rachel*; and she became a well-represented poet of the period. The Dunbar name was even more illustrious for Dunbar-Nelson. It, coupled with her earlier accomplishments and her multifarious involvements, especially in journalism and speaking, gave her high visibility. From today's vantage point, these writers still emerge as important, and for reasons that enlarge those recognized by their contemporaries. Johnson can be even better appreciated for her pseudonymous, multi-genred prolificacy. Grimké is burnished by the depth of her unpublished work, especially her lesbian poetry. The surfacing of Dunbar-Nelson's diary and discoveries about her other unpublished writing enhance her standing. For all of them, there can now be a vastly better comprehension of their lives as writers and remarkable women.

The vagaries of literary fortune further hold them together as a unit. Enough of their documents survived to make them major figures for study. Though Johnson's voluminous papers were summarily dumped on the day of her funeral, she had published enough to provide a substantial corpus, especially when it is supplemented by her long correspondence and contacts with luminaries from the period. Because of Dunbar-Nelson's connection with famous black poet Paul Laurence Dunbar and the consciousness of her historian-librarian niece about the worth of both Dunbar and her aunt, Dunbar-Nelson's papers have been treasured. Grimké's position as scion of the famous black Grimké family (which included lawyer-diplomat Archibald, cleric Francis, and diarist Charlotte Forten) led to her materials being preserved along with theirs. In a world where the remains of black women have not been universally valued and are relatively difficult to find, having a sizable body of original, archival material on a related group of three early writers is indeed a rare boon. (Anne Spencer, who kept her own rich collection until her death in 1975, would have accorded well with this trio. However, she had granted exclusive access to another researcher, J. Lee Greene.)[37]

A final point of general comparison among Dunbar-Nelson, Grimké, and Georgia Douglas Johnson is that no biography or literary criticism of any length or definitive significance has been written about them. They desperately need—and deserve—long overdue scholarly attention. Another related, unfortunate similarity is that too much of what they wrote is not easily and generally available because it either is out-of-print or was never published. Assessing them accurately requires one to consider both their published and unpublished writings, taking care to distinguish, especially when it is crucial, between them. It is hoped that, in the not-too-distant future, new editions and anthologies will present them in a freshly altered and fuller light.

Color defined the Harlem Renaissance. Philosophically and practically, it was a racial movement whose overriding preoccupation can be seen in all of its aspects and manifestations—the name of the era (where Harlem is synonymous with black), its debates and manifestos (Locke's "The New Negro"and Hughes's "The Negro Artist and the Racial Mountain"), book titles (Georgia Johnson's *Bronze*, Cullen's *Color*, *The Ballad of the Brown Girl*, and *Copper Sun*), artistic illustrations (the African motifs of Aaron Douglas and Gwendolyn Bennett), and so on. Indeed, during the 1920s, Alice Dunbar-Nelson, Angelina Grimké, and Georgia Douglas Johnson were participating in a literary movement that was, by self-definition, race oriented. How they were affected by this general reality emerged from their own specific realities as black women. Racial attitudes of the larger society, Harlem Renaissance dictates, and personal experience all combined to determine the handling of color in their writings.

Reflecting their nearness to the miscegenation of slavery, these three women were visibly mixed blooded. Grimké was a light brown quadroon, whose mother was white and father mulatto; Johnson herself said that she was born "a little yellow girl"; and Dunbar-Nelson could pass for white when she chose to. The Harlem Renaissance was preoccupied with the array of Afro-American skin tones, ranging across (in Claude McKay's catalogue) "chocolate, chestnut, coffee, ebony, cream, [and] yellow."[38] This rainbow began to be celebrated in art, even if the entire spectrum was still not as widely accepted in real life, where the same old light-minded hierarchy operated. Of course, the matter of color has always had a heavier impact on black women. Like McKay, men rhapsodized about their teasing browns, chocolate-to-the-bones, and lemon yellows, but many still preferred to marry the paler shades. Deep historical links between fair color and beauty, and fair color and class affiliation, are not easily broken. Even during this "natural"period that glorified blackness and exploited primitivism, the stage show chorines were creams and high browns (which was apparently what the promoters and public accepted), and Wallace Thurman, tortured himself by his own black skin, could relevantly present the agony of a self-hating dark heroine in his 1929 novel, *The Blacker the Berry*.

Though not of the "tragic mulatto" variety, these three women writers' situations came from ambivalences different from but no less complicated than those of Thurman's Emma Lou. The roots of their color complexes and preoccupations can be traced to their personal history; the roots of their racial consciousness to the combination of personal history and American racism. Grimké's attitudes seem to have been simpler and clearer than either Dunbar-Nelson's or Johnson's. Growing up with liberal and politically committed white and black people who—though themselves privileged—actively strove for racial betterment, she understood well intra- and interracial prejudice. These sympathies she translated directly into her literary work.

Lynching and the sorrow of having children are the dual themes of the drama and fiction that she produced before the Renaissance heyday, so much so that even a radical partisan wonders about her absolute fixation upon these subjects. For the 1925 *Opportunity* contest, she sent Charles Johnson a never-published story that expanded her militant focus into other race themes of the period. "Jettisoned" is about a black woman domestic named Miss Lucy, who decides not to pose as "old Black mammy" in order to visit her passing daughter in Long Island, New York. Her option is to remain with her sweet, young surrogate daughter, Mary Lou. In addition to this incidental treatment of the popular passing motif, the story also features average black folk characters who are, in Johnson's enthusiastic judgment, "real, unpretensious, and lovable."[39] Both these facts situated the piece firmly in the literary mode of the age. In "Jettisoned," Grimké used dialect to aid in picturing Miss Lucy, a racial-literary strategy that she had attempted years earlier in some Dunbar-derivative poetry.

Miscegenation was a major factor in Georgia Douglas Johnson's life and art. Undoubtedly because of her own identity, she "nourished a whole generation of Eurasians and other 'Mixed breeds,'"in the words of Cedric Dover.[40] Her involvement is further indicated by such works as two lost novels entitled *One and One Makes Three* and *White Men's Children*, and a poem called "Aliens," a neo-treatment of the tragic mulatto that she passionately dedicated "To You—Everywhere!"[41] Treated comically, miscegenation also underlay her prize-winning play *Blue Blood* (1926). During the Renaissance years, her creativity focused heavily on racial themes, especially in her realistic one-act plays. *Plumes*, a "folk tragedy," fulfilled the contemporary requirements for "real Negro literature"—"a Negro author, a Negro subject, and a Negro audience."[42] A *Sunday Morning in the South* survives from among her dramatic protests against lynching, while a primitive African melodrama called *Popoplikahu*, which was being rehearsed in 1926, has been lost. Johnson also wrote what she called plays of "average Negro life"and historical dramas such as *William and Ellen Craft*. Later, she continued her racial slant in war and brotherhood poems and songs, and in other interracial projects. Her political activity was not, however, as relentlessly race-oriented as Dunbar-Nelson's.

Perhaps she was referring only to her poetry, but Johnson told Arna Bontemps in 1941 that she really did not enjoy "writing racially": "Whenever I can, I forget my special call to sorrow and live as happily as I may."[43] This remark is strikingly similar to Anne Spencer's statement introducing herself in *Caroling Dusk:* "I write about some of the things I love. But have no civilized articulation for the things I hate."[44] Like Spencer, other women writers eschewed "hateful" topics of prejudice and injustice. Choosing to do so placed them out of the fashionable mainstream (to the detriment of their contemporary and posthumous reputations). Johnson succumbed to external pressure and wrote a volume of obligatory race poetry, *Bronze: A Book of Verse*, in 1922. Using a self-conscious and indirect style, she speaks here with the voice of a black woman-mother for her persecuted but rising race. However, this is her weakest book. Johnson later confessed that she attempted *Bronze* because someone had said, after she published *The Heart of a Woman* (1918), that she had "no feeling for the race."[45] In times of black political consciousness, writers are pressured to toe the racial line. Unfortunately, these post-Victorian black women authors could not always effectively reconcile their color, sex, and poetry, poetry here encompassing also their poetics (concepts of literature) and their imaginative writing in general.

Dunbar-Nelson was the most uncomfortable of all with mixing race and belletristic literature. Throughout her career, she maintained a sharp demarcation between black concerns and her literary work. Though race was the keynote and unification for practically everything else that she did, it rarely sounded in her poems and stories. In her two pre-Renaissance volumes of Creole stories, the fiction, as one critic put it, "has no characteristics peculiar to her race."[46] Even in poetry that she wrote during the Renaissance, the thematic separation is basically maintained, although she did make some slight attempt to modernize her subjects and style. At the same time, her articles and newspaper columns had the militantly black ring of the period. She advocates "Negro Literature for Negro Pupils,"exposes the racism on Mississippi levees during the floods, discusses black theater, and praises black sororities and fraternities for fostering race pride.

Interestingly, two of her unpublished Creole stories written during the first of the century tackle the more daring, racial topic of black Creole males who problematically decide to pass as white. When she proposed enlarging one of them, "The Stones of the Village," into a novel, Bliss Perry of the *Atlantic Monthly* discouraged her in 1900 by saying that the present American public disliked "color-line" fiction.[47] Maybe Perry spoke as a white reader who was tiring, say, of Charles Chesnutt, who had explicitly treated the color line in his 1899 collection. *The Wife of His Youth*, and more realistically dealt with racial concerns (passing and an interracial romance in the Reconstruction South) in his just-published novel, *The House Behind the Cedars* (1900). When the subject achieved fresh popularity in the 1920s,

Dunbar-Nelson did not resurrect her old manuscripts. It would have been informative to see their reception.

Dunbar-Nelson's split authorial personality suggests the duality (not to say confusion) of her own attitudes regarding blackness. She was secretly ashamed of some aspect of her birth and parentage, and ambivalent about dark-skinned, lower-class blacks. As a "brass ankles," that is, a "white nigger," she resented intraracial animosity directed at those of her caste. Yet, she worked with zeal for black people as a race in political parties and the black women's club movement. Allegiance to Afro-American heritage can also be discerned in other aspects and activities of her life—for example, the foods she loved and her immersion in a black oratorical tradition. Yet, even in the receptive atmosphere of the Harlem Renaissance, she did not creatively use such material.

Large amounts of ambivalence, white blood, and caste privilege did not obliterate the basic race-color reality of these three women's existence. They were all touched by it and all responded in their lives and writing. However, only Johnson contributed significantly to the race literature of the Harlem Renaissance period. Grimké had passed her creative peak, and Dunbar-Nelson hardly ever treated race themes in the imaginative genres that counted. Clearly if one narrowly judges the worth of writers associated with the era by what they produced on race during those specific years, then these and other women writers will be devalued.

The lives of Afro-American women have always been determined as much by their gender as by their race. Not surprisingly, Dunbar-Nelson, Grimké, and Johnson were all three schoolteachers trained in female fields (English and music). Their domestic configurations are varied, but still show women's limited options in a patriarchal society. Johnson's situation (the most traditional) was that of wife to a husband who discouraged her writing, and mother of two sons whose care emotionally and financially burdened her. Dunbar-Nelson acted out romances with her first two husbands before settling down in a rather egalitarian marriage with a man whose sexist attitudes were not stifling. Despite her marriages, however, her home base was almost always a gynocentric arrangement involving her mother and sister. A motherless child, Grimké was the daughter of a stern father; she chose not to marry and ended her life alone.

Johnson seemed to have rested easiest in her sexual roles. Dunbar-Nelson suspected her of having an affair in the early 1920s, and her friend the playwright-poet Owen Dodson commented that, even at eighty, she did not hide her "wrinkled bosom." Dunbar-Nelson experienced difficulty finding satisfying outlets for her passionate nature, especially since she was sexually attracted to both men and women. Grimké was a thwarted lesbian who forswore lasting intimacy at an early age. What she and her father diagnosed as laziness in her character may really have been an understandable psychological listlessness.

At the outset of this study, no data suggested that these three writers were anything other than conventionally heterosexual women. What emerged regarding their sexuality prompts further speculation about the hidden nature of women's sexual lives in general and, more specifically, about lesbian invisibility. It also highlights some of the difficulties of doing lesbian-feminist scholarship, where the subjects feel constrained even in their private utterances from expressing themselves clearly and fully. For the sensitive researcher, there is often a gap between what one knows and what can be "proved," especially to those readers who demand a kind of evidence about the individual and the meaning of her work that could not be produced for heterosexual subjects. Yet, it is obvious that both Grimké and Dunbar-Nelson had sexual psyches that cut across the usual grain and were manifested in their lives and writing.

In part because of their female status, Johnson and Dunbar-Nelson waged a running battle with the wolf of financial hardship. For example, during the Renaissance, Johnson was "in the grip of genteel poverty,"[48] and in 1942 at the age of sixty-two, found herself hoping for a few hours work in a clerical pool. With this and indeed all of their problems, they were sustained by their intuitive strength and spirituality (a resource that Grimké lacked). In particular, Johnson, who acted more like the "crazy lady" she was as she grew older, radiated a living energy that made people speak of her "soothing balm" and "basking in deep spirituality" at her home, which she had christened "Half-Way House." Unlike Dunbar-Nelson's predominantly female support groups, Johnson's circle included women friends and a homosexual coterie that she "mothered."

These three women writers are as feminine as they were aracial in their poetry. As her contemporary critics noted, Georgia Johnson sang "the heart of a woman" in her gemlike lyrics, although they failed to hear the irony, discontent, and quiet sedition that undercut some of their apparent sentimentality. Women characters also hold center stage in her 1920s plays, while her later short short story "Free" is a remarkable vignette of female bonding. Dunbar-Nelson's poetry—which she viewed as secondary and wrote sporadically—also mined feminine and traditional lyric topics such as nature and love, with one poem, "I Sit and Sew," being feminist in spirit. Generally speaking, how she handled gender in her work betrays the same kind of ambivalence that marked her treatment of race. For Dunbar-Nelson, there was always a dichotomy—fostered perhaps by female role and self-image conflicts—between the "inside" and the "outside." Externally, she was liberated in her carriage, doing radical women's work and making her way in the male journalistic profession. Yet, she succumbed to playing the good little helpless woman, and assumed poses of modest authorship—although less so as she matured. Almost all of the women in her work are depicted as traditional, with none of the interests and mettle that she herself possessed.

Dunbar-Nelson's general problem may simply have been a deep inability to use her own real experience as raw material for realistic art—even during the Renaissance, which encouraged such. One wonders if a modern, feminist acceptance of the "personal" as legitimate literary subject matter would have made her any more capable of doing so. All three of these women were released into the freedom of the self only through the lyric "I" persona. It should be said, however, that Johnson's work was not negatively affected by the fact that she did not draw from a more real autobiographical base. But creating in this way—had she been able to—could only have enhanced Dunbar-Nelson's output. Her colorful life would have produced writing in the same way that, say, the adventures of Hughes and McKay (safe and accepted because they were males) were translated into their poetry and fiction.

Like Johnson, Grimké is more feminine and personal in her poetry, and more racial in her drama and fiction. To the usual universal lyric topics, she adds the theme of lesbian love, predominantly in her unpublished poems. Not being able to write openly from her sexual self, as well as not being able to print whatever she did manage to write, blighted her creativity and reputation as a poet. If she and Dunbar-Nelson could have penned their lesbian poetry unfettered by internal or external constraints, their corpus would have benefited. The peculiarly female image of cloistering appears in Grimké's work, suggesting her own narrow, sheltered life and recalling similar images in Dunbar-Nelson's stories. Her two major characters (Rachel and Mara) are women, whose depiction is idealized and faintly autobiographical.

Contrasting widely as female personalities, Grimké, Dunbar-Nelson, and Georgia Douglas Johnson shared definite similarities as lyric, women poets. Evaluated solely by the poems that were published in Harlem Renaissance magazines and anthologies, they appear as traditional, feminine verse-makers who treated themes of love, death, sorrow, nature, selfhood, and identity, with a smattering of indirectly handled racial material (Johnson's "Old Black Men" and "Suppliant"; Grimké's "Tenebris"; and Dunbar-Nelson's "April Is on the Way"). Furthermore, male anthologists like James Weldon Johnson used some of their most sex-stereotyped work. Thus, Georgia Johnson is always represented by "I Want to Die While You Love Me" and never by "Ivy," which ironically addresses the usual "clinging vine" definition of women. That women, poetry, and women poets were not accorded maximum status did not improve the situation.

To varying degrees, women were important in all three writers' authorial lives and literary imaginations. They are positively evoked, from the outmoded feminine ideals that Dunbar-Nelson strangely enshrined, to Johnson's realistic black female folk characters, to Grimké's sensitive young delicate women. Expanding the view of this trio as women writers to fields beyond their poetry shows them in a truer light. It is difficult to say whether they saw themselves as part of a female literary tradition. During her heyday, Johnson was compared with Sara Teasdale and Edna St. Vincent Millay. Locke, at least, saw them as belonging to the same school of "modern feminist realism."[49] Dunbar-Nelson and Johnson, especially, knew themselves to be part of a contemporary group that included women as well as men. And the women sometimes aided each other. In Johnson's own words, Jessie Fauset "very generously helped her to gather together material for her first book,"[50] while Dunbar-Nelson wrote her an unavailing Harmon Foundation recommendation. Grimké's ceasing to write was almost certainly caused in part by her relative isolation. Like Nella Larsen (also after 1930), she secluded herself and was never artistically heard from again.

Yet, it required considerable courage for these early twentieth-century women to put themselves forth as writers. This they bravely did, despite their deferent gestures, their securing males to "offer their books" to publishers, and so forth. Johnson dedicated *An Autumn Love Cycle* to white woman writer and critic Zona Gale in gratitude for her encouragement. But all of her books are prefaced by men—poet-anthologist William Stanley Braithwaite, W.E.B. DuBois, and Alain Locke, respectively. However, any contrary evidence notwithstanding, on some basic and indispensable level, these three black women were serious about themselves as writers.

Certain features of their poetics further help to explain them and their positions as female literary artists of the Harlem Renaissance. Dunbar-Nelson held an exalted, high-art concept of literature that complemented her generally classical and orthodox taste. In fact, this ivory-tower conception contributed as much as her personal ambivalence to her not using her real self and experience in her art. Judging from their work, it appears that Grimké and Johnson operated from a broader, but still basically orthodox, position. Certainly, the three of them subscribed to romantic philosophies and notions of poetry. Grimké most fully articulated these ideas in a 1925 statement that she wrote. She declares that her poems arise from within herself as the reflection of moods that find symbolic analogues in nature, and even employs the image of the harp favored in romantic critical theory: "And what is word? May it not be a sort of singing in the harp strings of the mind? Then on the principle of sympathetic vibration is there not in nature a harp singing also to be found...." [51] Romantic concepts help account for their use of poetry as a vehicle for brief expression of intense emotion, a concentration on the ideal, and a lavish use of nature and natural images.

Generally speaking, they shied away from experimentation with more modern styles and modes of verse. Of course, in the 1920s, Carl Sandburg, William Carlos Williams, the imagists, Harriet Monroe, and others were introducing *vers libre* and similar flexible poetic forms. The black writers were adding to this their ethnically derived innovations of rhythm, dialect, jazz, and blues. In one poem, "At April," Grimké uses a kind of syncopation to admonish "brown girl trees" to "toss your gay lovely heads."[52] Dunbar-Nelson tried to capture the new, more colloquial and direct tone in a few of her poems of the period. But Johnson adhered to rhymed and metered stanzas throughout, never even developing a facility for free verse.

The gender-class-literary dimensions of how they wrote gain illuminating perspective when placed alongside the song lyrics of the period's black blueswomen. Critic Barbara Christian suggests:

> It might be said that the genuine poetry of the black woman appeared not in literature but in the lyrics of blues singers like Bessie Smith.... Perhaps because the blues was seen as "race music" and catered to a black audience, black women were better able to articulate themselves as individuals and as part of a racial group in that art form.[53]

Cheryl Wall puts the matter even more forcefully when she says: "Free of the burdens of an alien tradition, a Bessie Smith could establish the standard of her art; in the process she would compose a more honest poetry than any of her literary sisters'."[54] One aspect of Bessie Smith's "honesty" was a raunchy, woman-proud sexuality that echoed the explicitness of this licentious era. Reared as proper, middle-class, almost Victorian black women who were trained to be proofs of black female morals and modesty, Dunbar-Nelson, Grimké, and Johnson could only treat sex romantically and obliquely in their work—although, as Dunbar-Nelson vividly proves, they could be quite "naughty" in private life. The younger Helene Johnson was able to say to her "brown boy," "I loves you all over"; but this is a far cry from Bessie Smith's

"I'm gonna drink good moonshine and run these browns down."[55] Their restrained treatment of sex also helped to place them outside the sensational mainstream.

The lack of formal innovation exhibited by these three poets (were women conditioned to be less daring?) combined with their conventional, age-old themes (were these deemed more suitable for the lyric feminine sensibility?) made their work relatively unexciting in a renaissance awakening that required some flash and newness. Because of temperament and socialization, they did not loudly raise their voices in protest, pride, or primitivism. The quality of their achievement could not obliterate this difference. Nor could the fact that, for the first time in Afro-American literary history, women were entering the scribal tradition in more than token fashion, and largely as poets. Before, there had been the anomalous Phillis Wheatley, Harriet Wilson, Francis Ellen Watkins Harper, some exslave narrators (Harriet Brent Jacobs, Ellen Craft, and Elizabeth Keckley), and documentary writers such as Charlotte Forten, Ida B. Wells, and Mary Church Terrell. Perhaps the women writers of the Harlem Renaissance were truly having more of a nascence than a re-nascence.

Dunbar-Nelson, Grimké, and Johnson knew that winning their way as authors necessitated demonstrating talent in genres other than poetry that were considered more major and difficult, and that also carried greater rewards. To be perfectly accurate, Dunbar-Nelson considered the short story her most representative genre and also wrote plays. Grimké expended almost as much effort on drama as poetry and wrote a few short stories, even planning at one point to take a short-story writing course. Johnson focused on drama for a major portion of her career and wrote a little fiction. Her success in the three forms is more even, for Grimké's gifts really were lyrical while a latter-day assessment shows that Dunbar-Nelson's excellence came in noncanonical forms. Grimké was the only one who did not write a novel. Dunbar-Nelson worked on four throughout her life, and Johnson on one or two. A problem they had in common was not conceiving ideas and plots that were inherently of novel proportions. They found themselves making up word counts and "rounding up"necessary pages. Having been destroyed, Johnson's "White Men's Children"(which she described as "a novel dealing with the interplay of bloods") cannot be evaluated. Publishers considered but apparently did not accept it. In 1942, a Rosenwald Foundation executive volunteered that he had "taken a great deal of pleasure" in reading the work,[56] thus leaving behind the only documented opinion about it. Dunbar-Nelson's loosely written novels—which do not fall predominantly in the Renaissance period—did not sustain reader interest as tight fictional constructs. In the early 1900s, one of them, "Confessions of a Lazy Woman,"was accepted for publication, but the contract was canceled when the firm underwent changes. "This Lofty Oak," the final one she wrote at the end of her life, merits attention as fictionalized biography, with her, a woman writer, setting down for posterity the fascinating life history of another self-made woman who was her intimate friend

None of them—except Dunbar-Nelson—wrote modern realistic fiction that utilized the increasingly important urban setting. However, the experience of the two women novelists who did, Fauset and Larsen, is instructive. The first is disparaged for her proper, bourgeoise characters, milieu, tone, and point of view. In actuality, other novels by male writers—for example, those by Wallace Thurman and McKay's *Home to Harlem*—are as badly flawed in their way as Fauset's were in hers. However, because her faults were seen as sex-related ones that put her out-of-step with the avant-garde of her era, she is disproportionately minimized. David Lewis states further that "respectable critical reaction to the fiction of DuBois, Fauset, and Larsen was no match, in the short term, for the commercial success of *Home to Harlem*, [or] the controversy of *The Blacker the Berry*."[57] Larsen, who wrote good psychological fiction from a black female perspective, was generally appreciated but not truly understood. Interestingly, some of Dunbar-Nelson's best unpublished stories rely on psychological probing of her characters.

Final pieces of individual data further explain these three women's work. Again, Grimké is easiest of all to summarize. She could not really write or publish her lesbian poems and never collected a volume of her work, although she projected one sometime around 1920. Because of mainly personal factors, she was not prolific—not even in her métier, poetry. She leaves the impression of a talented writer whose potential was never realized. Her strengths were her fine sensibility, descriptive power, and quiet drama.

Inadequate volume was certainly not one of Georgia Douglas Johnson's problems. In 1944, she catalogued the unpublished work she had on hand: "three new books of poetry, thirty plays both one and three act, thirty short stories, a novel, a book of philosophy, a book of exquisite sayings, ... twenty songs."[58] There was, in addition, a biography of her late husband entitled "The Black Cabinet" and her reminiscences of her Renaissance Saturday Nighters, which she called "Literary Salon." When publication proved vain, she consoled herself by recalling that Balzac had left behind forty unpublished novels at his death. Unfortunately, with one or two exceptions, only what she published during her lifetime survived her. Based on this, she emerges as the most well-rounded, well-realized in the traditional literary genres. Erlene Stetson summarizes her major poetry like this:

> Over-all, all three volumes as musical lyrics form a sonata. The
> movement is from the intensely subjective world of the woman in
> the spring of life who is yet naive enough to shout her pain, to the
> summer of life, the red and fire of *Bronze* when motherhood,
> marriage and race exacts its toll on the female psyche and finally,
> to the autumnal season of realism and objectivity "when love's
> triumphant day is done" (*Autumn*, p. 47).[59]

This sonata displays her poetic literateness and aptly chosen images and
conceits.

She used her admirable dramaturgical skills in one-act plays that
focused on racial issues, mostly through female characters. One really wishes
that other of her short stories had survived to see if she customarily reached
the achievement level of "Free." Being definitive about her is short-circuited
by the work of hers lost to pseudonymous publication. Also, her poignant,
late lyrical admission that "one lives too long" could be applied to her as a
writer. Though she strove to remain current (like Dunbar-Nelson, going so
far as to attempt a filmscript), her themes of miscegenation, passing, and
brotherhood—even more so than her poetic style—were anachronistic in the
years before her death in 1966.

Of these three women writers, it is Dunbar-Nelson whose literary
position calls for the most radical revision. Long noted as a romantic poet
and writer of local-color sketches, she reemerges as a unique chronicler of
black female experience in her diary, a first-rate essayist and journalist, and a
fictionist whose total output (including unpublished stories) reveals a breadth
and interest beyond her recognized Creole pieces. Unfortunately, the work
that she excelled in is noncanonical, ephemeral, and unavailable. She is the
only one who approached the status of professional writer. Thus,
publication, which was important to all three women for self-realization, was
more critical to her for economic livelihood. Trying to earn money by her
pen (something she once bitterly remarked that fate had decreed should not
happen) was an ambition that her marriage to litterateur Paul Laurence
Dunbar helped to set. That it was more necessary did not make it happen.
How she was affected by the marketplace is partially indicated by the fact
that she found outlets for her slighter, color-less stories quicker than for her
meatier ones. Like Georgia Douglas Johnson she also wrote pulp romance.
Hers was embarrassingly poor; Johnson's may have been published under
pen names in magazines like *Tan Confessions*.

Dunbar-Nelson did not resort to self-subsidized publication, even
though at the time, and especially for black writers, it was not so heavily

stigmatized as a "vanity" enterprise (just as contemporary self-publication by women writers has taken on different meaning). By the time of the Harlem Renaissance, however, mainstream channels were opening (albeit selectively and unimpartially). Therefore, in 1925, Charles Johnson dissuaded Grimké from paying to have "Jettisoned" printed, saying, "A story such as this should sell itself."[60] In 1919, she had shared the initial cost of publishing *Rachel* with the Cornhill Company. Georgia Johnson's unprecedented three books of poetry owed their existence to her own money (for example, her 1918 *Heart of a Woman* was also published by Cornhill). Pleading for herself with reference to the Harmon awards in 1928, she said, "[I] cannot pay for another volume being published."[61]

Dunbar-Nelson's rejections were sometimes caused by the weakness of her work. As reviewers accurately noted, she is good at description but not with plot, while her matter is diverting but her style commonplace. Her ease with language and journalistic habits often betrayed her into hasty, prolix writing, which she did not strenuously revise. In poetry, she relied heavily on thematic and stylistic contrast. The twin subject of war and peace is one of her major motifs—in all genres. Her living through three wars (both hot and cold), being black and political (at a time when whether Afro-Americans should fight for the United States was a controversial racial debate), and working as executive secretary for the Friends American Inter-Racial Peace Committee help to explain this choice. Perhaps because it is the only forum where she starred herself, Dunbar-Nelson's diary presents her strongest and most distinctive voice.

This, then, introduces the three women writers of the Harlem Renaissance who constitute this study: Alice Dunbar-Nelson, Angelina Weld Grimké, and Georgia Douglas Johnson. The unearthing of hitherto unknown biographical and critical material about them corrects the prevailing myopic view of them as women and as writers. Generally speaking, their reputations are enhanced. But even those sceptics or resolute traditionalists who choose not to revise their opinions will now know more precisely how these figures came to be who they were. However, it would require a willful blindness to continue to see Dunbar-Nelson only as Paul Laurence Dunbar's elegant, poetic appendage, or Grimké as a shy lyricist who simply did not publish enough, or Georgia Douglas Johnson as the contented "poet-housewife."

Concomitantly, focusing on them has brought with it a changed perspective on other Harlem Renaissance writers; male and female. Though not a part of this study, Anne Spencer, for instance, is also explained by what has been learned about the core three. The four of them form a coherent contrast to the younger women poets and the female novelists of the period. Grimké, Johnson, and Dunbar-Nelson were certainly elder stateswomen and literary foremothers for the succeeding generation to reckon with. Blanche Taylor Dickinson suggested this when she named Johnson as one of her favorite poets.[62] In that genre, Johnson holds her place as "foremost," since the designation implies productivity and reputation, as well as achievement. However, in many ways, Grimké and Spencer are better and more original. It is interesting to see affinities between Gwendolyn Bennett and Grimké, while Helene Johnson and Gladys Hayford become all the more singular when placed alongside the rest of their sisters. Only secondarily poets, Fauset and Dunbar-Nelson push a consideration of these women into other forms. When this happens, the two of them and Johnson can receive more of the credit that they are due, and Grimké and Bennett can, too, be appreciated for their multi-genred achievement. These women poets wrought well in drama and fiction, and in nonliterary forms.

Directly comparing Johnson, Dunbar-Nelson, and Grimké with male poets and writers of the period would force them into a competition whose rules were formulated without them in mind. In colloquial parlance, it was not their "ball game." They themselves could not help playing it, but conscious critics do not have to tally a traditional score. It is far more instructive to imagine how Hughes's and Johnson's careers would have differed if they could have exchanged sexes, or whether Cullen's love and nature lyrics and poems of attenuated protest would have received the same favorable treatment had he been a woman writer. Certainly, it becomes harder to casually place these three in some inferior echelon below such of their contemporaries as Frank Horne or Arna Bontemps.

This matter of comparison symbolizes how much has been learned about the sexual-literary politics of the New Negro era. In myriad ways, both subtle and blatant, women were penalized for their gender. These ranged from "blaming the victim" for the inevitable results of her female socialization to outright sexist exclusion. Though Locke may still be respected for his erudition and insightful criticism, his iconic status as cultural entrepreneur has been tarnished. For reasons beyond those previously thought, Charles S. Johnson emerges as a much more important and admirable mentor. Posterity also has a better sense of the gender-related "breaks" that boosted the careers and permanent reputations of "major" writers like Hughes and McKay. Whatever these women were not able to accomplish was exacerbated by the age and has been further multiplied by their perennial critical treatment. Even David L. Lewis, who wrote a brilliant and indispensable social history of the period, *When Harlem Was in Vogue* (1982), largely ignores the women poets. And though he later supplemented his statement with more positive information, Lewis slurs Georgia Johnson's literary salon as one of the places in Philadelphia or Washington, D.C., "where belles-lettres meant Saturday night adventures in tidy parlors, among mostly tidy-minded literati."[63] Although she was a woman, neither Johnson's house nor her mind was tidy. And some of the same people who glittered on the Harlem scene attended her affairs.

To speak more positively, looking at these three writers enables one to see the "Harlem Renaissance" (if that designation is maintained) as a large and diverse movement in Afro-American literary history that went beyond what a small "in-crowd" was helping one another to do in New York City. Encompassing it requires a broadening of temporal, geographical, and critical boundaries. More literarily still, it becomes clear that women writers are tyrannized by periodization, the hierarchy of canonical forms, critical rankings of major and minor, and generalizations about literary periods. Indeed, generalizations about the characteristics of an era are often arrived at without weighting women's work. In this case, Dunbar-Nelson, Grimké, and Johnson sometimes pick up—and even extend—the dominant temper of the age, as when Johnson explores the black female folk psyche in *Plumes* or Grimké combines imagist and Renaissance racial techniques in her poem "The Black Finger." At other times, the pure fact of their being and what they write constitute an implicit challenge to the more visible modes. Dunbar-Nelson's diary, which she kept in 1921 and then from 1926 to 1931, is an excellent example. Generally, studying these women writers and the way they have been handled fosters a wariness about superficial, incomplete knowledge, oversimplifications, and the "band-wagoning" approach to criticism and teaching.

Without women writers, the Harlem Renaissance would have been a bleaker place. Though not blindingly vivid, the color they added completed the total spectrum. Not only did women play their usual and some additional special roles, but the work that they produced clearly—if sometimes "slantwise"—embodied the female half of human experience and swelled the ranks of the New Negro artists. Poetry, in particular, would have suffered had they not been writing. Johnson's plays and Dunbar-Nelson's essays and columns would also have left lacunae. When their lifetime of work is included, Dunbar-Nelson, Grimké, and Georgia Johnson become even more important. Their writings are significant as notable literary responses of earlier twentieth-century Afro-American women writers to the determining facts of race and gender as filtered through their personal and artistic consciousness. The resulting beauty and complexity is valuable for both historical and literary reasons.

One final word *in propria persona*. Even though it is neat and convenient to continue doing so, we need to stop hyper-emphasizing the Harlem Renaissance, often by repeating the same handful of works and critical clichés. Or, if we decide to use it as an originating point of focus, we must remember that there was significant literature both before and after, and that, in all three periods, black women writers live.

NOTES

1. Alice Dunbar-Nelson, "As in a Looking Glass," the Washington *Eagle*, February 25–September [?], 1927. "April Is on the Way," *ebony and Topaz*, ed. Charles S. Johnson (*Opportunity*, 1927).

2. Letter from Langston Hughes to Angelina Weld Grimké, May 8, 1927. The AWG Collection, Moorland-Spingam Research Center, Howard University, Washington, D.C. *Caroling Dusk: An Anthology of Verse by Negro Poets*, ed. Countee Cullen (New York: Harper & Brothers, 1927).

3. Gwendolyn Bennett, "The Ebony Flute," *Opportunity* (July 1927): 212. *Give Us Each Day: The Diary of Alice Dunbar-Nelson*, ed. Gloria T. Hull (New York: W. W. Norton, 1984), p. 185.

4. Nathan I Huggins, Introduction to his anthology *Voices from the Harlem Renaissance* (New York: Oxford University Press, 1976), p. 9. The following general information about the period draws from this source as well as from two others: *Black Writers of America*, ed. Richard Barksdale and Keneth Kinnamon (New York: The Macmillan Company, 1972); Darwin T. Turner's Introduction to Jean Toomer, *Cane* (New York: Liverights, 1975).

5. Alice Dunbar-Nelson, "As in a Looking Glass" column, the Washington *Eagle*, June 14, 1929. Unprocessed Dunbar-Nelson materials, Morris Library, University of Delaware, Newark, Delaware.

6. Huggins, *Voices From the Harlem Renaissance*, p. 5.

7. Elise Johnson McDougald, "The Task of Negro Womanhood," in *The New Negro*, ed. Alain Locke (1925; New York: Atheneum, 1974), p. 369.

8. Langston Hughes, "Madam's Past History," in his *Selected Poems* (New York: Alfred A. Knopf, 1959), p. 201.

9. Blanche Taylor Dickinson, "Revelation," in *Caroling Dusk*, p. 108.

10. This information comes from an interview of Ethel Ray Nance conducted by Ann Allen Shockley in 1970. Fisk University Library Oral History, Nashville, Tennessee.

11. David Levering Lewis, *When Harlem Was in Vogue* (New York: Alfred A. Knopf, 1981), p. 123. Lewis's extensively researched, eminently readable work is an

invaluable reference for the social-literary history of the period, and functioned as an important sourcebook for this introductory chapter.

12. Ibid., p. 127.

13. Biographical sketch of Anne Spencer taken from the program of the landmark dedication of her home, February 26, 1977. Biography file, Fisk University, Nashville, Tennessee.

14. Langston Hughes, *The Big Sea* (New York: Hill & Wang, 1932), p. 218.

15. Lewis, p. 96.

16. Owen Dodson interviewed by James V. Hatch, December 3, 1971. Tape collection, Atlanta University Library, Atlanta, Georgia. My transcription.

17. Hurston's comments about Locke are contained in a letter to James Weldon Johnson. Quoted from Jervis Anderson, *This Was Harlem: A Cultural Portrait, 1900–1950* (New York: Farrar, Straus & Giroux, 1982), p. 201.

18. Lewis, pp. 81, 85, 87, 88, 153.

19. Ibid., p. 196.

20. Ibid., p. 209.

21. A description of Van Vechten's parties given by Allen Churchill in *The Literary Decade*. Quoted from Jervis Anderson, *This Was Harlem*, p. 214. The succeeding quotation also comes from Anderson, p. 214.

22. Letter from James Weldon Johnson to Charles W. Chesnutt, January 31, 1928. Chesnutt Collection, Fisk University Library, Nashville, Tennessee.

23. Letter from James Weldon Johnson to Edwin R. Embree, August 22, 1931. Rosenwald Papers, Fisk University Library, Nashville, Tennessee.

24. Lewis, p. 293.

25. This information about McKay comes from Lewis, pp. 140–42, 225–26.

26. *Give Us Each Day: The Diary of Alice Dunbar-Nelson*, p. 313.

27. The Pittsburgh *Courier*, July [5, 16 7], 1928.

28. Lewis, p. 167.

29. Statement prepared for the Harold Jackman Memorial Committee by Regina M. Andrews, the Schomburg Center Vertical File; Lewis, p. 213.

30. Lewis, p. 266.

31. Ibid., p. 140.

32. Ethel Ray Nance interview with Ann Allen Shockley.

33. Cited in the Introduction to Robert Hemenway's edition of Hurston's autobiography, *Dust Tracks on a Road* (1942; Urbana: University of Illinois Press, 1984), pp. x–xi. Professor Cheryl Wall has discovered that Hurston was born on January 7, 1891, rather than January 1, 1901.

34. Georgia Douglas Johnson, "Welt." Quoted from *The Book of American Negro Poetry*, ed. J. W. Johnson (New York: Harcourt, Brace, 1931), p. 183.

35. Johnson, *The Book of American Negro Poetry*, p. 279. The poets discussed here are

best represented in Johnson's anthology, Cullen's *Caroling Dusk*, and *The Poetry of the Negro*, ed. Langston Hughes and Ama Bontemps. The Hayford poem quoted below is taken from *Caroling Dusk*, p. 200.

36. Lewis, p. 140.

37. Greene's work resulted in *Time's Unfading Garden: Ann Spencer's Life and Poetry*, (Baton Rouge: Louisiana State University Press, 1977).

38. McKay in *Home to Harlem*. Quoted from Arthur P. Davis, *From the Dark Tower: Afro-American Writers 1900–1960* (Washington, D.C.: Howard University Press, 1974), p. 40.

39. Letter from Charles S. Johnson to Angelina W. Grimké, January 6, 1925. AWG Collection, Collection, Moorland-Spingam Research Center, Howard University, Washington, D.C.

40. Cedric Dover, "The Importance of Georgia Douglass Johnson," *The Crisis* 59 (December 1952): 635.

41. This poem is included in her *Bronze: A Book of Verse* (Boston: B. J. Brimmer Co., 1922).

42. Review of *Plumes*, new York *Amsterdam News*, November 23 {?}, 1927.

43. Letter from Georgia Douglas Johnson to Ama Bontemps, July 6, 1941. The Cullen-Jackman Collection, Trevor Arnett Library, Atlanta University, Atlanta, Georgia.

44. *Caroling Dusk*, p. 47.

45. Letter from Georgia Douglas Johnson to Ama Bontemps, July 19, 1941. GDJ Papers, the Cullen-Jackman Collection.

46. The New York *Ecclesiastical Review*, February 1900.

47. Letter from Bliss Perry to Alice Dunbar-Nelson, August 22, 1900. AD-N Papers, the University of Delaware Library, Newark, Delaware.

48. Lewis, p. 94.

49. Alain Locke, Foreword to Georgia Douglas Johnson's *An Autumn Love Cycle* (New York: Harold Vinal, Ltd., 1928), p. xviii.

50. Johnson's third-person headnote in *Caroling Dusk*, p. 74.

51. This statement exists in an incomplete holograph draft. Grimké wrote it in response to a November 28, 1925, request for information from a student studying her work.

52. Reprinted in *The World Split Open: Four Centuries of Women Poets in England and America, 1552–1950*, ed. Louise Bernikow (New York: Vintage Books, 1974), p. 262.

53. Barbara Christian, "Afro-American Women Poets: A Historical Introduction," in *Black Feminist Criticism: Perspectives on Black Women Writers* (New York: Pergamon Press, 1985), p. 122.

54. Cheryl A. Wall, "Poets and Versifiers, Singers and Signifiers: Women of the Harlem Renaissance," in *Women, the Arts and the 1920's in Paris and New York*, ed.

Kenneth W. Wheeler and Virginia Lee Lussier (New Brunswick: N. J.: Transaction Books, 1982), p. 75.

55. Helene Johnson, "Poem," in *Caroling Dusk*, p. 219. Bessie Smith, "Young Women's Blues," quoted from Cheryl A. Wall, pp. 90–91.

56. Letter from William Haygood to GDJ, October 7, 1942. Rosenwald Collection, Fisk University, Nashville, Tennessee.

57. Lewis, p. 238.

58. Letter from GDJ to Harold Jackman, August 8, 1944. Cullen-Jackman Collection.

59. Erlene Stetson, "Rediscovering the Harlem Renaissance: Georgia Douglas Johnson, 'The New Negro Poet,'" *Obsidian* 5 (Spring/Summer, 1979): 33.

60. Letter from Charles S. Johnson to Angelina W. Grimké, May 28, 1925. AWG Collection.

61. Letter from Georgia Douglas Johnson to George E. Haynes, July 26, 1928. The Harmon Foundation Records, Manuscript Division, Library of Congress, Washington, D.C.

62. *Caroling Dusk*, p. 105.

63. Lewis, pp. 120–21.

RICHARD K. BARKSDALE

Black Autobiography and the Comic Vision

In Vernon Loggins's *The Negro Author*, a work which appeared just as the Harlem Renaissance was beginning to drift into the Depression years, the author observed that "With the exception of his folk songs, the Negro's most valuable contributions to American literature have been in the form of personal memoirs."[1] Today, almost fifty years later, few would argue with such a criticial assessment. Beginning with the earliest published slave narrative—John Saffin's *Adam Negro's Tryall* in 1703—and continuing to this day, black Americans have produced more autobiographical statements than any other American minority. And these have come from a wide spectrum of black America—all the way from distinguished leaders like Douglass, Washington, Du Bois, Daniel Payne, and Benjamin Mays to Icepick Slim, the king of the pimps on Chicago's Southside. Sometimes the titles of these autobiographies are simple and direct, like Richard Wright's *Black Boy* or Babs Gonzales's *I Paid My Dues;* at other times they are both evocative and provocative, like Daniel T. Grant's *When the Melon Is Ripe* or Robert Lee Grant's *The Star Spangled Hustle*. Sometimes, like some of the slave narratives written for abolitionist propaganda purposes between 1830 and 1860, some autobiographies are written with the collaboration and assistance of a second party (particularly true of successful athletes and entertainers who want to take advantage of a large captive audience but do not have the requisite writing skills to exploit such an advantage). Some, like *All God's Dangers* and

From *Praisesong of Survival: Lectures and Essays*, 1957-89. ©1992 by The Board of Trustees of the University of Illinois.

The Autobiography of Malcolm X, are not collaborative works but transmitted directly through a second party. Theodore Rosengarten is listed as the author of *All God's Dangers*, but there is no doubt that the one authentic voice in the work is that of Nate Shaw, or Nate Cobb as he was known in his home in black rural Alabama. Similarly, although Alex Haley transmitted the story of Malcolm X, the authentic voice is that of the Muslim leader himself.

So black autobiography is rich and varied. It represents the collective self-appraisal of a rich variety of Afro-Americans—a challenging melange that cuts across all groups, sects, and classes in black America. Robert Brignano, who published an annotated bibliography of black autobiographies in 1974, estimated that 459 such works had been published since the Civil War.[2] The overwhelming question to be answered, however, is not how many, but why so many? Do we have here a racially indigenous genre for which black Americans have a unique and special capability? Is the urge to tell one's story a racial urge to testify or bear witness—to be spiritually accountable? Or is the autobiographical urge a racial trait with African roots, like blues and jazz and the love of yams?

The obvious answer to all of these questions is no. Benjamin Franklin and Benvenuto Cellini have through their autobiographies supplied abundant evidence that the gift for writing in this genre was not transmitted from Africa nor has it ever been the special literary forte of black Americans only. The inescapable conclusion then is that the roots of the black autobiography syndrome lie deep in a soil fertilized by American racism and watered by the tears of the oppressed. Other literary critics substantiate this general conclusion with more subtle and sophisticated argument. For instance, Sidonie Smith, author of *Where I'm Bound*, a study of patterns of slavery and freedom in black American autobiography, argues that all writing in this category was and is motivated by the black man's or black woman's search for identity.[3] Just as the fugitive slave wrote his story and thereby gained a political and social identity, so a Baldwin, suffering from an identity crisis, began to find and know himself as he wrote *Nobody Knows My Name*. Other critics, noting that blacks in America suffer from a kind of cultural schizophrenia, say that the autobiographical statement is a therapeutic catharsis that heals the black psyche, making cohesive and unitary what Du Bois called "two warring selves in one dark skin."[4] In addition, there is a school of critical thought which asserts that black autobiography is a form of historical writing and the product of a genuinely creative historical imagination.[5] Having been excluded from involvement in the creation of history as history is defined by Western tradition, black people have, through their autobiographies, provided their own histories—stories of their journey from "can't to can" and their flight from oppression to an ever elusive quasi-freedom.

It is difficult to conclude which one of these theories explaining the nature and origin of the black autobiography is *the* explanation. Possibly, all have some degree of critical legitimacy. But one can safely conclude that, because each autobiography records a given persona's encounter with racism, each autobiography directly or indirectly reacts to the violence, anger, confusion, and psychological chaos that accompanies that racism. Chester Himes's *The Quality of Hurt*, for instance, is a book full of anger and the violence that is engendered by the implacably hostile environments that Himes encountered on his journey from "can't to can." And this anger and violence infect all of Himes's relationships, making him paranoid and suspicious about both friend and foe alike. Even his attitude toward his mother is strained and, at times, surly and intractable. For Richard Wright's initial kindnesses in helping him get settled in Paris he is not in any way grateful but, instead, elaborates at some length on the baser and less angelic side of his fellow writer's character and personality. On one occasion, the violence even invades the bedroom, and the hero emerges therefrom with a broken toe, self-inflicted when a poorly directed kick missed the intended victim and smashed against an unyielding piece of sturdy furniture. This last event does bring to an otherwise humorless and darkly somber work a smidgen of humor, especially when we note how maladroitly our broken-toed persona maneuvers in the service of Venus immediately after the self-inflicted fracture.

It should be pointed out in this context that in those autobiographies which recount the persona's ascent to success, anger, woe, and violence are usually muted. There are few of these so-called negative factors, for instance, in Booker T. Washington's *Up from Slavery*, a work obviously modeled on Franklin's success-story *Autobiography*. The violence of a reconstructionist South ever lurks in the background of Washington's story, but this is carefully masked and screened from the reader's view; in the foreground we have Washington, the stalwart Christian, a man of ingenuity, industry, and enterprise—making his journey from "can't to can" not on the backroads of earlier fugitive flights but on the bright highway of personal achievement. And Du Bois in his *Autobiography* travels on a similar high road. Man's inhumanity to man based on color is ever present in this work which Du Bois completed in the final years of his long and distinguished career, but the violence engendered by racism is kept in the background. The patterns of international travel are important in this work; admittedly the traveling is done to serve the ends of racial justice, but oftentimes for the reader of this autobiography, "where" becomes more important than "why."

Over and above these general characteristics, however, there is one additional feature of black autobiography that merits further probing and analysis. This I choose to call the literary device of comic distancing. This occurs when autobiographers who have the gift of comic vision rise above racism's drab and cruel realities and inject a note that lightens the mood of the reader and lifts the tone of the narrative. Needless to say, black autobiographers with this gift are by no means numerous. Very few of the nineteenth-century slave narrators, for instance, demonstrated any evidence of this kind of comic vision. Undoubtedly, the circumstances under which they were forced to survive were so horrendous and dehumanizing that there was no opportunity for comic detachment or comic distancing from the daily routine of pain and suffering which all slaves had to endure. Similarly, the great autobiographers of the Reconstruction and post-Reconstruction periods—Douglass, Payne, Washington, and John Langston—were seriously involved in recounting their achievements in the face of racism's overwhelming odds; hence, they were unable to detach themselves from the flow of events and objectively note the social ironies and subtle comic nuances that make the *comédie humaine* what it is. These were men who, according to the general consensus of history, "had crossed the broad rivers of racial discrimination and climbed the towering peaks of racial prejudice"; so their lives reflected the kind of moral commitment that demanded involvement and precluded detachment. One must admit that Douglass did have a pronounced penchant for heavy irony and sarcasm in his ever-running fight with American racism, but he used the sledge hammer of denunciation and not the scalpel of wit. By and large, then, autobiographers who have demonstrated an ability to employ a comic vision are twentieth-century authors. The three writers who provide the best examples of comic distancing in their autobiographical statements are Langston Hughes, Zora Neale Hurston, and Rosengarten's Nate Cobb in *All God's Dangers*. Before analyzing their autobiographies for evidence of this phenomenon, however, I would like to discuss two minor instances of what I choose to call comic authorial detachment from the pain and woe of racial experience.

The first instance, surprisingly, is found in one of the slave narratives recorded by the WPA Writers Project in the late 1930s and published in Botkin's *Lay My Burden Down*[6] in 1945. The narrator is Ellen Betts, a ninety-year-old ex-slave who, at the time of the interview, resided in Opelousas, Louisiana. In general, her memory of "slave times" was like the "remembrances" of the other old ex-slaves who were interviewed in the WPA Writers Project. Slavery was remembered as a time of cruel "tribulation," sorrow, and woe. Families were broken up and children sold down river from grieving mothers; grown women and men were, for the slightest offenses, strung up and given the customary thirty-nine lashes with a bull whip or with a cat-o'-nine-tails. Despite her painful memories, however, Ellen Betts provides a comic lilt as she recalls her years as a child and a young adult before "surrender come."

> Miss Sidney was Marse's first wife, and he had six boys by her. Then he marry the widow Cornelia, and she give him four boys. With ten children springing up quick like that and all the colored children coming 'long fast as pig litters, I don't do nothing all my days, but nurse, nurse, nurse. I nurse so many childrens it done went and stunt my growth, and that's why I ain't nothing but bones to this day....When the colored women has to cut cane all day till midnight come and after, I has to nurse the babies for them and tend the white children, too. Some them babies so fat and big I had to tote the feet while 'nother gal tote the head. I was such a little one, 'bout seven or eight year old. The big folks leave some toddy for colic and crying and such, and I done drink the toddy and let the children have the milk. I don't know no better. Lawdy me, it a wonder I ain't the biggest drunker in this here country, counting all the toddy I done put in my young belly! (pp. 125–26)

There is the same amount of comic detachment as well as the exaggeration that usually accompanies comic distancing in Ellen Betts's account of her adult years as a wet nurse on the Parsons' plantation:

> Two years after the war, I git marry and git children of my own and then I turn into a wet nurse. I wet-nursed the white children and black children, like they all the same color. Sometime I have a white one pulling the one side and a black one the other. (p. 126)

It is conceivable that the time that had elapsed since slavery helped Ellen Betts achieve some comic distancing from her experiences as a slave. Nevertheless, in her account of those bitter times, she was able to apprehend certain comic relationships that others, engrossed in pain and misery, were unable to see. She also had a distinct knack for graphic description. In her account of the devastation dealt the Parsons' sugar plantation after a Yankee attack, she said, "Lasses run in the bayou, and blood run in the ditches."

A second example of comic detachment in autobiographical writing resulted from an unusual "happening" at Williams College when Sterling Brown, distinguished literary scholar and Afro-American folklorist, returned to his alma mater in Williamstown, Massachusetts, for his fiftieth anniversary. The speech which he gave on this occasion is full of memories of his four-year stay at the small New England college. It was recorded and is now in print in an anthology.[7] Entitled "A Son's Return: 'Oh, Didn't He Ramble,'" the speech recounts, with wit and wisdom and levity, the major events of Brown's undergraduate years. One might add that the speech was apparently an impromptu piece of autobiographia, and the author rambles, just as the title of the old folksong promised that he would. The tone is established when Sterling Brown, commenting on his long association with Howard University, says: " ... I was hired, I was fired, I was rehired, I was retired, I was again rehired. If I tell many lies tonight and you get them taped, I may be refired" (p. 3). What is interesting about the speech for my purposes are the comments made by Brown about the racial experiences at Williams. He remarks how he had been told before leaving Washington, D.C., the so-called hub of black upper society in the 1920s, that his stay at Williams was going to be racially traumatic. His fellow undergraduates at the prestigious institution were to be graduates of Andover, Exeter, and Groton; they, the young Washingtonian was told, had never seen and associated with anyone of his racial group, and he had never been associated with a white man of comparable age and standing. So the young Brown traveled from Washington to Williamstown in 1919 with considerable foreboding. When he arrived, however, somewhat to his apparent disappointment, he found that he was treated with "benign neglect." In fact, nothing overtly racial happened; there were no searing racial crises. Says Brown:

> I did not meet with anything blatant. I did not meet with anything flagrant. Carter Marshall was called a "nigger" on Main Street, and he knocked the guy down. And I was right behind him to help on that. I was not a fighter, but I had my race to defend.... One of the big shots in my class from Louisiana would come to us (we wore knickerbockers in those days), and he would say "Look at the little 'knickers'" but you didn't know whether it was *ck* or *gg*. And the last lie I want to tell is that they used to call me Brownie. But how the hell could I object to them calling me Brownie? My name was Brown.... (p. 8)

Sterling Brown then goes on to relate how he converted, for his own less than honorable purposes, an excessive chapel-cutting experience into a minor racial crisis.

> ... you could not cut consecutively, you could not overcut ... and I had overcut and consecutively, and Dean Howes said, "Mr. Brown, you have got to go. You have got to be suspended." I knew that as much beating as my fraternity brothers had given me that was nothing to what my father was going to give me. I (then) committed one of the worst deeds of racism in my career. I said to Dean Howes, "You would not do this if I were not a Negro." It was the college law ... I had broken the law. I threw race at him and said he (was) picking on a poor little Negro. And it worked. He was the descendant of abolitionists. This man's grandfather had probably fought at Chickamauga or something, and he nearly cried. He said, "Mr. Brown, do you really feel that?" I said, "Yes, and the other fellows feel it too." From then on I not only consecutively cut, you know, I ain't thought about chapel. (p. 10)

Not only was Sterling Brown's anti-chapel ploy an early example of reverse racism, but it also illustrates some comic distancing from an incident of racial import.

Of the three twentieth-century autobiographers whose works provide further examples of comic distancing or the use of comic vision, Langston Hughes is undoubtedly the most interesting. This very versatile man of letters made his living as a writer and published in every literary genre during his forty-seven-year career. He wrote poetry, drama, fiction, and literary criticism, assembled anthologies, and collaborated on musicals and operas. And he also completed two autobiographies, *The Big Sea*[8] in 1940 and *I Wonder as I Wander*[9] in 1949. In the first he related his travels and experiences up to his twenty-ninth year. In the second, he gave an accounting up to and including his thirty-fifth year. Thus, Hughes, who lived from 1902 to 1967, covered his life in the two autobiographies from his boyhood in Kansas and the Middle West in the early years of the century up through 1937, the year he spent in Spain covering the Spanish Civil War for the *Baltimore Afro-American Newspaper*.

Critics in general and Hughesian specialists in particular have never been happy with either of these autobiographies as sources of information about the poet. They complain that both volumes contain too little about

Hughes and too much about others. In fact, Blanche Knopf, when considering the manuscripts for publication, raised a question about the kind of noncoverage Hughes provided about himself in the two autobiographies. Her company finally published *The Big Sea* with some reluctance but rejected *I Wonder as I Wander* when it was offered for consideration in 1949. It was finally published in 1956.

Essentially, the critics were right regarding the dearth of information about Hughes in these two autobiographies. For instance, the circumstances concerning the collapse of Hughes's friendship with Zora Neale Hurston over *Mule Bone*, a play on which the two writers collaborated, are only lightly touched upon in two pages at the end of *The Big Sea*. On the other hand, Robert Hemenway's biography of Zora Neale Hurston devotes an entire chapter, including eleven rather comprehensive footnotes, to the incident.[10] Nor is the *Goodbye Christ* episode, considered by many to be of focal significance in the development of Hughes's literary career in the 1930s, even mentioned in *I Wonder as I Wander*. Apparently, Hughes purposely masked his interior personal world and, instead, devoted full attention to the flotsam of the world in which he moved and had his social being.

Actually, Hughes as autobiographer reflected the same authorial demeanor that he revealed as Hughes the poet. He was not a poet driven and dominated by moods and inner states of feeling. In fact, because he was so personally detached, he became a master of comic vision, and the literary products of his comic vision were five volumes of the Simple stories and the numerous poems describing Harlem's rich gallery of characters.

In other words, Hughes's penchant for detachment improved and enriched his comic vision in the two autobiographies. As a result, *The Big Sea* is filled with wonderful characters who are portrayed with deftness and dramatic finesse. One is Maria, Hughes's English student in Cuernavaca, "a very delicate little woman ... with a great mass of heavy black hair and very bright but sad eyes" (p. 68); another is Bruce, the one-eyed black chef at Bricktop's restaurant in Paris who was moved to a knife-throwing frenzy when his boss suggested that he be terminated because of his surliness, hostility, and general inefficiency in the culinary arts (p. 183). Of even greater interest are Hughes's portraits of the so-called Harlem literati who were involved with him in the Harlem Renaissance. There was Rudolph Fisher who, although he died prematurely at the peak of his literary career in 1934, was both "a good writer" and "an excellent singer" and was the wittiest among the literati. Then there was Wallace Thurman, the brilliant and mercurial author of *The Blacker the Berry* who drank gin excessively and always threatened "to jump out of windows at people's parties and kill himself" (p. 235). And one cannot forget Hughes's portrait of Zora Neale Hurston. She is described as a pleasant, vivacious young woman who traveled throughout Harlem with an anthropologist's ruler measuring heads for Franz Boas, Columbia University's great anthropologist. Hughes also presented "downtown" literati who were involved in the Renaissance—Van Vechten, Ernestine Evans, Jake Baker (he had the dubious distinction of owning the largest erotic library in New York), Rebecca West, and George Viereck. About all of them Hughes provided some colorful incident or bit of memorabilia. He described the annual birthday party that Van Vechten staged for himself, James Weldon Johnson, and Alfred Knopf, Jr., because their birthdays fell on the same day. Every year there were three cakes, "one red, one white, and one blue—the colors of our flag. They honored a Gentile, a Negro, and a Jew" (p. 254). Hughes adds that "the differences of race did not occur to me until days later when I thought back about the three colors and the three men" (p. 255). Finally, Hughes described a bon voyage party given by Van Vechten in the Prince of Wales suite aboard the Cunarder:

> As the champagne flowed, Nora Holt, the scintillating Negro blonde entertainer de lux from Nevada, sang a ribald ditty called "My Daddy Rocks Me with One Steady Roll." As she ceased, a well-known New York matron cried ecstatically, with tears in her eyes: "My dear! Oh, my dear! How beautifully you sing Negro spirituals!"   (p. 254)

So Hughes's autobiographies are crowded with people and incidents molded and formed by his comic vision of life. We see nothing or very little of Hughes per se; he is a detached observer—a disciplined reactor and rarely an actor—almost an invisible man. At one point in *The Big Sea* he observed that he felt his second book of poems, *Fine Clothes to the Jew*, was a better book than his first, *The Weary Blues*, "because it was more impersonal, more about other people than myself" (p. 241). His autobiographies have that same quality of impersonality and objectivity and hence are comic in the best sense of the term.

Zora Neale Hurston's autobiography, *Dust Tracks on a Road*,[11] was published two years after *The Big Sea* appeared. Although it sold well, critics have been as unhappy with the Hurston autobiography as they have been with the Hughes autobiographies. Robert Hemenway, in his epochal study of the life and works of Hurston, says that it is a "discomfiting" work—that it is difficult to determine whether the authentic voice in the autobiography is

that of a folksy figure from black Eatonville, Florida, or the voice of the
successful writer who graduated from sophisticated Barnard College (p. 283).
Another critic, Darwin Turner, claims that *Dust Tracks on a Road* is a
"disappointing blend of artful candor and coy reticence" and full of
"contradictions and silences."[12] His conclusion appears to be that the
autobiography reveals far too little about Zora Neale Hurston. Of course,
this duplicates the charge made against the Langston Hughes
autobiographies. Instead of being clearly visible, the subject of the
autobiography tends at times to be almost invisible.

Hemenway has provided some information that helps to explain why
Dust Tracks on a Road became a "discomfiting" disappointment. First,
Hurston herself did not want to write it—because she found it difficult to
reveal "her inner self." To a large degree, the book proves that Hurston's
statement was a self-fulfilling prophecy. Secondly, her Lippincott editor
demanded an extensive revision of the first manuscript draft and demanded,
as well, deletion of all matters relating either to international politics or to
American race relations.[13] The result was a work in which the author
cautiously avoided any subjects bearing on integration, discrimination, or
colonialism. In other words, Lippincott's very conservative editorial policy
left Hurston alternately floating on a cloud of down-home folksiness or
hidden in a fog of personal anonymity.

Fortunately, something of critical value is retrievable from this rather
parlous state of affairs. For, even if *Dust Tracks on a Road* does have a low
critical rating as a useful and functional autobiography, it does provide
several excellent examples of how the comic vision can enliven
autobiographical writing. In this sense, Hurston as autobiographer is
comparable to Hughes as autobiographer. Hurston's description of her own
birth is a good case in point. Although she related an incident fraught with
potential tragedy, the story as it develops provides considerable comic
alleviation—

> My mother had to make it alone. She was too weak after I rushed
> out to do anything for herself.... She was so weak, she couldn't
> even reach down to where I was. She had one consolation. She
> knew I wasn't dead, because I was crying strong. (p. 37)

The "birthing" incident continues with the arrival of a white neighbor who,
hearing "me spread my lungs all over Orange County," rushed in, whipped
out his trusty "Barlow knife" to cut the navel cord, and then sponged off the
newly born Zora. Keeping her comic distance from the event and masking

the pain and misery of an untended birth, Hurston concludes the incident with the arrival of Aunt Judy, the midwife:

> She complained that the cord had not been cut just right.... She was mighty scared I was going to have a weak back, and that I would have trouble holding my water.... I did. (p. 38)

This passage has a tone of intimate folksiness, but it is also comic. As Langston Hughes once wrote:

> Birthin is hard
> And dyin is mean
> So get yourself a
> Little lovin in between.[14]

In reality, "birthing" was hard for Zora Neale Hurston too; but, by gaining some distance from the trauma of the event, she got herself a little autobiographical comedy "in between."

There are two other incidents in *Dust Tracks on a Road* that have comic significance. The first involves Zora's philandering Uncle Jim who, bearing gifts of sugar cane and peanuts, sneaks off to visit his secret love. He is followed by his axe-bearing spouse, Aunt Caroline. When she returns, she is not only carrying the axe, but draped on one shoulder are Uncle Jim's pants, shirt, and coat, and on the other, two sticks of sugar cane. It should be noted that this incident gives the reader little or no information about Zora Neale Hurston except that she apparently enjoyed that good old down-home humor which apparently also appealed to her Lippincott editor. The incident provides no comic masking from trauma, unless marital infidelity can be considered a trauma. One gathers that in Eatonville it was not.

The second incident in the autobiography which I wish to discuss is comic because it describes, with mock-heroic gusto, a fight between Zora and her new step-mother. The fight rages for four pages. Of course, Zora emerges as the victor and, if the reader has no stomach for a fight filled with hair-pulling fury, he or she emerges as the loser. It should also be noted that this mock-heroic extravaganza provides no comic masking from racial trauma, but it does show how vulnerable step-mothers were in Eatonville and how exuberantly Zora Neale Hurston could play the role of "La Belle Sauvage," again to the apparent delight of her Lippincott editor.

As I have noted above, *Dust Tracks on a Road* was purposely purged of matters of racial concern, so it contained little or no intentional comic masking of racial trauma. This was not true of *All God's Dangers*.[15] In this work, Nate Shaw tells the story of his life as a black tenant farmer in east-central Alabama, and racial tension and trauma abound throughout the book. Shaw grew to young manhood in the early years of this century, a time when rural Alabama was a hard and bitter land for the illiterate black tenant farmer. Despite this fact, he was able to achieve some comic distancing from the pain and misery that engulfed him. For instance, a delightful comic scenario develops when a youthful Shaw becomes embroiled in a fight with a neighbor named Luke Millikin. The fight develops when Luke attempts, for some minor reason, to knife Shaw and Shaw responds by smashing him on the head with a rock. The comedy begins when the victim's mother, stricken with grief, summons her lover forth from sleep to assist in avenging what she thinks is her son's foul murder. Her lover, a Mr. Flint, who just happens to be white, responds to the mother's screams for aid. Shaw relates the incident as follows:

> What you reckon that white man done? He grabbed his double barrel breech-loader and runned out there in his drawers, me peepin around the corner of the house lookin at him.... Old man Flint standin there, double barrel breech-loader in his hands, didn't have nothin on but his sleepers and them was his drawers, two piece worth. (pp. 44–45)

Fortunately, the incident ends without bloodshed, but it indicates that the potential for bloody violence was ever-present in Nate Shaw's rural Alabama.

Nate Shaw was also able to squeeze some comic relief out of a second incident which had even greater potential racial violence. This occurred when he walked into a country store called Sadler's Store in a town near his farm to buy some shoes for his children. While the clerk was waiting on him, a white man in the store became exasperated when he noted the white woman clerk climbing up and down ladders trying to serve a black customer. The white man, a Mr. Chase, grabbed a shovel and attempted to drive Shaw from the store. When Shaw refused to move, Chase then grabbed a rifle off the store's gun rack and loaded it. Fortunately, he was restrained from using it. In the meantime Shaw noted:

> There was a old colored fellow down at the door at Sadler's Store the whole time this ruckus was goin on inside ... he beckoned me to run out ... the old man tickled me ... heavy built old colored

man. And he had on one of these old frock-tail coats and it hit him just below the knee and it was cut back like a bug's wings. And he just stood there and bowed and beckoned for me to run out there. And ev'ry time he'd bow, that ol coat would fly up behind him and when he straightened up it would hit him right back there below the bend in his legs. Tickled me, it tickled me. I thought it was the funniest thing I ever saw. He was scared for me and wanted me to run out of there. I didn't run nowhere. I stood just like I'm standin today ... when I know I'm right and I ain't harmin nobody and nothin, I'll give you trouble if you try to move me. (pp. 169–70)

This passage proves that Shaw had a discerning eye for the comic, even as he stood surrounded by "All God's Dangers."

Four conclusions can be drawn from this discussion of black autobiographies and comedy. First, some of black America's best autobiographical statements contain no comedy. Second, some of those autobiographies which do contain comedy are mediocre autobiographies. Third, comedy tends to be an impersonal art. Those writers who are more impersonal tend to employ comic devices more often. And, fourth, there is no such thing as a good impersonal autobiography.

NOTES

Reprinted with permission from *Black American Literature Forum* 15, no. 1 (Spring 1981): 12–27.

1. Vernon Loggins, *The Negro Author: His Development in America to 1900* (New York: Columbia University Press, 1931), p. 4.

2. Russell C. Brignano, *Black Americans in Autobiography* (Durham, N.C.: Duke University Press, 1974), p. 91.

3. Sidonie Smith, *Where I'm Bound* (Westport, Conn.: Greenwood Press, 1974), p. ix.

4. Stephen Butterfield, *Black American Autobiography* (Amherst: University of Massachusetts Press, 1974), p. 94.

5. Albert E. Stone, "Patterns in Recent Black Autobiography," *Phylon* 29 (March 1978): 21.

6. B.A. Botkin, *Lay My Burden Down* (Chicago: University of Chicago Press, 1945). Subsequent references to this book are noted parenthetically in the text.

7. Michael Harper and Robert Stepto, eds., *Chant of Saints* (Urbana: University

of Illinois Press, 1979). Subsequent references to this book are noted parenthetically in the text.

8. Langston Hughes, *The Big Sea* (New York: Alfred Knopf, 1940). Subsequent references to this book are noted parenthetically in the text.

9. Langston Hughes, *I Wonder as I Wander* (New York: Hill and Wang, 1956).

10. Robert Hemenway, *Zora Neale Hurston* (Urbana: University of Illinois Press, 1977), pp. 136–58.

11. Zora Neale Hurston, *Dust Tracks on a Road* (New York: Lippincott, 1942). Subsequent references to this book are noted parenthetically in the text.

12. Darwin Turner, *In a Minor Chord* (Carbondale: Southern Illinois University Press, 1971), p. 91.

13. Hemenway, *Hurston*, p. 288.

14. Langston Hughes, *Selected Poems* (New York: Vintage Books, 1974), p. 264.

15. Theodore Rosengarten, *All God's Dangers* (New York: Knopf, 1974). Subsequent references to this book are noted parenthetically in the text.

EVA LENNOX BIRCH

Harlem and the First
Black Renaissance

The abolition of slavery after the Civil War had not brought automatic acceptance of the black people into the family of white America. The war's cessation in 1865 was the point at which the blacks' struggle for their full participation in and enjoyment of the promises enshrined in the Declaration of Independence was begun in earnest. Various spokespeople for the American blacks emerged, the most notable of whom was Frederick Douglass. Born into slavery in 1818, and spending half of his life in that condition, Douglass was the first black leader to capture the respect and attention of white Americans, and he progressed to become a federal administrator and eventually Consul-General to Haiti before his death in 1895. His guiding ideal, pursued without compromise throughout his life, had been the assimilation of his people into American society by the assertion of their political rights. This was not facilitated during the post-war period of reconstruction when efforts to repair the devastated Southern economy were accompanied by a hardening of the Southern whites' attitudes towards blacks, expressed in the violence of Ku Klux Klan lynchings and a determined move to disenfranchise the emancipated Negro. Douglass died in 1895 with his dreams for his people unrealised and the mantle of black leadership fell on the shoulders of a younger man, Booker T. Washington, who believed that black social and economic improvement would come

From *Black American Women's Writing: A Quilt of Many Colours.* © 1994 by Harvester Wheatsheaf.

gradually and naturally through accommodation and compromise rather than self-assertion, and only if the blacks were educated.

In his ghosted autobiography, *Up From Slavery*, first published in 1901 (from which date it has never been out of print), Washington describes his own rise from a slave childhood begun in 1856, to an unlooked-for position as leader of his people. A man of prodigious determination and diligence, his rise to prominence came not through the pulpit or the legislature, but through an education at Hampton Normal Institute, a school for the industrial training of blacks, established and administered by a Northern ex-general of the Civil War. Having imbibed and embraced the self-help ethic of the Victorian Samuel Smiles on which Hampton was founded, Washington perpetuated it in his principalship of the Tuskegee Institute, which was the first industrial school for blacks to be run by a black man. His aim—to educate the freed black to fulfil a productive role in the reconstruction of the South—was a laudable one, although later leaders like W.E.B. DuBois and Alain Locke were to point to the self-set limitations of such an education, based as it was on transforming the black male at least into a tradesman and the black woman into a proficient laundress. Washington tirelessly sought white patronage as well as the donations of poor blacks to establish and maintain Tuskegee, confessing to 'a strong feeling that what our people most needed was to get a foundation in education, industry, and property, and for this I felt that they could better afford to strive than for political preferment' (*Up From Slavery*, p. 93). Tuskegee encouraged industry, self-reliance and a faith in the power of materialism which Washington astutely recognised as becoming the dominant creed in late nineteenth-century America. In Washington's system of education, the Puritan ethics of labour and thrift went hand-in-hand with the use of a toothbrush and regular bathing, as essential requirements for the Negro who was to make himself indispensable to a Southern community through his 'skill, intelligence and character' (p. 202). Washington was convinced that industrial education would enable the blacks to become 'fit' members of the larger, white society whose approval they would slowly win. His autobiography stresses that such a gradual improvement of his people's condition would reassure the Southern whites and secure friendly interracial relations. His was a policy of conciliation rather than confrontation taken to such an extent that of the Ku Klux Klan he could write at the turn of the century: 'Today there are no such organisations in the South, and the fact that such ever existed is almost forgotten by both races. There are few places in the South now where public sentiment would permit such organisations to exist' (p. 79). Such seeming sycophancy was the product of his determination to placate Southern hostility and so afford his people an opportunity and a space to acquire the skills he believed they needed for social and economic advancement. His address in 1895 to a mixed audience in Atlanta was a masterly exercise in verbal tightrope-walking, designed to encourage the blacks without alarming the whites. It was such a summation of his policy of conciliation that the whole of his speech is now known as 'The Atlanta Compromise'. In this very carefully manipulated address, whilst stressing the advantages to both black and white of an educated black people, he promised that 'In all things that are purely social we can be as separate as the fingers, yet one as the hand in all things essential to mutual progress'. What he seemed to be promising was an undemanding, unthreatening, segregated and submissive black people who would gradually earn, rather than demand as a right, their place in American society.

With hindsight it is easy to diminish Washington's real achievements in his role as race leader, and to describe his deference to whites as demeaning, but this would be to ignore the deftness of a political strategy that had succeeded in giving his people a sense of purpose and belief in their own potential which two centuries of slave experience had sapped and stifled. Inevitably his educational aims were limited by their tailoring to his own experience of the condition of the rural black in the South where Tuskegee was founded, and which could not satisfy the different demands made by life in the industrial North to which many blacks were attracted. Seeking an imagined opportunity for economic and political improvement in the expanding industrial cities of the North, many Southern blacks migrated there. In the early 1900s, those who flooded into New York followed the typical pattern of migrating groups, gravitating towards areas where people of their own culture have already established themselves. In New York that place was Harlem. Similar groupings of racially different communities are found in many European cities where migrants were initially welcomed as a convenient labour force. British society is changing under the impact of Commonwealth immigrants whose contribution has been recognised as not simply economic, but cultural. What we see is a struggle by immigrants to preserve their own culture as a sign of identity, this being a necessary step towards a multi-cultural society. However, the struggle of blacks born in America was different. Their need was to find an identity previously denied them. Harlem offered them a place to do this.

Nathan Huggins[1] describes the twenties in Harlem as 'a point of change' (p. 3). Certainly this time is identified with a burgeoning of black creativity in what has retrospectively become known as the Harlem Renaissance, the vanguard of which was literary in nature. Harlem represented a spirit of advancement, at source motivated by the political impulse to improve the social position of all blacks, founded on a dream of possibilities rather than a cohesive creed. Artists, musicians and writers found in Harlem a climate congenial to their creative energy, and were encouraged by the philosophies of previous as well as emerging race leaders. As the demographic disposition of the American blacks changed in their move from agrarian to industrial occupations, so there was a plethora of often conflicting black voices advocating different routes to black self-expression and political power. The ideas of Booker T. Washington still commanded popular appeal, and his autobiography was a source of inspiration to his people, although even before his death in 1915 these ideas had been challenged and questioned by younger black intellectuals. In 1903 W.E.B. DuBois was to write:

> Mr Washington distinctly asks that black people give up, at least
> for the present, three things—
> First, political power,
> Second, insistence on civil rights,
> Third, higher education of Negro youth,—
> and concentrate all their energies on industrial education, the
> accumulation of wealth, and the conciliation of the South.[2]

In 1905 W.E.B. DuBois founded the Niagara Movement which was dedicated to outspoken protest against racial injustice, the active pursuit of civil rights and an implicit rejection of the accommodationist impulse of Washington's philosophy. Although it started with only 250 members this movement marked a shift in political strategies for black advancement. By 1909 some of Washington's white allies had deserted him to join the Niagara Movement blacks in their formation of the National Association for the Advancement of Colored People, an organisation which Washington steadfastly refused to join. Clearly Washington's strategies could not be accommodated successfully into the political aims of the Northern, urban black.

On Washington's death, the banner he dropped was raised anew by Alain Locke, who proclaimed hopefully that blacks could be reborn, and take their rightful place in twentieth-century American society. Locke was one of the emerging political thinkers whose analysis of the new social structure which transformed rural blacks into urban, industrialised citizens, emphasised that in transplantation the Negro had been transformed. Removed from their place of Southern enslavement, the new Northern blacks sought a new social identity. Harlem afforded a space in which this self-definition could develop, and also gave black intellectuals and political leaders a chance to raise the consciousness of people drawn from all over the South. The concept of the 'New Negro' was born and articulated by Alain Locke who wrote in the periodical *The New Negro*, published in 1925, that 'the younger generation is vibrant with a new psychology; the new spirit is awake in the masses'.[3] This 'new' psychology focused on the problem of identity, recognising that blackness was not simply a colour, but a state of mind engendered by generations of institutionalised slavery given justification, sought from science and religion, by the supposed racial inferiority of blacks. The uprooting and replanting of Southern blacks into the expanding industrial centres in the North did not dispel white opinion that even the educated black was their racial or intellectual inferior. The blacks were relegated to the lowest socio-economic strata in American society, but even those black union leaders who foregrounded class rather than race as a determinant in their people's disadvantaged state, and advocated a joining with the white proletariat in the class struggle, were forced to recognise the racism of the equally dispossessed, poor whites. A. Philip Randolph sadly admitted that such a union was an impossible dream because 'Black America is a victim of both class and race prejudice and oppression'.[4] The continuance of slavery in the South had depended upon the assumption of the racial inferiority of blacks and, despite the work done by the anthropologist Franz Boas to show that environmental and not hereditary factors were cultural determinants, prejudice was deep-seated. It also survived by the denial of facts. White opinion was not to be changed by Boas who attacked the Jim Crow laws 'which are based simply upon public prejudice, without the shadow of knowledge of the underlying biological facts'.[5]

To disprove this inscription of black inferiority, black political leaders pointed to the black artists in Harlem as evidence of the mistaken white view. James Weldon Johnson was quick to grasp the propaganda potential of the Harlem writers, whom he charged with the serious task of re-educating white opinion:

> But these younger writers must not be mere dilettantes; they have serious work to do. They can bring to bear a tremendous force for breaking down and wearing away the stereotyped ideas about the Negro, and for creating a higher and more enlightened opinion about the race.[6]

Johnson was convinced that art and propaganda were inextricably interrelated, a view with which today's literary critics who interrogate the canon—and question its validity as anything more than a perpetuation of vested interests—would not quarrel. He found support for his argument in W.E.B. DuBois, who urged the channelling of political energy into the arts. DuBois, along with other black intellectuals, subscribed to the idea of 'Negritude' as a celebration of the artistic and spiritual qualities of black Americans, which involved the recognition of experience encapsulated in black oral culture. Yet, conscious of white opinion, he wanted that oral tradition to be translated into a form that accorded with white cultural standards. Like many of the new black bourgeoisie, he did not want his people portrayed as 'low' characters. This attitude informed some black critics who rejected any unflattering depiction of the Negro. Arna Bontemps' novel *God Sends Sunday* was described by Alice Dunbar Nelson as having left a sour taste in her mouth, because 'The characters are low, loose in morals, frivolous in principles, and in many instances even criminal ... Bontemps, undoubtedly has portrayed some ambitions of Negro life—but in my opinion Negro literature has not benefited thereby'.[7] The attitude expressed in this review suggests that in keeping with DuBois—who saw black art as one way of convincing the whites of the reality of black intellectual and imaginative power—Alice Dunbar Nelson's criticism was influenced by extra-aesthetic considerations. Houston A. Baker identifies this as being dependent upon race theories that when joined with 'the use of the word *culture* in a slanted manner have allowed Whites to state that Black men are part of an inferior race and possess no cultural capabilities'.[8] In truth, Alain Locke's concept of the 'New Negro' could only be realised if the artists were free to develop their own black aesthetic and not simply direct their efforts to achieving incorporation within dominant white culture. Black identity could not be affirmed if it entailed the rejection of the oral culture which was an expression of their shared experience, and which had been accorded no place of value within the dominant white culture—although Mark Twain's use of white vernacular in *Huckleberry Finn* had been acclaimed as an authentic American voice. According to Richard Ellison,[9] if black contribution to American culture was to be recognised, black artists needed to cherish, reclaim and build upon the oral culture which had preserved their sense of identity and self-esteem during their years of enslavement.

Searching for the roots that made their cultural inheritance unique, the Harlem Renaissance writers turned to the art and music of their African ancestors, in an effort to prove that the black American was not a cultural orphan. Some, like Hughes and Hurston, believed that the authenticity of their own voices depended upon their deliberate use of the hitherto 'non-literary' language and idiom of the blacks, as well as the standard English then associated with the literary. They argued that the exclusion from their writing of the particularly expressive use of English by black Americans would not only be a constraint upon their creativity, but also would give credence to the idea of white supremacy. Although hailed by Alain Locke as part of the 'talented tenth' of the black population whose responsibility it was to speak for the silenced majority, these writers resisted this idea of an artistic elite. At a time when 90 per cent of black Americans lived in poverty in the Deep South, the philosophy of the 'talented tenth' was not without dangers. The elevation of the intellectual above the ordinary person can lead to a separation of the artist from the roots of experience. In his article on 'The Negro Artist and the Racial Mountain' in *The Nation* in 1926, Langston Hughes warned that the 'urge within the race towards Whiteness'—to be as little Negro and as much American as possible—was a self-denying, suicidal aspiration. With Wallace Thurman and Zora Neale Hurston he founded a magazine called *Fire!* In this, Harlem writers voiced their resistance to white standardisation as well as their fears that art founded on a propagandist or elitist base would become vitiated. They, too, wanted the advancement of the Negro, yet at the same time attempted to resist an over-politicising of their work which could lead to the loss of personal recognition for themselves as individual artists. In the aforementioned article in *The Nation*, Hughes expressed the aims of these Harlem writers:

> We younger Negro artists who create now intend to express our individual dark-skinned selves, without fear or shame. If White people are pleased, we are glad. We know we are beautiful. And ugly too.... if colored people are pleased, we are glad. If they are not, their displeasure doesn't matter either. We build our temples for tomorrow, strong as we know how, and we stand on top of the mountain free within ourselves.[10]

In the same article, Hughes identified the double-bind in which the Harlem writers found themselves. They were constrained by political pressures from black leaders, and by their financial dependence upon white patrons. Hughes and Hurston both depended upon the financial assistance of a rich white woman, Mrs Osgood Mason. She gave money to support their writing; in return she insisted upon being called 'Godmother', as well as claiming editorial rights to their work. It is not surprising that in her autobiography Hurston refers to the Renaissance in Harlem as 'so-called'.

The 'rebirth' was limited. In *The Big Sea*, Hughes describes the gradual appropriation of Harlem by whites coming in droves to the Cotton Club to listen to black musicians. Moneyed whites brought Jim Crow to the very heart of Harlem, 'flooding the little cabarets and bars where formerly only colored people laughed and sang, and where now the strangers were given the best ring-side tables to sit and stare at the Negro customers—like amusing animals in a zoo'.[11]

Arna Bontemps reminisced to the scholar Robert E. Hemenway about that particular period in black cultural history when black artists were 'shown off and exhibited and presented' to all sorts of white people.[12] The terms used here can be applied to valuable works of art, but also to freaks or performing animals. This feature of the Renaissance, when blacks were lionised and petted, illustrates the constraints under which the writers worked. As 'exhibits' they were 'owned', or at least controlled, by their own political leaders or by rich white patrons. What had begun in the Harlem of the 1920s as an exciting, vibrant explosion of black creativity, with the possibility of regeneration and self-definition, had become considerably muted by the mid-1930s. The race riots of 1935 were both an expression of black discontent and an acknowledgement that Booker T. Washington's dream of full and equal status for the blacks in American society was still just that—a dream.

Yet despite its constraints, the Harlem Renaissance was an important seed-bed for the black writers who came later. In that brief period, certain preoccupations and ideas took root that were seminal to the literature that followed. The Renaissance gave substance to Marcus Garvey's pronouncement that 'Black is beautiful'; it expressed a pride in a hitherto ignored black identity; it established a black aesthetic founded on suppressed and hitherto discounted Afro-American culture; it gave voice to a 'talented tenth' that included women as well as men. Of the women writers who came to prominence at that time, I have singled out Zora Neale Hurston for sustained discussion, believing that her efforts to record the richness of black life and culture were a significant advance in the development of a distinct literary tradition. She was not the only woman writer in Harlem, and she certainly shared with Nella Larsen a concern about the clash in cultures that Harlem witnessed. Like Larsen, Hurston pondered and explored the dilemma of the educated mulatta and her search for a meaningful place in American society; engaged with sexual and racial politics; and opened up the problematic area of the ambiguous nature of female sexuality. Both Hurston and Larsen came to prominence in Harlem within a literary milieu that was male dominated, and both had to combat the sexism and racism in their lives which they used as the stuff of their fictions. Both died in relative obscurity in the middle of this century. Larsen had abandoned a sustained career in writing and returned to nursing, after being accused of plagiarism in 1922, from the shock of which it is said she never recovered. Hurston, having combated in a court of law an accusation that she had sexually corrupted a juvenile, was still writing at the end of her life, although she was reportedly working as a chambermaid to survive financially. It is strange and sad that these women who had received so much early acclaim as writers, should have been forced eventually by adverse circumstances into the stereotypical roles of carer and cleaner to others which had been the lot of so many black women.

Unlike Jean Toomer, whose *Cane* was heralded as the black masterpiece of the Harlem Renaissance, Hurston never denied her allegiance to her own black people, and yet literary history was to silence her voice far more effectively than it did Toomer's. Perhaps Hurston's cynical dismissal of the black literati as the 'niggerati' is a significant comment, revealing her shrewd assessment of those intellectuals who were in danger of losing contact with the roots of black experience. I feel she deserves particular attention in this limited review because, above all else, her work is a sustained celebration of the rich inventiveness of black creativity and the will to survive which characterises much of the writing by black women who came later. Her engagement with the Harlem Renaissance was significant too, because it illustrated that her position as a black woman and aspiring writer was one of extreme vulnerability. In many ways she was like Booker T. Washington, whose strategies for survival in a white world she had learned well. She too was an accommodationist when it suited, and like him she would have one opinion for white consumption and another for black. She emerges as a complex, tragic and talented figure; a woman who had to combat the societal pressures exercised by class, race, gender and religion. Langston Hughes, her friend at that time, has left a personal record:

> Of this 'niggerati' Zora Neale Hurston was certainly the most amusing. Only to reach a wider audience, need she ever write books—because she is a perfect book of entertainment in herself. In her youth she was always getting scholarships and things from wealthy White people, some of whom simply paid her just to sit around and represent the Negro race for them, she did it in such a racy fashion. She was full of side-splitting anecdotes, humorous tales and tragicomic stories, remembered out of her life in the

South as a daughter of a travelling minister of God, she could make you laugh one minute and cry the next. To many of her White friends, no doubt, she was a perfect 'darkie', in the nice meaning they gave the term—that is a naive, childlike, sweet, humorous and highly colored Negro. But Miss Hurston was clever too—a student who didn't let college give her a broad 'a' and who had a great scorn for all pretensions, academic or otherwise.[13]

Her laughter was remembered, but it was a laughter born of the pain of being poor, black and female.

NOTES

1. Nathan A Huggins (ed.), *Voices from the Harlem Renaissance* (Oxford, Oxford University Press, 1976).

2. DuBois, W.E.B., 'Of Mr Booker T. Washington and Others', from *The Seven Souls of Balck Folk* reprinted in Julius Lested (ed.), *The Seventh Son: The Thought and Writing of W.E.B. Du Bois* (New York, Random House, 1971), Volume I, p. 74.

3. Alain Locke, 'The New Negro' (Huggins, *op. cit.*), p. 47.

4. Quoted in James O. Young, *Black Writers of the Thirties* (Baton Rouge, Louisiana State University Press, 1973), p. 65.

5. Franz Boas, *Race Language and Culture* (New York, Macmillan, 1940), p. 51.

6. James Weldon Johnson, Foreword to 'Challenge', Vol. 1, March 1934, in Huggins, *op. cit.*, p. 390.

7. Young, *op. cit.*, p. 135.

8. Houston A. Baker Jr, *Long Black Song* (Charolottesville, University Press of Virginia, 1972), p. 135.

9. Ralph Ellison, *Shadow and Act* (New York, New American Library, 1966), p. 172: '[folk-lore ... embodies those values by which the group lives or dies. These drawings may be crude, but they are nonetheless profound in that they represent the group's attempt to humanize the world. It's no accident that great literature, the products of individual artists, is erected upon so humble a base.'

10. Michael G. Cooke, *Afro-American Literature in the Twentieth Century* (New Haven, Yale University Press, 1984), p. 32.

11. Langston Hughes, *The Big Sea*, quoted in Huggins, *op. cit.*, p. 370.

12. Robert E. Hemenway, *Zora Neale Hurston: A literary biography* (London, Camden Press, 1986), p. 38.

13. Langston Hughes, *The Big Sea*, in Huggins, *op. cit.*, p. 380.

DAVID LEVERING LEWIS

Reading the Harlem Renaissance

The Harlem Renaissance was a somewhat forced phenomenon, a cultural nationalism of the parlor, institutionally encouraged and directed by leaders of the national civil rights establishment for the paramount purpose of improving race relations in a time of extreme national backlash, caused in large part by economic gains won by Afro-Americans during the Great War. W.E.B. Du Bois labeled this mobilizing elite the "Talented Tenth" in a seminal 1903 essay. He fleshed out the concept that same year in "The Advance Guard of the Race," a piece in *Booklover's Magazine* in which he identified the poet Paul Laurence Dunbar, the novelist Charles W. Chesnutt, and the painter Henry O. Tanner, among a small number of other well-educated professionals, as representatives of this class. The Talented Tenth formulated and propagated a new ideology of racial assertiveness that was to be embraced by the physicians, dentists, educators, preachers, businesspeople, lawyers, and morticians who comprised the bulk of the African American affluent and influential—some ten thousand men and women out of a total population in 1920 of more than ten million. (In 1917, traditionally cited as the natal year of the Harlem Renaissance, there were 2,132 African Americans in colleges and universities, probably no more than fifty of them attending "white" institutions.)

It was, then, the minuscule vanguard of a minority—a fraction of 0.1 percent of the racial total—that jump-started the New Negro Arts

From *The Portable Harlem Renaissance Reader*, edited by David Levering Lewis. © 1994 by David Levering Lewis.

Movement, using as its vehicles the National Association for the Advancement of Colored People (NAACP) and the National Urban League (NUL), and their respective publications, *The Crisis* and *Opportunity* magazine. The Harlem Renaissance was not, as some students have maintained, all-inclusive of the early twentieth-century African American urban experience. Not everything that happened between 1917 and 1935 was a Renaissance happening. The potent mass movement founded and led by the charismatic Marcus Garvey was to the Renaissance what nineteenth-century populism was to progressive reform: a parallel but socially different force related primarily through dialectical confrontation. Equally different from the institutional ethos and purpose of the Renaissance was the Black Church. If the leading intellectual of the race, Du Bois, publicly denigrated the personnel and preachings of the Black Church, his animadversions were merely more forthright than those of other New Negro notables James Weldon Johnson, Charles S. Johnson, Jessie Redmon Fauset, Alain Locke, and Walter Francis White. An occasional minister (such as the father of poet Countee Cullen) or exceptional Garveyites (such as Yale-Harvard man William H. Ferris) might move in both worlds, but black evangelism and its cultist manifestations, such as Black Zionism, represented emotional and cultural retrogression in the eyes of the principal actors in the Renaissance.

When Du Bois wrote a few years after the beginning of the New Negro movement in arts and letters that "until the art of the black folk compels recognition they will not be rated as human," he, like most of his Renaissance peers, fully intended to exclude the blues of Bessie Smith and the jazz of "King" Oliver. Spirituals sung like *Lieder* by the disciplined Hall Johnson Choir—and, better yet, *Lieder* sung by conservatory-trained Roland Hayes, 1924 recipient of the NAACP's prestigious Spingarn Medal—were deemed appropriate musical forms to present to mainstream America. The deans of the Renaissance were entirely content to leave discovery and celebration of Bessie, Clara, Trixie, and various other blues-singing Smiths to white music critic Carl Van Vechten's effusions in *Vanity Fair.* When the visiting Russian film director Sergei Eisenstein enthused about new black musicals, Charles S. Johnson and Alain Locke expressed mild consternation in their interview in *Opportunity* magazine. As board members of the Pace Phonograph Company, Du Bois, James Weldon Johnson, and others banned "funky" artists from the Black Swan list of recordings, thereby contributing to the demise of the African American–owned firm. But the wild Broadway success of Miller and Lyles's musical *Shuffle Along* (which helped to popularize the Charleston) or Florence Mills's *Blackbirds* revue flouted such artistic fastidiousness. The very centrality of music in black life, as well as of black musical stereotypes in white minds, caused popular musical forms to impinge inescapably on Renaissance high culture. Eventually, the Renaissance deans made a virtue out of necessity; they applauded the concert-hall ragtime of "Big Jim" Europe and the "educated" jazz of Atlanta University graduate and big-band leader Fletcher Henderson, and took to hiring Duke Ellington or Cab Calloway as drawing cards for fund-raising socials. Still, their relationship to music remained beset by paradox. New York ragtime, with its "Jelly Roll" Morton strides and Joplinesque elegance, had as much in common with Chicago jazz as Mozart did with "Fats" Waller.

Although the emergence of the Harlem Renaissance seems much more sudden and dramatic in retrospect than the historic reality, its institutional elaboration was, in fact, relatively quick. Because so little fiction or poetry had been produced by African Americans in the years immediately prior to the Harlem Renaissance, the appearance of a dozen or more poets and novelists and essayists seemed all the more striking and improbable. Death from tuberculosis had silenced poet-novelist Dunbar in 1906, and poor royalties had done the same for novelist Chesnutt after publication the previous year of *The Colonel's Dream*. Since then, no more than five African Americans had published significant works of fiction and verse. There had been *Pointing the Way* in 1908, a flawed, fascinating civil rights novel by the Baptist preacher Sutton Griggs. Three years later, Du Bois's sweeping sociological allegory *The Quest of the Silver Fleece* appeared. The following year came James Weldon Johnson's well-crafted *The Autobiography of an Ex-Colored Man*, but the author felt compelled to disguise his racial identity. A ten-year silence fell afterward, finally to be broken in 1922 by Claude McKay's *Harlem Shadows*, the first book of poetry since Dunbar.

Altogether, the Harlem Renaissance evolved through three stages. The first phase, ending in 1923 with the publication of Jean Toomer's unique prose poem *Cane*, was deeply influenced by white artists and writers—Bohemians and Revolutionaries—fascinated for a variety of reasons with the life of black people. The second phase, from early 1924 to mid-1926, was presided over by the Civil Rights Establishment of the NUL and the NAACP, a period of interracial collaboration between Zora Neale Hurston's "Negrotarian" whites and the African American Talented Tenth. The last phase, from mid-1926 to the Harlem Riot of March 1935, was increasingly dominated by the African American artists themselves—the "Niggerati," in Hurston's pungent phrase. The movement, then, was above all literary and self-consciously an enterprise of high culture well into its middle years. When Charles S. Johnson, new editor of *Opportunity*, sent invitations to some dozen young and mostly unknown African American poets and writers to attend a celebration at Manhattan's Civic Club of the sudden outpouring of "Negro" writing, on March 21, 1924, the Renaissance shifted into high gear. "A group of the younger writers, which includes Eric Walrond, Jessie Fauset, Gwendolyn Bennett, Countee Cullen, Langston Hughes, Alain Locke, and some others," would be present, Johnson promised each invitee. All told, in addition to the "younger writers," some fifty persons were expected: "Eugene O'Neill, H.L. Mencken, Oswald Garrison Villard, Mary Johnston, Zona Gale, Robert Morss Lovett, Carl Van Doren, Ridgely Torrence, and about twenty more of this type. I think you might find this group interesting enough to draw you away for a few hours from your work on your next book," Johnson wrote almost coyly to the recently published Jean Toomer.

Although both Toomer and Langston Hughes were absent in Europe, approximately 110 celebrants and honorees assembled that evening; included among them were Du Bois, James Weldon Johnson, and the young NAACP officer Walter Francis White, whose energies as a literary entrepreneur would soon excel even Charles Johnson's. Locke, a professor of philosophy at Howard University and the first African American Rhodes scholar, served as Civic Club master of ceremonies. Fauset, the literary editor of *The Crisis* and a Phi Beta Kappa graduate of Cornell University, enjoyed the distinction of having written the second fictional work and first novel of the Renaissance, *There Is Confusion*, just released by Horace Liveright. Liveright, who was present, rose to praise Fauset as well as Toomer, whose prose poem *Cane* his firm had published in 1923. Speeches followed pell mell—Du Bois, James Weldon Johnson, Fauset. White called attention to the next Renaissance novel—his own, *The Fire in the Flint*, shortly forthcoming from Knopf. Albert Barnes, the crusty Philadelphia pharmaceutical millionaire and art collector, described the decisive impact of African art on modern art. Poets and poems were commended—Hughes, Cullen, and Georgia Douglas Johnson of Washington, D.C., with Gwendolyn Bennett's stilted yet appropriate "To Usward" punctuating the evening: "We claim no part with racial dearth,/We want to sing the songs of birth!" Charles Johnson wrote the vastly competent Ethel Ray Nance, his future secretary, of his enormous gratification that Paul Kellogg, editor of the influential *Survey Graphic*, had proposed that evening to place a special number of his magazine "at the service of representatives of the group."

Two compelling messages emerged from the Civic Club gathering: Du Bois's that the literature of apology and the denial to his generation of its authentic voice were now ending; Van Doren's that African American artists were developing at a uniquely propitious moment. They were "in a remarkable strategic position with reference to the new literary age which seems to be impending," Van Doren predicted. "What American literature decidedly needs at this moment," he continued, "is color, music, gusto, the free expression of gay or desperate moods. If the Negroes are not in a position to contribute these items," Van Doren could not imagine who else could. The African American had indisputably moved to the center of Mainstream imagination with the end of the Great War, a development nurtured in the chrysalis of the Lost Generation—Greenwich Village Bohemia. Ready conversance with the essentials of Freud and Marx became the measure of serious conversation in MacDougal Street coffeehouses, Albert Boni's Washington Square Book Shop, or the Hotel Brevoort's restaurant, where Floyd Dell, Robert Minor, Matthew Josephson, Max Eastman, and other *enragés* denounced the social system, the Great War to which it had ineluctably led, and the soul-dead world created in its aftermath, with McKay and Toomer, two of the Renaissance's first stars, participating. The first issue of Randolph Bourne's *Seven Arts* (November 1916)—which featured, among others of the "Lyrical Left," Waldo Frank, James Oppenheim, Robert Frost, Paul Rosenfeld, Van Wyck Brooks, and the French intellectual Romain Rolland—professed contempt for "the people who actually run things" in America. Waldo Frank, Toomer's bosom friend and literary mentor, foresaw a revolutionary new America emerging "out of our terrifying welter or steel and scarlet." The Marxist radicals (John Reed, Floyd Dell, Helen Keller, Max Eastman) associated with *Masses* and its successor magazine, *Liberator*, edited by Max and Crystal Eastman, were theoretically much more oriented to politics. The inaugural March 1918 issue of *Liberator* announced that they would "fight for the ownership and control of industry by the workers."

Among the Lyrical Left writers gathered around *Broom*, *S4N*, and *Seven Arts*, and the political radicals associated with *Liberator*, there was a shared reaction against the ruling Anglo-Saxon cultural paradigm. Bourne's concept of a "trans-national" America, democratically respectful of its ethnic, racial, and religious constitutents, complemented Du Bois's earlier concept of divided racial identity in *The Souls of Black Folk*. From such conceptions, the Village's discovery of Harlem followed both logically and, more compellingly, psychologically, for if the factory, campus, office, and corporation were dehumanizing, stultifying, or predatory, the African American, largely excluded because of race from all of the above, was a perfect symbol of cultural innocence and regeneration. He was perceived as an integral, indispensable part of the hoped-for design, somehow destined to aid in the reclamation of a diseased, dessicated civilization.

Public annunciation of the rediscovered Negro came in the fall of 1917 with Emily Hapgood's production at the old Garden Street Theatre of three one-act plays by her husband, Ridgely Torrence. *The Rider of Dreams, Simon the Cyrenian,* and *Granny Maumee* were considered daring because the casts were black and the parts were dignified. The drama critic from *Theatre Magazine* enthused of one lead player that "nobody who saw Opal Cooper— and heard him as the dreamer, Madison Sparrow—will ever forget the lift his performance gave." Du Bois commended the playwright by letter, and James Weldon Johnson excitedly wrote his friend, the African American literary critic Benjamin Brawley, that *The Smart Set's* Jean Nathan "spoke most highly about the work of these colored performers." From this watershed flowed a number of dramatic productions, musicals, and several successful novels by whites—yet also, with great significance, *Shuffle Along,* a cathartic musical by the African Americans Aubry Lyles and Flournoy Miller. Theodore Dreiser grappled with the explosive subject of lynching in his 1918 short story "Nigger Jeff." Two years later, the magnetic African American actor Charles Gilpin energized O'Neill's *Emperor Jones* in the 150-seat theater in a MacDougal Street brownstone taken over by the Provincetown Players.

The year 1921 brought *Shuffle Along* to the 63rd Street Theatre, with music, lyrics, choreography, cast, and production uniquely in African American hands, and composer Eubie Blake's "I'm Just Wild About Harry" and "Love Will Find a Way" entered the list of all-time favorites. Mary Hoyt Wiborg's *Taboo* was produced that year, with a green Paul Robeson making his theatrical debut. Clement Wood's 1922 sociological novel *Nigger* sympathetically tracked a beleaguered African American family from slavery through the Great War into urban adversity. *Emperor Jones* (revived in 1922 with Robeson in the lead part) showed civilization's pretentions being mocked by forces from the dark subconscious. That same year T. S. Stribling's *Birthright* appeared, a novel remarkable for its effort to portray an African American male protagonist of superior education (a Harvard-educated physician) martyred for his ideals after returning to the South. "Jean Le Negre," the black character in E. E. Cummings's *The Enormous Room* (1922), was another Noble Savage paradigm observed through a Freudian prism.

But Village artists and intellectuals were aware and unhappy that they were theorizing about Afro-America and spinning out African American fictional characters in a vacuum—that they knew almost nothing firsthand about these subjects. Sherwood Anderson's June 1922 letter to H. L. Mencken spoke for much of the Lost Generation: "Damn it, man, if I could really get inside the niggers and write about them with some intelligence, I'd be willing to be hanged later and perhaps would be." Anderson's prayers were answered almost immediately when he chanced to read a Jean Toomer short story in *Double-Dealer* magazine. With the novelist's assistance, Toomer's stories began to appear in the magazines of the Lyrical Left and the Marxists, in *Dial*, *S4N*, *Broom*, and *Liberator*. Anderson's 1925 novel *Dark Laughter* bore unmistakable signs of indebtedness to Toomer, whose work, Anderson readily admitted, had given him a true insight into the cultural energies that could be harnessed to pull America back from the abyss of fatal materialism. Celebrity in the Village brought Toomer into Waldo Frank's circle, and with it criticism from Toomer about the omission of African Americans from Frank's sprawling work *Our America*. After a trip with Toomer to South Carolina in the fall of 1922, Frank published *Holiday* the following year, a somewhat overwrought treatment of the struggle between the two races in the South, "each of which ... needs what the other possesses."

Claude McKay, whose volume of poetry *Harlem Shadows* (1922) made him a Village celebrity (he lived in Gay Street, then entirely inhabited by nonwhites), found his niche among the *Liberator* group, where he soon became co-editor of the magazine with Michael Gold. The Eastmans saw the Jamaican poet as the kind of writer who would deepen the magazine's proletarian voice. McKay increased the circulation of *Liberator* to sixty thousand, published the first poetry of E. E. Cummings (over Gold's objections), introduced Garvey's Universal Negro Improvement Association (UNIA), and generally treated the readership to experimentation that had little to do with proletarian literature. "It was much easier to talk about real proletarians writing masterpieces than to find such masterpieces," McKay told the Eastmans and the exasperated hard-line Marxist Gold. Soon all manner of Harlem radicals began meeting, at McKay's invitation, in West 13th Street, while the Eastmans fretted about Justice Department surveillance. Richard B. Moore, Cyril Briggs, Otto Huiswood, Grace Campbell, W. A. Domingo, inter alia, represented Harlem movements ranging from Garvey's UNIA and Briggs's African Blood Brotherhood to the CPUSA with Huiswood and Campbell. McKay also attempted to bring the Village to Harlem, in one memorable sortie taking Eastman and another Villager to Ned's, his favorite Harlem cabaret. Ned, notoriously anti-white, expelled them.

This was part of the background to the Talented Tenth's abrupt, enthusiastic, and programmatic embrace of arts and letters after the First World War. With white Broadway audiences flocking to O'Neill plays and shrieking with delight at *Liza*, *Runnin' Wild*, and other imitations of *Shuffle*

Along, Charles Johnson and James Weldon Johnson, Du Bois, Fauset, White, Locke, and others saw a unique opportunity to tap into the American mainstream. Harlem, the Negro Capital of the World, filled up with successful bootleggers and racketeers, political and religious charlatans, cults of exotic character ("Black Jews"), street-corner pundits and health practitioners (Hubert Harrison, "Black Herman"), beauty culturists and distinguished professionals (Madame C.J. Walker, Louis T. Wright), religious and civil rights notables (Reverends Cullen and Powell, Du Bois, Johnson, White), and hard-pressed, hardworking families determined to make decent lives for their children. Memories of the nightspots in "The Jungle" (133rd Street), of Bill "Bojangles" Robinson demonstrating his footwork on Lenox Avenue, of raucous shows at the Lafayette that gave Florenz Ziegfeld some of his ideas, of the Tree of Hope outside Connie's Inn where musicians gathered as at a labor exchange, have been vividly set down by Arthur P. Davis, Regina Andrews, Arna Bon-temps, and Langston Hughes.

If they were adroit, African American civil rights officials and intellectuals believed they stood a fair chance of succeeding in reshaping the images and repackaging the messages out of which Mainstream racial behavior emerged. Bohemia and the Lost Generation suggested to the Talented Tenth the new approach to the old problem of race relations, but their shared premise about art and society obscured the diametrically opposite conclusions white and black intellectuals and artists drew from them. Harold Stearns's Lost Generation *revoltés* were lost in the sense that they professed to have no wish to find themselves in a materialistic, mammon-mad, homogenizing America. Locke's New Negroes very much wanted full acceptance by Mainstream America, even if some, like Du Bois, McKay, and the future *enfant terrible* of the Renaissance, Wallace Thurman, might have immediately exercised the privilege of rejecting it. For the whites, art was the means to change society before they would accept it. For the blacks, art was the means to change society in order to be accepted into it. For this reason, many of the Harlem intellectuals found the white vogue in Afro-Americana troubling, although they usually feigned enthusiasm about the new dramatic and literary themes. Despite the insensitivity, burlesquing, and calumny, however, the Talented Tenth convinced itself that the civil rights dividends were potentially greater than the liabilities. Benjamin Brawley put this potential straightforwardly to James Weldon Johnson: "We have a tremendous opportunity to boost the NAACP, letters, and art, and anything else that calls attention to our development along the higher lines."

Brawley knew that he was preaching to the converted. Johnson's preface to his best-selling anthology *The Book of American Negro Poetry* (1922) proclaimed that nothing could "do more to change the mental attitude and raise his status than a demonstration of intellectual parity by the Negro through his production of literature and art." Putting T. S. Stribling's *Birthright* down, an impressed Jessie Fauset nevertheless felt that she and her peers could do better. "We reasoned," she recalled later, "'Here is an audience waiting to hear the truth about us. Let us who are better qualified to present that truth than any white writer, try to do so.'" The result was *There Is Confusion*, her novel about genteel life among Philadelphia's aristocrats of color. Similarly troubled by *Birthright* and other two-dimensional or symbolically gross representations of African American life, Walter White complained loudly to H.L. Mencken, who finally silenced him with the challenge "Why don't you do the right kind of novel? You could do it, and it would create a sensation." White did. And the sensation turned out to be *The Fire in the Flint* (1924), the second novel of the Renaissance, which he wrote in less than a month in a borrowed country house in the Berkshires. Meanwhile, Langston Hughes, whose genius (like that of Toomer's) had been immediately recognized by Fauset, published several poems in *The Crisis* that would later appear in the collection *The Weary Blues*. The euphonious "The Negro Speaks of Rivers" (dedicated to Du Bois) ran in *The Crisis* in 1921. With the appearance of McKay's *Harlem Shadows* and Toomer's *Cane* the next year, 1923, the African American officers of the NAACP and the NUL saw how a theory could be put into action. The young New York University prodigy Countee Cullen, already published in *The Crisis* and *Opportunity*, had his Mainstream breakthrough in 1923 in *Harper's* and *Century* magazines. Two years later, with Carl Sandburg as one of the three judges, Cullen won the prestigious Witter Bynner poetry prize. Meanwhile, Paul Kellogg's *Survey Graphic* project moved apace under the editorship of Locke.

Two preconditions made this unprecedented mobilization of talent and group support in the service of a racial arts-and-letters movement more than a conceit in the minds of a handful of leaders: demography and repression. The Great Black Migration from the rural South to the industrial North produced the metropolitan dynamism undergirding the Renaissance. The Red Summer of 1919, a period of socialist agitation and conservative backlash following the Russian Revolution, produced the trauma that led to the cultural sublimation of civil rights. In pressure-cooker fashion, the increase in its African American population caused Harlem to pulsate as it pushed its racial boundaries south below 135th Street to Central Park and north beyond 139th ("Strivers' Row"). In the first flush of Harlem's

realization and of general African American exuberance, the Red Summer of
1919 had a cruelly decompressing impact upon Harlem and Afro-America in
general. Charleston, South Carolina, erupted in riot in May, followed by
Longview, Texas, in July, and Washington, D.C., later in the month. Chicago
exploded on July 27. Lynchings of returning African American soldiers and
expulsion of African American workers from unions abounded. In the North,
the white working classes struck out against perceived and manipulated
threats to job security and unionism from blacks streaming north. In
Helena, Arkansas, where a pogrom was unleashed against black farmers
organizing a cotton cooperative, and outside Atlanta, where the Ku Klux
Klan was reconstituted, the message of the white South to African
Americans was that the racial *status quo ante bellum* was on again with a
vengeance. Twenty-six race riots in towns, cities, and counties swept across
the nation all the way to Nebraska. The "race problem" became definitively
an American dilemma in the summer of 1919, and no longer a remote
complexity in the exotic South.

The term "New Negro" entered the vocabulary in reaction to the Red
Summer, along with McKay's poetic catechism—"Like men we'll face the
murderous, cowardly pack/Pressed to the wall, dying, but fighting back!"
There was a groundswell of support for Marcus Garvey's UNIA. Until his
1924 imprisonment for mail fraud, the Jamaican immigrant's message of
African Zionism, anti-integrationism, working-class assertiveness, and
Bookerite business enterprise increasingly threatened the hegemony of the
Talented Tenth and its major organizations, the NAACP and NUL, among
people of color in America (much of Garvey's support came from the West
Indians). "Garvey," wrote Mary White Ovington, one of the NAACP's white
founders, "was the first Negro in the United States to capture the
imagination of the masses." *The Negro World*, Garvey's multilingual
newspaper, circulated throughout Latin America and the African empires of
Britain and France. Locke spoke for the alarmed "respectable" civil rights
leadership when he wrote, in his introductory remarks to the special issue of
Survey Graphic, that, although "the thinking Negro has shifted a little to the
left with the world trend," black separatism (Locke clearly had Garveyism in
mind) "cannot be—even if it were desirable." Although the movement was
its own worst enemy, the Talented Tenth was pleased to help the Justice
Department speed its demise.

No less an apostle of high culture than Du Bois, initially a Renaissance
enthusiast, vividly expressed the farfetched nature of the arts-and-letters
movement as early as 1926: "How is it that an organization of this kind [the
NAACP] can turn aside to talk about art? After all, what have we who are

slaves and black to do with art?" It was the brilliant insight of the men and women associated with the NAACP and NUL that, although the road to the ballot box, the union hall, the decent neighborhood, and the office was blocked, there were two untried paths that had not been barred, in large part because of their very implausibility, as well as irrelevancy to most Americans: arts and letters. They saw the small cracks in the wall of racism that could, they anticipated, be widened through the production of exemplary racial images in collaboration with liberal white philanthropy, the robust culture industry primarily located in New York, and artists from white Bohemia (like themselves marginal and in tension with the status quo). If, in retrospect, then, the New Negro Arts Movement has been interpreted as a natural phase in the cultural evolution of another American group, as a band in the literary continuum running from New England, Knickerbocker New York, Hoosier Indiana, to the Village's Bohemia, to East Side Yiddish drama and fiction, and then on to the Southern Agrarians, such an interpretation sacrifices causation to appearance. Instead, the Renaissance represented much less an evolutionary part of a common experience than it did a generation-skipping phenomenon in which a vanguard of the Talented Tenth elite recruited, organized, subventioned, and guided an unevenly endowed cohort of artists and writers to make statements that advanced a certain conception of the race, a cohort of men and women most of whom would never have imagined the possibility of artistic and literary careers.

Toomer, McKay, Hughes, and Cullen possessed the rare ability combined with personal eccentricity that defined the artist, but the Renaissance not only needed more like them but a large cast of supporters and extras. American dropouts heading for seminars in garrets and cafés in Paris were invariably white and descended from an older gentry displaced by new moneyed elites. Charles Johnson and his allies were able to make the critical Renaissance mass possible. Johnson assembled files on prospective recruits throughout the country, going so far as to cajole Aaron Douglas, the artist from Kansas, and others into coming to Harlem, where a network manned by his secretary, Ethel Ray Nance, and her friends Regina Anderson and Louella Tucker (assisted by gifted Trinidadian short-story writer Eric Walrond) looked after them until a salary or a fellowship was secured. White, the very self-important assistant secretary of the NAACP, urged Paul Robeson to abandon law for an acting career, encouraged Nella Larsen to follow his own example as a novelist, and passed the hat for artist Hale Woodruff. Fauset continued to discover and publish short stories and verse, such as those of Wallace Thurman and Arna Bontemps. Shortly after the Civic Club evening, both the NAACP and the NUL announced the creation of annual awards ceremonies bearing the titles of their respective publications, *Crisis* and *Opportunity*.

The award of the first *Opportunity* prizes came in May 1925 in an elaborate ceremony at the Fifth Avenue Restaurant with some three hundred participants. Twenty-four distinguished judges (among them Carl Van Doren, Zona Gale, Eugene O'Neill, James Weldon Johnson, and Van Wyck Brooks) had ruled on the worthiness of entries in five categories. The awards ceremony was interracial, but white capital and influence were crucial to success, and the white presence, in the beginning, was pervasive, setting the outer boundaries for what was creatively normative. Money to start the *Crisis* prizes had come from Amy Spingarn, an accomplished artist and poet, and wife of Joel Spingarn, chairman of the NAACP's board of directors. The wife of the influential attorney, Fisk University trustee, and Urban League Board chairman, L. Hollingsworth Wood, had made a similar contribution to initiate the *Opportunity* prizes. These were the whites Zora Neal Hurston, one of the first *Opportunity* prizewinners, memorably dubbed "Negrotarians." There were several categories: Political Negrotarians like progressive journalist Ray Stannard Baker, and maverick socialist types associated with *Modern Quarterly* (V.F. Calverton, Max Eastman, Lewis Mumford, Scott Nearing); salon Negrotarians like Robert Chanler, Charles Studin, Carl and Fania (Marinoff) Van Vechten, and Eleanor Wylie, for whom the Harlem artists were more exotics than talents. They were kindred spirits to Lost Generation Negrotarians, drawn to Harlem on their way to Paris by a need for personal nourishment and confirmation of a vision of cultural health, in which their romantic or revolutionary perceptions of African American vitality played a key role—Anderson, O'Neill, Georgia O'Keefe, Zona Gale, Waldo Frank, Louise Bryant, Sinclair Lewis, Hart Crane. The commercial Negrotarians like the Knopfs, the Gershwins, Rowena Jelliffe, Horace Liveright, V.F. Calverton, and Sol Hurok scouted and mined Afro-American like prospectors.

The May 1925 *Opportunity* gala showcased the steadily augmenting talent in the Renaissance—what Hurston characterized as the "Niggerati." Two laureates, Cullen and Hughes, had already won notice beyond Harlem. The latter had engineered "discovery" as a Washington, D.C., bellhop by placing dinner and three poems on Vachel Lindsay's hotel table. Some prizewinners were barely to be heard from again: Joseph Cotter, G.D. Lipscomb, Warren MacDonald, Fidelia Ripley. Others, like John Matheus (first prize in the short-story category) and Frank Horne (honorable mention in short-story writing), fell short of first-rank standing in the Renaissance. Most of those whose talent had staying power were introduced that night: E. Franklin Frazier, who won the first prize for an essay on social equality; Sterling Brown, who took second prize for an essay on the singer Roland Hayes; Hurston, awarded second prize for a short story, "Spunk"; and Eric Walrond, third-prize winner for his short story "Voodoo's Revenge." James Weldon Johnson read the poem that took first prize, "The Weary Blues," Langston Hughes's turning-point poem, combining the gift of a superior artist and the enduring, music-encased spirit of the black migrant. Comments from Negrotarian judges ranged from O'Neill's advice to "be yourselves," to novelist Edna Worthley Underwood's exultant anticipation of a "new epoch in American letters," and Clement Wood's judgment that the general standard "was higher than such contests usually bring out."

The measures of Charles S. Johnson's success were the announcement of a second *Opportunity* contest to be underwritten by Harlem "businessman" (and numbers king) Caspar Holstein, former *Times* music critic Carl Van Vechten's enthusiasm over Hughes and subsequent arranging of a contract with Knopf for Hughes's first volume of poetry, and, one week after the awards ceremony, a prediction by the New York *Herald Tribune* that the country was "on the edge, if not already in the midst of, what might not improperly be called a Negro renaissance"—thereby giving the movement its name. Priming the public for the Fifth Avenue Restaurant occasion, the special edition of *Survey Graphic*, "Harlem: Mecca of the New Negro," edited by Locke, had reached an unprecedented 42,000 readers in March 1926. The ideology of cultural nationalism at the heart of the Renaissance was crisply delineated in Locke's opening essay, "Harlem," stating that, "without pretense to their political significance, Harlem has the same role to play for the New Negro as Dublin has had for the New Ireland or Prague for the New Czechoslovakia." A vast racial formation was under way in the relocation of the peasant masses ("they stir, they move, they are more than physically restless"), the editor announced. "The challenge of the new intellectuals among them is clear enough." The migrating peasants from the South were the soil out of which all success must come, but soil must be tilled, and the Howard University philosopher reserved that task exclusively for the Talented Tenth in liaison with its Mainstream analogues—in the "carefully maintained contacts of the enlightened minorities of both race groups." There was little amiss about America that interracial elitism could not set right, Locke and the others believed. Despite historic discrimination and the Red Summer, the Rhodes scholar assured readers that the increasing radicalism among African Americans was superficial. At year's end, Albert and Charles Boni published Locke's *The New Negro*, an expanded and polished edition of the poetry and prose from the *Opportunity* contest and the special *Survey Graphic*.

The course of American letters was unchanged by the offerings in *The New Negro*. Still, it carried several memorable works, such as the short story "The South Lingers On" by Brown University and Howard Medical School graduate Rudolph Fisher; the acid poem "White House(s)" and the euphonic "The Tropics in New York" by McKay, now in European self-exile; and several poetic vignettes from Toomer's *Cane*. Hughes's "Jazzonia," previously published in *The Crisis*, was so poignant as to be almost tactile as it described "six long-headed jazzers" playing while a dancing woman "lifts high a dress of silken gold." In "Heritage," a poem previously unpublished, Cullen outdid himself in his grandest (if not his best) effort with its famous refrain, "What is Africa to me." The book carried the distinctive silhouette drawings and Egyptian-influenced motifs by Aaron Douglas, whose work was to become the artistic signature of the Renaissance. With thirty-four African American contributors (four were white), Locke's work included most of the Renaissance regulars. The notable omissions from *The New Negro* were Asa Randolph, George Schuyler, and Wallace Thurman. These were the gifted men and women who were to show by example what the potential of some African Americans could be and who proposed to lead their people into an era of opportunity and justice.

By virtue of their symbolic achievements and their adroit collaboration with the philanthropic and reform-minded Mainstream, their augmenting influence would ameliorate the socioeconomic conditions of their race over time and from the top downward. Slowly but surely, they would promote an era of opportunity and justice. It was a Talented Tenth conceit, Schuyler snorted in Asa Randolph's *Messenger* magazine, worthy of a "high priest of the intellectual snobbocracy," and he awarded Locke the magazine's "elegantly embossed and beautifully lacquered dill pickle." Yet it seemed to work, for although the objective conditions confronting most African Americans in Harlem and elsewhere were deteriorating, optimism remained high. Harlem recoiled from Garveyism and socialism to applaud Phi Beta Kappa poets, university-trained painters, concertizing musicians, and novel-writing officers of civil rights organizations. "Everywhere we heard the sighs of wonder, amazement and sometimes admiration when it was whispered or announced that here was one of the 'New Negroes,'" Bontemps recalled.

By summer of 1926, Renaissance titles included *Cane* (1923), *There Is Confusion* (1924), *Fire in the Flint* (1924), *Flight* (1926), McKay's *Harlem Shadows* (1922), Cullen's *Color* poetry volume (1924), and *The Weary Blues* volume of poetry (1926). The second *Opportunity* awards banquet, April 1926, was another artistic and interracial success. Playwright Joseph Cotter was honored again, as was Hurston, for a short story. Bontemps, a

California-educated poet struggling in Harlem, won first prize for "Golgotha Is a Mountain," and Dorothy West, a Bostonian aspiring to make a name in fiction, made her debut, as did essayist Arthur Fauset, Jessie's able brother. The William E. Harmon Foundation transferred its attention at the beginning of 1926 from student loans and blind children to the Renaissance, announcing seven annual prizes for literature, music, fine arts, industry, science, education, and race relations, with George Edmund Haynes, African American official in the Federal Council of Churches, and Locke as chief advisors. That same year, the publishers Boni & Liveright offered a thousand-dollar prize for the "best novel on Negro life" by an African American. Casper Holstein contributed one thousand dollars that year to endow *Opportunity* prizes. Van Vechten made a smaller contribution to the same cause. Amy Spingarn provided six hundred dollars toward the *Crisis* awards. Otto Kanh underwrote two years in France for the young artist Hale Woodruff. There were Louis Rodman Wanamaker prizes in music composition.

The third *Opportunity* awards dinner was a vintage one for poetry, with entries by Bontemps, Sterling Brown, Hughes, Helene Johnson, and Jonathan H. Brooks. In praising their general high quality, the white literary critic Robert T. Kerlin added the revealing comment that their effect would be "hostile to lynching and to jim-crowing." Eric Walrond's lush, impressionistic collection of short stories *Tropic Death* appeared from Boni & Liveright at the end of 1926, the most probing exploration of the psychology of cultural underdevelopment since Toomer's *Cane*. If *Cane* recaptured in a string of glowing vignettes (most of them about women) the sunset beauty and agony of a preindustrial culture, *Tropic Death* did much the same for the Antilles. Hughes's second volume of poetry, *Fine Clothes to the Jew* (1927), spiritedly portrayed the city life of ordinary men and women who had traded the hardscrabble of farming for the hardscrabble of domestic work and odd jobs. Hughes scanned the low-down pursuits of "Bad Man," "Ruby Brown," and "Beale Street" and shocked Brawley and other Talented Tenth elders with the bawdy "Red Silk Stockings." "Put on yo red silk stockings,/Black gal," it began, urging the protagonist to show herself to white boys. It ended wickedly with "An' tomorrow's chile'll/Be a high yaller."

A veritable Ministry of Culture now presided over Afro-America. McKay, viewing the scene from abroad, spoke derisively of the artistic and literary autocracy of "that NAACP crowd." The Ministry mounted a movable feast to which the anointed were invited, sometimes to Walter and Gladys White's apartment at 409 Edgecombe Avenue, where they might share cocktails with Sinclair Lewis or Mencken; often (after 1928) to the famous 136th Street "Dark Tower" salon maintained by beauty culture heiress A'Lelia Walker, where guests might include Sir Osbert Sitwell, the Crown Prince of Sweden, or Lady Mountbatten; and very frequently to the home of Carl and Fania Van Vechten, to imbibe the host's sidecars and listen to Robeson sing or Jim Johnson recite from "God's Trombones" or George Gershwin play the piano. Meanwhile, Harlem's appeal to white revellers inspired the young physician Rudolph Fisher to write "The Caucasian Storms Harlem," a satiric piece in the August 1927 *American Mercury*.

The third phase of the Harlem Renaissance began even as the second had only just gotten under way. The second phase (1924 to mid-1926) was dominated by the officialdom of the two major civil rights organizations, with its ideology of civil rights advancement of African Americans through the creation and mobilization of an artistic-literary movement. Its essence was summed up in blunt declarations by Du Bois that he didn't care "a damn for any art that is not used for propaganda" or in exalted formulations by Locke that the New Negro was "an augury of a new democracy in American culture." The third phase of the Renaissance, from mid-1926 to the end of 1934, was marked by rebellion against the Civil Rights Establishment on the part of many of the artists and writers whom that Establishment had assembled and promoted. Three publications during 1926 formed a watershed between the genteel and the demotic Renaissance. Hughes's "The Negro Artist and the Racial Mountain," which appeared in the June 1926 issue of *The Nation*, served as manifesto of the breakaway from the arts-and-letters party line. Van Vechten's *Nigger Heaven*, released by Knopf that August, drove much of literate Afro-America into a dichotomy of approval and apoplexy over "authentic" versus "proper" cultural expression. Wallace Thurman's *Fire!!*, available in November, assembled the rebels for a major assault against the Civil Rights Ministry of Culture.

Hughes's turning-point essay had been provoked by Schuyler's essay in *The Nation*, "The Negro-Art Hokum," ridiculing "eager apostles from Greenwich Village, Harlem, and environs" who made claims for a special African American artistic vision distinct from that of white Americans. "The Aframerican is merely a lamp-blacked Anglo-Saxon," Schuyler had sneered. In a famous peroration, Hughes answered that he and his fellow artists intended to express their "individual dark-skinned selves without fear or shame. If white people are pleased we are glad.... If colored people are pleased we are glad. If they are not, their displeasure doesn't matter either." There was considerable African American displeasure; and it was complex. Much of the condemnation of the license for expression Hughes, Thurman, Hurston, and other artists arrogated to themselves was generational or puritanical, and usually both. "Vulgarity has been mistaken for art," Brawley spluttered after leafing the pages of the new magazine *Fire!!*, which contained among other shockers Richard Bruce Nugent's extravagantly homoerotic short story "Smoke, Lillies and Jade!" Du Bois was said to be deeply aggrieved.

But much of the condemnation stemmed from racial sensitivity, from sheer mortification at seeing uneducated, crude, and scrappy black men and women depicted without tinsel and soap. Thurman and associate editors John Davis, Aaron Douglas, Gwendolyn Bennett, Arthur Huff Fauset, Hughes, Hurston, and Nugent took the Renaissance out of the parlor, the editorial office, and the banquet room. With African motifs by Douglas and Nordic-featured African Americans with exaggeratedly kinky hair by Nugent; poems to an elevator boy by Hughes; a taste for the jungle by Edward Silvera; short stories about prostitution ("Cordelia the Crude") by Thurman, gender conflict between black men and women at the bottom of the economy ("Sweat") by Hurston, and a burly boxer's hatred of white people ("Wedding Day") by Gwendolyn Bennett; a short play about pigment complexes within the race *(Color Struck)* by Hurston—the focus shifted to Locke's "peasant matrix," to the sorrows and joys of those outside the Talented Tenth. "Let the blare of Negro jazz bands and the bellowing voice of Bessie Smith ... penetrate the closed ears of the colored near-intellectuals," Hughes exhorted in "The Negro Artists and the Racial Mountain."

Carl Van Vechten's influence decidedly complicated the reactions of otherwise worldly critics like Du Bois, Fauset, Locke, and Cullen. While the novel's title alone enraged many Harlemites who felt their trust and hospitality betrayed, the deeper objections of the sophisticated to *Nigger Heaven* lay in its message that the Talented Tenth's preoccupation with cultural improvement was a misguided affectation that would cost the race its vitality. It was the "archaic Negroes" who were at ease in their skins and capable of action, Van Vechten's characters demonstrated. Significantly, although Du Bois and Fauset found themselves in the majority among the Renaissance leadership (ordinary Harlemites burned Van Vechten in effigy at 135th Street and Lenox Avenue), Charles Johnson, James Weldon Johnson, Schuyler, White, and Hughes praised the novel's sociological verve and veracity and the service they believed it rendered to race relations.

The younger artists embraced Van Vechten's fiction as a worthy model because of its ribald iconoclasm and iteration that the future of African American arts and letters lay in the culture of the working poor and even of the underclass—in bottom-up drama, fiction, music, and poetry, and painting. Regularly convening at the notorious "267 House," the brownstone an indulgent landlady provided Thurman rent-free on 136th Street (alternately known as "Niggerati Manor"), the group that came to produce *Fire!!* saw art not as politics by other means—civil rights between covers or from a stage or an easel—but as an expression of the intrinsic conditions most men and women of African descent were experiencing. They spoke of the need "for a truly Negroid note," for empathy with "those elements within the race which are still too potent for easy assimilation," and they openly mocked the premise of the Civil Rights Establishment that (as a Hughes character says in *The Ways of White Folks)* "art would break down color lines, art would save the race and prevent lynchings! Bunk!" Finally, like creative agents in society from time immemorial, they were impelled to insult their patrons and to defy conventions.

To put the Renaissance back on track, Du Bois sponsored a symposium in late 1926, "The Criteria of Negro Art," inviting a spectrum of views about the appropriate course the arts should take. His unhappiness was readily apparent, both with the overly literary tendencies of Locke and with the bottom-up school of Hughes and Thurman. The great danger was that politics were dropping out of the Renaissance, that the movement was turning into an evasion, sedulously encouraged by certain whites. "They are whispering, 'Here is a way out. Here is the real solution to the color problem. The recognition accorded Cullen, Hughes, Fauset, White and others shows there is no real color line,'" Du Bois charged. He then announced that *Crisis* literary prizes would henceforth be reserved for works encouraging "general knowledge of banking and insurance in modern life and specific knowledge of what American Negroes are doing in these fields." Walter White's own effort to sustain the civil-rights-by-copyright strategy was the ambitious novel *Flight*, edited by his friend Sinclair Lewis and released by Knopf in 1926. Kind critics found White's novel (a tale of near-white African Americans of unusual culture and professional accomplishment who prove their moral superiority to their oppressors) somewhat flat. The reissue the following year of *The Autobiography of an Ex-Colored Man* (with Johnson's authorship finally acknowledged) and publication of a volume of Cullen poetry, *Copper Sun*, continued the tradition of genteel, exemplary letters. In a further effort to restore direction, Du Bois's *Dark Princess* appeared in 1928 from Harcourt, Brace, a large, serious novel in which the "problem of the twentieth century" is taken in charge by a Talented Tenth International whose prime mover is a princess from India. But the momentum stayed firmly with the rebels.

Although Thurman's magazine died after one issue, respectable Afro-America was unable to ignore the novel that embodied the values of the

Niggerati—the first Renaissance best-seller by a black author—McKay's *Home to Harlem*, released by Harper & Brothers in spring 1928. Its milieu is wholly plebeian. The protagonist, Jake, is a Lenox Avenue Noble Savage who demonstrates (in marked contrast to the book-reading Ray) the superiority of the Negro mind uncorrupted by European learning. *Home to Harlem* finally shattered the enforced literary code of the Civil Rights Establishment. Du Bois confessed to feeling "distinctly like needing a bath" after reading McKay's novel about the "debauched tenth." Rudolph Fisher's *The Walls of Jericho*, appearing that year from Knopf, was a brilliant, deftly executed satire which upset Du Bois as much as it heartened Thurman. Fisher, a successful Harlem physician with solid Talented Tenth family credentials, satirized the NAACP, the Negrotarians, Harlem high society, and easily recognized Renaissance notables, while entering convincingly into the world of the working classes, organized crime, and romance across classes.

Charles Johnson, preparing to leave the editorship of *Opportunity* for a professorship in sociology at Fisk University, now encouraged the young rebels. Renaissance artists were "now less self-conscious, less interested in proving that they are just like white people.... Relief from the stifling consciousness of being a problem has brought a certain superiority" to the Harlem Renaissance, Johnson asserted. Meanwhile, McKay's and Fisher's fiction inspired the Niggerati to publish an improved version of *Fire!!*. The magazine, *Harlem*, appeared in November 1928. Editor Thurman announced portentously, "The time has now come when the Negro artist can be his true self and pander to the stupidities of no one, either white or black." While Brawley, Du Bois, and Fauset continued to grimace, *Harlem* benefitted from significant defections. It won the collaboration of Locke and White, and lasted two issues. Roy de Coverly, George W. Little, and Schuyler signed on, and Hughes contributed one of the finest short stories, based on his travels down the West Coast of Africa—"Luani of the Jungles," a polished genre piece on the seductions of the civilized and the primitive.

The other Renaissance novel that year from Knopf, Nella Larsen's *Quicksand*, achieved the distinction of being praised by Du Bois, Locke, and Hughes. Larsen claimed to have been the daughter of a Danish mother and an African American father from the Danish Virgin Islands. In fact, her father was probably a chauffeur who lived in New York; and Larsen was probably born in New York, rather than in Chicago as she claimed. Trained in the sciences at Fisk, she never pursued further studies, as has been reported, at the University of Copenhagen. She would remain something of a mystery woman, helped in her career by Van Vechten and White but somehow always receding, and finally disappearing altogether from the Harlem scene. *Quicksand* was a triumph of vivid yet economic writing and rich allegory. Its very modern heroine experiences misfortunes and ultimate destruction from causes that are both racial and individual. She is not a tragic mulatto but a mulatto who is tragic for reasons that are both sociological and existential. Helga Crane, Larsen's protagonist, was the Virginia Slim of Renaissance fiction. If there were reviews *(Crisis, New Republic, New York Times)* that were as laudatory about Fauset's *Plum Bun*, also a 1928 release, they were primarily due to the novel's engrossing reconstruction of rarefied, upper-class African American life in Philadelphia, rather than to special literary merit. Angela Murray (Angele, in her white persona), the heroine of Fauset's second novel, was the Gibson Girl of Renaissance fiction. *Plum Bun* continued the second phase of the Renaissance, as did Cullen's second volume of poetry, published in 1929, *The Black Christ*. Ostensibly about a lynching, the lengthy title poem lost its way in mysticism, paganism, and religious remorse. The volume also lost the sympathies of most reviewers.

Thurman's *The Blacker the Berry*, published by Macaulay in early 1929, although talky and awkward in spots (Thurman had hoped to write the Great African American Novel), was a breakthrough novel. The reviewer for the Chicago *Defender* enthused, "Here at last is the book for which I have been waiting, and for which you have been waiting." Hughes praised it as a "gorgeous book," mischievously writing Thurman that it would embarrass those who bestowed the "seal-of-high-and-holy approval of Harmon awards." The Ministry of Culture found the novel distinctly distasteful, *Opportunity* judging *The Blacker the Berry* to be fatally flawed by "immaturity and gaucherie." For the first time in African American fiction, color prejudice within the race was the central theme of a novel. Emma Lou, its heroine (like the author very dark and conventionally unattractive), is obsessed with respectability as well as tortured by her pigment, for Thurman makes the point on every page that Afro-America's aesthetic and spiritual center resides in the unaffected, unblended, noisome common folk and the liberated, unconventional artists. With the unprecedented Broadway success of *Harlem*, Thurman's sensationalized romp through the underside of Harlem, the triumph of Niggerati aesthetics over Civil Rights arts and letters was impressively confirmed. Another equally sharp smell of reality irritated Establishment nostrils that same year, with the publication of McKay's second novel, *Banjo*, appearing only weeks after *The Blacker the Berry*. "The Negroes are writing against themselves," lamented the reviewer for the *Amsterdam News*. Set among the human flotsam and jetsam of Marseilles and

West Africa, the message of McKay's novel was again that European civilization was inimical to Africans everywhere.

The stock market collapsed, but reverberations from the Harlem Renaissance seemed stronger than ever. Larsen's second novel, *Passing*, appeared. Its theme, like Fauset's, was the burden of mixed racial ancestry. But, although *Passing* was less successful than *Quicksand*, Larsen's novel again evaded the trap of writing another tragic-mulatto novel by opposing the richness of African American life to the material advantages afforded by the option of "passing." In February 1930, Marc Connelly's dramatization of Roark Bradford's book of short stories opened on Broadway as *The Green Pastures*. The Hall Johnson Choir sang in it, Richard Harrison played "De Lawd," and scores of Harlemites found parts during 557 performances at the Mansfield Theatre, and then on tour across the country. The demanding young critic and Howard University professor of English Sterling Brown pronounced the play a "miracle." After *The Green Pastures* came *Not Without Laughter*, Hughes's glowing novel from Knopf. Financed by Charlotte Osgood Mason (the often tyrannical bestower of artistic largesse nicknamed "Godmother") and Amy Spingarn, Hughes had resumed his college education at Lincoln University and completed *Not Without Laughter* his senior year. The beleaguered family at the center of the novel represents Afro-America in transition in white America. Hughes's young male protagonist learns that proving his equality means affirming his distinctive racial qualities. Not only Locke admired *Not Without Laughter*; the *New Masses* reviewer embraced it as "our novel." The Ministry of Culture decreed Hughes worthy of the Harmon gold medal for 1930. The year ended with Schuyler's ribald, sprawling satire *Black No More*, an unsparing demolition of every personality and institution in Afro-America. Little wonder that Locke titled his retrospective piece in the February 1931 *Opportunity* "The Year of Grace."

Depression notwithstanding, the health of the Renaissance appeared to be more robust than ever. The first Rosenwald fellowships for African Americans had been secured largely due to James Weldon Johnson's influence the previous year. Since 1928, advised by Locke, the Harmon Foundation had mounted an annual traveling exhibition of drawings, paintings, and sculpture by African Americans. The 1930 participants introduced the generally unsuspected talent and genius of Palmer Hayden, William H. Johnson, Archibald Motley, Jr., James A. Porter, and Laura Wheeler Waring in painting. Sargent Johnson, Elizabeth Prophet, and Augusta Savage were the outstanding sculptors of the show. Both Aaron Douglas and Romare Bearden came to feel that the standards of the foundation were somewhat indulgent and, therefore, injurious to many young artists, which was undoubtedly true even though the 1931 Harmon Travelling Exhibition of the Work of Negro Artists was seen by more than 150,000 people.

Superficially, Harlem itself appeared to be in fair health well into 1931. James Weldon Johnson's celebration of the community's strengths, *Black Manhattan*, was published near the end of 1930. "Harlem is still in the process of making," the book proclaimed, and the author's confidence in the power of the "recent literary and artistic emergence" to ameliorate race relations was unshaken. In Johnson's Harlem, redcaps and cooks cheered when Renaissance talents won Guggenheim and Rosenwald fellowships; they rushed to newstands whenever the *American Mercury* or *New Republic* mentioned activities above Central Park. It was much too easy for Talented Tenth notables like Johnson, White, and Locke not to notice in the second year of the Great Depression that, for the great majority of the population, Harlem was in the process of unmaking. Still, there was a definite prefiguration of Harlem's mortality when A'Lelia Walker suddenly died in August 1931, a doleful occurrence shortly followed by the sale of Villa Lewaro, her Hudson mansion, at public auction. By the end of 1929, African Americans lived in the five-hundred block of Edgecombe Avenue, known as "Sugar Hill." The famous "409" overlooking the Polo Grounds was home at one time or another to the Du Boises, the Fishers, and the Whites. Below Sugar Hill was the five-acre Rockefeller-financed Dunbar Apartments complex, its 511 units fully occupied in mid-1928. The Dunbar eventually became home for the DuBoises, E. Simms Campbell (illustrator and cartoonist), Fletcher Henderson, the A. Philip Randolphs, Leigh Whipper (actor), and (briefly) Paul and Essie Robeson. The complex published its own weekly bulletin, the *Dunbar News*, an even more valuable record of Talented Tenth activities during the Renaissance than the *Inter-State Tattler*.

The 1931 *Report on Negro Housing*, presented to President Hoover, was a document starkly in contrast to the optimism found in *Black Manhattan*. Nearly 50 percent of Harlem's families would be unemployed by the end of 1932. The syphilis rate was nine times higher than white Manhattan's; the tuberculosis rate was five times greater; pneumonia and typhoid were twice that of whites. Two African American mothers and two babies died for every white mother and child. Harlem General Hospital, the single public facility, served 200,000 African Americans with 273 beds. A Harlem family paid twice as much of their income for rent as a white family. Meanwhile, median family income in Harlem dropped 43.6 percent by 1932. The ending of Prohibition would devastate scores of marginal speakeasies, as well as prove fatal to theaters like the Lafayette. Connie's Inn would eventually migrate downtown. Until then, however, the clubs in "The Jungle" (133rd Street)— Bamville, Connor's, Clam House, Nest Club—and elsewhere (Pod's and Jerry's, Smalls' Paradise) continued to do a land-office business. With the repeal of the Eighteenth Amendment, honorary Harlemites like Van Vechten sobered up and turned to other pursuits. Locke's letters to Charlotte Osgood Mason turned increasingly pessimistic in the winter of 1931. In June 1932, he perked up a bit to praise the choral ballet presented at the Eastman School of Music—*Sahdji*, with music by William Grant Still and scenario by Nugent, but most of Locke's news was distinctly downbeat. The writing partnership of two of his protégés, Hughes and Hurston, their material needs underwritten in a New Jersey township by "Godmother" Charlotte Mason, collapsed in acrimonious dispute. Each claimed principal authorship of the only dramatic comedy written during the Renaissance, *Mule Bone*, a three-act folk play unperformed (as a result of the dispute) until 1991. Locke took the side of Hurston, undermining the tie of affection between Godmother and Hughes and effectively ending his relationship with the latter. The part played in this controversy by their brilliant secretary, Louise Thompson, the strong-willed, estranged wife of Wallace Thurman, remains murky, but it seems clear that Thompson's Marxism had a deep influence on Hughes in the aftermath of his painful breakup with Godmother, Locke, and Hurston.

In any case, beginning with "Advertisement for the Waldorf-Astoria" published in the December 1931 *New Masses*, Hughes's poetry became markedly political. "Elderly Race Leaders" and "Goodbye Christ," as well as the play "Scottsboro, Limited," were irreverent, staccato offerings to the coming triumph of the proletariat. The poet's departure in June 1932 for Moscow, along with Louise Thompson, Mollie Lewis, Henry Moon, Loren Miller, Theodore Poston, and thirteen others, ostensibly to act in a Soviet film about American race relations, *Black and White*, symbolized the shift in patronage and accompanying politicization of Renaissance artists. *One Way to Heaven*, Cullen's first novel, badly flawed and clearly influenced by *Nigger Heaven*, appeared in 1932, but it seemed already a baroque anachronism with its knife-wielding Lotharios and elaborately educated types. An impatient Du Bois, already deeply alienated from the Renaissance, called for a second Amenia Conference to radicalize the movement's ideology and renew its personnel. Jessie Fauset remained oblivious to the profound artistic and political changes under way. Her final novel, *Comedy: American Style* (1933), was technically much the same as *Plum Bun*. Her subject, once again, was skin pigment and the neuroses of those who had just enough of it to spend their lives obsessed by it. James Weldon Johnson's autobiography, *Along This*

Way, an elegantly written review of his sui generis public career as archetypal renaissance man in both meanings of the word, was the publishing event of the year. McKay's final novel also appeared that year. He worried familiar themes, but *Banana Bottom* represented a philosophical advance over *Home to Harlem* and *Banjo* in its reconciliation through the protagonist, Bita Plant, of the previously destructive tension in McKay between the natural and the artificial—soul and civilization.

The publication at the beginning of 1932 of Thurman's last novel, *Infants of the Spring*, had already announced the end of the Harlem Renaissance. The action of Thurman's novel is in the ideas of the characters, in their incessant talk about themselves, Booker T. Washington, Du Bois, racism, and the destiny of the race. Its prose is generally disappointing, but the ending is conceptually poignant. Paul Arbian (Richard Bruce Nugent) commits suicide in a full tub of water, which splashes over and obliterates the pages of Arbian's unfinished novel on the bathroom floor. A still legible page, however, contains this paragraph, which was, in effect, an epitaph:

> He had drawn a distorted, inky black
> skyscraper, modeled after Niggerati Manor,
> and on which were focused an array of
> blindingly white beams of light. The
> foundation of this building was composed
> of crumbling stone. At first glance it
> could be ascertained that the skyscraper
> would soon crumple and fall, leaving the
> dominating white lights in full possession
> of the sky.

The literary energies of the Renaissance finally slumped. McKay returned to Harlem in February 1934 after a twelve-year sojourn abroad, but his creative powers were spent. The last novel of the movement, Hurston's beautifully written *Jonah's Gourd Vine*, went on sale in May 1934. Charles Johnson, James Weldon Johnson, and Locke applauded Hurston's allegorical story of her immediate family (especially her father) and the mores of an African American town in Florida called Eatonville. Fisher and Thurman could have been expected to continue to write, but their fates were sealed by professional carelessness. Thurman died a few days before Christmas 1934, soon after his return from an abortive Hollywood film project. Ignoring his physician's strictures, he hemorrhaged after drinking to excess while hosting a party in the infamous house at 267 West 136th Street. Four days later,

Fisher expired from intestinal cancer caused by repeated exposure to his own X-ray equipment.

Locke's *New Negro* anthology had been crucial to the formation of the Renaissance. As the movement ran down, another anthology, English heiress Nancy Cunard's *Negro*, far more massive in scope, recharged the Renaissance for a brief period, enlisting the contributions of most of the principals (though McKay and Walrond refused, and Toomer no longer acknowledged his African American roots), and captured its essence in the manner of expert taxidermy. A grieving Locke wrote Charlotte Mason from Howard University, "It is hard to see the collapse of things you have labored to raise on a sound base."

Arthur Fauset, Jessie's perceptive brother, attempted to explain the collapse to Locke and the readers of *Opportunity* at the beginning of 1934. He foresaw "a socio-political-economic setback from which it may take decades to recover." The Renaissance had left the race unprepared, Fauset charged, because of its unrealistic belief "that social and economic recognition will be inevitable when once the race has produced a sufficiently large number of persons who have properly qualified themselves in the arts." Du Bois had not only turned his back on the movement, he had left the NAACP and Harlem for a university professorship in Atlanta after an enormous row over civil rights policy. Marxism had begun to exercise a decided appeal for him, but as the 1933 essay "Marxism and the Negro Problem" had made abundantly clear, Du Bois ruled out collaboration with American Marxists because they were much too racist. James Weldon Johnson's philosophical *tour d'horizon* appearing in 1934, *Negro Americans, What Now?*, asked precisely the question of the decade. Most Harlemites were certain that the riot exploding on the evening of March 19, 1935, taking three lives and costing two million dollars in property damage, was not an answer. By then, the Works Progress Administration (WPA) had become the major patron of African American artists and writers. Writers William Attaway, Ralph Ellison, Margaret Walker, Richard Wright, and Frank Yerby would emerge under its aegis, as would painters Romare Bearden, Jacob Lawrence, Charles Sebree, Lois Maillou Jones, and Charles White. The Communist Party was another patron, notably for Richard Wright, whose 1937 essay "Blueprint for Negro Writing" would materially contribute to the premise of Hughes's "The Negro Artist and the Racial Mountain." For thousands of ordinary Harlemites who had looked to Garvey's UNIA for inspiration, then to the Renaissance, there was now Father Divine and his "heavens."

In the ensuing years, much was renounced, more was lost or forgotten, yet the Renaissance, however artificial and overreaching, left a positive mark.

Locke's *New Negro* anthology featured thirty of the movement's thirty-five stars. They and a small number of less gifted collaborators generated twenty-six novels, ten volumes of poetry, five Broadway plays, countless essays and short stories, three performed ballets and concerti, and a considerable output of canvas and sculpture. If the achievement was less than the titanic expectations of the Ministry of Culture, it was an arts-and-letters legacy, nevertheless, of which a beleaguered and belittled Afro-America could be proud, and by which it could be sustained. If more by osmosis than conscious attention, Mainstream America was also richer for the color, emotion, humanity, and cautionary vision produced by Harlem during its Golden Age.

"If I had supposed that all Negroes were illiterate brutes, I might be astonished to discover that they can write good third rate poetry, readable and unreadable magazine fiction," wrote one contemporary white Marxist passing flinty judgment upon the Renaissance. Nevertheless there were many white Americans—perhaps the majority—who found the African American artistic and literary ferment of the period wholly unexpected and little short of incredible. If the judgment of the Marxist observer soon became a commonplace, it was because the Harlem Renaissance demonstrated—finally, irrefutably, during slightly more than a decade—the considerable creative capacities of the best and brightest of a disadvantaged racial minority.

JAMES WELDON JOHNSON

From *Black Manhattan*

With thousands of negroes pouring into Harlem month by month, two things happened: first, a sheer physical pressure for room was set up that was irresistible; second, old residents and new-comers got work as fast as they could take it, at wages never dreamed of, so there was now plenty of money for renting and buying. And the Negro in Harlem did, contrary to all the burlesque notions about what Negroes do when they get hold of money, take advantage of the low prices of property and begin to buy. Buying property became a contagious fever. It became a part of the gospel preached in the churches. It seems that generations of the experience of an extremely precarious foothold on the land of Manhattan Island flared up into a conscious determination never to let that condition return. So they turned the money from their new-found prosperity into property. All classes bought. It was not an unknown thing for a coloured washerwoman to walk into a real-estate office and lay down several thousand dollars on a house. There was Mrs. Mary Dean, known as "Pig Foot Mary" because of her high reputation in the business of preparing and selling that particular delicacy, so popular in Harlem. She paid $42,000 for a five-story apartment house at the corner of Seventh Avenue and One Hundred and Thirty-seventh Street, which was sold later to a coloured undertaker for $72,000. The Equitable Life Assurance Company held vacant for quite a while a block of 106 model private houses, designed by Stanford White, which the company had been

From *The Portable Harlem Renaissance Reader*, edited by David Levering Lewis. © 1994 by David Levering Lewis.

obliged to take over following the hegira of the whites from Harlem. When they were put on the market, they were promptly bought by Negroes at an aggregate price of about two million dollars. John E. Nail, a coloured real-estate dealer of Harlem who is a member of the Real Estate Board of New York and an appraisal authority, states that Negroes own and control Harlem real property worth, at a conservative estimate, between fifty and sixty million dollars. Relatively, these figures are amazing. Twenty years ago barely a half-dozen coloured individuals owned land on Manhattan. Down to fifteen years ago the amount that Negroes had acquired in Harlem was by comparison negligible. Today a very large part of the property in Harlem occupied by Negroes is owned by Negroes.

It should be noted that Harlem was taken over without violence. In some of the large Northern cities where the same sort of expansion of the Negro population was going on, there was not only strong antagonism on the part of whites, but physical expression of it. In Chicago, Cleveland, and other cities houses bought and moved into by Negroes were bombed. In Chicago a church bought by a coloured congregation was badly damaged by bombs. In other cities several formerly white churches which had been taken over by coloured congregations were bombed. In Detroit, mobs undertook to evict Negroes from houses bought by them in white neighbourhoods. The mob drove vans up to one house just purchased and moved into by a coloured physician, ordered him out, loaded all his goods into the vans, and carted them back to his old residence. These arrogated functions of the mob reached a climax in the celebrated Sweet case. A mob gathered in the evening round a house in a white neighbourhood which Dr. O. H. Sweet, a coloured physician, had bought and moved into the day before. When the situation reached a critical point, shots fired from within the house killed one person in the crowd and seriously wounded another. Dr. Sweet, his wife, and eight others, relatives and friends, who were in the house at the time, were indicted and tried for murder in the first degree. They were defended in two long trials by the National Association for the Advancement of Colored People, through Clarence Darrow and Arthur Garfield Hays, assisted by several local attorneys, and were acquitted. This was the tragic end of eviction by mob in Detroit.

Although there was bitter feeling in Harlem during the fifteen years of struggle the Negro went through in getting a foothold on the land, there was never any demonstration of violence that could be called serious. Not since the riot of 1900 has New York witnessed, except for minor incidents, any inter-racial disturbances. Not even in the memorable summer of 1919—that summer when the stoutest-hearted Negroes felt terror and dismay; when the race got the worst backwash of the war, and the Ku Klux Klan was in the ascendant; when almost simultaneously there were riots in Chicago and in Longview, Texas; in Omaha and in Phillips County, Arkansas; and hundreds of Negroes, chased through the streets or hunted down through the swamps, were beaten and killed; when in the national capital an anti-Negro mob held sway for three days, in which time six persons were killed and scores severely beaten—not even during this period of massacre did New York, with more than a hundred thousand Negroes grouped together in Harlem, lose its equanimity....

At any rate, there is no longer any apparent feeling against the occupancy of Harlem by Negroes. Within the past five years the colony has expanded to the south, the north, and the west. It has gone down Seventh Avenue from One Hundred and Twenty-seventh Street to Central Park at One Hundred and Tenth Street. It has climbed upwards between Eighth Avenue and the Harlem River from One Hundred and Forty-fifth Street to One Hundred and Fifty-fifth. It has spread to the west and occupies the heights of Coogan's Bluff, overlooking Colonial Park. And to the east and west of this solid Negro area, there is a fringe where the population is mixed, white and coloured. This expansion of the past five years has taken place without any physical opposition, or even any considerable outbreak of antagonistic public sentiment.

The question inevitably arises: Will the Negroes of Harlem be able to hold it? Will they not be driven still farther northward? Residents of Manhattan, regardless of race, have been driven out when they lay in the path of business and greatly increased land values. Harlem lies in the direction that path must take; so there is little probability that Negroes will always hold it as a residential section. But this is to be considered: the Negro's situation in Harlem is without precedent in all his history in New York; never before has he been so securely anchored, never before has he owned the land, never before has he had so well established a community life. It is probable that land through the heart of Harlem will some day so increase in value that Negroes may not be able to hold it—although it is quite as probable that there will be some Negroes able to take full advantage of the increased values—and will be forced to make a move. But the next move, when it comes, will be unlike the others. It will not be a move made solely at the behest of someone else; it will be more in the nature of a bargain. Nor will it be a move in which the Negro will carry with him only his household goods and utensils; he will move at a financial profit to himself. But at the present time such a move is nowhere in sight.

On December 15, 1919 John Drinkwater's *Abraham Lincoln* had its American *première* at the Cort Theatre in New York, and Charles Gilpin, formerly with both the Lincoln and the Lafayette companies, was drafted to create the role of the Rev. William Custis, a Negro preacher who goes to the White House for a conference at the request of Lincoln, this conference between the President and the black man constituting one of the strongest and most touching scenes in the play. The character of Custis was intended by the playwright to be a representation of Frederick Douglass. Drinkwater in writing the play had largely followed Lord Charnwood's life of Abraham Lincoln, in which Douglass is erroneously set down as "a well-known Negro preacher." The playwright also made the error of putting Custis's lines into dialect. He may, as a dramatist, have done this intentionally to heighten the character effect; or he may, as an Englishman, have done it through unfamiliarity with all the facts. In either case, the dialect was such as no American Negro would ever use. It was a slightly darkened pidgin-English or the form of speech a big Indian chief would be supposed to employ in talking with the Great White Father at Washington. However, Gilpin was a success in the role.

Meanwhile Eugene O'Neill was experimenting with the dramatic possibilities of the Negro both as material and as exponent. He had written a one-act play, *The Moon of the Caribbees*, in which the scene was laid aboard a ship lying in a West Indian harbour, and the characters were members of the ship's crew and Negro natives of the island. The play was produced at the Provincetown Playhouse, New York, in 1918, with a white cast. He had also written a one-act tragedy, *The Dreamy Kid*, in which all of the four characters were Negroes. *The Dreamy Kid* was produced at the Provincetown Playhouse, October 31, 1919, with a Negro cast and with Harold Simmelkjaer—who, despite the Dutch name, is a Negro—in the title-role. This play was later revived with Frank Wilson as the Dreamy Kid. In the season of 1919–20 Butler Davenport's Bramhall Players produced at their playhouse in East Twenty-seventh Street a play called *Justice* with a mixed cast. Frank Wilson and Rose McClendon played important parts.

None of these efforts, so far as the Negro is concerned, evoked more than mildly favourable comment. But on November 3, 1920 O'Neill's *The Emperor Jones* was produced at the Provincetown Playhouse, with Charles Gilpin in the title-role, and another important page in the history of the Negro in the theatre was written. The next morning Gilpin was famous. The power of his acting was enthusiastically and universally acclaimed. Indeed, the sheer physical feat of sustaining the part—the whole play is scarcely more than a continuous monologue spoken by the principal character—demanded admiration. The Drama League voted him to be one of the ten persons who had done most for the American theatre during the year; and some of the readers of these pages will recall the almost national crisis that was brought on as a consequence of this action. As was the custom, the Drama League gave a dinner in honour of the ten persons chosen; and, as seemed quite natural to do, invited Mr. Gilpin. Thereupon there broke out a controversy that divided the Drama League, the theatrical profession, the press, and the public. Pressure was brought to have the invitation withdrawn, but those responsible for it stood firm. Then the pressure was centred upon Mr. Gilpin to induce him not to attend the dinner. The amount of noise and heat made, and of serious effort expended, was worthy of a weightier matter than the question of a dinner with a coloured man present as a guest. This incident occurred only ten years ago, but already it has an archaic character. It is doubtful if a similar incident today could provoke such a degree of asininity. Mr. Gilpin attended the dinner.

By his work in *The Emperor Jones* Gilpin reached the highest point of achievement on the legitimate stage that had yet been attained by a Negro in America. But it was by no sudden flight; it was by a long, hard struggle. Before being dined by the Drama League as one of those who had done most for the American theatre, he had travelled with small road shows playing one-night stands, been stranded more than once, been compelled to go back to work at his trade as a printer, been a member of a minstrel show, worked in a barber-shop, joined a street fair company, gone out with a concert company, tried being a trainer of prize-fighters, sung with a company of jubilee singers, worked as an elevator-boy and switch-board operator in an apartment house on Riverside Drive, been a railroad porter, played vaudeville, held a job as a janitor, and hesitated greatly about giving it up. His real theatrical career can be traced from Williams and Walker's company to Gus Hill's *Smart Set*, to the Pekin stock-company, to the Anita Bush Players at the Lincoln in Harlem, to the Lafayette Players, to John Drinkwater's *Abraham Lincoln*, and to *The Emperor Jones*. Mr. Gilpin was awarded the Spingarn Medal in 1920. He died May 6, 1930....

In the summer of 1921 along came *Shuffle Along*, and all New York flocked to the Sixty-third Street Theatre to hear the most joyous singing and see the most exhilarating dancing to be found on any stage in the city. *Shuffle Along* was a record-breaking, epoch-making musical comedy. Some of its tunes—"I'm Just Wild about Harry," "Gipsy Blues," "Love Will Find a Way," "I'm Cravin' for That Kind of Love," "In Honeysuckle Time," "Bandana Days," and "Shuffle Along"—went round the world. It would be difficult to name another musical comedy with so many song hits as *Shuffle*

Along had. Its dances furnished new material for hundreds of dancing performers. *Shuffle Along* was cast in the form of the best Williams and Walker, Cole and Johnson tradition; but the music did not hark back at all; it was up to the minute. There was, however, one other respect in which it did hark back; it was written and produced, as well as performed, by Negroes. Four men—F. E. Miller, Aubrey Lyles, Eubie Blake, and Noble Sissle— combined their talents and their means to bring it about. Their talents were many, but their means were limited, and they had no easy time.

They organized the show in New York and took it on a short out-of-town try-out, with Broadway as their goal. It was booked for an opening at the Howard Theatre, a coloured theatre in Washington. When the company assembled at the Pennsylvania Station, it was found that they did not have quite enough money for transportation, and there had to be quick scurrying round to raise the necessary funds. Such an ominous situation could not well be concealed, and there were misgivings and mutterings among the company. After all the tickets were secured, it took considerable persuasion to induce some of its members to go so far away from New York on such slim expectations.

They played two successful weeks at the Howard Theatre and so had enough money to move to Philadelphia, where they were booked to play the Dunbar Theatre, another coloured house. Broadway, their goal, looked quite distant even from Philadelphia. The managers, seeking to make sure of getting the company to New York, suggested to the owner of the Dunbar Theatre that it would be a good investment for him to take a half-interest in the show for one thousand dollars, but he couldn't see it that way. They played two smashing weeks at the Dunbar and brought the company intact into New York, but, as they expressed it, on a shoe-string. They went into the Sixty-third Street Theatre, which had been dark for some time; it was pretty far uptown for Broadway audiences. Within a few weeks *Shuffle Along* made the Sixty-third Street Theatre one of the best-known houses in town and made it necessary for the Traffic Department to declare Sixty-third Street a one-way thoroughfare. *Shuffle Along* played New York for over a year and played on the road for two years longer. It was a remarkable aggregation. There was a chorus of pretty girls that danced marvellously. The comedians were Miller and Lyles, and a funny black-face pair they were. Their burlesque of two ignorant Negroes going into "big business" and opening a grocery-store was a never-failing producer of side-shaking laughter. There was a quartet, the Four Harmony Kings, that gave a fresh demonstration of the close harmony and barber-shop chords that are the chief characteristics of Negro quartets. There was Lottie Gee, jauntiest of *ingénues*, and Gertrude

Saunders, most bubbling of comediennes. There was Noble Sissle with his take-it-from-me style of singing, and there was Eubie Blake with his amazing jazz piano-playing. And it was in *Shuffle Along* that Florence Mills, that incomparable little star, first twinkled on Broadway.

Shuffle Along pre-empted and held New York's interest in Negro theatricals for a year. In the fall of 1921 another venture was made, when Irving C. Miller, a brother of the Miller of *Shuffle Along*, produced *Put and Take*, a musical comedy, at Town Hall (New York). *Put and Take*, by all ordinary standards, was a good show, but it was overshadowed by the great vogue of *Shuffle Along*. In the spring of 1923 Irving C. Miller had better success with *Liza*, a tuneful and very fast dancing show that he produced at a downtown theatre.

In the fall Miller and Lyles came out with a new play, *Runnin' Wild*, and opened at the Colonial Theatre, on upper Broadway, on October 29. The old combination had been broken. Miller and Lyles had remained together; Sissle and Blake had formed a separate partnership, and Florence Mills was lost to both sides; she was heading a revue at the Plantation, a downtown night-club. Notwithstanding, *Runnin' Wild*, even in the inevitable comparison with its predecessor, was a splendid show. It had a successful run of eight months at the Colonial. *Runnin' Wild* would have been notable if for no other reason than that it made use of the "Charleston," a Negro dance creation which up to that time had been known only to Negroes; thereby introducing it to New York, America, and the world. The music for the dance was written by Jimmie Johnson, the composer of the musical score of the piece. The Charleston achieved a popularity second only to the tango, also a Negro dance creation, originating in Cuba, transplanted to the Argentine, thence to the world via Paris. There is a claim that Irving C. Miller first introduced the Charleston on the stage in his *Liza*; even so, it was *Runnin' Wild* that started the dance on its world-encircling course. When Miller and Lyles introduced the dance in their show, they did not depend wholly upon their extraordinarily good jazz band for the accompaniment; they went straight back to primitive Negro music and had the major part of the chorus supplement the band by beating out the time with hand-clapping and foot-patting. The effect was electrical. Such a demonstration of beating out complex rhythms had never before been seen on a stage in New York. However, Irving C. Miller may indisputably claim that in his show *Dinah*, produced the next year at the Lafayette Theatre, he was the first to put another Negro dance, the "Black Bottom," on the stage. The "Black Bottom" gained a popularity which was only little less than that of the Charleston.

The Sissle and Blake show of this same year was *Chocolate Dandies*. In comparison with *Runnin' Wild*, its greatest lack lay in the fact that it had no comedians who approached the class of Miller and Lyles. But *Chocolate Dandies* did have Johnny Hudgins, and in the chorus a girl who showed herself to be a comedienne of the first order. Her name was Josephine Baker.

On May 7, 1923 there was witnessed at the Frazee Theatre what was the most ambitious attempt Negroes had yet made in the legitimate theatre in New York. The Ethiopian Art Players, organized by Raymond O'Neil and Mrs. Sherwood Anderson, presented Oscar Wilde's *Salome;* an original interpretation of Shakespere's *The Comedy of Errors;* and *The Chip Woman's Fortune*, a one-act Negro play by Willis Richardson. The acting of Evelyn Preer in the role of Salome, and her beauty, received high and well-deserved praise from the critics; and the work of Sidney Kirkpatrick, Laura Bowman, Charles Olden, and Lionel Monagas, all formerly of the Lafayette Players, won commendation. But the only play on the bill that was fully approved was *The Chip Woman's Fortune*. Some of the critics said frankly that however well Negroes might play "white" classics like *Salome* and *The Comedy of Errors*, it was doubtful if they could be so interesting as they would be in Negro plays, if they could be interesting at all. The Ethiopian Art Players had run up against one of the curious factors in the problem of race, against the paradox which makes it quite seemly for a white person to represent a Negro on the stage, but a violation of some inner code for a Negro to represent a white person. This, it seems, is certain: if they had put into a well-written play of Negro life the same degree of talent and skill they did put into *Salome* and *The Comedy of Errors*, they would have achieved an overwhelming success. But it appears that at the time no such play was available for them. Beginning June 4, the company played for a week at the Lafayette in Harlem....

But on May 15, 1924 Eugene O'Neill produced at the Provincetown Playhouse a Negro play that made New York and the rest of the country sit up and take notice. The play was *All God's Chillun Got Wings*. The cast was a mixed one, with Paul Robeson in the principal role, playing opposite Mary Blair, a white actress. Public excitement about this play did not wait for the opening in the theatre, but started fully three months before; that is, as soon as it was seen through the publication of the play in the *American Mercury* that the two chief characters were a coloured boy and a white girl, and that the boy falls in love with the girl and marries her. When it was learned that the play was to be produced in a New York theatre with a coloured and a white performer in these two roles, a controversy began in the newspapers of the city that quickly spread; and articles, editorials, and interviews filled columns upon columns in periodicals throughout the country. The discussion in the press was, as might be expected, more bitter than it had been in the incident of the Drama League dinner to Charles Gilpin. The New York *American* and the *Morning Telegraph* went further than other New York publications. For weeks they carried glaring headlines and inciting articles. They appeared to be seeking to provoke violence in order to stop the play.

The New York *American* on March 18, eight weeks before the opening, carried an article headed: "Riots Feared From Drama—'All God's Chillun' Direct Bid for Disorders, the View of George G. Battle—Thinks City Should Act." In the article George Gordon Battle was quoted as saying: "The production of such a play will be most unfortunate. If the Provincetown Players and Mr. O'Neill refuse to bow before public opinion, the city officials should take action to ban it from the stage." In the same article Mrs. W. J. Arnold, "a founder of the Daughters of the Confederacy," was quoted as saying: "The scene where Miss Blair is called upon to kiss and fondle a Negro's hand is going too far, even for the stage. The play may be produced above the Mason and Dixie [*sic*] line, but Mr. O'Neill will not get the friendly reception he had when he sent 'Emperor Jones' his other coloured play into the South. The play should be banned by the authorities, because it will be impossible for it to do otherwise than stir up ill feeling between the races."

An issue of the Hearst publication said editorially:

> Gentlemen who are engaged in producing plays should not make it any harder for their friends to protect them from censorship. They should not put on plays which are, or threaten to become, enemies of the public peace; they should not dramatize dynamite, because, while helping the box office, it may blow up the business.
>
> We refer to the play in which a white woman marries a black man and at the end of the play, after going crazy, stoops and kisses the Negro's hand.
>
> It is hard to imagine a more nauseating and inflammable situation, and in many communities the failure of the audience to scrap the play and mutilate the players would be regarded as a token of public anemia.

It would be still harder to imagine yellower journalism than this, or why a thing that has happened more than once in actual life should be regarded as so utterly beyond conception as a theatrical situation.

The opening night came, the theatre was crowded—the attacks had served as publicity—there was some feeling of tenseness on the part of the audience and a great deal on the part of the performers, but the play proceeded without any sign of antagonistic demonstration, without even a hiss or a boo. None of the appeals to prejudice, hate, and fear had had the intended effect. The pressure brought on Mayor Hylan and the Police Department got no further result than the refusal of permission to allow a group of children to appear in the opening scene. The public at large failed to be moved to any sense of impending danger to either the white or the black race because of this play. The outcome of the whole business proved that the rabid newspapers were not expressing public sentiment, but were striving to stir up a public sentiment.

All God's Chillun Got Wings did not prove to be another *Emperor Jones*. One sound reason why it did not was because it was not so good a play. It was dramatic enough, but the incidents did not link up along the inevitable line that the spectator was made to feel he must follow. It may be that as the play began to grow, Mr. O'Neill became afraid of it. At any rate, he side-stepped the logical question and let his heroine go crazy; thus shifting the question from that of a coloured man living with a white wife to that of a man living with a crazy woman; from which shift, so far as this particular play was concerned, nothing at all could be demonstrated. The play, as a play, did not please white people, and, on the other hand, it failed to please coloured people. Mr. O'Neill, perhaps in concession to public sentiment, made the white girl who is willing to marry the black student, and whom he is glad to get, about as lost as he could well make her. Coloured people not only did not consider this as any compliment to the race, but regarded it as absolutely contrary to the essential truth. However, the play ran for several weeks, and Paul Robeson increased his reputation by the restraint, sincerity, and dignity with which he acted a difficult role.

Mr. Robeson's reputation is now international. He played the leading Negro character in the London production of *Show Boat*. He played the title role in a successful revival of *The Emperor Jones* in Berlin early in 1930. And it has been announced that he will play Othello in a production to be made of Shakspere's immortal tragedy at the Savoy Theatre, London, in May 1930.

Perhaps it was now time for New York again to sing and dance and laugh with the Negro on the stage; and it soon had the opportunity. On October 29, 1924, exactly one year after the opening of *Runnin' Wild*, Florence Mills came to the Broadhurst Theatre in *Dixie to Broadway*, and New York had its first Negro revue. For the Florence Mills show broke away entirely from the established traditions of Negro musical comedy. Indeed, it had to, because she was the star; and the traditions called for a show built around two male comedians, usually of the black-face type. The revue was actually an enlarged edition of the one in which Miss Mills had been appearing at the Plantation. It was also the same revue that had been played in London the season before under the title of *Dover to Dixie* with her as the star. On the night of the production of *Dixie to Broadway* New York not only found itself with a novelty in the form of a Negro revue, but also discovered that it had a new artist of positive genius in the person of Florence Mills. She had made a name in *Shuffle Along*, but in *Dixie to Broadway* she was recognized for her full worth.

ALAIN LOCKE

The New Negro

Harlem was perceived by its inhabitants as a world entire unto itself, the cradle of a culture that would perform much the same role, proclaimed Alain Locke, as Dublin and Prague had performed in the creation of the new Ireland and new Czechoslovakia. Yet Harlem was also said to be distinctive only the better to make its contribution to the American whole. "Separate as it may be in color and substance," Locke announced confidently in The New Negro, *"the culture of the Negro is of a pattern integral with the times and with its cultural setting." Thus, its music was distinctive (Rogers on jazz), its very existence a source of creative exploration (Robeson on O'Neill), its future the recapitulation and fulfillment of glories in the distant African past (Schomburg), and, in the words of Elise Johnson McDougald, its "progressive and privileged groups of Negro women," like Harlem's Talented Tenth men, inspired by the finest American ideals of personal character and social mobility.*

In the last decade something beyond the watch and guard of statistics has happened in the life of the American Negro and the three norns who have traditionally presided over the Negro problem have a changeling in their laps. The Sociologist, the Philanthropist, the Race-leader are not unaware of the New Negro, but they are at a loss to account for him. He simply cannot be swathed in their formulae. For the younger generation is vibrant with a new psychology; the new spirit is awake in the masses, and under the very eyes of the professional observers is transforming what has been a perennial problem into the progressive phases of contemporary Negro life.

From *The Portable Harlem Renaissance Reader*, edited by David Levering Lewis. © 1994 by David Levering Lewis.

Could such a metamorphosis have taken place as suddenly as it has appeared to? The answer is no; not because the New Negro is not here, but because the Old Negro had long become more of a myth than a man. The Old Negro, we must remember, was a creature of moral debate and historical controversy. His has been a stock figure perpetuated as an historical fiction partly in innocent sentimentalism, partly in deliberate reactionism. The Negro himself has contributed his share to this through a sort of protective social mimicry forced upon him by the adverse circumstances of dependence. So for generations in the mind of America, the Negro has been more of a formula than a human being—a something to be argued about, condemned or defended, to be "kept down," or "in his place," or "helped up," to be worried with or worried over, harassed or patronized, a social bogey or a social burden. The thinking Negro even has been induced to share this same general attitude, to focus his attention on controversial issues, to see himself in the distorted perspective of a social problem. His shadow, so to speak, has been more real to him than his personality. Through having had to appeal from the unjust stereotypes of his oppressors and traducers to those of his liberators, friends and benefactors he has had to subscribe to the traditional positions from which his case has been viewed. Little true social or self-understanding has or could come from such a situation.

But while the minds of most of us, black and white, have thus burrowed in the trenches of the Civil War and Reconstruction, the actual march of development has simply flanked these positions, necessitating a sudden reorientation of view. We have not been watching in the right direction; set North and South on a sectional axis, we have not noticed the East till the sun has us blinking....

There is, of course, a warrantably comfortable feeling in being on the right side of the country's professed ideals. We realize that we cannot be undone without America's undoing. It is within the gamut of this attitude that the thinking Negro faces America, but with variations of mood that are if anything more significant than the attitude itself. Sometimes we have it taken with the defiant ironic challenge of McKay:

Mine is the future grinding down to-day
Like a great landslip moving to the sea,
Bearing its freight of débris far away
Where the green hungry waters restlessly
Heave mammoth pyramids, and break and roar
Their eerie challenge to the crumbling shore.

Sometimes, perhaps more frequently as yet, it is taken in the fervent and almost filial appeal and counsel of Weldon Johnson's:

> O Southland, dear Southland!
> Then why do you still cling
> To an idle age and a musty page,
> To a dead and useless thing?

But between defiance and appeal, midway almost between cynicism and hope, the prevailing mind stands in the mood of the same author's *To America*, an attitude of sober query and stoical challenge:

> How would you have us, as we are?
> Or sinking 'neath the load we bear,
> Our eyes fixed forward on a star,
> Or gazing empty at despair?

> Rising or falling? Men or things?
> With dragging pace or footsteps fleet?
> Strong, willing sinews in your wings,
> Or tightening chains about your feet?

More and more, however, an intelligent realization of the great discrepancy between the American social creed and the American social practice forces upon the Negro the taking of the moral advantage that is his. Only the steadying and sobering effect of a truly characteristic gentleness of spirit prevents the rapid rise of a definite cynicism and counter-hate and a defiant superiority feeling. Human as this reaction would be, the majority still deprecate its advent, and would gladly see it forestalled by the speedy amelioration of its causes. We wish our race pride to be a healthier, more positive achievement than a feeling based upon a realization of the shortcomings of others. But all paths toward the attainment of a sound social attitude have been difficult; only a relatively few enlightened minds have been able as the phrase puts it "to rise above" prejudice. The ordinary man has had until recently only a hard choice between the alternatives of supine and humiliating submission and stimulating but hurtful counter-prejudice. Fortunately from some inner, desperate resourcefulness has recently sprung up the simple expedient of fighting prejudice by mental passive resistance, in other words by trying to ignore it. For the few, this manna may perhaps be effective, but the masses cannot thrive upon it.

Fortunately there are constructive channels opening out into which the balked social feelings of the American Negro can flow freely.

Without them there would be much more pressure and danger than there is. These compensating interests are racial but in a new and enlarged way. One is the consciousness of acting as the advance-guard of the African peoples in their contact with Twentieth Century civilization; the other, the sense of a mission of rehabilitating the race in world esteem from that loss of prestige for which the fate and conditions of slavery have so largely been responsible. Harlem, as we shall see, is the center of both these movements; she is the home of the Negro's "Zionism." The pulse of the Negro world has begun to beat in Harlem. A Negro newspaper carrying news material in English, French and Spanish, gathered from all quarters of America, the West Indies and Africa has maintained itself in Harlem for over five years. Two important magazines, both edited from New York, maintain their news and circulation consistently on a cosmopolitan scale. Under American auspices and backing, three pan-African congresses have been held abroad for the discussion of common interests, colonial questions and the future co-operative development of Africa. In terms of the race question as a world problem, the Negro mind has leapt, so to speak, upon the parapets of prejudice and extended its cramped horizons. In so doing it has linked up with the growing group consciousness of the dark-peoples and is gradually learning their common interests. As one of our writers has recently put it: "It is imperative that we understand the white world in its relations to the non-white world." As with the Jew, persecution is making the Negro international.

As a world phenomenon this wider race consciousness is a different thing from the much asserted rising tide of color. Its inevitable causes are not of our making. The consequences are not necessarily damaging to the best interests of civilization. Whether it actually brings into being new Armadas of conflict or argosies of cultural exchange and enlightenment can only be decided by the attitude of the dominant races in an era of critical change. With the American Negro, his new internationalism is primarily an effort to recapture contact with the scattered peoples of African derivation. Garveyism may be a transient, if spectacular, phenomenon, but the possible rôle of the American Negro in the future development of Africa is one of the most constructive and universally helpful missions that any modern people can lay claim to.

Constructive participation in such causes cannot help giving the Negro valuable group incentives, as well as increased prestige at home and abroad. Our greatest rehabilitation may possibly come through such channels, but for the present, more immediate hope rests in the revaluation by white and black alike of the Negro in terms of his artistic endowments and cultural contributions, past and prospective. It must be increasingly recognized that the Negro has already made very substantial contributions, not only in his folk-art, music especially, which has always found appreciation, but in larger, though humbler and less acknowledged ways. For generations the Negro has been the peasant matrix of that section of America which has most undervalued him, and here he has contributed not only materially in labor and in social patience, but spiritually as well. The South has unconsciously absorbed the gift of his folk-temperament. In less than half a generation it will be easier to recognize this, but the fact remains that a leaven of humor, sentiment, imagination and tropic nonchalance has gone into the making of the South from a humble, unacknowledged source. A second crop of the Negro's gifts promises still more largely. He now becomes a conscious contributor and lays aside the status of a beneficiary and ward for that of a collaborator and participant in American civilization. The great social gain in this is the releasing of our talented group from the arid fields of controversy and debate to the productive fields of creative expression. The especially cultural recognition they win should in turn prove the key to that revaluation of the Negro which must precede or accompany any considerable further betterment of race relationships. But whatever the general effect, the present generation will have added the motives of self-expression and spiritual development to the old and still unfinished task of making material headway and progress. No one who understandingly faces the situation with its substantial accomplishment or views the new scene with its still more abundant promise can be entirely without hope. And certainly, if in our lifetime the Negro should not be able to celebrate his full initiation into American democracy, he can at least, on the warrant of these things, celebrate the attainment of a significant and satisfying new phase of group development, and with it a spiritual Coming of Age.

CHARLES S. JOHNSON

The Negro Renaissance
and Its Significance

There is a double presumptuousness about this presentation: It is not only a sort of history, constructed in large part from memory; but it is presented as history in the presence of rigid and exacting historians who regard the proper and unchallengeable enlightenment of future generations as their sacred trust.

There are, however, some compensating factors for this boldness: We are, in a sense, memorializing Alain Locke, an important maker of history who is himself inadequately recorded. And while some of the fragments of memory and experience may be compounded with a prejudiced aura of friendship, this fact itself from a collateral contemporary may have some value.

As a sociologist rather than an historian, it is expected that particular events would be viewed in the light of broader social processes, thus offering greater illumination to what has come to be recognized as a dramatic period in our national history.

American Negroes in the 1920's were just a little more than a half century on their rugged course to citizenship. This period was the comet's tail of a great cultural ferment in the nation, the "melting pot" era, a period of the ascendancy of unbridled free enterprise, of the open beginnings of class struggle and new and feeble mutterings of self-conscious labor; of muckrakers and social settlements, of the open and unabashed acceptance of

From *The Portable Harlem Renaissance Reader*, edited by David Levering Lewis. © 1994 by David Levering Lewis.

"inferior and superior races and civilizations." Likewise, the era just preceding the 1920's was a period of the sullen and frustrated gropings of the agrarian and culturally sterile South, in its "colonial" dependence upon the industrial North. It had been left in indifference to settle its problem of democracy in its own way.

In the wake of Reconstruction in the South there had been for the Negro, almost total political disfranchisement, economic disinheritance, denial of, or rigid limitation of, educational opportunity, complete racial segregation, with a gaudy racial philosophy to defend it, cultural isolation with its bitter fruit of inner personal poison, followed by mass migrations and revolt, and the tortuous struggle to slough off the heavy handicaps in order to achieve more completely a new freedom.

These were a part of the backdrop of what we have called the "Negro Renaissance," that sudden and altogether phenomenal outburst of emotional expression, unmatched by any comparable period in American or Negro American history.

It is well to point out that this was not a crisis and trauma affecting only the Negroes. It was fundamentally and initially a national problem.

James Weldon Johnson, who, with W.E.B. Du Bois emerged in the period just preceding the epochal 1920's, recognized this relationship and said this:

> A good part of white America frequently asks the question, "What shall we do with the Negro?" In asking the question it completely ignores the fact that the Negro is doing something with himself, and also the equally important fact that the Negro all the while is doing something with America.

Before Johnson there had been only a few Negroes capable of articulat the inner emotional turmoil of the race in full consciousness of its role in a nation that was itself in great stress.

Frederick Douglass had been a powerful oratorical force for the abolition of slavery, convincing to a sector of the nation in his own superiority as a person. Booker T. Washington had been a social strategist, speaking to the nation from the heavy racial miasma of the deep South, with wise words of economic counsel and even wiser words of tactical racial strategy. He parried the blows of the skeptical ones and the demagogues, who spoke hopelessly and menacingly of the destiny of the millions of ex-slaves in the South, still very largely unlettered and sought the armistice of tolerance during a vital period of regional gestation, as he negotiated with the industrial strength and benevolence of the North that was in being and the industrial dreams of the South, as yet unrealized.

W.E.B. Du Bois, brilliant, highly cultured, and racially sensitive, wrote with such bitter contempt for the American racial system that his flaming truths were invariably regarded as incendiary. He got attention but scant acceptance. And there was the poet Paul Laurence Dunbar who, like Booker T. Washington, came at a dark period, when with the release of the white working classes the independent struggle of Negroes for existence had become almost overwhelming in its severity. Dunbar caught the picture of the Negro in his pathetic and contagiously humorous moods and invested him with a new humanity. He embellished a stereotype and made likeable, in a homely way, the simple, joyous creature that was the mass Southern Negro, with the soft musical dialect and infectious rhythm. William Dean Howells, in an article in *Harper's Magazine*, hailed Dunbar as the first Negro to feel Negro life esthetically and express it lyrically. But in his candid moments, Dunbar confessed to Johnson that he resorted to dialect verse to gain a hearing and then nothing but his dialect verse would be accepted. He never got to the things he really wanted to do.

The acceptability of Dunbar's verse inspired many followers, including, for a brief spell, Johnson himself. The period of Johnson, however, was one that permitted bolder exploration and he turned forthrightly to poetry of race-consciousness. They were poems both of revelation and of protest. William Stanley Braithwaite was able to say of him that he brought the first intellectual substance to the context of poetry by Negroes, and a craftsmanship more precise and balanced than that of Dunbar. His Negro sermons symbolized the transition from the folk idiom to conscious artistic expression. In naive, non-dialect speech, they blend the rich imagery of the uneducated Negro minister with the finished skill of a cultured Negro poet. In a curiously fascinating way both style and content bespoke the meeting and parting of the old and new in Negro life in America.

The commentators even farther removed from today will be able to define more clearly the influence of these social and economic forces shortly after World War I, moving beneath the new mind of Negroes, which burst forth with freshness and vigor in an artistic "awakening." The first startlingly authentic note was sounded by Claude McKay, a Jamaican Negro living in America. If his was a note of protest it came clear and unquivering. But it was more than a protest note; it was one of stoical defiance which held behind it a spirit magnificent and glowing. One poem, "If We Must Die," written at the most acute point of the industrialization of Negroes when sudden mass contact in the Northern states was flaming into riots, voiced for Negroes, where it did not itself create, a mood of stubborn defiance. It was reprinted in practically every Negro newspaper, and quoted wherever its audacious lines could be remembered. But McKay could also write lyrics utterly divorced from these singing daggers. "Spring in New Hampshire" is one of them. He discovered Harlem and found a language of beauty for his own world of color.

> Her voice was like the sound of blended flutes
> Blown by black players on a picnic day.

Jean Toomer flashed like a meteor across the sky, then sank from view. But in the brilliant moment of his flight he illuminated the forefield of this new Negro literature. *Cane*, a collection of verse and stories, appeared about two years ahead of its sustaining public mood. It was significantly a return of the son to the Southland, to the stark, natural beauties of its life and soil, a life deep and strong, and a virgin soil.

More than artist, he was an experimentalist, and this last quality carried him away from what was, perhaps, the most astonishingly brilliant beginning of any Negro writer of his generation.

With Countee Cullen came a new generation of Negro singers. Claude McKay had brought a strange geographical background to the American scene which enabled him to escape a measure of the peculiar social heritage of the American Negro which similarly lacked the impedimenta of an inhibiting tradition. He relied upon nothing but his own sure competence and art; one month found three literary magazines carrying his verse simultaneously, a distinction not to be spurned by any young poet. Then came his first volume, *Color*. He brought an uncannily sudden maturity and classic sweep, a swift grace and an inescapable beauty of style and meaning. The spirit of the transplanted African moved through his music to a new definition—relating itself boldly to its past and present.

> Lord, not for what I saw in flesh or bone
> Of fairer men; not raised on faith alone;
> Lord, I will live persuaded by mine own.
> I cannot play the recreant to these;
> My spirit has come home, that sailed the doubtful seas.

He spoke, not for himself alone, but for the confident generation out of which he came. White gods were put aside and in their place arose the graces of a race he knew.

> Her walk is like the replica
> Of some barbaric dance
> Wherein the soul of Africa
> Is winged with arrogance.

and again:

> That brown girl's swagger gives a twitch
> To beauty like a queen.

No brief quotations can describe this power, this questioning of life and even God; the swift arrow thrusts of irony curiously mingled with admiration; the self-reliance and bold pride of race; the thorough repudiation of the double standard of literary judgment. He may have marvelled "at this curious thing to make a poet black and bid him sing," but in his *Heritage* he voiced the half-religious, half-challenging spirit of an awakened generation. "He will be remembered," said the *Manchester Guardian*, "as one who contributed to his age some of its loveliest lyric poetry."

Langston Hughes, at twenty-four, had published two volumes of verse. No Negro writer so completely symbolizes the new emancipation of the Negro mind. His was a poetry of gorgeous colors, of restless brooding, of melancholy, of disillusionment:

> We should have a land of sun
> Of gorgeous sun,
> And a land of fragrant water
> Where the twilight
> Is a soft bandana handkerchief
> And not this land where life is cold.

Always there is, in his writing, a wistful undertone, a quiet sadness. That is why, perhaps, he could speak so tenderly of the broken lives of prostitutes, the inner weariness of painted "jazz-hounds" and the tragic emptiness beneath the glamour and noise of Harlem cabarets. His first volume, *The Weary Blues*, contained many moods; the second, *Fine Clothes to the Jew*, marked a final frank turning to the folk life of the Negro, a striving to catch and give back to the world the strange music of the unlettered Negro—his "Blues." If Cullen gave a classic beauty to the emotions of the race, Hughes gave a warm glow of meaning to their lives.

I return again more comfortably to my role as a sociologist in recording this period following the deep and disrupting crisis of a world war, with its uprooting of customs and people in which there developed two movements with clashing ideologies. There was reassertion with vigor of the old and shaken racial theories, with "racial purity clubs," intelligence tests "proving" the unchangeable inferiority of the Negro and other darker peoples, Congressional restrictions of immigration according to rigid racial formulas, race riots, dark foreboding prophecies of the over-running of the white race by the dark and unenlightened hordes from Asia and Africa, in Lothrop Stoddard's *Rising Tide of Color*.

These were only reflections of the new forces set loose in the world and finding expression in such mutterings as "India for the Indians," "A Free Ireland," self-determination for the smaller countries of the world.

For the just-emerging Negro who had freed himself geographically at least, there was much frustration. Perhaps the most dramatic phase of this was the Garvey movement. Here were hundreds of thousands of Negroes who had reached the promised land of the North and found it a bitter Canaan. Having nowhere else to seek haven in America their dreams turned to Africa under the powerful stimulation of the master dream-maker from the West Indies, Marcus Garvey. They would find haven in their ancestral homeland, and be free from the insults and restrictions of this nation and England, on their chance for greatness. Provisionally there were created Dukes of the Nile, Princesses of Ethiopia, Lords of the Sudan, for the weary and frustrated people whose phantom freedom in the North was as empty as their explicit subordination in the South.

Of this desperate and pathetic mass fantasy I find an editorial note in *Opportunity Magazine* in 1923 in a mood of brooding concern for the present and apprehension for the future:

It is a symbol, a symptom, and another name for the new psychology of the American Negro peasantry—for the surge of race consciousness felt by Negroes throughout the world, the intelligent as well as the ignorant.

It is a black version of that same one hundred per cent mania that now afflicts white America, that emboldens the prophets of a Nordic blood renaissance, that picked up and carried the cry of self-determination for all people, India for the Indians, A Free Ireland.

The sources of this discontent must be remedied effectively and now, or the accumulating energy and unrest, blocked off from its dreams, will take another direction. Perhaps this also will be harmless, but who knows.

To this note of 1923 might be added the observation of what is happening in the Asian-African Conference in Bandung in 1955; what happened in this long interval to make it possible for twenty-nine nations that in 1923 were only muttering against colonial imperialism and now are speaking as free and independent nations collectively to preserve the peace and security of the world.

It was out of forces of such magnitude that the voices of the Negro Renaissance made themselves heard and felt. It was a period, not only of the quivering search for freedom but of a cultural, if not a social and racial emancipation. It was unabashedly self-conscious and race-conscious. But it was race-consciousness with an extraordinary facet in that it had virtues that could be incorporated into the cultural bloodstream of the nation.

This was the period of the discovery by these culturally emancipated Negroes of the unique esthetic values of African art, of beauty in things dark, a period of harkening for the whispers of greatness from a remote African past. This was the period of Kelly Miller's Sanhedrin to reassess the lost values and build upon newly-found strengths. It was the period of the reaching out of arms for other dark arms of the same ancestry from other parts of the world in a Pan-African Conference.

Significantly, Dr. W.E.B. Du Bois made his first talk after returning from the Pan-African Conference of 1923 at the first *Opportunity Magazine* dinner, sponsoring the fledgling writers of the new and lively generation of the 1920's.

The person recognized as the Dean of this youthful group was Alain Locke. A brilliant analyst trained in philosophy, and an esthete with a flair for art as well as letters, he gave encouragement and guidance to these young writers as an older practitioner too sure of his craft to be discouraged by failure of full acceptance in the publishing media of the period.

Perhaps this is the point at which to add a previously unwritten note to the history of the period. The importance of the *Crisis Magazine* and *Opportunity Magazine* was that of providing an outlet for young Negro writers and scholars whose work was not acceptable to other established media because it could not be believed to be of standard quality despite the superior quality of much of it. What was necessary was a revolution and a revelation sufficient in intensity to disturb the age-old customary cynicisms. This function became associated with *Opportunity Magazine*.

Alain Locke recognized the role and possibility of this organ for creating such a revolution and associated himself with it, first as a reviewer and appraiser of various literary and sociological efforts and later as a contributor of major articles. As a by-product of his acquaintance with France, England and Germany through frequent visits, he wrote articles on current issues affecting Negroes from the perspective of Europe: "The Black Watch on the Rhine" (1921), "Apropos of Africa" (1924) and "Back Stage on European Imperialism" (1925). These articles were of such mature sophistication and insight that *Opportunity* offered to share their publication with the *Survey Magazine* to get a larger reading public. This magazine not only published the articles jointly with *Opportunity* but requested special ones for the *Survey* readers. Thus began an important relationship with the editor of the *Survey* and *Survey Graphic*.

The first *Opportunity* contest had Alain Locke's enthusiastic support and assistance. It was a dual venture in faith: faith in the creative potential of this generation in its new cultural freedom; and faith in the confidence of the nation's superior mentalities and literary creators. Both were justified. Locke's mellow maturity and esthetic sophistication were the warrant of confidence in the possibilities of these youth as well as the concrete evidence of accomplishment. The American scholars and writers who stretched out their arms to welcome these youthful aspirants to cultural equality were, without exception, the intellectual and spiritual leaders of the nation's cultural life and aspirations. They served as judges in these contests and in this role gave priceless assistance to this first and vital step in cultural integration. They were such great figures of American literary history as Van Wyck Brooks, Carl Van Doren, Eugene O'Neill, James Weldon Johnson, Paul Kellogg, Fannie Hurst, Robert Benchley, Zona Gale, Dorothy Canfield Fisher, Witter Bynner, W.E.B. Du Bois, Alexander Woolcott, John Macy, John Dewey, Carl Van Vechten, John Farrar and others.

They not only judged the poetry, essays, short stories and plays, but lent a supporting hand to their development in the best literary traditions.

At the first *Opportunity* dinner at the Civic Club in New York, Alain Locke was as a matter of course and appropriateness, moderator. It happens that this was one of the most significant and dramatic of the announcements of the renaissance. It marked the first public appearance of young creative writers in the company of the greatest of the nation's creative writers and philosophers. Out of this meeting came some of the first publications in the best publication tradition.

I cannot refrain from quoting briefly a poem read at this dinner by Gwendolyn Bennett:

TO USWARD

And some of us have songs to sing
Of purple heat and fires
And some of us are solemn grown
With pitiful desires;
And there are those who feel the pull
Of seas beneath the skies;
And some there be who want to croon
Of Negro lullabies.
We claim no part with racial dearth
We want to sing the songs of birth.
And so we stand like ginger jars,
Like ginger jars bound round
With dust and age;
Like jars of ginger we are sealed
By nature's heritage.
But let us break the seal of years
With pungent thrusts of song
For there is joy in long dried tears
For whetted passions of a throng.

For specific identification, it should be noted that Frederick Allen of
Harper's Magazine made a bid for Countee Cullen's poems for publication as
soon as he had finished reading them at this *Opportunity* dinner; and Paul
Kellogg of the *Survey* sought to carry the entire evening's readings in an issue
of the magazine. This fumbling idea led to the standard volume of the
period, *The New Negro*.

Winold Reiss, a German artist of extraordinary skill in pictorial
interpretation had just completed some drawings for the *Survey* of Sea
Island Negroes. The publishers Boni and Boni who were interested in a
book of Winold Reiss' drawings decided to carry the literary content along
with the pictures. This literary content had been carried first in the *Survey
Graphic* in a special issue under the editorship of Alain Locke. As a book it
became *The New Negro*, also edited by Locke, and expanded from the special
issue of the *Survey Graphic* to the proportions that now make brilliant
history.

The impetus to publication backed by the first recognition of creative
work in the best literary tradition, swept in many if not most of the budding
writers of this period, in a fever of history-making expression.

Removed by two generations from slavery and in a new cultural environment, these Negro writers were less self-conscious and less interested in proving that they were just like white people; in their excursions into the fields of letters and art, they seemed to care less about what white people thought, or were likely to think, than about themselves and what they had to say. Relief from the stifling consciousness of being a problem had brought a certain superiority to it. There was more candor, even in discussions of themselves about weaknesses, and on the very sound reasoning that unless you are truthful about your faults, you will not be believed when you speak about your virtues. The emancipation of these writers gave them freedom to return to the dynamic folk motives.

Carl Van Doren, in commenting upon this material said:

> If the reality of Negro life is itself dramatic there are, of course, still other elements, particularly the emotional power, with which Negroes live—or at least to me they seem to live. What American literature needs at this moment is color, music, gusto, the free expression of gay, or desperate moods. If the Negroes are not in a position to contribute these items, I do not know which Americans are.

As a rough cultural yardstick of the continuing repercussions of the period called the Renaissance, I have looked up the record of the youthful writers and commentators of this period for evidences of their effect upon the present state of the American culture.

An anthology called *Ebony and Topaz* carried about twenty young Negro writers, previously unknown to the great and critical public. Of those still living Langston Hughes and Sterling Brown are established poets, Arna Bontemps is a major novelist, having left his poetry with his youth; Aaron Douglas is one of the country's best-known artists; Zora Neale Hurston is a writer-anthropologist; Allison Davis is a distinguished psychologist and Abram Harris an equally distinguished economist, and both are on the faculty of the University of Chicago. Ira Reid heads the Department of Sociology at Haverford; Frank Horne is a national housing official. E. Franklin Frazier is one of the nation's most notable sociologists and a former president of the American Sociological Society, George Schuyler is a well-known columnist and John P. Davis is publisher of *Our World Magazine*.

There are others, of course, but the important thing is to show some end result of the striving.

As master of ceremonies for the first *Opportunity* dinner Alain Locke had this to say about these young spirits being launched on their careers: "They sense within their group—spiritual wealth which if they can properly expound, will be ample for a new judgment and re-appraisal of the race."

Whether or not there has been a reappraisal of the race over these past thirty years rests with our estimates of the contributions of those who began their careers in the 1920's. It is my opinion that the great fire and enthusiasm of the earlier period, and the creative dynamism of self-conscious racial expression are no longer present. They have faded with the changed status of Negroes in American life.

With the disappearance of many of the barriers to participation in the general culture the intense race-consciousness has been translated into contributions within the accepted national standards of the special professional fields.

One of Goethe's commentators referred to his literary art as the practice of living and pointed out that his life was as much worth studying as his work. Goethe in one of his diaries said:

> People who are always harping on the value of experience tend to forget that experience is only the one-half of experience. The secret of creative living consists in relating the rough and tumble of our contact with the world outside ourselves to the work which our minds put in on this stuff of experience. The full value of experience is in seeing the significance of what has happened. Without this awareness we do not really live. Life lives us.

This, it seems to me, is the essence of the shift in Negro life and Negro appraisals of life.

The infectious race-conscious movement of the period of the "Renaissance" has been transmited into less race-conscious scholarship. The historical research of John Hope Franklin, Benjamin Quarles and Rayford Logan appears as aspects of American history even though the subject matter may be Negroes. Similarly the sociological writing of E. Franklin Frazier, Ira de A. Reid, and Oliver Cox is in the broader context of the American society. Frank Yerby's romantic novels are best sellers and deal only incidentally with Negroes, if at all.

The most recent books by Negro authors, interestingly enough, are travel studies of other lands and people. Saunders Redding and Carl Rowan have written about India, Richard Wright and Era Belle Thompson about Africa. Meanwhile the kind of writing done by American Negroes in the

1920's is reflected in the books today by Peter Abrahams of South Africa and George Lamming of Trinidad, in the British West Indies.

In 1923 Franklin Frazier who was one of the first *Opportunity* prize winners with a bold essay on "Social Equality and the Negro" had this to say:

> The accomplishment of a consciously built-up culture will depend upon leaders with a vision and understanding of cultural processes. Nevertheless, spiritual and intellectual emancipation of the Negro awaits the building of a Negro university, supported by Negro educators, who have imbibed the best that civilization can offer, where its savants can add to human knowledge and promulgate those values which are to inspire and motivate Negroes as a cultural group.

We have in this present period, and out of the matrix of the Renaissance period, scholars who know the cultural process, and savants who have imbibed the best that civilization can offer and can and are aiding human knowledge, within the context, not of a special culture group, but of the national society and world civilization.

AMY HELENE KIRSCHKE

The Pulse
of the Negro World

As early as 1917, a new "white curiosity" about the culture and characteristics of black America appeared in the United States, especially in the center of culture, New York City.[1] After World War I this interest grew, and whites were increasingly attracted to Harlem. Some blacks had misgivings, but leaders such as the writer James Weldon Johnson and Charles Johnson, the head of the National Urban League, regarded white interest as a positive development. Charles Johnson in particular hoped that white interest in black arts would lead to public exposure and more professional opportunities for Negro painters and sculptors. This desire did not take long to materialize. In March 1924 Harlem leaders held a dinner attended by influential figures in the New York cultural community and young black artists. The guest speaker was W.E.B. Du Bois, who explained that although his generation had been denied its true voice, the time had come for the end of the "literature of apology." In particular Du Bois praised James Weldon Johnson for providing an inspiration to young black artists. By the end of the evening, Du Bois's message moved one of the white participants, Paul Kellog, to make a unique offer. Addressing Charles Johnson, Kellog, the editor of *Survey Graphic*, offered to devote an entire issue of his "mainstream cultural magazine" to the new black artists, an offer Johnson gladly accepted.[2]

From Aaron Douglas: *Art, Race, and the Harlem Renaissance*. © 1995 by the University Press of Mississippi.

179

Why would such a magazine wish to do a special issue on Harlem? The offer was unprecedented but not as unusual as it might seem. The magazine *Survey* appeared twice a month, a "graphic" issue on the first, with a decorated cover, and a "midmonthly" issue on the fifteenth, printed on lighter stock and unbound. Although the magazine's subscribers were predominantly white, its editors were open to the forces of change they saw sweeping the world. Comparing the cultural development of black America with newly independent Ireland and revolutionary Russia and Mexico, the editors sought

> month by month and year by year to follow the subtle traces of race growth and interaction through the shifting outline of social organization and by the flickering light of individual achievement. There are times when these forces that work so slowly and so delicately seem suddenly to flower—and we become aware that the curtain has lifted on a new act in the drama of part or all of us.... If The Survey reads the signs right, such a dramatic flowering of a new race-spirit is taking place close at home—among American Negroes, and the stage of that new episode is Harlem.[3]

The special issue of *Survey Graphic*, with Alain Locke as chief editor, appeared in March 1925. It was titled "Harlem: Mecca of the New Negro."

Survey Graphic had an extraordinary impact on Aaron Douglas. In later interviews, he always insisted that one of the main reasons he came to Harlem was the inspiration he derived from this one magazine. What could an issue of *Survey Graphic* possibly contain that would make Harlem seem so inviting and interesting, so open to a young artist? It was the first comprehensive study devoted entirely to Harlem, and it contained the viewpoints of blacks and whites, women and men, scholars, sociologists, civil leaders, and poets. It explored every aspect of life there, including the opportunities and excitement and the disappointments and problems.

More important, this issue of *Survey Graphic* offers an extraordinary look into the cultural milieu in which Aaron Douglas would work and provides detail on some of the important influences on his work. In four important areas—the discussion of the New Negro, the problems and opportunities of the city of Harlem, the importance of Africa for the black artist, and the highlighting of the work of Winold Reiss—*Survey Graphic* merits special attention.

The New Negro was a product of a world created in the aftermath of World War I, when a host of new nations replaced former empires and kingdoms. At the Versailles Peace Conference, President Woodrow Wilson had proclaimed America's support for the principle of self-determination for colonial peoples, and although the United States did not join the new League of Nations, Americans were sympathetic observers of the movements for independence around the world. In many of these new states, leaders faced the problem of instilling a separate and distinct national identity among predominantly rural and peasant populations. Artists and intellectuals played key roles in the creation of these nationalist movements, emphasizing culture and language to strengthen national identity and liberate their peoples from the psychology of colonial dependency. Irish writers and poets were important leaders in the independence movement and the revival of the Gaelic language, while in Czechoslovakia and Poland, a new generation of intellectuals broke away from the dominant German cultural traditions.

The concepts of self-determination, separatism, and cultural identity influenced American black leaders during the 1920s, although they adapted them to their particular circumstances. The urbanization of blacks during World War I, along with their participation in the war and their disappointment with its results, encouraged a greater spirit of independence, while at the same time many American blacks demanded recognition from white society. One of the foremost spokesmen for these ideas was Alain Locke, and his writings clearly had a great impact on Douglas's perception of the role of an artist in the black community. Locke was identified by the magazine's editors as a foremost example of the "Talented Tenth," the leaders who African-Americans were hoping could improve the image and estimation of the race in the eyes of the uninformed and frequently indifferent white public. They praised him as a graduate of Harvard, Oxford, and Berlin Universities, now a professor of philosophy at Howard University, "and himself a brilliant exemplar of that poise and insight which are happy omens for the Negro's future."[4] Locke was determined to bring to the public eye black poetry, music, art, and literature, and he encouraged artists to explore their African heritage through the arts. He became a spokesman for these artists. In Locke's essay "The Legacy of the Ancestral Arts" in *The New Negro*, he argued that the black artist lacked a mature tradition and might consider the newfound African arts as his real and exploitable heritage. He stated: "There is a real and vital connection between this new artistic respect for African idiom and the natural ambition of Negro artists for a racial idiom in their art expression.... The Negro physiognomy must be freshly and objectively conceived on its own patterns if it is ever to be seriously and importantly interpreted.... We ought and must have a school of Negro art, a local and racially representative tradition."[5]

In the opening essay of the 1925 special issue of *Survey Graphic*, Locke equated Harlem's role for the American Negro with Dublin's for the new Ireland or Prague's for the new Czechoslovakia. Locke coined the term "New Negro," praising the younger generation of blacks as a vibrant group with a new psychology and a new spirit. Locke argued that sociologists, philanthropists, and race leaders could not account for the emergence of the New Negro. For generations, in the mind of America, the Negro had been "more of a formula than a human being—a something to be argued about, condemned or defended, to be 'kept down,' or 'in his place,' or 'helped up,' to be worried with or worried over, harassed or patronized, a social bogey or a social burden." Locke proclaimed that a sudden reorientation was necessary, a spiritual emancipation. A renewed self-respect and self-dependence had arisen in Harlem. These life attitudes appeared in the "self-expression of the Young Negro, in his poetry, his art, his education and his new outlook ... poise and greater certainty of knowing what it is all about."[6] Locke placed the future of the New Negro movement in the new generation, the young Negro, the artist. The artist would communicate the ideals of the movement to the masses. (Such an opportunity for artistic expression must have been a primary lure for Douglas.) Locke proclaimed that the Negro problem was no longer exclusively or predominantly southern.[7]

The massive migration from the South to the urban North and Midwest had brought racial unrest to these areas as well. Yet Locke believed that problems which rural blacks faced in adjusting to their new urban environments were not particularly racial and were similar to those faced by Eastern and Southern European immigrants. The Negro had too often unnecessarily excused himself because of the way group and personal experience, had at his hand almost the conditions to produce classical art. "Negro genius today relies upon the race-gift as a vast spiritual endowment from which our best developments have come and must come."[12] Poets no longer spoke for the Negro, they spoke *as* Negroes. They spoke to their own and tried to express the essence of Negro life and spirit. Race added enriching adventure and discipline, giving subtler overtones to life, making it more beautiful and interesting, even if more poignant.

To Locke, race was now a source of inspiration for black artists. Being black helped the artist to express both joy and suffering more poignantly. Locke agreed with Du Bois that blacks were innately and permanently different from whites and that color consciousness needed to be promoted, developed, and refined, even in the arts.[13] The artist's struggle had not been so much to acquire an outer mastery of form and technique as to achieve an inner mastery of mood and spirit. The artists of the New Negro movement were particularly fortunate because they had predecessors who helped lay the groundwork for them, a generation of "creative workmen who have been pioneers and path-breakers," such as sociologist and *Crisis* editor Du Bois, poet Paul Laurence Dunbar, and writer James Weldon Johnson; in painting, Henry Tanner and William Scott; in sculpture, Meta Warrick and May Jackson; and in acting, Paul Robeson. Locke regarded the youngest generation, which included writers Jessie Fauset, Claude McKay, and Jean Toomer and poets Langston Hughes and Countee Cullen, as the legitimate heirs to a tradition that was ready to acquire new energy. These people constituted a new generation not because of their youth but because of their new aesthetic and philosophy of life. They had gained more recognition from literary circles and the general public than Negro creative artists had ever before received in an entire working lifetime. It was a time of spiritual quickening, when "the heart beats a little differently." "There is in it all the marriage of a fresh emotional endowment with the finest niceties of art."[14]

Locke discussed a new poetry of social protest and a fiction of calm, dispassionate social analysis. Instead of the wail and appeal, there was challenge and indictment. The new artists had an "instinctive love and pride of race ... and ardent respect and love for Africa, the motherland." The brands and wounds of social persecution were becoming the proud stigmata of spiritual immunity and moral victory. Locke closed the essay with the poignant words, "Indeed, by the evidence and promise of the cultured few, we are at last spiritually free, and offer through art an emancipating vision to America."[15]

Intimately connected with the theme of the New Negro was the concept of Harlem as a "race capital," the largest black city in the world. Locke explained the significance of this development. He proclaimed Harlem as the "new race capital," where "the pulse of the Negro world has begun to beat.... A Negro newspaper, carrying the news material in English, French and Spanish, gathered from all quarters of America, the West Indies and Africa has maintained itself in Harlem for over two years."[16] Locke compared Harlem's meaning for blacks to that of the Statue of Liberty for European immigrants. The volume of migration to Harlem had made it "the greatest Negro community the world has known" without counterpart in the South or in Africa. Harlem also represented the Negro's latest thrust toward democracy. White New Yorkers, according to Locke, thought of Harlem merely as a rough rectangle of commonplace city blocks, unaccountably full of Negroes. A few saw Harlem as a place to savor for its racy music and racier dancing, of cabarets notorious for their amusements, of abandon and sophistication. This Harlem drew in both the entertainment connoisseur and the undiscriminating sightseer. This was the "shufflin' " and "rollin' " and "runnin' wild" Harlem on the exotic fringe of the metropolis. There was also the Harlem of the newspapers, a Harlem of monster parades and political flummery, swept by revolutionary oratory and flashy black millionaires.

In the final analysis, Locke saw Harlem not as a slum, ghetto, resort, or colony, but rather as place that was, or promised to be, "a race capital."[17] Locke explained that the tide of Negro migration could not be adequately interpreted as a blind flood started by the demands of war industry coupled with the shutting off of foreign migration or by the pressure of poor crops. Neither labor demand, the boll weevil, nor the Ku Klux Klan was a determining factor. This migration northward represented a new vision of opportunity, of social and economic freedom, of a spirit to seize, despite an extortionate and heavy toll, a chance to improve conditions. With each wave, the Negro migrants became more and more like the European waves at their crests, moving toward the democratic chance, a deliberate flight from medieval America to modern.[18]

Not only was Harlem the largest Negro community in the world, but it was also the first concentration of so many diverse elements of Negro life. It attracted the African, the West Indian, the Negro American, the northerner and southerner, the man from city, town, and village. Harlem had become home to the peasant, the student, the businessman, the professional man, the artist, poet, musician, adventurer, and social outcast. The greatest experience of all had been finding one another. This was a laboratory of a great race welding: "Hitherto, it must be admitted that American Negroes have been a race more in name than in fact ... more in sentiment than in experience. The chief bond between them has been that of a common condition rather than a common consciousness.... In Harlem, Negro life is seizing upon its first chances for group expression and self-determination."[19]

Locke and many of his colleagues saw the positive in Harlem more than the negative. Subsequent historical treatments tended to stress the negative dimensions of Harlem's emergence as an all-black community, focusing on the creation of slum conditions and a ghetto pathology. Harlem became a slum in the 1920s because of the high cost of rent, poor employment possibilities, poor salaries, congestion, substandard health care, crime, and poor sanitation. Why would Locke and others have viewed Harlem in such a positive light, largely ignoring its troubles?

Locke and the artists he worked with were not average migrants. They were educated, they were united as a group in search of opportunities, and many of them were backed by the wealth of white patrons. Locke was discussing the opportunities available, and there were many, for the artists of the New Negro movement. It was the first time such artists had come together in an urban center, no longer isolated in rural communities as a peasant class. Harlem offered them tremendous opportunities just as American cities had attracted European immigrants despite the negative aspects of urban life. The members of the Renaissance accentuated the positive because much of their personal experience was more positive than was the average Harlemite's. Their experience in Harlem was also frequently a vast improvement over that in their places of origin. They believed that problems of race could be solved through art and cultural acceptance. Artists like Douglas were looking for different things in Harlem than the average laborer who migrated to the area.

For Locke, a new order had been created, and Harlem voiced these new aspirations of a people, the new condition, new relationships, a stage of the pageant of contemporary Negro life. Although Locke's view of Harlem was clearly skewed, his words of encouragement were inspirational. To Locke, Harlem was the center of a new cultural revolution for the Negro, a place open to new leaders, new ideas, and, most important, new artistic talent.

One of Douglas's primary reasons for moving to Harlem was to find other artists who shared the race consciousness he was developing. Douglas had met only one person in Kansas City to whom he could relate, and he felt isolated and longed to be part of a community. James Weldon Johnson's article "The Making of Harlem" showed men and women like Douglas, who were often isolated, well-educated blacks, that such a community of support existed. Johnson was listed in the beginning of the issue as a journalist, editor, poet, and executive secretary of the National Association for the Advancement of Colored People (NAACP), as well as editor of the *Book of American Negro Poetry* and author of *Fifty Years and After* and *The Autobiography of an Ex-Coloured Man*. Johnson described Harlem as the Negro metropolis, the mecca for the sightseer, the pleasure seeker, the curious, the adventurous, the enterprising, the ambitious, and the talented of the Negro world. Harlem was a city within a city, one of the most beautiful and healthy sections of the city, with its own churches, social and civic centers, shops, theaters, and other places of amusement. It contained more Negroes per square mile than any other place on earth, beginning on 125th Street and covering twenty-five solid blocks. The Harlem of 1925, wrote Johnson, was practically a development of the past decade, although there had always been colored people in New York. Entertainment spots famous for showcasing Negro talent appeared in Harlem, such as the Marshall Hotel, where actors, musicians, composers, writers, singers, dancers, and vaudevillians gathered. Famed actors such as Paul Robeson frequented the Marshall when visiting New York. (This kind of Harlem establishment would become a source of inspiration for the visual imagery in Douglas's works.) Again, Johnson saw the positive side of Harlem, emphasizing the positive and excluding certain glaring realities. Like Locke, Johnson saw Harlem as a land of opportunity.

In Johnson's view, Harlem was becoming more and more a self-supporting community, where blacks were able to branch out steadily into new businesses and enterprises. Negroes were experiencing a constant growth of group consciousness, the sense of community that Aaron Douglas was searching for. It had movement, color, gaiety, singing, dancing, boisterous laughter and loud talk, and outstanding brass band parades. Harlem was not a mere quarter in New York City, for several reasons Johnson listed. First, the language of Harlem was not a foreign tongue, it was English. Second, Harlem was not physically a quarter, but rather a zone through which four main arteries of the city ran. Third, because there was little or no gang labor, Negroes could lose their former identity and quickly assimilate: "A thousand Negroes from Mississippi put to work as a gang in a Pittsburgh steel mill will for a long time remain a thousand Negroes from Mississippi. Under the conditions that prevail in New York they would all within six months become New Yorkers. The rapidity with which Negroes become good New Yorkers is one of the marvels to observers." Optimistically—and somewhat naively—Johnson thought there was little chance that Harlem would ever be a point of race friction in New York. Old white residents lived peacefully side by side with black tenants, and he could see no reason why problems would arise, especially with the large proportion of Negro police on duty. To Johnson, Harlem was more than just a Negro community: "It is a large scale laboratory experiment in the race problem."[20]

Although Johnson admitted that the Negro still met with discrimination in Harlem, it was more important to recognize that blacks possessed basic civil rights and could be confident that discrimination would eventually be abolished. Johnson ended his essay with the following statement: "I believe that the Negro's advantages and opportunities are greater in Harlem than in any other place in the country, and that Harlem will become the intellectual, the cultural and the financial center for Negroes of the United States, and will exert a vital influence upon all Negro peoples."[21] An opportunity to combine the tasks of self-fulfillment and race betterment was what Aaron Douglas sought, and Harlem seemed qualified on both counts.

The anthropologist Melville Herskovits's essay, "The Dilemma of

Social Pattern," in the same *Survey Graphic* issue, described Negro newspapers, intellectuals, churches, and social groups. Harlem offered a busy, whirring cycle of life, with doctors, lawyers, teachers, nurses, student waiters, and more. It was the same pattern found in any community in America, only a different shade![22] It was a community that a white would find familiar, with vitality and opportunities; the only difference was the skin color of its members. Herskovits applauded the vigor of Harlem and all it had to offer men like Aaron Douglas.

For all of its problems, Harlem was the first American city that blacks could claim as their own. Even though it was located within the larger political entity of New York, it encouraged among blacks a sense of power and possibilities, providing the opportunity to forge a new sense of identity. If the move to Harlem led to poverty and hardship for many blacks, it also provided a much-needed sense of community and support for those like Aaron Douglas who sought to forge a new racial identity. His creativity and innovation cannot be understood apart from the dynamic community that was Harlem in the 1920s.

One of the most distinctive aspects of Aaron Douglas's work would be his attempt to draw upon the African heritage of American blacks. *Survey Graphic* helped stimulate his interest in this subject. Alain Locke discussed the importance of African art, paying tribute to the Barnes Foundation's collection of African art. Locke noted the influence of African art on modernist art in both France and Germany, including the works of Matisse, Picasso, Amedeo Modigliani, Alexander Archipenko, Jacques Lipchitz, Wilhelm Lehmbruck, and others, centering in Paris around the pioneer exponent, Paul Guillaume. Thus far, the Negro in his American environment had turned predominantly to the arts of music, dance, and poetry, and the influence of African culture was either unconscious or indirect. Locke hoped that the "plastic arts" would allow Africa a more direct influence on the artistic development of the American Negro, an influence that had already manifested itself in modern European art: "It [African Art] may very well be taken as the basis for a characteristic school of expression in the plastic and pictorial arts, and give to us again a renewed mastery of them ... and a lesson in simplicity and originality of expression. Surely this art, once known and appreciated, can scarcely have less influence upon the blood descendants than upon those who inherit by tradition only."[23]

Locke wanted to emphasize that the Negro was not a cultural foundling without an inheritance. His essay was accompanied by reproductions of four African sculptures, three masks and one male figure. (Other African art pieces from the Barnes Foundation collection were included in the issue to accompany poems such as Countee Cullen's on the African heritage.[24]) The need for the Negro to go back to his own unique heritage, a heritage others had tried to claim, was repeated throughout the *Survey Graphic* issue.

The Harlem of the 1920s was also home to other pan-African sentiments. The pan-African movement, which attempted to unite African-origin blacks worldwide, was a growing phenomenon, part of a new internationalism that aspired to reestablish contact among the scattered peoples of Africa. Marcus Garvey, a West Indian insurgent, was perhaps the most flamboyant spokesman for the pan-African cause, though in 1923 he was convicted of mail fraud, jailed, and later deported. Not surprisingly, Locke referred to Garvey's Universal Negro Improvement Association movement in a less than flattering manner, but he agreed with Garvey that the American Negro needed to be involved in the future development of Africa. Such involvement would give the Negro valuable prestige at home and abroad.

Before he came to Harlem, race had not been a part of Douglas's artistic work. Although his pre-Harlem paintings no longer exist, he does refer to them in his letters as traditional studies of human anatomy, not based on racial issues or stylistically influenced by modernist trends. Nor does it appear that there were any significant visual artists in Harlem before Douglas who were incorporating African ideas in their work. In this area Douglas was clearly an innovator, and he was quick to seize upon this challenge after his arrival in Harlem. (Indeed, Locke called Douglas, who illustrated some chapters of *The New Negro* in 1925, "a pioneering Africanist.") With Douglas's arrival in Harlem, a whole new chapter of Africanism in African-American art was opened. It comes as no surprise that Douglas would earn the title of "the father of Black American art."[25]

The final aspect of *Survey Graphic* that affected Aaron Douglas was the artwork and style of Winold Reiss. The very first illustration was Reiss's portrait of Roland Hayes, "whose achievement as a singer symbolizes the promise of the younger generation." Drawn in a straightforward, realistic manner, with Hayes's head floating on a plain white page, it shows no neck or body. This was the "splendid portrait of a Black man by the famous German artist Fritz Winold Reiss" that Douglas referred to when discussing the impact *Survey Graphic* had on him.[26] Hayes is looking off to the side thoughtfully and seriously. Reiss had proudly displayed Hayes's African traits, including a full nose and lips (Figure I).

The magazine also contained a brief discussion of the significance of Reiss's work, probably written by Locke. The author asserted that conventions stood doubly in the way of the artistic portrayal of Negro folk:

certain narrow, arbitrary conventions of physical beauty and "that inevitable inscrutability of things seen but not understood." Caricature had put upon the countenance of the Negro the mask of the comic and the grotesque, whereas in actuality, based on life experience, the very opposite should have been included, namely, the serious, the tragic, the wistful. The Negro artist was still confronting his own material timidly. His best development, according to the essayist, would most likely come in the pictorial arts, "for his capacity to express beauty depends vitally upon the capacity to see it in his own life and to generate it out of his own experience."[27] Using one's own life experiences and heritage as a source of inspiration for creating art was the credo of Winold Reiss, with whom Aaron Douglas would study for two years and find encouragement to paint things African and explore a vein of artistic experience that was uniquely his.

Winold Reiss was born in 1886 in Karlsruhe in southwestern Germany, the son of a Bavarian landscape painter.[28] He studied at the Kunstgewerbe Schule in Munich under Franz von Stuck, as well as under the direction of his father, respected artist Fritz Mahler Reiss. The elder Reiss had trained at the Düsseldorf Academy, studying natural history, German landscape, and peasant portraiture, and he passed these traditions down to his son. Reiss's teacher Franz von Stuck, master at the Munich Academy, exposed him to the modern art movements of fauvism and cubism and eventually encouraged him to enroll at the School of Applied Arts, where he would study commercial design and poster design under Julius Diez. Reiss painted folk groups in Sweden, Holland, and Germany before his immigration to the United States in 1913. He probably became aware of cubism and African art at least by 1913, when he most likely saw an exhibition of Picasso's African-inspired cubist works in Munich. Von Stuck also introduced Reiss to *Jugendstil* (youth style), the German decorative arts movement which was rooted in France's Art Nouveau. Reiss had worked as a designer in Munich and would take these talents to New York, where he worked as an illustrator for magazines, books, and advertising, using his commercial and poster art training. Reiss was also no doubt familiar with the German folk art technique *Scherenschnitt*, which influenced his simple black and white designs and often resembled cutouts or collages.

Reiss, along with other Munich modernists, was attracted to ethnography. He was aware of the 1912 Blaue Reiter almanac, which contained numerous photographs of the art of the Cameroons, Egypt, and Japan, as well as Bavarian and Russian folk art. Reiss therefore developed an interest in both ancient and modern art and an awareness of contemporary experiments of modern artists.

Before becoming a premier artist in Harlem, Reiss spent a great deal of time traveling in the American West, Canada, and Mexico, as well as in Central America, painting Indians and aspects of Indian life. He was particularly fascinated by the Blackfoot Indians, the Pueblo people, Mexicans, and the American Negro. Reiss had always been interested in documenting various racial groups "as a means to illuminate the distinctions and integrity of different ethnic groups." Reiss went to communities that were undergoing dramatic social changes, visiting the heirs of the Aztecs in Mexico in 1921 and the last survivors of the intertribal wars of the nineteenth century in Browning, Montana. Harlem provided similar opportunities for documentation, a community that author Jeffrey Stewart states Reiss "stumbled onto," finding it "brimming with racial consciousness and a desire for dignified self-representation."[29]

Reiss's art owed its success "as much to the philosophy of his approach as to his technical skill."

> He is a folk-lorist of the brush and palette, seeking always the folk character back of the individual, the psychology behind the physiognomy. In design also he looks not merely for decorative elements, but for the pattern of the culture from which it sprang. Without loss of naturalistic accuracy and individuality, he somehow subtly expresses the type, and without being any the less human, captures the racial and local.[30]

To Locke, Reiss's attention to American blacks was particularly welcome: "What Gauguin and his followers have done for the Far East, and the work of Ufer and Blumenschein and the Taos school for the Pueblo and Indian, seems about to become for the Negro and Africa: in short, painting, the most local of arts, in terms of its own limitations even, is achieving universality."[31] For Reiss, the Negro, without humor or caricature, was an acceptable subject.

The drawings that surrounded the essay about Reiss consisted first of a young, somber mother with clear, straightforward black facial features including a prominent, wide nose and full lips, holding a young girl perhaps two years old, with loose, kinky, natural hair. The original drawings were done in pastel crayon and charcoal, with very little paint added to just a few of the garments. The young girl bears only the slightest smile. Most of Reiss's drawings showed serious and thoughtful facial expressions. The next page contained three more portraits, *A Boy Scout* in profile, *A woman lawyer,* and *Girl in the white blouse.* All of Reiss's portraits show detail in the face and hands, and in the originals color pastel crayons are used for the face and hands. The clothing and bodies are not detailed and are almost sketches, further emphasizing the sensitive, serious, and dignified nature of the sitter. There is no effort to caricature or overemphasize black features, nor is there an attempt to hide features particular to African-Americans. Reiss's work provided a source of pride and inspiration for the black artist, who often in this time period did not choose to paint black subject matter. Reiss's final portrait in this section of *Survey Graphic* was *A college lad*, clad in a fine suit and tie, intelligent, thoughtful, handsome, and dignified.

Reiss influenced Douglas not only in his eventual turn to his black heritage and Africanism but also in stylistic ways. Reiss's illustration *Dawn in Harlem* (Figure 2) shows modern skyscrapers, à la Charles Sheeler or Joseph Stella, without the same strong influence of cubism. Progress in 1925 is depicted by skyscrapers towering over the city, most of them topped by smokestacks, some illuminated by the morning sun, others hidden in shadow. The sun is rising along the horizon, surrounded by concentric circles of energy. Douglas would use a very similar, clear style in his works, undoubtedly under the influence of Reiss's tutelage, including skyscrapers, smokestacks, and concentric circles, a motif he would take much further.

An article by J. A. Rogers, "Jazz at Home," provided the opportunity for more of Reiss's illustrations. Rogers, the author of *From Superman to Man*, reviewed the history of jazz, calling it one part American, three parts Negro, a spirit that could express itself in almost any way. It was joyous revolt, the revolt of the emotions against repression.[32] His article was accompanied by two of Reiss's drawings, *Interpretations of Harlem Jazz* (Figure 3). One drawing included a Negro dancer in a cabaret, dancing with a young woman, their faces accented only by thick, overaccentuated lips, their bodies flat silhouettes. The piece has the stylized qualities of Art Deco, Egyptian art, and a touch of cubism, all of which would influence Douglas. An African mask, a booze bottle, and another dancer's leg appear in the background. All of the black silhouette figures are accentuated by thick features, slightly slanted eyes (reminiscent of Dan sculpture of the Ivory Coast of Africa), thick lips, and black faces. Here Reiss uses flat patterns and silhouettes of figures in black and white, giving the illusion of a cutout work similar to *Scherenschnitt*, or scissors-cut images. This was the folk art silhouette technique of black cutouts, with no depth or perspective. This technique was also used in Germany with marionettes and puppet theater, employing cutout forms behind a transparent screen. This technique may have influenced Reiss, who in turn taught Douglas. Again, Douglas's stylistic connection to Reiss is particularly clear in these drawings. Douglas would turn to jazz and cabaret life as a source of inspiration in his works, including book illustrations and murals.

In a series of moving portraits titled *Four Portraits of Negro Women*, Reiss used the same style, with a clearly drawn, detailed, realistic face and sketchier body, which in some cases consisted of only a few simple black lines. These are titled *The Librarian, Two Public School Teachers*, and *Elise Johnson McDougald* (Figures 4, 5, 6). All of the portraits are extremely thoughtful, indeed almost solemn, with the trademark dignity Reiss gave his sitters.

Survey Graphic offered the reader a remarkable insight into Harlem as a place of opportunity, of educated leaders of the arts and letters, of race betterment. It also depicted the less attractive side of Harlem as a place of exploitation and disappointments. Overall, the issue left a distinctly positive view of Harlem and its environs. It provided a lure for many young, striving blacks like Aaron Douglas to come and participate in this new movement with all the great leaders of the time. Douglas would become close friends with many of the issue's contributors and would study under Winold Reiss. The issue was eventually expanded into the volume *The New Negro* edited by Alain Locke, to which Douglas would contribute, later that same year. Both the magazine and the book would announce to the world the new self-awareness, artistic consciousness, and race pride of the Negro of the Renaissance. Like *Survey Graphic*, *The New Negro* focused on Harlem as the symbol of a new chapter in the history of the black race, "the laboratory of a great race-welding."[33]

Douglas wrote Locke upon his arrival in New York City. He told of his personal background and training, explaining:

> There isn't much romance there. No, but under it all there is a great deal of pathos. Now, why do I speak of pathos as if it were a point of great merit; as if it were an exception; as if black America has known ought but pathos; as if pathos is not now one of the most vital elements in the genius of the race. Yes, and we must let down our buckets into our own souls where joy and pain, mirth and sadness, still flows swift and deep and free, and drink until we are drunk as with an overpowering desire for expression.
>
> If you should find it possible to use one of my drawings I am flattered beyond measure. I am sure they merit no such distinction.[34]

Douglas would find abundant opportunities to express "the joy and pain, mirth and sadness" of black life, shortly after his arrival in Harlem.

Notes

1. Mary Schmidt Campbell, *Harlem Renaissance: Art of Black America* (New York: Abrams, 1987), pp. 62–63.

2. Ibid., p. 63. Along with this issue, Charles Johnson decided to institute in the Urban Leagues's magazine *Opportunity* new awards for outstanding achievement as incentive for the new artists. He announced this innovation in his September editorial, saying the awards would commence the following May (1925). The *Crisis*, the NAACP's monthly magazine, also announced that it would award literary prizes backed by the NAACP.

3. *Survey Graphic* 6 (March 1925): 628.

4. *Survey Graphic* 6 (March 1925): 627. The magazine actually listed Locke as professor of philosophy at Harvard University.

5. Alain Locke, ed., *The New Negro* (New York: Albert and Charles Boni, 1925), p. 254.

6. Alain Locke, "Enter the New Negro," *Survey Graphic* 6 (March 1925): 631.

7. Although Locke was correct to note these changes, the vast majority of black Americans remained in the South.

8. Locke, "Enter the New Negro," p. 632.

9. Ibid.

10. Ibid., p. 633.

11. Ibid.

12. Alain Locke, "Youth Speaks," *Survey Graphic* 6 (March 1925): 659.

13. For the German-educated Du Bois, such a celebration of what was unique and honorable about blacks derived from Hegelian philosophy. A similar celebration of white genius in the beginning of the twentieth century as been termed by historian Joel Williamson, "Volksgeistian Conservatism" (*A Rage for Order: Black/White Relations in the American South Since Emancipation* [New York: Oxford University Press, 1986], pp. 65–69, 206–7]}.

14. Locke, "Youth Speaks," p. 660.

15. Ibid.

16. Ibid.

17. For another view, see Gilbert Osofsky, *Harlem, The Making of a Ghetto: Negro New York, 1890–1930* (New York: Harper & Row, 1966). Osofsky is far more negative than *Survey Graphic*, although many of the same points—about price gouging in rents, discrimination in employment, poor housing, substandard health care, crime, and poor sanitation—are raised in the special issue.

18. James Grossman, *Land of Hope: Chicago, Black Southerners and the Great Migration* (Chicago: University of Chicago Press, 1989), pp. 27–31, discusses the desire of black migrants to better their economic opportunities by migrating north. This is also chronicles in painter Jacob Lawrence's migration series, sixty panels dating to 1942, now in the Phillips Collection and Museum of Modern Art.

19. Alain Locke, "Harlem," *Survey Graphic* 6 (March 1925): 630. The social problems are discussed by several contributors to the *Survey Graphic* issue, among them Eunice Hunter, Winthrop Lane, Charles S. Johnson, W.E.B. Du Bois, and Rudolf Fisher.

20. James Weldon Johnson, "The Making of Harlem," *Survey Graphic* 6 (March 1925): 639.

21. Ibid.

22. Melville Herkovits, "The Dilemma of Social Pattern," *Survey Graphic* 6 (March 1925): 676.

23. Alain Locke, "The Art of Ancestors," *Survey Graphic* 6 (March 1925): 673. This article was only a page, with four illustrations. Locke expanded this essay for the November 1925 publication of *The New Negro* and included it under the heading "The Negro Digs Up His Past."

24. Countee Cullen, "Heritage," a series of poems and reproductions of Barnes Foundation African art in *Survey Graphic* 6 (March 1925): 674–75.

25. David Driskell, "Aaron Douglas," in Campbell, *Harlem Renaissance*, p. 110.

26. Douglas, Personal writings, Box 3, Folder 15, Douglas Papers, Fisk.

27. *Survey Graphic* 6 (March 1925): 652–53.

28. This discussion of Reiss is based on Jeffrey Stewart, *To Color America: Portraits of Winold Reiss* (Washington D.C.: National Portrait Gallery, 1989), pp. 17–23.

29. Ibid., p. 17.

30. Ibid.

31. *Survey Graphic* 6 (March 1925): 653. Some of these drawings are today housed in the Fisk University Library on the first floor, a gift to Fisk by Winold Reiss in 1953, at the urging of Aaron Douglas.

32. J.A. Rogers, "Jazz at Home," *Survey Graphic* 6 (March 1925): 666.

33. Locke, ed., *The New Negro*, p. 7.

34. Douglas to Locke, n.d., Box 164–25, Correspondence, Alain Locke Papers, Moorland-Spingarn Research Center, Manuscript Division, Howard University, Washington, D.C.

STERLING A. BROWN

The Negro Author
and His Publisher

One truth concerning the Negro author and his publisher seems to be that before Richard Wright's success with *Native Son* no Negro writer has made a living from creative writing. Phillis Wheatley's poetry went into numerous editions, but many of these editions were posthumous. Her brief years of writing could hardly be considered a professional author's career. The narratives of ex-slaves in frequent instances had wide sales, but it is likely that some of the authors shared profits with "ghost" writers who edited and "doctored" these autobiographies, and that those fugitives who wrote authentic autobiographies returned a goodly portion of their receipts into the coffers of antislavery organizations, more honor to them. Frederick Douglass and William Wells Brown made money from their writing certainly, Douglass telling us that at the end of the Civil War he still had some money saved from his royalties on *My Bondage and My Freedom*. But they had supplemented this out with lecturing and journalism, and could hardly be considered men of letters making a livelihood from writing. After her eloquent lecturing and readings, Frances Watkins Harper sold large numbers of her poems printed as small throwaways. The audience for this type of work was composed largely of people already or willing to be convinced, and propaganda rather than profit was the high motive of the authors.

From *Remembering the Harlem Renaissance*. © 1996 by Cary D. Wintz.

Dunbar and Chesnutt are generally considered to be our first professional authors. But Dunbar in his tragically brief life-span had to get money (little enough at that) by writing for the Broadway musical comedy bargain counter, by working at the Library of Congress, and by occasional patronage. Chesnutt's income from his several highly praised books was insufficient for a livelihood. Chesnutt's daughter writes in *Breaking Into Print:*[1]

> Practically all of Mr. Chesnutt's creative work was done after business hours. He followed his profession of court reporter throughout his life except for two years in 1900 and 1901, when he devoted himself exclusively to literary work. In that period he did a great deal of lecturing and reading, and much writing, but the needs of a growing family, the education of four children— two at Smith, one at Harvard, and one at Western Reserve— made it imperative that he earn more money than his literary work produced. So that at the end of the two years, his literary work again took second place.

In the early years of our century there were produced a number of "door-to-door" novels, so-called because the authors or their agents sold them from door to door or at least took upon themselves the problems of sale, distribution, and advertising. Sutton Griggs, was one of these author-agents. For the audience that we must encourage and in turn rely upon, there is much to be said for this method of sale and distribution. J. A. Rogers, irritated by commercial publishing practices, is doing this, just as Upton Sinclair did for so long.

W.E.B. DuBois, whose total works fill a shelf of great importance to all, has still had to depend upon editing of magazines, scholarly grants, and teaching for a livelihood. William Stanley Braithwaite did newspaper work before his present teaching. Benjamin Brawley, who produced many books, was preeminently the teacher. James Weldon Johnson did organizational work for the N.A.A.C.P.; only in his last years, those of teaching, did he have the requisite leisure for writing the books he had long planned. Similarly Walter White has devoted most of his energies to the program of the Association.

Of the younger authors, Countee Cullen is now teaching; Zora Hurston has done secretarial work and has lectured and taught; and Langston Hughes has relied upon grants, prizes, and patronage, in addition to his royalties. Rudolph Fisher wrote books in the few off-hours possible to the medical practitioner. George Schuyler and Frank Marshall Davis are practising journalists; Jessie Fauset, Arna Bontemps, and Waters Turpin are teachers.

Now, of course, the economically hard way is not segregated, is not marked "For Negroes Only." Authorship in America, and perhaps almost everywhere in the world, is a risky business, with great rewards for the fortunate few, and little or no rewards for the many. The *Partisan Review* recently sent out a questionnaire to several fairly well-known writers. One of the questions reads:[2]

> Have you found it possible to make a living by writing the sort of thing you want to and without the aid of such crutches as teaching and editorial work? Do you think there is any place in our present economic system for literature as a profession?

Sherwood Anderson, certainly one of the most influential writers of our time, whose *Winesburg, Ohio, Poor White, Tar, A Story-Teller's Story*, and *Dark Laughter* sold sufficiently well to warrant being included in many reprint series, and whose *I Want to Know Why* and *I'm a Fool* seem to be the keystones of anthologies of the modern short story, answered:[3]

> It seems to me that the answer to this depends upon what you mean by making a living. I have had to do all sorts of things to keep going but believe also that men working seriously in any of the arts have always had a hard time making a living. Now that I have been writing for twenty or twenty-five years enough does usually trickle in to keep me going. It has, however, been a long, hard pull.

The poet, Louise Bogan, now on the staff of the *New Yorker*, answers that she has not made a living by writing poetry and that "it has never entered my mind that I could do so ... The place in our present American set-up for the honest and detached professional writer is both small and cold." Lionel Trilling states that he never tried to make a living out of writing, which he considers next to impossible. His further remarks, which may not seem quite so pertinent to this paper, I shall quote for their pertinence to our general purpose: [4]

> I should like to say ... that I have found teaching something more than a "crutch." Perhaps I have been exceptionally lucky, but I have found it not only a pleasant but exciting and instructive kind

of work despite its bad reputation. For criticism, at any rate, it seems invaluable to have to deal, on the one hand, with freshmen who are relatively intelligent but either ignorant of literature, or naive about it or even inimical to it, for it forcibly reminds the critic how small a part literature plays in our world and it makes him bring his assumptions out of their professional cave; then, on the other hand, it is very salutary to have to face talented seniors who will give one no quarter; and the subject matter, the most interesting work of the past, is always a refreshment.

Trilling considers the problems of literary economics to be "too complex to be written about briefly." He thinks that literature will aways be, in one sense:

> ... a most competitive profession ... always forced to face social resistance. Any artist in the degree that he is notable must always be making minor revolutions or supporting them, revolutions in taste and feeling. He is therefore always going to be rejected and resisted both by some part of his profession and by some part of society. No doubt this entails a certain amount of social waste.[5]

Concerning the WPA Writers' Project or "some more rational and thorough-going alternative," he writes: "It is hard to imagine a condition in which, as someone said, the state will pay the piper and the piper will call his own tune."

Robert Fitzgerald, poet and translator, answers the double question succinctly, "No. Yes, obviously." Horance Gregory, certainly one of the best of contemporary poets, has not made his living from writing and sees as alternative only

> ... a system of patronage, whether from individuals or grants or funds or publishers.... It depends upon the character or moral strength of the writer as to whether or not either alternative (patronage or earning one's living) becomes dishonourable.[6]

The critic R.P. Blackburn knows of no writers, except a few successful novelists, and no painters or composers or sculptors who have earned their living by creating what they prefer to create. They have all had to engage in journalism, lecturing, teaching, and editorial work. He blames "part of the rub" on the weakness of the individual.[7]

The average man who thinks of himself as a writer wants to live like his betters in money, and so far thinks he ought to that he deserts his own profession for theirs; that is the great reason why the average writer does not count much as a writer. The bumbs of the literary world, who do no work at all, seem to me better examples of the profession than that.... (The economic system) gives a place to the writer exactly as precarious as to the lobster-fisherman, and with less investment, or any man of odd jobs. I do not mean that I think this situation laudable or comfortable; I mean that the writer who has talent and a little recognition has a pretty good chance of getting along as well as the lobster-man with only a few odd jobs thrown in. The writer with talent or without recognition has no chance at all.

Thus it is that writers of our times bear added witness to a story familiar to students of American literature, or for that matter, of any modern literature; the story of Poe, harassed by economic as well as other griefs, dying in a Baltimore alley; of Hawthorne in his countinghouse; of Melville dying comparatively unknown, unappreciated, and poor; of Stephen Crane, dependent on the largesse of English friends; of Edwin Arlington Robinson saved by Theodore Roosevelt and others from a life of want edging over into vagrancy; of Vachel Lindsay, trading songs for bread. Ring Lardner expended much valuable creative energy as a sports journalist. Theodore Dreiser edited women's magazines for an audience that would probably have repudiated his *Sister Carrie* and *Jennie Gerhardt*. Carl Sandburg, after the great successes of the past few years, is back in harness as a newspaperman, according to report. Perhaps (and we hope and believe it) he is now well fixed for life, and is merely drawn back to a calling he loves. But there is a chance that even a best-seller in biography and poetry can use more money.

Against such examples, of course, can be set those writers who by merit, by high pressure advertisement, or by both, enter the ranks of the best-sellers. One such aid to a large prospective audience is afforded by the several book-of-the-month clubs. Such authors of distinction as Ernest Hemingway and Ellen Glasgow, selling well in the ordinary course of events, have prospered from having works chosen by these clubs. There is a large group of novelists—Edna Ferber, Booth Tarkington, Fannie Hurst, Kathleen Norris, Octavus Roy Cohen among them—who are steadily best or at least better selling novelists. But the real money comes from the drugstore trade where novels of the purple sage or of purple passion continue the tradition of the blood and tears romance dear to America, and from the newsstand where the Shadow hovers and the Lone Ranger does not ride alone over the pulpwoods.

Some American writers, upon all levels of sincerity and skill, do well financially. But the majority have their troubles with the wolf at the door. Is the difference between the economic returns of Negro authors and white authors merely quantitative, then? That is: since we have so few writers (let us say fifty who are producing books), if one out of those fifty does well (and Richard Wright must be doing well), is that not the same percentage as one hundred white authors out of five thousand? Is the Negro author, therefore, in no worse plight than his fellow white author?

Such statistical discussion is not especially pertinent here. Even though so many white authors find difficulty in making a living from writing, Negro authors are even more handicapped. The chief of these besetting factors, it goes without saying, is the factor of race prejudice.

In *Breaking Into Print*, Chesnutt wrote that *The House Behind The Cedars*, the first novel he submitted to his publishers, was rejected with the softening suggestion that

> ... perhaps a collection of the conjure stories might be undertaken by the firm with a better prospect of success. I was in the hands of my friends, and submitted the collection. After some omissions and additions, all at the advice of Mr. Page, the book was accepted and announced.[8]

There is a great deal, it seems, between those lines. Let us remember that the Mr. Page mentioned was Walter Hines Page, a Southern liberal—almost the antithesis to Thomas Nelson Page, and that his publishing associates were of staunch Yankee stock. But this was the era of compromise. Bringing out a book by a Negro, now that the anti-slavery struggle was happily over, did seem to call for the courage of pioneers. Pioneers need caution, also, if they are to stay alive. Chesnutt wrote interestingly:[9]

> At that time a literary work by an American of acknowledged color was a doubtful experiment, both for the writer and for the publisher, entirely apart from its intrinsic merit. Indeed, my race was never mentioned by the publishers in announcing or advertising the book ... (one critic) learned of my race and requested leave to mention it as a matter of interest to the literary public. Mr. Page demurred at first on the ground that such an

announcement might be harmful to the success of my forthcoming book, but finally consented. ...

Chesnutt contrasted the changed conditions from the time of his first book to the time of his reminiscences (he wrote these a decade ago): [10]

> Negro writers no longer have any difficulty in finding publishers. Their race is no longer a detriment but a good selling point, and publishers are seeking their books, sometimes, I am inclined to think, with less regard for quality than in the case of white writers.

Writing of the present, and acquainted with publishing conditions of the time of which the above was written, Langston Hughes differs from Chesnutt. The following quotation is taken from *Fighting Words*, an account of the proceedings of the third Congress of the League of American Writers: [11]

> Here are our problems: In the first place, Negro books are considered by editors and publishers as exotic. Negro material is placed, like Chinese material or Bali material or East Indian material into a certain classification. Magazine editors will tell you, "We can use but so many Negro stories a year." (That "so many" meaning very few.) Publishers will say, "We already have one Negro novel on our list this fall."

The market for Negro writers, then, is definitely limited as long as we write about ourselves. And the more truthfully we write about ourselves, the more limited our market becomes. Those novels about Negroes that sell best, by Negroes or whites, those novels that make the best-seller lists and receive the leading prizes, are almost always books that touch very lightly upon the facts of Negro life, books that make our black ghettos in the big cities seem very happy places indeed, and our plantations in the deep south idyllic in their pastoral loveliness.... When we cease to be exotic, we do not sell well.

I know, of course, that very few writers of my race make a living directly from their writing.... But a great many American writers—who are not Negroes—may make a living in fields more or less connected with writing.... Whether their books are good or bad, they may work in editorial offices, on publishers' staffs, in publicity firms, in radio, or in motion pictures. Practically never is such employment granted to a Negro writer though he be as famous as the late James Weldon Johnson or as excellent a craftsman as the living Richard Wright. Perhaps an occasional prize or a fellowship may come a Negro writer's way—but not a job. It is very hard for a Negro to become a professional writer. Magazine offices, daily newspapers, publishers' offices are as tightly closed to us in America as if we were pure non-Aryans in Berlin.

This is the best statement of the economic problems facing the Negro writer. Remembering his own hardships and impatient with the Harlem school of fiction, Chesnutt had overstated the easy lot of contemporary Negro writers.

Opposition to honest treatment of Negro life in literature is certain and it is strong. In other fields it exists quite much. The anecdote of the Broadway entrepreneur, though exaggerated a bit, is in order here. Reading a play of the grim experiences of a sharecropper's family, he demanded the insertion of "hot spots," so the chorus girls could swing into their numbers— he had some silk bandannas and sateen overalls (shortened of course) in the stock room. Reviewing the National Urban League Radio Program, *Time Magazine* has this to say:

> (Negroes) are welcome on sustaining shows and in bit parts on
> sponsored programs. But no advertiser will buck racial prejudice
> to back a colored show or let a Negro star shine too brightly.

Of course, social protest, even about Negro experience, can sell widely, as the phenomenal and deserved success of Richard Wright's *Native Son* demonstrates. In the wake of this economic success, Wright's *Uncle Tom's Children* has been brought out in an enlarged edition, with much new material that has greater drive than even the first strong stories. Wright is a craftsman who can tell a story with the best of them today; he can reach and hold an audience. He is a publisher's find, and these do not turn up every year. Whatever he has to say, and he has a great deal, will find publishers ready for it. It remains true, however, that if a publisher is going to publish unpopular views on Negro life, and many others did this before Harpers brought out *Native Son*, he would prefer to risk his money on a book that he thinks will sell, on a novel, for instance, rather than on short stories, or essays, or poetry.

One of our leading critics used to characterize the New Negro movement as the time when "every publisher wanted a Negro book." This was peeved exaggeration. A few new and liberal publishers were genuinely interested in Negro expression; a few attempted to create and/or cash in on a fad; but when all was said and done, comparatively few books on the Negro were published. The New Negro movement has been overpraised, but it has been unduly blamed as well. One important thing that it did, even though incompletely, was to open publishers' doors to Negro authors. If a Negro enters a publisher's waiting room today, he does not have to be considered a delivery boy.

Lord Byron called his publisher Barabbas. But other names suit other publishers better; no single name can comprise the class. Publishers range from right to left, from conservative to experimental, from narrow to tolerant, from Barabbas to Saint Francis of Assisi. One cannot and should not want to indict the whole publishing fraternity; the only constant seems to be that publishers are business men who must make money to survive.

As a case in point, the Modern Age Publishers, definitely a liberal, democratic house, producing books to sell for a low price to a wide audience, do not have on their list, to my knowledge, a book by a Negro author or one treating Negro life in America in any fullness. What is the reason? Probably that no Negro has submitted a book to them. And favorable or not to the cause of the Negro in America, they must be more favorable to this: to a writer's technical ability to produce a work that will sell in huge lots.

Regardless of racial tolerance, publishers must ask, in self preservation, the size of the Negro reading public, necessarily one of the chief markets for books by Negroes. One of the few generalizations about American Negroes that are hard to disprove is this one: "Negroes just do not buy books." Race defenders may hasten forth with the rejoinder "Why should they? Why should poor people, needing their money for necessities such as bread and shoes, rent and coal, pay from two dollars to five dollars for a book?" The argument has point, of course. Nevertheless, even among the Negro middle class, only a small proportion buy books.

We should expect the potential Negro book-buying audience to come largely from the ranks of the college graduates. In the hundred years between 1826 and 1936 there were, according to Charles S. Johnson, only 43,821 college graduates, of whom 18,918 are living. Three thousand more graduates could be expected in 1940, according to this authority. It is worth pointing out that if every one of these college graduates were to buy one copy of a book by a Negro, the total number would not equal one twentieth of the sale of such popular fiction as *Anthony Adverse* and *Gone With The Wind*. But there is no need to talk of impossibilities. The number of Negroes buying books in the field of their special interest is certainly not high. The number of those who buy books about Negro life by Negro authors is certainly low.

With a small proportion of a small middle class able to afford books, a smaller proportion of readers, and a smaller proportion still of book-buyers, the likelihood of a Negro audience for books by Negro authors is not promising. Even this potential audience is less than it might be. There is on the part of many a dislike for books about Negroes and books by Negroes. Some of this is based upon an understandable desire to escape the perplexities and pressures of the race situation in America. Some of it is based upon the ineptitude of immature authors dealing with difficult subject matter. Quite as much is based upon a caste-ridden disdain of Negro life and character, and anguish at being identified with an ignorant and exploited people to whom many "upper class" Negroes are completely unsympathetic. "I don't intend to paint Negroes," said a young artist of my acquaintance; "I intend to paint human beings." He meant by human beings white people of the middle class. Many young student writers seem to believe that when they create "raceless" individuals they touch upon "universality."

More than once the assertion has been made that our writers are not American writers, but "Negro" writers. I cannot agree with either the assertion or its implications. I do not see why Dunbar when he deals with Negro farmers on the Eastern Shore is less American than is James Whitcomb Riley when dealing with Hoosier farmers, or Mike Gold when dealing with Jews on the East Side, or James Farrell when dealing with Irish boys in Chicago. To say that Dunbar is not a great American poet is another thing. But he is as American as any other, unless our criteria are those of the Klan.

Charges are levelled against many of our authors of "selling the race down the river." This is an easy charge, generally raised when our authors write something we may not happen to like. The use of dialect and of characters from the lower economic levels, for instance, causes some critics to cry treason. The sounder way of criticism, it seems, would be to approach the product and evaluate it, not to attribute motives too easily. If the author has sold out, the untruthfulness of the work will be obvious; and it is the critic's job to point out that untruthfulness. Many of our critics, however, still condemn without reading, because they do not approve the way of life portrayed. Yet they might hesitate to say that Erskine Caldwell and John Steinbeck have not sold out their crackers and Oakies just because they present unflattering pictures of them.

The American publisher does not yet believe in the Negro market. As a case in point, let us look at *The Negro In Virginia*. Receiving uniformly favorable reviews, considered by many to be one of the best products of the Federal Writers' Project, a good job of social history for the general reader on a subject little known about, told by Negroes with accuracy and warmth, well printed and illustrated, *The Negro In Virginia* has not yet sold a thousand copies. Those who would cavalierly dismiss it as another Writers' Project book are ignorant of the real achievement of the Project as attested by all of the leading cultural journals of the country.

As the Negro author matures, learning to be publishable and interesting as well as honest and informative, I believe that he will be accepted, and will help to build his own audience. Should he write propaganda? If by propaganda is meant the self-pity and self-justication of adolescents, the question answers itself. If by propaganda is meant the revealing of the exploitation, oppression and ignominy, the struggle and the dream, and that is what many do mean by the word, I should answer yes. But I consider the author's task to be the revelation of what he believes, after long thought, to be the truth; and the truth of Negro experience in America is strong enough propaganda for anyone. The complete picture will not be one of unalloyed tragedy. To present counter-stereotypes of villainous whites and victimized Negroes is a temptation, but it is not worthy of our best creative and interpretative powers. One favored belief, for instance, is that Negro laughter is always "laughin' jes' to keep from cryin.'" That type of laughter does exist in abundance. But I have heard laughter that is just laughter, high spirited enjoyment of living, and not always—or mainly, among the lucky few, but rather among the harassed many. Truth to Negro experience must consider the Negro's ability to take it, to endure, and to wring out of life something of joy.

One aspect of the Negro and his publisher and audience that must be noticed is the work of Negro publishers. Preeminent among these is the fine achievement of Carter G. Woodson, who, probably more than any other single figure, has encouraged a Negro audience to buy books by Negroes about Negro life and history. He is running our most successful Negro publishing concern. He deserves our staunch support. Other ventures are the Wendell Malliet Company and the Negro Publication Society, both of New York City. Aiming to publish books within the purchasing power of a poor people and to develop an audience, these Negro enterprises are highly commendable.

But the Negro must also work within the present publishing framework. If prejudice does exist, denying complete and honest treatment of Negro life and character, and of course it does, the individual Negro writer must act as far as possible as if the prejudice did not exist. He cannot afford to fall into what is so often the bane of Negro achievement, i.e., self pity: the "if only I had been white," the "ain't it hard to be an Ethiopian," "the world's against me because I am a Negro." The way of the artist is long and arduous; he has a hard enough task to learn his craft, to learn to report, to understand, to communicate, to interpret. The Negro artist especially cannot afford the enervating luxury of seeking excuses for not achieving what he fears he may not be able to achieve. If he is worth his salt, he is trying to enter a company of men who have struggled against odds to create work of integrity. The job ahead of the Negro author is challenging. It is the job of developing a critical but interested reading public. To have great poets, says Whitman, we must have great audiences, too.

NOTES

1. Elmer Adler, *Breaking Into Print.* New York: Simon and Schuster. 1927. p. 48.

2. "The Situation in American Writing," *Partisan Review*, Vol. VI, No. 5, p. 103.

3. *Ibid.*, p. 106.

4. *Ibid.*, p. 111.

5. "The Situation in American Writing." Partisan Review, Vol. VI, No. 5, p. 112.

6. *Ibid.*, p. 122.

7. *Ibid.*, p. 119.

8. Adler, op. cit., p. 52.

9. *Ibid.*, p. 54.

10. *Ibid.*, p. 56.

11. Donald Ogden Stewart, Fighting Words. New York: Harcourt, Brace & Co. (1940), pp. 58ff.

CHERYL A. WALL

Aspects of Identity
in Nella Larsen's Novels

At the height of the Harlem Renaissance, Nella Larsen published two novels, *Quicksand* (1928) and *Passing* (1929). They were widely and favorably reviewed. Applauded by the critics, Larsen was heralded as a rising star in the black artistic firmament. In 1930 she became the first Afro-American woman to receive a Guggenheim Fellowship for Creative Writing. Her star then faded as quickly as it had risen, and by 1934 Nella Larsen had disappeared from Harlem and from literature.[1] The novels she left behind prove that at least some of her promise was realized. Among the best written of the time, her books comment incisively on issues of marginality and cultural dualism that engaged Larsen's contemporaries, such as Jean Toomer and Claude McKay, but the bourgeois ethos of her novels has unfortunately obscured the similarities. However, Larsen's most striking insights are into psychic dilemmas confronting certain black women. To dramatize these, Larsen draws characters who are, by virtue of their appearance, education, and social class, atypical in the extreme. Swiftly viewed, they resemble the tragic mulattoes of literary convention. On closer examination, they become the means through which the author demonstrates the psychological costs of racism and sexism.

For Larsen, the tragic mulatto was the only formulation historically available to portray educated middle-class black women in fiction.[2] But her protagonists subvert the convention consistently. They are neither noble nor

From *Analysis and Assessment*, 1980–1994. © 1996 by Cary D. Wintz.

long-suffering; their plights are not used to symbolize the oppression of blacks, the irrationality of prejudice, or the absurdity of concepts of race generally. Larsen's deviations from these traditional strategies signal that her concerns lie elsewhere, but only in the past decade have critics begun to decode her major themes. Both *Quicksand* and *Passing* contemplate the inextricability of the racism and sexism which confront the black woman in her quest for a wholly integrated identity. As they navigate between racial and cultural polarities, Larsen's protagonists attempt to fashion a sense of self free of both suffocating restrictions of ladyhood and fantasies of the exotic female Other. They fail. The tragedy for these mulattoes is the impossibility of self-definition. Larsen's protagonists assume false identities that ensure social survival but result in psychological suicide. In one way or another, they all "pass." Passing for white, Larsen's novels remind us, is only one way this game is played.

Helga Crane, the protagonist of *Quicksand*, never considers racial passing, but she is keenly aware of playing a false role. Her inability to assume it comfortably leads her to ponder her "difference." As the novel opens, Helga is teaching at Naxos, a Southern black college where she is doomed to be an outsider, unable to conform or to be happy in her nonconformity. Initially, the self-righteous, stultifying atmosphere of the school seems to be at fault. Clearly modeled on Tuskegee Institute where Larsen herself was once employed, Naxos tolerates neither innovation nor individualism. Moreover, the institution, for all its rhetoric of race consciousness and race pride, seems intent on stamping out in its students those qualities which Helga characterizes as racial. On reflection, however, Helga realizes that her problems go deeper than conditions at Naxos. She understands that her battles with school authorities and snobbish co-workers are symptomatic of her personal struggle to define herself.

Helga recognizes that, superficially, her more sophisticated taste in clothing and furnishings sets her apart at Naxos and conditions the way in which others respond to her. For example, when she mentions resigning, a colleague urges her to stay because "'we need a few decorations to brighten our sad lives'" (43). The darkskinned young woman making this statement reveals not only a negative self-image, but the expectation that light-skinned "pretty" women like Helga should assume an ornamental role. Helga's interracial parentage—her father is black and her mother white—troubles her too, but it is not the primary cause of her unease. Her real struggle is against imposed definitions of blackness and womanhood. Her "difference" is ultimately her refusal to accept society's terms even in the face of her inability to define alternatives.

In the class-conscious community of Naxos, however, her heritage is a practical liability, and Helga is concerned lest it jeopardize her engagement to James Vayle, the son of prominent black Atlantans. Vayle, whose name evokes the "veil" of Du Bois's famous metaphor, lives shrouded by the narrow, petty ideas of the college; his only ambition is to rise within its ranks. He is as impatient with Helga's inability to win the acceptance of their peers as she is contemptuous of his self-satisfaction. She analyzes their relationship thus: "She was, she knew, in a queer indefinite way, a disturbing factor. She knew too that something held him, something against which he was powerless. The idea that she was in but one nameless way necessary to him filled her with a sensation amounting almost to shame. And yet his mute helplessness against that ancient appeal by which she held him pleased her and fed her vanity—gave her a feeling of power" (34). Here is an incipient realization that sexuality is political; it is "power." But Helga mistakenly assumes it is hers to wield. Actually she is trapped by the need to repress her sexuality, to assume the ornamental, acquiescent role of "lady," which not only Vayle but the entire Naxos community expects. Her reflection that "to relinquish James Vayle would most certainly be social suicide ... " is followed by a scene in Helga's rather ornately furnished room in which "faintness closed about her like a vise" (35). Revealingly, the words which force Helga's actual departure are not spoken by Vayle, but by the "apparently humane and understanding" administrator, Robert Anderson, who argues that she is needed there because she is "a lady."[3]

The next important setting of the novel is Harlem, where, in happy contrast to Naxos, Helga Crane meets people who share her tastes and ideas. "Their sophisticated cynical talk, their elaborate parties, the unobtrusive correctness of their clothes and homes, all appealed to her craving for smartness, for enjoyment" (84-85). Better yet, they are extremely scornful of institutions like Naxos, and Helga feels her own actions have been vindicated. Even Robert Anderson has traded Naxos for New York. Then there is the "continuously gorgeous panorama of Harlem," which to Helga is so fascinating that she rarely finds occasion to venture to other areas of the city. In short, she feels a sense of freedom in Harlem, she is accepted there, and she chooses not to risk the rejection of the white world. Besides, she is convinced that Harlem offers a complete, self-contained life. "And she was satisfied, unenvious. For her this Harlem was enough" (87).

Of course, Larsen's point is that Harlem is not enough. Life there is "too cramped, too uncertain, too cruel" (163). Shallow and provincial, Helga's Harlemites are possessed of a race consciousness at once consuming and superficial, proud and ineffectual. They immerse themselves in the race problem, scanning newspapers to tabulate every injustice against the race, yet they keep their distance from the suffering masses. Indeed, though they proclaim their love of blackness, they imitate the values and ways of white folks down to the smallest detail. They dislike Afro-American songs and dances, the rhythms of black speech, and "like the despised people of the white race, ... preferred Pavlova to Florence Mills, John McCormack to Taylor Gordon, Walter Hampden to Paul Robeson" (92). Floundering in this maze of contradictions, these New Negroes are unable to confront themselves and their situation honestly.

The peculiar demands of the Jazz Age further complicated matters for the Harlem bourgeoisie. As more and more white New Yorkers, like Americans generally, were drawn to black Culture—or at least what they believed to be black culture—, the New Negroes felt compelled to increase their own identification with their traditions. Unfortunately, they were often as ignorant of these traditions as anyone else and embraced the popular imitations instead. Larsen uses a nightclub scene, an almost obligatory feature in Harlem novels, to examine the packaging of manufactured blackness:

> For the while, Helga was oblivious of the reek of flesh, smoke, and alcohol, oblivious of the oblivion of other gyrating pairs, oblivious of the color, the noise, and the grand distorted childishness of it all. She was drugged, lifted, sustained by the extraordinary music, blown out, ripped out, beaten out, by the joyous, wild, murky orchestra. The essence of life seemed bodily motion. And when suddenly the music died, she dragged herself back to the present with a conscious effort; and a shameful certainty that not only had she been in the jungle, but that she had enjoyed it, began to taunt her. She hardened her determination to get away. She wasn't, she told herself, a jungle creature. (107–08)

Of course Helga is correct about not being a jungle creature, but then neither are any of the club's other patrons. This image was nonetheless foisted on blacks as Harlem barrooms were refurbished to resemble African jungles, and as bands, even the best ones, like that of Duke Ellington, began advertising the latest in "jungle music." It all made Harlem a more exotic tourist attraction while it increased the confusion of some local residents. In Larsen's interpretation, the ersatz culture marketed to blacks as their own was clearly insufficient. It borrowed enough of the authentic traditions to retain some power, but it existed dysfunctionally in a vacuum. The reference to the "grand distorted childishness of it all" applies to the spectacle of these urbane, middle-class New Yorkers attempting to find their cultural roots in the basement of a Harlem speakeasy. For Helga, the artifice is repelling.[4]

Both Vayle and Anderson reappear in the Harlem sequences of the novel, thereby demonstrating that the expectations for women remain the same there. Helga's meeting with Vayle confirms the wisdom of her decision to reject him, social suicide being preferable to spiritual death. For his part, he wants to resume the engagement and tries to impress upon Helga her obligation as a member of the Talented Tenth to marry and have children. "Don't you see that if we—I mean people like us—don't have children, the others will still have. That's one of the things that's the matter with us. The race is sterile at the top'" (173). This is a responsibility Helga neither recognizes nor accepts, and she is happy to leave Vayle to Naxos. Robert Anderson is another matter, however. On seeing him again, she becomes aware of a strong and mutual sexual attraction. Taught too well to repress any sexual feelings, she denies them. Anderson's behavior is equally circumspect.

Larsen introduces a minor character named Audrey Denney to highlight the psychic cost of Helga's self-denial. Audrey is glamorous and bold, ignoring the outraged reactions her appearance and behavior elicit from respectable Harlemites like Anne Grey, the wealthy young widow with whom Helga lives. Most objectionable is her refusal to limit her socializing to Harlem; Audrey has white friends and possibly white lovers. However disreputable her character, she is the object of eager attention from black men as well. In the nightclub scene Robert Anderson joins her circle of admirers. When he does, Helga's envious approbation gives way to jealousy. Larsen concludes the scene with well-placed references to asphyxiation, as her heroine escapes the smoke-filled cabaret for the brisk night air.

Helga is emerging too from the restricting definitions of ladyhood so accepted in the middle-class black world. She does not consider chastity the supreme virtue the women at Naxos insist it to be, though she notes that, as "sophisticated" as Anne Grey is, she has preferred a passionless marriage. Helga is also aware of the energy black women waste trying to conform to a white standard of beauty. Straightened hair, she reflects, does not beautify, though as her own is naturally straight, she cannot voice this opinion. Ever conscious of clothes, she resents the prohibition of bright colors by those who want it understood that black women do not love red. She does. She further seeks the adventure that color usually symbolizes. That is what makes Audrey Denney so appealing to her. Audrey is unencumbered by the norms that define Negro ladies. Having white friends is the least of her daring.

More to the point, Audrey has declaimed to play the husband-hunting game. She need not marry to find someone to pay for all those tasteful, elegant things with which real ladies surround themselves.

Eventually, Harlem becomes as oppressive an environment as Naxos. The constant, superficial race consciousness seems to demand that Helga deny a part of herself, and when a white uncle gives her five thousand dollars she uses his conscience money to escape to Copenhagen. Denmark promises "no Negroes, no problems, no prejudice" (103), though Helga is slightly wary of the reception she will receive from relatives there. Her fears prove unfounded, her well-to-do aunt and uncle welcome her warmly, but the kind reception is proffered with an eye to the role the young woman can play in advancing the couple's social fortunes. Immediately, they inform Helga that she should capitalize on her "difference." She should wear "'striking things, exotic things'" (120) so she will make an impression. They are more than happy to supply the necessary wardrobe. Though she recognizes their motives and resents being a decoration, a curio with which her relatives hope to capture the notice of influential people, Helga enjoys, as always, the expensive clothes, the physical freedom, and the fact that her dark skin, so despised in America, makes her the sourse of endless fascination to the Danes. Forced to discover and parade her own beauty, she feels new confidence and self-acceptance.

Her satisfaction does not last. Not only does she tire of being continuously exhibited, but she finds that she is much more race conscious than she had realized. One telling incident occurs at a theater, where a minstrel act featuring two black Americans upsets her greatly. By turns moved and embarrassed by their "stage Negro" antics, she is infuriated by the audience's gleeful response to the performance. Without fully understanding why, she returns to the vaudeville house again and again. The reason is clear to the reader who sees the extent to which Helga has become a "stage Negro" herself. After this experience, her thoughts of America are filled with outrage at the way blacks are abused; in fact, she never thinks of the United States except in relation to race.

In Copenhagen, no one requires that Helga be a lady; instead she is made into an exotic female Other—symbol of the unconscious, the unknowable, the erotic, and the passive.[5] Although her aunt and uncle are among those who conspire to this end, by dressing her in batik dresses, leopard-skin coats, and glittering jewelery, it is Axel Olsen who most fervently wants to recreate her. Olsen is a fashionable portrait painter and an odd man, given to overwrought, theatrical gestures. It is he who demonstrates most sharply the confluence of racism and sexism, in both the way he paints Helga and the way he courts her. In their first meeting he examines the specimen before him and pronounces her "'amazing'" and "'marvelous'"; her smile becomes a "mask" as he announces his findings to his audience (125). Larsen borrows vocabulary from anthropology throughout the Copenhagen section, but never to greater effect than when Olsen is present. Helga's role, as she realizes, is to be exhibited, to "incite" a voluptuous impression in sedate Danish drawing rooms. Soon she finds herself enjoying "the fascinating business of being seen, gaped at, desired" (130). When she sees the resulting impression reproduced on Olsen's canvas, she disowns the image. "It wasn't, she contended, herself at all, but some disgusting sensual creature with her features" (152). Olsen is, of course, sure that he has captured the essential Helga; but although he has discerned the sensuality she had concealed in America, his portrait is not the mirror of Helga's soul he believes it to be. He has confused the image and the woman. He is so in love with her image that, after Helga ignores his insinuations that they have an affair, he proposes marriage. He is mystified by her refusal.

Critic Hortense Thornton has suggested that because Helga stresses their racial differences in her rejection of Olsen, perhaps "her acknowledgment of race is used as a mask for her sexual repression" (299). In my view, this scene more than any other shows how inextricably bound sexual and racial identity are. Olsen follows his marraige proposal with a frank admission that he would have preferred that she be his mistress. At that point she protests, "' ... in my country the men, of my race at least, don't make such suggestions to decent girls'" (148). Olsen cannot hear her objection. He rants instead about her "'deliberate lure,'" and declares that for him marrying her will be "'an experience.'" And finally, he sums up her character:

> "You know, Helga, you are a contradiction. You have been, I suspect, corrupted by the good Fru Dahl, which is perhaps as well. Who knows? You have the warm impulsive nature of the woman of Africa, but, my lovely, you have, I fear, the soul of a prostitute. You sell yourself to the highest buyer. I should of course be happy that it is I. And I am." (149)

Only the spell of racial mythology could lead a man to mistake such insults for gallantry. Olsen knows nothing of African women, but that does not shake his belief in their exotic primitivism. Black women, he feels, are completely sentient, sexual beings. Helga Crane should confirm that belief. When she does not, it proves she has been contaminated by the West, has suffered the primordial female corruption. Yet even so damaged, she is the closest approximation of the exotic female Other he is likely to find. He is willing to settle.

Olsen makes explicit the connection between prostitution and marriage Larsen had earlier implied in the scene with Audrey Denney and in Helga's musings about marriage as a means to acquire things. His words evoke a declaration of independence from Helga which is echoed in any number of current novels. "'But you see, Herr Olsen, I'm not for sale. Not to you. Not to any white man. I don't care at all to be owned'" (150). Shortly after this confrontation, Helga leaves Denmark. Olsen's accusations linger, however, and influence her behavior upon her return to Harlem. Determined not to sell herself, she gives herself away.

Unwilling to repress her sexuality any longer, she misconstrues Robert Anderson's intentions when he drunkenly kisses her. She is ready to have an affair, but Anderson, now married to Anne Grey, declines. Helga's subsequent turmoil is marked by an increasing number of asphyxiation metaphors. Nella Larsen, like many women writers, found rooms to be appropriate symbols of female confinement and frustration.[6] She uses Helga's room in Naxos, a Chicago subway car, and a Harlem cabaret among other examples. With the narrowing of choices available to Helga, such references redouble and intensify. A Harlem church becomes, for example, a kind of transcendent women's room. In its heightened emotional atmosphere, the predominantly female congregation purges itself of discontent and despair. The church sisters attend Helga until she too achieves a temporary catharsis. As drawn by Larsen, this scene resembles that of the cabaret, except this time Helga has lost the ability to be critical. Despite some badly overwritten and patronizing description of the service, the scene as a whole is credible.

The calm that descends upon the restless Helga and the promise of serenity bulwarked by faith presents an alternative to the materially rich but spiritually impoverished life she has led in Harlem and Copenhagen; it seems to offer a resolution. This resolution, more accurately a retreat, is personified by the aptly named Reverend Pleasant Green, whom she hurriedly marries. In rural Alabama Rev. Green's female parishioners assume the role played by the women in the Harlem mission. But their ministrations cannot sustain her neither can the sexual release she finds in marriage. Reality is too harsh, and the confinement of the birthing room is inescapable. Her five children tie her permanently to a life she loathes.[7]

Helga has fought against the white world's definition of a Negro knowing she is neither exotic nor primitive, neither "savage" no sharecropper. At the same time she has resisted male definitions of her womanhood. Having no foundation on which to base one Helga never achieves true self-definition. If her quest ends in defeat her struggle is nonetheless admirable. Larsen's depiction of a memorable protagonist, her adept narration, and her skillful development of the central metaphor expressed by the novel's title have all won praise. Most critics agree that *Quicksand* is one of the best novels of the Harlem Renaissance.

Response to Larsen's second novel, *Passing*, has been less favorable. From one perspective, critics argue that *Passing* fails to exploit fully the drama of racial passing and declines instead into a treatment of sexual jealousy. If, from another perspective, the novel is the best treatment of its subject in Afro-American literature then the topic of blacks passing for white is dated and trivial.[8] In Larsen's novel, however, "passing" does not refer only to the sociological phenomenon of blacks crossing the color line. It represents instead both the loss of racial identity and the denial of self required of women who conform to restrictive gender roles. Like "quicksand," "passing" is a metaphor of death and desperation, and both central metaphors are supported by images of asphyxiation, suffocation, and claustrophobia. Unlike "quicksand," "passing" provokes definite associations and expectations that Larsen is finally unable to transcend. Looking beyond these associations, one sees that *Passing* explores the same themes as its predecessor. Though less fully developed than Helga Crane, the main characters of this novel likewise demonstrate the price black women pay for their acquiescence and, ultimately, the high cost of rebellion.

Two characters, Irene Redfield and Clare Kendry, dominate the novel: Both are attractive, affluent, and able to "pass." Irene identifies with blacks, choosing to "pass" only for occasional convenience, while Clare has moved completely into the white world. Each assumes a role Helga Crane rejects: Irene is the perfect lady, and Clare, the exotic Other. A chance meeting in the tearoom of an exclusive Chicago hotel, on an occasion when both women are "passing," introduces the action of the novel. Clare recognizes the childhood friend she has not seen in twelve years, and she is eager to renew the acquaintance. Irene, assured and complacent in her life as the wife of a Harlem physician, is more cautious. Reluctantly, she accepts Clare's invitation to tea, where they are joined by another school friend, Gertrude, who is married to a white man, and by Clare's husband Jack Bellew. Bellew proves to be a rabid racist, and Irene vows never to see Clare again. Two years later, her resolve is shaken. While visiting New York, and partly in response to her husband's bigotry, Clare longs for the company of blacks. She presents herself at Irene's home uninvited and, over Irene's objections, makes increasingly frequent jaunts to Harlem. Distressed by the unsettling effect produced by Clare's presence, Irene begins to suspect that Clare is having an affair with Dr. Red-field. But before Irene can act on her suspicions, Bellew follows Clare to Harlem and confirms his. Clare Kendry falls through a sixth-story window to her death.

Although her death is typical of the tragic mulatto's fate, the Clare Kendry character breaks the mold in every other respect.[9] Her motives for "passing" are ambiguous. Though she seeks the freedom to define herself, she also wants the material comforts the white world offers. As she explains, "' ... I was determined to get away, to be a person and not a charity or a problem, or even a daughter of the indiscreet Ham. Then, too, I wanted things. I knew I wasn't bad-looking and that I could "pass"' (56). The psychic rewards are few, but at first Clare is sure the money is worth its price. Bellew is an international banking agent, apparently as rich as Croesus, who indulges his wife's love of luxury. Clare can chat glibly of travels to pre-War Paris and post-War Budapest. She can also refer to herself as a "'deserter,'" yet Irene looks in vain for traces of pain, fear, or grief on her countenance. Even when Clare begins to doubt the wisdom of her choice, she claims no noble purpose, merely loneliness and a vague yearning for "'my own people.'" In fact, her trips to Harlem involve more pleasure-seeking than homecoming. At one point, she confesses to Irene: "'Why, to get the things I want badly enough, I'd do anything, hurt anybody, throw anything away. Really, 'Rene, I'm not safe'" (139). In drawing such an unsympathetic character, Larsen seems initially merely to flout the tragic-mulatto convention.

Rather than emphasize the pathos of the "passing" situation, Larsen stresses its attractive veneer. Clare Kendry always looks exquisite, whether wearing a "superlatively simple cinammon-brown frock" with a "little golden bowl of a hat" or a stately black taffeta gown. Clothes, furnishings, notepaper—all the accoutrements of Clare's life are painstakingly described. At times Larsen's intentions seem definitely satirical, as when on one occasion Clare chooses a dress whose shade not only suits her but sets off her hotel room's decor! But at other points Larsen seems to solicit the reader's admiration for the graceful, elegant Clare.

Annis Pratt's analysis of patterns in women's fiction offers a tenable explanation for such inconsistency: "It is as if the branch of women's fiction that deals most specifically with society were incapable of either fully rejecting it or fully accommodating to it, the result being the disjunction of narrative structure, ambivalence of tone, and inconclusive characterizations typical of this category" (168). *Passing* displays all of these features with its abrupt and unearned ending, its often arch and stilted dialogue, and the author's wavering response to her characters. To be sure, Larsen's own social world was mirrored in her novel, and she evidently found it difficult to reject it out of hand. Nevertheless, what seems at first an annoying preoccupation with "minutiae" (to borrow Hoyt Fuller's apt term [18]) becomes instead a statement on the condition of women in the book.

Clare's survival depends literally on her abiltity to keep up appearances. She must look like the white society matron she pretends to be. But her looks, clothes, and facile conversation are the envy of the other female characters. They too spend an inordinate amount of time shopping and preening. In their lives, maintaining the social niceties is an obligation, and pouring tea is, in the words of one, "'an occupation.'" Each of these characters, like Clare, relies on a husband for material possessions, security, identity. Each reflects and is a reflection of her husband's class status. Clare's is merely an extreme version of a situation all share.

An analysis of the Irene Redfield character supports this reading. The novel is told from her point of view, and she consistently calls attention to the differences between herself and Clare. More often than not, Nella Larsen minimizes these differences to great effect. For example, Irene craves stability and abhors the risks Clare thrives on; she is a devoted mother, whereas Clare professes little interest in the welfare of her daughter, and she prides herself on her loyalty to the race. However, Irene's world is barely more secure than that of her friend, and when it is threatened, she is every bit as dangerous. The parallels are established in the first encounter described above, when, because both are "passing," they are playing the same false role. Indeed it is Irene who fears detection; her alarmed, defensive reaction contrasts ironically with the cool demeanor assumed by Clare, whose only concern is recognizing an old friend. In the subsequent meeting with Bellew, Irene is horrified that Clare, whom he jokingly calls "Nig," tolerates her husband's bigotry; but Irene herself listens to his insults. She even imagines that "under other conditions" she could like the man. Her attempt to excuse her cowardice by claiming to have acted out of loyalty to race and to Clare as a member of the race is entirely specious. Although Irene does volunteer work for the "Negro Welfare League," the race is important to her only insofar as it gives the appearance of depth to a shallow life.

What Irene does value is her marriage, not out of any deep love for her husband Brian, but because it is her source of security and permanence. Much like Anne Grey's in *Quicksand*, the Redfields' marriage is passionless;

the couple sleep in separate bedrooms, and Brian argues that the sooner their children learn that sex is "'a grand joke,'" the better off they will be. The Redfields' life is one Irene has "arranged." She has dissuaded Brian from pursuing his dream of a new life in Brazil. She has spun a cocoon around her sons, forbidding discussion of racism and of sex as too disagreeable, and she plans someday to send the boys to European boarding schools (like the one Clare's daughter attends in Switzerland). Nothing is allowed to encroach upon the sanctuary of home and family.

When Clare enters this safe harbor, she upsets the order Irene cherishes. She visits unannounced, plays with the children, and chats with the servants. She poses other threats as well. Typically, Irene bolsters her self-image by defining herself in relation to her "inferiors": Her comments on women whose husbands are less successful than hers evidence this snobbery. When, for example, Gertrude expresses her anger at Bellew's racism—a deeper anger than Irene can muster—Irene dismisses her. After all, Gertrude looks like the butcher's wife she is; her feelings could not matter. Clare is too clearly Irene's equal, in many respects her superior, to be neutralized in this way. Compared to Clare, Irene feels at times "dowdy and commonplace" (128). Partly in self-defense and partly because Clare invites the role, Irene begins to view her friend as an exotic Other. Watching her, she has the sensation of "gazing into the eyes of some creature utterly strange and apart" (77). Then again, Clare's look was "unfathomable, utterly beyond any comprehension" of Irene's (85). Irene invents for Clare a complex inner life. But she is not responding to the person before her so much as to her own notions of Otherness. Clare's "Negro eyes" symbolize the unconscious, the unknowable, the erotic, and the passive. In other words, they symbolize those aspects of the psyche Irene denies within herself. Her confused sense of race becomes at last an evasion by which she avoids confronting her deepest feelings.

Clare's repeated assertions of her own dangerousness reinforce Irene's fears and allow her to objectify Clare completely. When her suspicions grow that Clare is interested in Brian, Clare becomes a menace she must eliminate; for without Brian, Irene believes she is nothing. Her opportunity comes during the confusion surrounding Bellew's unexpected appearance at a Harlem party. Although the evidence is all circumstantial, Larsen strongly implies that Irene pushes Clare through the window.[10] She is certainly capable of it, for by the end of the novel Irene is indeed Clare's double, willing to "'do anything, hurt anybody, throw anything away'" to get what she wants. A psychological suicide, if not a murderer, she too has played the game of "passing" and lost.

Passing, like *Quicksand,* demonstrates Larsen's ability to explore the psychology of her characters. She exposes the sham that is middle-class security, especially for women whose total dependence is morally debilitating. The absence of meaningful work and community condemn them to the "walled prison" of their own thoughts. In this cramped enclosure, neurosis and fantasy breed. She exposes as well the fears and self-contempt experienced by those, like Helga, who seek to escape the constrictions of middle-class life. Helga is an admirable character because she recognizes early on that "passing" is not worth the price. Her integrity earns her no victory; her rebellion is as ineffectual as the dishonorable Clare's. As these characters deviate from the norm, they are defined—indeed too often define themselves—as Other. They thereby cede control of their lives. But, in truth, the worlds these characters inhabit offer them no possibility of autonomy or fulfillment.

Nathan Huggins has observed that of the Harlem Renaissance writers "Nella Larsen came as close as any to treating human motivation with complexity and sophistication. But she could not wrestle free of the mulatto condition that her main characters had been given" (236). I would argue that Larsen achieves a good measure of complexity and sophistication, yet Huggins' point has merit, especially in regard to *Passing.* Much more than *Quicksand,* this novel adheres to the pattern: the victim caught forever betwixt and between until she finds in death the only freedom she can know. The inevitable melodrama weakens the credibility of the narrative and diverts attention from the author's real concerns. Still, the plot reveals something of the predicament of the middle-class black woman, and the book itself illuminates problems facing the black woman novelist.

Among the images of black women presented in fiction before the Harlem Renaissance, the tragic mulatto character was the least degrading and the most attractive, which partly explains its prominence in Jessie Fauset's novels and in those of her predecessors, dating back to Harriet Wilson and Frances Watkins Harper. Nella Larsen's personal history doubtless increased the character's appeal for her, as the reality behind the image was her own story. Besides, depicting the tragic mulatto was the surest way for a black woman fiction writer to gain a hearing. It was also an effective mask. In a sense Nella Larsen chose to "pass" as a novelist; not surprisingly, readers who knew what they were seeing—that is, reading—missed the point.

NOTES

1. Biographical material may be found in my entry on Larsen in *American Women Writers*; in Adelaide Cromwell Hill's "Introduction" to *Quicksand*; and in Mary

Helen Washington's "Nella Larsen: Mystery Woman of the Harlem Renaissance."

2. For a full discussion of the tragic mulatto convention in novels by black women, see Barbara Christian's *Black Women Novelists* (35–61).

3. Sexism as an issue in the novel was first explored at length by Hortense Thornton in "Sexism As Quagmire: Nella Larsen's *Quicksand*." My reading of the novel owes much to Thornton's essay.

4. Nathan I. Huggins notes Larsen's rejection of black primitivism in his *Harlem Renaissance* (160–61). See also Addison Gayle's *The Way of the New World* (130–35).

5. A classic statement on female Otherness is found in Simone de Beauvoir's The *Second Sex* (viii–xxix).

6. See, for example, Annis Pratt's *Archetypal Patterns in Women's Fiction* (41–70), and Sandra Gilbert's and Susan Gubar's *The Madwoman in the Attic* (83–92).

7. The novel illustrates the pattern in women's fiction whereby the confinement of pregnancy replicates the confinement of society for women (see Gilbert and Gubar 88).

8. These conclusions reflect the views, respectively, of Amaritjit Singh in *The Novels of the Harlem Renaissance* (99), of Robert Bone in *The Negro Novel in America* (102), and of Hoyt Fuller in his "Introduction" to *Passing* (14).

9. Most commentators have read *Passing* as a tragic-mulatto story, but two critics offer sharply different views. Mary Mabel Youmans argues in "Nella Larsen's *Passing*: A Study in Irony" that Irene is the one who actually "passes" because she gives up her racial heritage for middle-class security. And in "Nella Larsen's *Passing*: A Problem of Interpretation," Claudia Tate argues that *Passing* is an intriguing romance in which Irene Redfield is the heroine and the unreliable center of consciousness.

10. Tate insists that the evidence is adequate to determine Irene's guilt or innocence (145).

Works Cited

Beauvoir, Simone de. *The Second Sex*. 1949. New York: Bantam, 1961.

Bone, Robert. *The Negro Novel in America*. Rev. ed. New Haven: Yale UP, 1965. Christian, Barbara. *Black*

Women Novelists: The Development of a Tradition, 1892–1976. Westport: Greenwood, 1980.

Fuller, Hoyt. "Introduction." *Passing*. By Nella Larsen. New York: Collier, 1971. 11–24.

Gayle, Addison, Jr. *The Way of the New World: The Black Novel in America*. New York: Anchor, 1975.

Gilbert, Sandra M., and Susan Gubar. *The Madwoman in the Attic: The Woman Writer and the Nineteenth-Century Literary Imagination*. New Haven: Yale UP, 1979.

Hill, Adelaide Cromwell. "Introduction." *Quicksand*. By Nella Larsen. New York: Collier, 1971. 9–17.

Huggins, Nathan I. *Harlem Renaissance*. New York: Oxford UP, 1971.

Larsen, Nella. *Passing*. 1929. New York: Collier, 1971.

———. *Quicksand*. 1928. New York: Collier, 1971.

Pratt, Annis. *Archetypal Patterns in Women's Fiction*. Bloomington: Indiana UP, 1981.

Singh, Amaritjit. *The Novels of the Harlem Renaissance: Twelve Black Writers*, 1923–1933. University Park: Pennsylvania State UP, 1976.

Tate, Claudia. "Nella Larsen's *Passing*: A Problem of Interpretation."*Black American Literature Forum* 14 (1980): 142–46.

Thornton, Hortense. "Sexism As Quagmire: Nella Larsen's *Quicksand*." *CLA Journal* 16 (1973): 285–301.

Wall, Cheryl. "Nella Larsen." *American Women Writers: A Critical Reference Guide from Colonial Times to the Present*. Ed. Lina Mainero. New York: Frederick Ungar, 1980. 2: 507–09.

Washington, Mary Helen. "Nella Larsen: Mystery Woman of the Harlem Renaissance." *MS*. Dec. 1980: 44–50.

Youmans, Mary Mabel. "Nella Larsen's *Passing*: A Study in Irony." *CLA Journal* 18 (1974): 235–41.

MAUREEN HONEY

Survival and Song: Women poets of the Harlem Renaissance

Writers of the Harlem Renaissance occupy a crucial place in the history of Afro-American literature for the high artistic quality of such works as *Cane* by Jean Toomer and Nella Larsen's *Quicksand,* for the distinctive voices of Langston Hughes and Zora Neale Hurston, and for the defiant pride which their movement came to represent. With the exceptions of Hurston and possibly Larsen, however, the women writers of the period have been largely overlooked, at best accorded a minor status in this important literary episode. I wish to urge retrieval of their work from the obscurity into which it has fallen and suggest an intepretive approach that reveals its value for contemporary study.

I am focusing on poetry as it was the chosen genre of an overwhelming majority of Black women publishing during the 1920's.[1] Well known in Black intellectual circles of their day and widely published, women poets achieved the respect of their peers and were popular with a Black middle-class audience. Scholars who lived through the Renaissance generally write favorably of them. Sterling Brown, for instance, compares Anne Spencer to Emily Dickinson and calls Georgia Douglas Johnson's poetry "skillful and fluent."[2] James Weldon Johnson praises Gwendolyn Bennett for her "delicate, poignant" lyrics while calling attention to Jessie Fauset's "light and neat" touch.[3] Later critics, however, have tended to see women's verse as conventional and sentimental, out of step with the militant, rebellious race-

From *Women's Studies* 16 (1989). © 1989 by Gordon and Breach, Science Publishers, Inc.

consciousness of the period.[4] Those who accord it some artistic value nevertheless agree that most women poets remained within the genteel school of "raceless" literature, having largely confined themselves to the realm of private experience, love lyrics, and nature poetry reminiscent of the nineteenth century.[5] I wish to argue that the full import of women's imaginative choices has been obscured for most modern readers by their seemingly anachronistic subject matter. When placed in its historical context, however, women's poetry comes alive and its significance as the first modern Black female voice becomes clear. Furthermore, a new reading reveals that it is animated, not by an imitative impluse, but rather stems from a defiant sensibility reflective of the Black women who wrote it.

In his discussion of Renaissance poetry, Sterling Brown characterizes Gwendolyn Bennett, Helene Johnson, Carrie Clifford, and Allison Davis as "race conscious" writers.[6] By this he means that they exhibit the qualities most often associated with "New Negro" writing: identification with the race, a miltant proud spirit, overt anger at racism, rejection of white culture, an attempt to reconstruct a now invisible heritage, and determination to fight oppression. Bennett and Johnson appear frequently in early anthologies represented by selections that declare their independence from white standards. Johnson uses playful, bold street language to praise Black urban style as in this poem about male beauty: "Gee, boy, I love the way you hold your head, high sort of and a bit to one side, like a prince, a jazz prince."[7] Bennett, in "Hatred," one of the most widely reprinted of Renaissance poems, lays a curse on her enemies, the implacability of which is matched only by its assurance: "I shall hate you like a dart of singing steel ... while rekindled fires in my eyes shall wound you like swift arrows."[8] Both were known for their poetry exalting Black pride. In Bennett's "To A Dark Girl," for example, the speaker sees "something of old forgotten queens" in the way a young girl walks, while Johnson admires a "disdainful and magnificent" Black man sauntering down a Harlem street, his laughter "arrogant and bold."[9]

Two things are noteworthy about Brown's remarks. The first is that, until recently, women were considered part of the Renaissance mainstream and used as examples of modern "Black pride" writers. Indeed, fully half of the poetry by women in the pages of *Opportunity* and *The Crisis* from 1920 through 1931 dealt explicitly with race issues.[10] Prejudice, lynching, stereotypes, white cultural imperialism, finding strength in one's ancestors and culture, the beauty of Blackness, and the assertion of rights were all popular subjects during the decade for both men and women. Moreover, nearly as many women's poems were published as those by men.[11] Yet as time went on, the image of women's poetry grew to be that of the pastoral or romantic lyric with only occasional references to the vast amount of race poems produced.[12]

Second, in mentioning well known poets Anne Spencer and Georgia Douglas Johnson, Brown fails to indicate that they wrote on race themes even though they composed powerful pieces about political and racial issues. While the majority of their work is comparatively private, they were clearly interested in and supportive of the new militance. Spencer addressed lynching, female oppression, and racism in her writing.[13] Johnson reflected often on the ironies of race prejudice and imperialism, berating white men for being "weak-kneed ... afraid to face the counsel of their timid hearts."[14] Similarly, nature poet Effie Lee Newsome wrote of African boys as pathfinders for a new world while Mae V. Cowdery, known for her love poetry, ventured occasionally into political areas.[15] Conversely, the "race poets" tried their hand at personal topics.[16]

From looking at the output of each poet, it is clear that while a given woman might have preferred one kind of subject over another, he generally did not confine herself to it. As a group, these women hared a sensibility that transcended the categories into which they were placed. In part because the race poets were overshadowed by Langston Hughes, Claude McKay, and Sterling Brown, later criticism would focus on the lyricists, obscuring the implicit connection between the social and personal writing most of them did.

Jessie Fauset is one of the writers who concentrated on the private world of romantic love in her poetry yet she stated in 1922 that the issue of race was always with her: "I cannot if I will forget the fact of color in almost everything I do or say ... "[17] Anne Spencer, who excelled at lush descriptions of her garden, fought against racial discrimination in her small Virginia town and declared in the headnote to her verse in Countée Cullen's anthology: "I proudly love being a Negro woman."[18] Angelina Weld Grimké chose to write imagistic nature poems and at the same time admired her activist father and abolitionist aunt, Charlotte Forten Grimké. The seeming contrast between these women's personal struggles against racism and the nonracial quality of their writing is a characteristic shared by many female poets of the time and has been interpreted as an escapist impulse, evidence of a self-denying identification with white culture, or a declaration of independence from the role Black writers were expected to fill. Feeling constrained by the label "race writer," they opted for what they considered more universal themes appropriate to the art of poetry and insisted on the freedom to follow their individual muse.[19]

When viewed in the context of what women produced as a whole during the Renaissance, however, a more complex picture emerges of this nonracial poetry. Because the total work of each writer was small (with the exception of Georgia Douglas Johnson), the pattern of metaphors and themes characteristic of women's writing is not evident when looking at individual poets. The impulse behind the poetry, therefore, is unclear since the framework from which it emerged is invisible. Artistic choices were made repeatedly that give definition to individual poems seemingly divorced from a Black sensibility and that make it accessible to us today. Rather than representing a split consciousness, one that denies the Afro-American heritage of the writer, this poetry uses the landscape of nature and romantic love to affirm the humanity of women rendered invisible by the dominant culture. As will be explained later, these were areas with which Black women felt comfortable and that provided opportunities to counter the destructive effects of racism and sexism.

Erlene Stetson is one of the few critics to place these poets in a tradition of art characterized by subversive allusion to an oppressive social framework. In Black women's attempt to create a voice of their own, she maintains, they have addressed two key questions through subtle exploration of a personal landscape: "How do we assert ... our identities in a world that prefers to believe we do not exist? How do we balance and contain our anger and pain?"[20] It is in reference to these questions that the pattern of metaphors and subjects used by writers of the twenties takes on new meaning.

In the early years of this century, as now, Black women struggled to find images of themselves in a culture that glorified whiteness. Ridiculed by minstrel stereotypes, objectified as beasts of burden or docile servants, found wanting when measured against white standards of beauty or achievement, they attempted to counterpose a reality that affirmed their worth. The celebration of African heritage, folklore, and the deracinated personality were among the major strategies used by Renaissance writers of all kinds for asserting a self ignored or condemned by Anglo-Saxon civilization. Yet, as Nathan Huggins concludes, the focus on Africa and participation in a movement that came to be known as "primitivism" posed problems for Black artists, especially women.[21] Prevailing knowledge of Africa was one-dimensional and it was limited as a source of ethnic identity for a group native to America. Distorted into humiliating parodies by whites, rural folk culture, with a few notable exceptions, was something from which the mostly urban generation creating the new art wished to distance itself.[22] In addition, most of the women writing at the time did not live in Harlem, the inspirational source of new urban poetry being turned to by men.[23] Finally, celebration of the instinctual and "primitive" threatened to emprison Blacks in another stereotype, particularly women, who had long suffered from being identified with their sexuality. As the following lines indicate, white fascination with Black sensuality was suspect and perceived as objectifying by women:"Emerges now a hero new, a soul unknown to claim the horizon of your fancy ... souls of lust embroidered to your liking—not shaming gazing eyes but feeding them."[24]

While women did celebrate their nonEuropean roots and lifestyle, they found their primary symbols of identity in nature. Africa and Harlem appear in their writing yet the impulse was to turn away from these settings toward a garden, field, hill, horizon, or forest. Aside from affording them an alternative to subjects dimly glimpsed, focus on the natural world in part grew out of attitudes shared by Black women writers with other artists of the period. One of these was rebellion against the idea of progress as the principle moving force in history, an optimistic belief prevalent in the prewar period that the world was getting better through technological and moral advancement.[25] Accelerated by World War I, disillusionment with the notion that material and spiritual advancement coincided in America was characteristic of white intellectuals in the 1920's, so much so that many of them took up residence in Europe to escape what they saw as a poisonous malaise in their native land.[26] Despite writers' beliefs that art could humanize America, Blacks had even more compelling reasons for rejecting faith in the modern industrial world as a force for enlightenment since racism had viciously exploded on the scene in the immediate postwar years with a rash of lynchings and attacks on urban Black communities.[27] As a pristine counterpoint to the manmade machinery of an industrialized society, nature could provide an alternative vision and language.

The city was a symbol of freedom for these writers, but their poetry indicated that it also resonated with a power that felt alien and intrusive. In this poem, for example, the speaker likens skyscrapers to behemoths that block her vision: "Skylines are marking me in today, like huge arms ... locking out the world's eye, forgetting all about the stars."[28] A sense of the city as barrier to a female voice is also present in Marjorie Marshall's "Nostalgia," where she yearns for "fresh-blown winds that roam through silent hills" and declares: "I shall go forth from here; these burning streets shall know my songs no more—and I shall guard my ears against the rigid cry of steel on stones."[29] Similarly, Anne Spencer speaks of releasing her poetic song and thereby escaping manmade structures: "My thought leans forward ... quick! you're lifted clear of brick and frame to moonlit garden bloom."[30] Black women poets were inspired by and echo the nineteenth century English romanticists they studied in school in part because placing nature at the center of the imagination allowed them to get some distance on an urban world that attracted them yet represented a reality not of their making.

It is instead in a landscape untouched by man that these poets found mirrors. "My soul is like a tree lifting its face to the sun, flinging wide its branches ... to breathe into itself a fragrance of far-off fields of clover" (Mae Cowdrey).[31] "The river is a decrepit old woman shivering in her sombre shawl of fog" (Ethel Caution).[32] "I would be one with the morning to hold in my throat soft ecstasies of bird notes ... I would be one with the evening to clasp in my hands strange brilliancy of star dust" (Majorie Marshall).[33] This poetry locates the self in a setting not only of continual regeneration but one that has also suffered damage at the hands of men seeking to remake the world in their likeness. This connection is made explicit in Anne Spencer's "White Things," where the oppression of Blacks is seen as part of a long genocidal history wherein their tormentors destroy life in order to rule: "Most things are colorful things—the sky, earth and sea. Black men are most men; but the white are free! White things are rare things; so rare, so rare—They stole from out a silvered world—somewhere. Finding earth-plains fair plains, save greenly grassed, they strewed white feathers of cowardice, as they passed; The golden stars with lances fine, the hills all red and darkened pine, they blanched with their wand of power; and turned the blood in a ruby rose to a poor white poppy-flower."[34]

The connection between women and the land is clear in nature poetry with references to female-like valleys, hills, "the sable breast of earth," and soft ground pregnant with life. Whiteness, in contrast, is associated with power, control, and death. The poem "Chalk-dust," for example, concerns the desire of a teacher to escape her classroom and "roll in wet, green grass, plunge headfirst into youth, and music, and laughter." The dust permeates the air, her hair, and clothing and symbolizes the dry lifeless facts written in chalk on her blackboard: "It has the relentless persistence of the long dead. It gets between me and the rays of the sun ... It will strangle me slowly, quietly; and sift over my body when I, like it, am so dead as to be merely useful."[35] The world of book knowledge, figures, formal education is white and suffocating while colorful nature releases a life-giving joyous sensuality.

Similarly, the white light of the moon is portrayed as a force that will steal the soul of a mother's baby in African writer Aqua Laluah's poem "Lullaby": "Close your sleepy eyes, or the pale moonlight will steal you. Else in the mystic silence, the moon will turn you white, then you won't see the sunshine, nor smell the open roses, nor love your Mammy any more, whose skin is dark as night. Wherever moonlight stretches her arms across the heavens, you will follow ... till you become instead a shade in human draperies."[36] Here, Laluah creates an allegory for the process by which Black people become separated from their roots, culture, and true selves through using the moon as a symbol of white culture and appreciation of nature as a concomitant of self-love. If you gaze too long at images of whiteness, the mother warns her child, you will reject your racial heritage and conform to alien standards thereby becoming a shadow self living in the corners of people's minds.

The moon is a central element in two poems that link it to themes of destruction. Heba Jannath likens the moon to a nun in death who is impervious to the "bedeviled" comets dancing around her grave. She is for the speaker a reflection of her deadened spirit rendered lifeless in self-protection against the pain of lost passion: "O Moon, thy face is a frozen mirror wherein our Sun and Satellites behold themselves; and I, myself—and the chilling breath from off thy silent wastes relieves our passion fires."[37] While the poem expresses gratitude for this beacon of serenity, it is a calm dearly bought as the speaker is "self-lost in nothingness." A more complicated use is made of white metaphors in Esther Popel's "Theft."[38] The moon is described as an old woman looking in vain for her children, afraid of and taunted by the elements as she hurries home. She creeps along, huddled in an old black cape and tries to escape the wind who pelts her with snowballs "filling her old eyes with the flakes of them." Suddenly, she falls and is buried by the snow while jewels fall from their bag onto the earth where they are seized by tall trees which then sparkle with their "glittering plunder." The trees are uncharacteristically malevolent in this poem, but the usage of moon and snow are typical. The snow blinds this old woman, trips and envelopes her; it causes her to lose a small treasure carefully guarded. Finally, its companion, the wind, laughs at her piteous moans and turns her own children against her who, though found, prove to be an enemy. Negative white elements are present in a double sense here, for not only is the desperate mother defeated by them, she is herself white, or rather yellow, the color of old white paint. Popel's central figure is ambiguous in that she evokes pity, modifying the image of the moon as dangerous. At the same time, she represents weakness, debilitation, and devastating loss.

Allusions to white domination and danger abound yet the predominant message is that it can be resisted. Alice Dunbar Nelson's reflections on a snow-covered autumn tree, for instance, focus on its resilience to a force trying to claim it. "Today I saw a thing of arresting poignant beauty: a strong young tree, brave in its Autumn finery ... bending beneath a weight of early snow which ... spread a heavy white chilly afghan over its crested leaves./Yet they thrust through, defiant, glowing, claiming the right to live another fortnight."[39] The assertion of vitality against deathly stillness appears again in "Late Afternoon": "She snowshowed by ... following the hush that called her from the wood, finding in whiteness deep on leaves and sod a soundlessness she somehow understood. /The wood seemed waiting for the falling snow, breathless and still and lovely in its sure welcoming of further white, and so she found a beauty she could not endure. Her quick hand shut her eyes out from the sight: the woods would take the kiss of snow all night."[40]

Initially drawn by the soft still beauty of the snowfall, the wanderer is captivated by the silence with which it blankets the wood she is tempted to enter. The poem calls attention to the soundlessness of "whiteness deep on leaves and sod," the "breathless" welcoming posture of the trees, and the "hush" that beckons to the woman on snow-shoes. While beautiful, the snowfall has a sinister quality as it silences and covers a motionless stand of trees. Nearly seduced into stillness herself, the woman continues her journey: "her quick hand shut her eyes out from the sight." Both poems link whiteness to the covering of life with a suffocating pall, no less deathlike for its loveliness. Yet each poet places within her scene an act of resistance, one that preserves vibrancy and movement in the midst of a threatening storm.

Angelina Weld Grimké's well known piece, "Tenebris," echoes this subtle assertion of self against a white power: "There is a tree, by day, that. at night, has a shadow, a hand huge and black, with fingers long and black. All through the dark against the white man's house, in the little wind, the black hand plucks and plucks at the bricks. The bricks are the color of blood and very small. Is it a black hand, or is it a shadow?"[41] Grimké's poetry is deceptively free of direction in that she presents, without comment, a string of images connected by a logic outside the poem. One of her strengths is that her selection of elements seems to allude to a larger reality and lends itself to a variety of interpretations. In this case, by likening the branches of a tree to a hand "huge and black," whose shadow rests against "the white man's house." Grimké invites us to find in her image a statement about the relationship of Blacks to white society. One reading of the poem is that a sees Black struggle as a subterranean, persistent chipping away at white structures. The black hand "plucks and plucks" at the bricks which are "the color of blood and very small" at night, when the occupant is sleeping, falsely secure that the image on his house is only the shadow of a harmless tree. Yet the last line asks: 'Is it a black hand, or is it a shadow?" and we are left sensing that the white man's house is in danger. oh! my feet flew madly! My body whirled and swayed! My soul danced in its ecstacy untrammeled, unafraid!" (Ethel Caution)[49] "Within the shadow of the moon you danced ... Your dark flame-beauty challenging a glance, you flung a sob-caught laugh and leaped afar into the arms of night, with upturned face that mocked the waning beauty of the moon, its fragile curves ... lacked your Nileborn grace" (Majorie Marshall).[50] "To dance—in the light of the moon, a platinum moon poised like a slender dagger on the velvet darkness of night" (Mae Cowdery).[51] "In Alabama stars hand down so low, so low they purge the soul with their infinity" (Jessie Fauset).[52] While poets looked to natural settings in general for space in which to savor the abandonment of confining roles, night was sought most frequently as it was a time when the objectifying gaze was covered by sleep and the freedom to be at one with darkness could be safely enjoyed.

It is to night also that the poet turns for solace and restoration. Here, Mae Cowdery soothes her wounded heart by communing with the stars and moon: "I want to take down with my hands the silver stars that grow in heaven's dark blue meadows and bury my face in them./I want to wrap all around me the silver shedding of the moon to keep me warm."[53] Georgia Douglas Johnson also seeks the darkness when gripped by sorrow in "Escape:" "Shadows, shadows, hug me round in your solitude profound."[54] The reference to night as comforter can be seen as an affirmation of Black resilience. It also transforms the night from a setting of terror, a time when Black people were tormented by white vigilantes, into one of peace. Poems centered on lynching victims, for instance, commonly close on a note of relief wherein night mercifully descends to remove a man's soul from his tortured body.

The images of softness linked to night indicate its association with maternal caresses and a mother's comforting embrace. In the poem "Dark Madonna," for example, night is described as "an old Negro woman hovering above her sleeping children ... Along their brows she draws cool hands./Her breasts yearn for the hunger of their waking."[55] Consoler of the bruised and even broken spirit, guardian of the soul at rest, night serves as a metaphor for the restorative powers within to which the poet can turn when feelings of despair overwhelm her. Just as the death of each day is followed by a healing period of quiet repose, so too does the battered spirit find sustenance in womb like suspension of interaction with the outside world.

The impulse to protect oneself from a hurtful reality is not an admission of defeat, but rather an acknowledgement that the forces arrayed against a Black woman's dignity and development of her powers are formidable. Much of the poetry characterizes these forces as male as well as white. Blanche Taylor Dickinson, for instance, identifies with an icicle's short-lived brilliance in sunlight: "Chilled into a serenity as rigid as your pose you linger trustingly, but a gutter waits for you. Your elegance does not secure you favors with the sun. He is not to pity fragileness. He thinks all cheeks should burn and feel how tears can run."[56] Similarly, in "Magalu," Helene Johnson warns her African sister against a missionary's attempts to convert her: "Do not let him lure you from your laughing waters."[57] Finally, Gwendolyn Bennett relates the fate of a woman seduced by a man in "silvern armour" with "silver spurs and silken plumes a-blow" who finds that under his visor lies the face of death.[58]

Anne Spencer's poem, "Letter to My Sister," provides insight into the motif of retreat found in poetry concerning night and links it to these warnings about male destruction. Though the gods she mentions are not identified as male, it is made clear that women battle a common enemy and share a kind of bondage that sets them apart from men. "It is dangerous for a woman to defy the gods," she begins, "to taunt them with the tongue's thin tip ... or draw a lined daring them to cross." The speaker adds, however, that appeasement will not protect women from harm: "Oh, but worse still if you mince along timidly—dodge this way or that, or kneel, or pray." Instead, she recommends deftly removing one's treasured secrets from view and revealing them only under strict conditions of privacy: "Lock your heart, then quietly, and, lest they peer within, light no lamp when dark comes down. Raise no shade for sun."[59] Although the day's piercing light destroys, it can be thwarted by guarding the innermost recesses of the self in periodic flights to invisibility.

Another Spencer poem, "Lady, Lady," brings to the surface the three major themes of nature poetry: equation of Blackness and femaleness with strength, resistance to white and male oppression, and survival of the core self. Typical of Renaissance poetry, it studies a member of the working class made invisible by racism and classism. "Lady, Lady, I saw your face, dark as night withholding a star ... The chisel fell, or it might have been you had borne so long the yoke of men. Lady, Lady, I say your hands, twisted, awry, like crumpled roots, bleached poor white in a sudsy tub, wrinkled and drawn from your rub-a-dub. Lady, Lady, I saw your heart, and altared there in its darksome place were the tongues of flames the ancients knew, where the good God sits to spangle through."[60] The washerwoman's external appearance bears the stamp of her oppressor. Her face has been chiseled by pain borne from carrying "the yoke of men;" her hands are twisted "like crumpled roots" by the labor she does for white people, symbolizing the stunting of her growth and crippling of her true posture. They are also "bleached poor white," a mirror of the degree to which her race has consigned her to a draining exploited existence controlled by whites. Despite the harsh life she has led, however, there remains a sacred inviolable place within where her spirit burns brightly "altared there in its darksome place," host to a transcendent guiding force.

Nature furnished women with an objective correlative to articulate their aspirations, fears, wounds, and struggles to define themselves in a patriarchal racist society. Through exploring properties of the natural world, they found images that spoke to their condition and dreams. In a society with insufficient mirrors, poets constructed an imaginary reality which reflected their beauty, worth, and strength.

Another major subject of women's poetry was romantic love. Largely devoid of references to race or gender oppression, it concentrates on private affairs of the heart, the pain of loss, the ecstacy of union with another. Seemingly unconnected to the poet's relation to her society, it appears at first glance to be an anomalous feature of a literary movement to record authentically the Afro-American experienced and break free of stereotypes. Yet the love poetry reverberates with emotions that implicitly challenge the dehumanizing flat caricatures of Black people found in American culture.

One of the many misconceptions held by white people about Blacks at the time was that they were a happy race, perpetually childlike in their ability to laugh at woe and shrug off cares. Such an image served important psychological functions for whites, among them relief from guilt, avoidance of fears about rebellion, and escape from a sober model of propriety.[61] A laughing Black face put whites at ease and seemingly offered a world where troubles could be left behind. New Negro writers addressed this issue by making public their rage at the various forms racism took and exposing as a lie Black contentment with servility. These aspects of twenties militance are present in women's poetry. Anita Scott Coleman, for example, sees a beautiful anger in her people: "I love black faces ... They are full of smould'ring fire."[62] Others declare the era of smiling docility to be over: "Sambo's laugh used to ring out ... But now Sambo has lost his laugh, he doesn't guffaw any more."[63]

In addition to revealing their anger, writers protested the necessity to hide pain in order to fulfil white fantasies, a message running through Mary Jenness's poem, "The Negro Laughs Back:" "You laugh, and I must hide the wound your laughter cuts in me"; similarly, Clarissa Scott Delany bitterly describes the false front she is forced to present in "The Mask" where she emphasizes the distance from self this imposes by referring to herself in the third person: "So detached and cool she is, no notion e'er betrays the secret life within her soul, the anguish of her days."[64]

When read in this context, the love poetry takes on added significance for in it the poet reveals her pain, her human capacity to be vulnerable and suffer deep disappointment. She possesses the gift of laughter, but it is clear that sadness has shaped her as much as joy, that suffering is a big part of her life. The heartbreak over unrequited love that runs through this poetry is an affirmation of humanity in the face of injunctions to play a role. It also asserts that the personal realm of the poet need not be uplifting in order to be a proper subject for public verse. Her feelings are worthy of poetic expression in and of themselves. This claiming of the despondent self represented an important departure from nineteenth century Afro-American poetry which, according to Joan Sherman, followed that era's conception of art as something that should inspire and instruct.[65] It was therefore incumbent on the poet to be optimistic and end poems on a forward looking note. Insisting on the full range of human emotions for their province, poets of the twenties expanded the boundaries of acceptable subjects to include despair and woeful yearning after something dearly lost.

The right, indeed the necessity, to recognize anguish as a consequence of being fully alive is a theme often struck in this poetry of the heart. Refusing to take the safer yet diminishing path of a life without dreams or large emotional risks, the poet proclaims her suffering to be a growth-producing factor in her quest for vitality. Helene Johnson, for example, defines fulfillment as a willingness to endure pain in the passionate pursuit of meaningful experience: "Ah, life, to let your stabbing beauty pierce me ... to grapple with you, loving you too fiercely, and to die bleeding—consummate with Life."[66] Reflecting on a failed love affair, the speaker in Georgia Douglas Johnson's poem, "Afterglow," also affirms the value of opening oneself to hurt: "I smile across the backward way and pledge anew, my vow: For every glancing, golden gleam, I offer, gladly, Pain; and I would give a thousand worlds, to live it all again."[67] Here, emotional transport, whether toward joy or sorrow, is heralded as a lifeforce that brings the poet into contact with her humanity and the world around her. It is both her route to self-actualization as she is willing to encounter life directly, without masks, and her announcement that she is multidimensional, a woman of sensitivity and warmth.

Another aspect of Renaissance love poetry that simultaneously went beyond nineteenth century conventions and resisted contemporary stereotypes was the introduction of erotic passionate imagery. Mae Cowdrey mourns a lost lover by explicitly recalling scenes from their lovemaking: "No more the feel of your hand on my breast ... no more the lush sweetness of your lips."[68] In "Ecstacy," Virginia Houston similarly reminisces about a passion no longer hers: "I remember only the ecstacy of soft lips covering mine dragging my soul through my mouth."[69] Jessie Fauset holds close the memory of a fleeting kiss that nevertheless wrung from her. "a sharp caught cry."[70] Kathleen Tannkersley Young's poem, "Hunger," compares her lover's body to "dark wine" that she lifts to her "trembling lips," and Eda Lou Walton bids hers to "lower your lips and let them rest against the anguish of my breast."[71]

In some poems, passion for women too emerges, consistent with the woman-identification found in the nature poetry. Mae Cowdrey's "Insatiate" captures the urgent desire for sensual experience that appears in much of the period's poetry when she admits that even if her lover were exquisite as jewels, "if her lips were rubies red," she would still not be able to satisfy her appetite for pleasure.[72] Angelina Weld Grimké displays a similar urgency as she breathlessly describes a lover's kiss: "Yearning, yearning, languor, surrender; your mouth, and madness, madness, tremulous, ... flaming."[73] She longs explicitly for union with a woman in "A Mona Lisa," alluding to her intense hunger: "I should like to creep through the long brown grasses that are your lashes; I should like to poise on the very brink of the leaf-brown pools that are your shadowed eyes ... I should like to sink down and down and down ... and deeply drown."[74] Finally, "Rainy Season Love Song" celebrates the speaker's passionate encounter with a woman in the rain: "Into my hands she cometh, and the lightening of my desire flashes and leaps about her ... its warm electricity in you pulses wherever I may touch ... The thunder rumbles about us, and I feel its triumphant note as your warm arms steel around me; and I kiss your dusky throat."[75]

The highlighting of sensual passion was a legacy from what Henry May calls the Rebellion, a prewar movement away from Victorianism that, among other things, celebrated spontaneous free expression and release of the body from unnatural confinement.[76] At the same time, it constituted a reclaiming of Black women's sexuality, either denied by desexed images of the plantation mammy or debased in lewd portraits of the "primitive" African. To bring their bodies into public view under their own terms was a liberating act that allowed women the freedom to experience themselves as sentient complex beings.

This poetry has been criticized for its excess emotionality and sentimentality.[77] Much of it is to modern readers embarrassingly dramatic, almost Victorian in its melodramatic gestures and coy allusions to lovers. At the same time, it was important that poets venture into the forbidden territory of erotic passion and explore the world of sensation and spontaneous feeling. In doing so, they were insisting on the right to be human and resisting a society that worshipped machines, architects, engineers but seemed to have no room for love or understanding. If they had a tendency to go to extremes, it was in reaction to what they saw as an unfeeling culture primarily concerned with things and capable of wounding them casually, unthinkingly. Voicing their pain was one step toward authenticity as was celebrating their moments of ecstacy.

Contemporary criticism of the Harlem Renaissance provides a starting point for understanding neglect of women's poetry. When measured against the historical role Renaissance artists claimed for themselves, i.e. creators of a New Afro-American sensibility, the failures in much of their work become apparent. Nathan Huggins, for example, considers Claude McKay and Countée Cullen flawed poets because they embraced a European artistic tradition at odds with the heart of their own experience. Crippled by their notion that art should be more universal than a focus on race alone allowed and unable or unwilling to depart from traditional structures, they ironically fell short of the greatness they sought.[78] Saunders Redding also faults Cullen for adhering to verse modeled after nineteenth century romantic lyricists and concludes he contributed little to Afro-American literature, standing aloof as he did from the revolutionary currents flowing past him.[79] Finally, in his discussion of Renaissance novelists, Addison Gayle Jr. concludes that, while Black writers left a legacy of questioning rebellion, they were not able to develop fully their vision because they were insufficiently independent of white culture.[80]

Known primarily for their lyrical and pastoral verse, women too have been seen as imitating European traditions and devising little that was useful in the creation of a Black aesthetic. Hampered by devotion to a theory of art not their own, so the consensus goes, whatever talent some of these women had was snuffed out by conformity to inappropriate poetic models.

I think it is valid to recognize the limitations of artists who overtly tried to develop an indigenous literary canon and who were at the same time constrained by historical conditions militating against radically new visions. There were many ways in which Renaissance poets failed to provide the kind of legacy which they saw themselves creating. Yet, although much of women's poetry is sing-song, clichéd, and awkward, there is a body of work that has held up over time, that speaks with a modern voice and artfully expresses messages of substance. Anne Spencer, Mae Cowdery, Angelina Weld Grimké, Gwendolyn Bennett, and Helene Johnson produced poems of high aesthetic quality and their best pieces inspire careful examination. That their poetic strategies did not often include departure from conventional metaphors and models ought not distract us from the coherent rebellious messages in their verse.

Jean Wagner has drawn a parallel between the attitudes displayed by second and third generation Afro-Americans freed from slavery and those of descendents of immigrants: the second generation tends to reject markers of ethnic identity while the third embraces them.[81] His explanation for the emergence of a generation reclaiming its cultural heritage in the 1920's helps clarify the strain in women's poetry that is divorced from overt identification with the people and focused on subjects traditionally used by Anglo-Saxon male poets. The most influential women—Anne Spencer, Angelina Weld Grimké, Alice Dunbar Nelson, Georgia Douglas Johnson, Jessie Fauset— were all members of the second generation to experience emancipation and all wrote private poetry.[82] That they should turn away from folk or urban Afro-American expression is perhaps not surprising using Wagner's model.

Yet this kind of analysis cannot account fully for the vast amount of nature and love poetry produced by Black women during the Renaissance, for younger poets like Gwendolyn Bennett and Helene Johnson, while they did move into the new idiom being created by Langston Hughes, followed as well the direction of the older poets. Erlene Stetson asserts that one defining aspect of Black women's poetry is that the writer's quest for identity takes place within a personal landscape.[83] In this sense, then, Renaissance poets remained within a female rather than a white tradition as they explored their inner selves, intimate relations with lovers, and private connections to the natural world in an effort to make themselves visible. They found congenial poetic models in the imagists and English romantics because these forms allowed them access to a core self from which the dominant culture kept them alienated. Communing with nature in spontaneous, associative ways or unself-consciously exploring the intensity of their most initimate connections with people produced a vocabulary for describing the unborn self soon to burst upon the world.[84] It was a markedly female, as well as middle-class, strategy for claiming an authentic Afro-American worldview.

This period witnessed the most significant flowering of Black women's writing until the 1960's and, as such, requires extensive critical attention. Moreover, the poetry with which women came to be identified provided a number of key bridges: from nineteenth century oratorical and sentimental verse to a modern sensibility, from white art to Afro-American, and from the male-dominated New Negro movement to female experience. Despite the gaps, theirs are among the first voices that sound familiar to us and that anticipate contemporary issues. Women poets of the Harlem Renaissance went beyond their predecessors to find a form that spoke to their special needs as Afro-Americans with a new outlook and as modern women of strength, vision, and passion.

NOTES

1. Critics disagree on the starting date of the Harlem Renaissance but most agree it was over by the end of 1931. I have elected to study the poetry from 1920 through 1931 as it was not until 1924 that large numbers of poems were published by women and 1920 provides a neat beginning for a comprehensive view of the decade. Only a small amount of fiction was written by Black women during the Renaissance. Six novels were produced, four by Jessie Fauset and two by Nella Larsen, and around fifty short stories were published in *Opportunity* and *The Crisis*. Women's poetry was published in these important periodicals and also by A. Philip Randolph's socialist journal, *The Messenger,* and Marcus Garvey's *Negro World.* For a discussion of the latter, see Tony Martin *Literary Garveyism: Garvey, Black Arts and the Harlem Renaissance* (Massachusetts: Majority Press, 1983), p. 50-88.

2. Sterling Brown *Negro Poetry and Drama* (Washington D.C.: Assocs. in Negro Fold Education, 1937) p. 62 and 65.

3. James Weldon Johnson *The Book of American Negro Poetry* (N.Y.: Harcourt, Brace and World, 1959 © 1922) p. 243 and 205.

4. Margaret Perry *Silence to the Drums: A Survey of the Literature of the Harlem Renaissance* (Westport, CT: Greenwood Press 1976) p. 153; Margaret Just Butcher *The Negro in American Culture* (N.Y.: Alfred A. Knopf 1973) p. 123. Studies that omit women altogether include Saunders Redding *To Make A Poet Black* (Chapel Hill: Univ. of North Carolina Press 1939); Blyden Jackson and Louis Rubin *Black Poetry in America* (Baton Rouge: Louisiana State Univ. Press 1974); Jean Wagner *Black Poets of the United States* (Urbana: Univ. of Illinois Press 1973); Arthur P. Davis *From the Dark Tower* (Washington DC: Howard Univ. Press, 1974) discusses fiction writers but no women poets; Michael Cooke *Afro-American Literature in the Twentieth Century* (New Haven: Yale Univ. Press 1984) mentions only Larsen and Hurston; Arthur P. Davis and Saunders Redding *Cavalcade: Negro American Writing from 1760 to the Present* (Boston: Houghton Mifflin 1971) includes two women poets, Frances E.W. Harper and Anne Spencer; Wallace Thurman "Negro Poets and Their Poetry" in Addison Gayle, Jr. ed. *Black Expression* (N.Y.: City College of New York 1969).

5. Arthur P. Davis and Michael Peplow *The New Negro Renaissance*(N.Y.: Harper and Row 1975) place poems by Fauset, Spencer, Grimké, and Georgia Johnson under the category "Raceless Literature." Richard Barksdale and Kenneth Kinnamon *Black Writers of America: A Comprehensive Anthology* (N.Y.: Macmillan Co. 1972).

6. Brown, 1937, p. 65 and 74.

7. "Poem" in Countée Cullen *Caroling Dusk* (N.Y.: Harper and Row 1955 © 1927) p. 218.

8. *Ibid.*, p. 160.

9. *Ibid.*, p. 157; "Sonnet to a Negro in Harlem" p. 217.

10. This conclusion is based on a reading of all the poetry appearing by women in these two periodicals for the years in question.

11. Omitting names whose gender was not clearly marked, e.g. first names omitted in favour of initials, a total of 347 poems appears by men in both journals from 1925 through 1931 and 277 by women. The numbers are even for *The Crisis* where Jessie Fauset was literary editor until March 1927.

12. Exceptions to this trend are Davis and Peplow, 1975, who include poems by women under the category "Race Pride." Arna Bontemps *American Negro Poetry* (N.Y.: Hill and Wange 1963) anthologizes many poems concerning race by women; Nathan Huggins *Voices from the Harlem Renaissance* (N.Y.: Oxford Univ. Press 1976) is another anthology with poetry of this kind; William Adams, Peter Conn, Barry Slepian *Afro-American Literature* (Boston: Houghton Mifflin 1970) reprints racial poetry by Bennett, Helene Johnson, and Frances Harper.

13. There is a chapter on Spencer's political poetry in the excellent study J. Lee Greene *Time's Unfading Garden: Anne Spencer's Life and Poetry* (Baton Rouge: Louisianna State Univ. Press 1977) Chapter 8.

14. "Courier," *The Crisis* (November 1926) p. 29.

15. Newsome's poem is "Morning Light" in Cullen, 1955, p. 55.

16. See, for example, Gwendolyn Bennett's "Nocturne" *The Crisis* (November 1923) p. 20 and Helene Johnson's "Summer Matures" in Cullen, 1955, p. 217.

17. Quoted in Carolyn Sylvander *Jessie Redmon Fauset, Black American Writer* (Troy, N.Y.: The Whitson Pub. Co. 1981) p. 83.

18. Cullen, 1955, p. 47.

19. Butcher, 1973, p. 123.

20. Erlene Stetson *Black Sister: Poetry by Black American Women, 1746-1980* (Bloomington: Indiana Univ. Press 1981) p. xvii.

21. Nathan Huggins *The Harlem Renaissance* (N.Y.: Oxford Univ. Press 1971) p. 188.

22. Gregory Holmes Singleton provides a demographic chart demonstrating the urban origins of Renaissance writers in "Birth, Rebirth, and the 'New Negro' of the 1920s" *Phylon* XLIII No. 1 (March 1982): 29–45. Of the women for whom place of birth is known, Georgia Douglas Johnson was born in Atlanta, Jessie Fauset and Effie Lee Newsome in Philadephia, Alice Dunbar Nelson in New Orleans. Angelina Weld Grimké and Helene Johnson in Boston, Lucy Ariel Williams in Mobile, Alabama. Those born in rural areas include Gwendolyn Bennett, Giddings, Texas; Clarissa Scott Delaney, Tuskegee Institute, Alabama; and Blanche Taylor Dickinson, a Kentucky farm. Anne Spencer was born somewhere in Virginia.

23. Helene Johnson and Jessie Fauset lived in New York City at this time. Gwendolyn Bennett spent the early 1920's in New York, then moved to Washington D.C. in 1924. Angelina Weld Grimké, Georgia Douglas Johnson, and Clarissa Scott Delaney were all in Washington D.C. during the years of the Renaissance. Blanche

Taylor Dickinson was in Sewickley, Pennsylvania, Effie Lee Newsome in Wilberforce, Ohio, Lucy Ariel Williams in Oberlin, Ohio, Anne Spencer spent her entire adult life in Lynchburg, Virginia. Aquah Laluah, a.k.a. Gladys May Casely Hayford, lived in Sierra Leone, the African Gold Coast.

24. Ruth G. Dixon "Epitome" *The Crisis* (October 1930) p. 342. Gilbert Osofsky discusses the objectifying aspects of white interest in the "New Negro" in *Harlem: The Making of a Ghetto: Negro New York, 1890-1930* (N.Y.: Harper and Row 1963) p. 183.

25. Henry F. May *The End of American Innocence: A Study of the First Years of Our Own Time, 1912-1917* (N.Y.: Alfred A. Knopf 1959) p. 361.

26. Malcolm Cowley *Exile's Return: A Literary Odyssey of the 1920's* (N.Y.: Viking Press 1951).

27. May, 1959, p. 347; Paula Giddings *When and Where I Enter: The Impact of Black Women on Race and Sex in America* (N.Y.: William Morrow and Co. 1984) p. 145. The NAACP reported eighty-one lynchings in 1919 and sixty in 1920 *The Crisis* (February 1921) p. 160.

28. Bessie Mayle "Skylines" *The Crisis* (May 1930) p. 163.

29. *The Crisis* (November 1929)p. 378.

30. "Substitution" in Cullen, 1955, p. 48.

31. "The Wind Blows" *Opportunity* (November 1929) p. 299.

32. "The River" *The Crisis* (March 1930) p. 93.

33. "Desire" *The Crisis* (June 1928) p. 196.

34. *The Crisis* (March 1923) p. 204.

35. Lillian Byrnes *The Crisis* (August 1930) p. 273. Many of the women poets were teachers, for example, Alice Dunbar Nelson, Allison Davis, Angelina Weld Grimké, Lucy Ariel Williams, Georgia Douglas Johnson, Jessie Fauset, Clarissa Scott Delaney, Blanche Taylor Dickinson, Aquah Laluah, and Gwendolyn Bennett. Bennett was the only one to teach at a university (she was a professor at Howard University).

36. *The Crisis* (March 1929) p. 85.

37. "Moon Death" *Opportunity* (February 1931) p. 51.

38. *Opportunity* (April 1925) p. 100.

39. "Snow in October" in Cullen, 1955, p. 40.

40. Frances M. Frost, *The Crisis* (May 1929) p. 160.

41. Cullen, 1955 p. 40.

42. *Opportunity* (November 1923) p. 343.

43. *Opportunity* (May 1925) p. 147.

44. "Portraiture" *The Crisis* (June 1931) p. 199.

45. "What Do I Care for Morning" in Cullen, 1955, p. 216.

46. Bessie Mayle, "Poems," *The Crisis* (May 1930) p. 163.

47. *Opportunity* (May 1926) p. 152.

48. Esther Popel, "Night Comes Walking," *The Crisis* (August 1929) p. 249.

49. "Last Night" *The Crisis* (February 1929) p. 50.

50. "To A Dark Dancer" *The Crisis* (January 1928) p. 14.

51. "Longings" *The Crisis* (December 1927) p. 337.

52. "Stars in Alabama" *The Crisis* (January 1928) p. 14.

53. "Wants" *The Crisis* (November 1928) p. 372.

54. *The Crisis* (May 1925) p. 15.

55. Verna Bright *The Crisis* (March 1929) p. 85.

56. "To An Icicle" in Cullen, 1955, p. 110.

57. *Ibid.*, p. 223.

58. "Sonnet" *Ibid.*, p. 160.

59. Bontemps, 1963, p. 19.

60. *Survey Graphic* (March 1, 1925) p. 661.

61. Huggins, 1971, Chapter 6; Osofsky, 1963, p. 184.

62. "Black Faces" *Opportunity* (Octoer 1929) p. 320.

63. Grace P. White, "Sambo—Passing," *The Crisis* (July 1927) p. 158.

64. Jenness's poem is in *Opportunity* (August 1928) p. 233; Delaney's appears in Robert Kerlin *Negro Poets and Their Poems* (Washington D.C.: Associate Publishers 1923) p. 279.

65. Joan Sherman *Invisible Poets: Afro-Americans of the Nineteenth Century* (Urbana: Univ. of Illinois Press 1974) p. xxi.

66. "Fulfillment" *Opportunity* (June 1926) p. 194.

67. *The Crisis* (March 1920) p. 266.

68. "Farewell" *The Crisis* (February 1929) p. 50.

69. *Ibid.*

70. "Fragment" in Cullen, 1955, p. 70.

71. Young's poem is in *Opportunity* (June 1928) p. 168; Walton's is "A Kiss Requested" *The Crisis* (October 1927) p. 265.

72. This poem appears in Mae Cowdrey's anthology *We Lift Our Voices* (Philadelphia: Alpress 1936) p. 57. This is one of the few anthologies to be published by a woman poet from the Renaissance period. Others include three by Georgia Douglas Johnson *The Heart of a Woman* (Boston: The Cornhill Co. 1918), *Bronze* (Boston: B.J. Brimmer Co. 1922), and *An Autumn Love Cycle* (N.Y.: H. Vinal Ltd. 1928); and a later one by Lucy Ariel Williams *Shape Them Into Dreams: Poems* (N.Y.: Exposition Press 1955).

73. "El Beso" in Kerlin, 1923, p. 154.

74. Cullen, 1955, p. 42. Akasha Gloria Hull has done ground-breaking research on Black lesbian poets of the Renaissance. See "Under the Days:' The Buried Life

and Poetry of Angelina Weld Grimké" *Conditions: Five* Vol. II No. 2 (Autumn 1979): 17-25; and *Give Us Each Day* (N.Y.: Random House 1983), an edited diary by Alice Dunbar Nelson.

75. Gladys Casely Hayford (a.k.a. Aquah Laluah) in Cullen, 1955, p. 198.

76. May, 1959, p. 249.

77. Perry, 1976, p. 153.

78. Huggins, 1971, pp. 161-214.

79. J. Saunders Redding "The New Negro Poet in the Twenties" in Donald Gibson

ed. *Modern Black Poets* (Englewood Cliffs: Prentice-Hall 1973).

80. Addison Gayle, Jr. *The Way of the New World: The Black Novel in America* (Garden City, N.Y.: Anchor Press 1975) p. 5, 95, 107.

81. Wagner, 1973, p. 165. Robert Bone also adheres to this model in *The Negro Novel in America* (New Haven: Yale Univ. Press 1958) p. 56.

82. Spencer was born in 1882, Grimké in 1880, Nelson in 1875, Johnson in 1886, and Fauset in 1882.

83. Stetson, 1981, p. xxii.

84. The theme of birthing a new self was a key one for Renaissance writers according to Gregory Singleton "Rebirth," 1982.

PATTI CAPEL SWARTZ

Masks and Masquerade: The Iconography of the Harlem Renaissance

In some places the autumn of 1924 may have been an unremarkable season. In Harlem, it was like a foretaste of paradise. "A blue haze descended at night and with it strings of fairy lights on broad avenues" (Lewis, *Vogue*, 103). Arna Bontemps's description of Harlem provides an appropriate backdrop for a world of magic and masquerade. The Harlem of the twenties was such a world—a mecca for black artists and performers and their supporters, and for white as well as black audiences. The Harlem of the twenties created a space in which African-American artists had an unparalleled environment for creativity, an environment in which both production and artistry were controlled by the "actor."

The use of the term actor to designate the artists working in all areas of production—art, theatre, music, writing—implies control. The idea of control of production is vital to understanding the artistic creations of Harlem. The concept of artistic control also helps to reclaim the importance of what happened in Harlem, that world so often described as "almost heaven." In his forward to *Black Magic* Ossie Davis writes:

> Langston [Hughes] reminds us that our singing, our dancing, our music, our humor, our stories, our "entertainment"—spirituals, jazz, the blues, rap—was, and still is all too often, the one place where we have a chance to set standards and make definitions ...

From *Analysis and Assessment*, 1980–1994. © 1996 by Cary D. Wintz.

the one thing about us that could never be fully explained or explained away ... an island of self-sufficiency set in a sea of almost universal doubt. Our art, to us, was always, and still is, a form of self-assertion, a form of struggle, a repository of self-esteem that racism, Jim Crow, and the Ku Klux Klan could never beat out of us—the only authentic history that black folks have in America, because we made it ourselves.

Harlem brought together a large group of African-American artists in one location. Close to white culture, 1920s Harlem allowed a community of artists the freedom to maintain control of artistic production. The Harlem Renaissance has often been accused of failure. Central to any examination of the success or failure of this movement is who controlled production. In Harlem, it was the artist who controlled the audience and the gaze. Neither a failed economy that affected whites and blacks alike, or the later relative submersion (except for musical forms) by the white mainstream of the production of the Renaissance could change that tradition of reversal of artist control.

In an examination of control, several aspects of African-American culture are important, but two seem vital. Both concern African-Americans as marginal to a white society that has controlled or attempted to control them. One has to do with the idea of carnival, and the power reversals that carnival creates; the other concerns the idea of speaking from behind a mask.

In Arna Bontemps's description of Harlem—a "blue haze" and "fairy lights"—a feeling of a special space eluding time is created, the atmosphere often connected with carnival. The iconography of the Harlem Renaissance is akin to that of the masque or carnival—of perceptions and reversals, of expectations about the performer, and of a reversal of societal positions in that the normally marginalized person or group gains control. The idea of the mask, the masque, and the masquerade—what Russian literary theorist Bakhtin would describe as Carnival—illuminates the phenomenon of Harlem during the 1920s in fascinating ways and provides additional credence to Ossie Davis's statement of control from a performative view. It also creates a different view of spectators, of a white audience which becomes marginalized, losing ownership of the gaze rather than performing its usual function of marginalizing those others performing for it.

Examples of social reversals in instances of carnival appear in a long tradition of literary works—in Jonson's *Bartholomew Fair*, for instance, or in Hawthorne's description of carnival in his *The Marble Faun*. Annual examples of reversals through carnival occur in the festivals of Mardi Gras in New

Orleans or Carnival in Rio de Janeiro. In each, the carnival atmosphere creates a new freedom of action and permits new interactions and power reversals to occur; a suspension of the everyday, the creation of a mythic world with mythic performers peopling it—performers like Florence Mills, Bill Robinson, "Duke" Ellington, or the "Empress of the Blues," Bessie Smith.

In Harlem, a normally marginalized group of African-American artists and performers gained control and became the locus of power that expressed and created a space of another kind, a space freed from convention and sometimes laced with exoticism and a return to primitive motifs.

For the African-American, a return to the primitive was a search for or a return to roots. For the white audience the primitive implied exoticism and the African-American artist embodied an "exotic other," an escape from "civilization." This white audience was alienated from "civilization" by the horrors of trench warfare and gas and by an increasingly mechanistic industrial society with its accompanying machine-age iconography. Popular conceptions of Einstein's theories of relativity had shaken not only scientific circles with a restructuring of physical bases, but they appeared in popular magazine articles and were transferred to the social and philosophical worlds as well, causing a shifting relativity in interpersonal and individual relationships. This white audience also accepted the new psychological theories of Freud that presented the subconscious or the "id" as a repository of primitive and sexual desires wishing escape. Harlem, with its music and often primitive iconography, seemed a perfect escape for the tensions of modern life; an escape to the primitive with the promise of a freer sexuality to an audience whose paid guides took them on a safari to the clubs. This look to the "primitive other" was a circumstance the Harlem artist often used advantageously, turning the mask on the visitor and thus maintaining control of the production of art.

Masks have been essential to African-Americans. From the time of their importation as slaves, African-Americans have had to devise strategies for physical, emotional, and cultural survival. Any examination of the production of works in Harlem and the role of the artist or actor must take this history into account and examine two kinds of discourse or expression that arose out of "wearing the mask." The concept of the Signifying Monkey is vital to a discussion of masks and masquerade.

The Signifying Monkey is rooted in African folklore. The story was carried in stories from Africa to the United States, and it survived slavery. In fact, the idea of a signifying trickster became a survival technique for the African-American living in a white world. The Signifying Monkey was given new forms in slave tales, in both the Br'er Rabbit stories collected by white Joel Chandler Harris, and in African-American Charles Chestnutt's *Conjure Woman* stories. The Signifying Monkey is able to best a larger, more powerful creature through a quickness of wit and a false appearance of reality or desire. Through this ability, although appearing oppressed, the Signifying Monkey—or person—is often able to change circumstances and best the oppressor. Signifying's history extends through performances in Harlem to present-day rap and discourse in which the meaning of words often varies from the dictionary or "white" meaning. Signifying implies speaking from behind a mask to those who will not understand, and implies a complicit understanding of the wearing of the mask from those who do understand.

In his book, *Modernism and the Harlem Renaissance*, Houston Baker, Jr., speaks of the masks used in two kinds of discourse or signifying traditionally used by African-American writers and speakers. The first is the mask assumed, as Baker says Booker T. Washington assumed it, within the "form" or a discourse of race that satisfied white assumptions about racial stereotypes. Baker contends that in his speeches and appeals for funds, Washington was careful to frame his discourse within the stereotypical expectations of a white audience, then to go beyond those stereotypes to attain his goals. The context in which Washington acted was one that Baker says had slavery as a beginning historical precedent, even though the signifying that it implies reaches back to African roots. This discourse, however, looks no further for its images than those images of slavery—of blacks as childlike, often without ambition or "white" morals, "needing" white guidance and support for survival. It is from this tradition that the white conception of the African-American embodied in the minstrel show character or in the characters familiar to the white audience that were created in both the book and the play *Uncle Tom's Cabin*, a white northern woman's conception of the Negro, appeared and grew.

In representational iconography that was created in the Harlem Renaissance, this mask can be seen in some of the work of painter Palmer Hayden. David Driskell writes:

> Hayden saw no reason to refrain from borrowing from the popular images of Blacks by White artists. He often exaggerated Black features, stylizing eyes, noses, lips, and ears, and making the heads of many of his subjects look bald and rounded in form. But he insisted that he was not poking fun at Black people. (132)

Hayden was interested in folklore and felt his images were creating a visual representation of that folklore. Because of a lack of critical acceptance, however, he was often placed in a position of defending his work. Hayden actually repainted his autobiographical *The Janitor Who Paints*. The "Black man wearing a beret" and the "beautiful young black woman holding a child" cover the original painting in which "the janitor looks like a caricature of a Black person" and "the beautiful black woman and her lovely newborn are a minstrel-faced mammy and a grinnin' child" (Campbell, 33). In her introduction to *Harlem Renaissance: Art of Black America* Mary Campbell writes:

> Hayden's deliberately self-effacing interpretation of his efforts as an artist, his insistence on portraying Blacks with the masks of the minstrels—that is, as performers for a White audience—and his ingratiating reference to the benevolence of his liberators, are probably honest ... portrayals of Hayden's very real feelings about his efforts at making art. As such, they are poles apart from Meta Fuller's aristocratic defiance and political sophistication or Aaron Douglas's epic perspective on the history and origins of the African-American. (33)

Meta Fuller's work and that of Aaron Douglas better fit the second mask, or "veil," of which Baker writes, that of deformation (essentially de-formation), in which the act of speech or performance goes beyond, or de-forms expectations in a return to an ancient trope of form—in this case a return to African and primitive motifs. This de-formation creates a space in which new forms and tropes, based on transformations of older ones, are possible. Through the use of de-formation, many diverse sounds, images, and voices are possible. A polyphonic present that includes many past forms, ways of being, or ways of seeing can be created: For example, the return to primitive motifs in the painting of Aaron Douglas goes beyond the historical fact of slavery as the beginning point of his imagistic discourse, returning rather to African roots and to a long history that did not begin with, but included and survived, slavery. Douglas's flat, hard-edged style that harkens back to African motifs probably reached its greatest achievement in his thirties' mural "Aspects of Negro Life," a work that contains much reference not only to the history of the slave and to African roots, but also to the trope of music.

These divergent discourses, both Washington's style and DuBois's vision, have relationships to music. The musical form of jazz is transformative in the same sense as any other discourse for the melodies of jazz can be traced through combinations of syncopated marching bands, ragtime, blues, and spirituals—transformations of those African melodies imported with persons sold as slaves. Through the use of one or the other of these forms of discourse, a freed world is provided to the audience. The form used extends from that of the expectations of a white audience (or a black audience enjoying the actors'—and their own—ability to signify on the more powerful white world) to an interest in determining a past and rootedness through the tracing of roots and culture through slavery to African sources. The reversal, or the control that the performer holds, is contained in the private joke of the performers who act from behind this mask and in the vision of the black audience which is a party to the signifying being done. The signifying is not revealed to those outside. Performance, then, occurs to a greater or lesser degree as a masque depending on spectators' understanding and expectations.

Genevieve Fabre cites a historical precedent for such masquerade and reversal in her *Drumbeats, Masks and Metaphor:*

> From the time they boarded ships for the passage to the New World, slaves provided shows for the entertainment of whites.... From their very first appearances, these shows took on a subversive character. Similar in form to African ceremonies or festivals, they were clearly occasions to perpetuate certain customs and to preserve the cultural heritage.... Mimed songs that had all the appearance of praising whites actually satirized them. Slaves were thus able to express their dissatisfaction and unhappiness without risking punishment for their insolence. (4)

The issue of control raised by Fabre is vital, as is the issue of an African-American standard for judging African-American art. In *Black Theatre: Premise and Presentation*, Carlton and Barbara Molette state:

> There is presently a great deal of concern that many Afro-American concepts or aesthetics are so totally a product of white oppression that we ought not to glorify them. Some have taken the position that we should consciously reject traditional Afro-American art that is clearly connected to oppression. (43)

The Molettes however, feel that art must reflect the cultural experience of the maker and of the audience for that art. They stress the importance of who is in control of the form and production of art. In speaking of Black theatre they say:

Although the style of the language and other such surface characteristics may have changed through the years, there is no indication that the intended functions of Black theatre for Black audiences have changed concurrently. The combined use of double meaning and comic irony as a contributor to survival within an environment of systematic oppression appears to be a recurring function, as does the galvanizing of existing anti-slavery sentiment. (35)

Whenever a Black comic hero succeeds in controlling his destiny while exhibiting wit and comic irony, Black audiences seem to be willing to accept some accompanying racial cliches. So, as heroes in plays by Black playwrights are encountered, a key question must constantly be raised: Who is really in control? (113)

The question of control in theatre might best be looked at through a musical review that appealed strongly to both black and white audiences. "Shuffle Along," the first all-black musical play of the twenties to be seen on Broadway, appealed to both black and white audiences although it was conceived for black theatre. Written, directed, and acted by African-Americans, "Shuffle Along" was described as an "explosion" of energy, singing and dancing on stage. The plot was concerned with the campaign for mayor of one virtuous and one not-so-virtuous pair of candidates. Both black and white audiences loved the show. Stanley Green says "white audiences were happy to travel a bit north of the theatre district to enjoy the show's earthy humor, fast pacing, spirited dancing, and infectious rhythms" (1921 np).

We, looking back, are taken aback by the pictures of this production which show black actors in blackface. While familiar with Al Jolson's state renditions of black, minstrel-like characters in such plays as "Bombo" and "Sinbad," or his rendition of "Mammy," sung from his knees in the movie "The Jazz Singer," we do not expect to see black actors performing in blackface for a black audience. Yet the use of such a mask descends from the tradition of minstrel show where stereotypical portrayals of African-Americans were performed for white audiences and from which blacks were often barred as audience. As we do not expect Palmer Hayden's hidden janitor who paints, we do not expect such interpretations from black actors. Yet "Shuffle Along" had wide appeal for black audiences as well as white ones—for white audiences not only because of the power and energy of the performances, but also because expectations of black stereotypes were reinforced. The appeal for black audiences was because of excellence and energy of the performances and *the signifying irony* that bonded performers and audience members.

"Shuffle Along" as a musical revue differed from the Eugene O'Neill play that opened the white stage to black actors and that created white interest in Africa-American culture and theatre—the drama "The Emperor Jones." O'Neill's character Brutus Jones, while a fine psychological portrait of a disintegrating man, is a portrait of a black man whose descent and spiritual collapse is directly related to the misuse of power; a concept that many black critics call a Eurocentric rather than an Afrocentric view of the psyche. O'Neill's creation, then, is seen by many black critics as a white creation for a white audience. Loften Mitchell in his book *Black Drama* says that, during the twenties revival of the play in Harlem, when Jules Bledsoe, the actor who played Brutus Jones, ran fearfully through the jungle "negroes shouted from the audience: 'Man, you come on outa that jungle! This is Harlem!' " (84).

Despite excellent stock companies, the cost of tickets and the production of plays like "The Emperor Jones" or "In Abraham's Bosom" by white authors and a failure to speak to the daily life of African-Americans caused a decline in black theatre. Mitchell says "It was ... easy for people to turn from the lies and fairy tales placed on the American stage to those manufactured by Hollywood, especially since the latter were considerably less expensive" (84). Although black film companies were developed in Harlem, the stranglehold of Hollywood distribution made their continued existence problematic because of production costs and the limited revenues that could be gained without wide distribution. Images of blacks in Hollywood films were stereotypical and created for white audience expectations. The stereotypes of lazy, stupid, shiftless black male characters in the early silent films of "Rastas" and "Sambo," the later roles of Stepin Fetchit, the easily frightened, gullible black, or the singing mammy were the images that Hollywood projected for many years. Black audiences often had to create reversals in order to identify with movies. In Hollywood film, the locus of control was certainly not with the African-American performer engaging with an African-American audience. In *Black Magic* Langston Hughes and Milton Meltzer indicate the extent of Hollywood stereotyping, the lack of control of the black artist or writer, and the failure to recognize the potential of a black audience.

If film characters were stereotyped, the characters created by African-American writers during the Harlem Renaissance were not. Writing had a wide range. Claude McKay's *Home to Harlem*, a celebration of primitive sexuality and sensuality that caused W.E.B. DuBois to say that he felt he needed to take a bath (Lewis, "Harlem," 72) explored a world of sex, clubs, and music that was entirely black. Like the artist Douglas, McKay was concerned with a primitive motif, but with a very different outlook and outcome, one greatly concerned with sexual prowess.

While McKay was criticized for the blatant sexuality of *Home to Harlem*, the Harlem community felt that white writer and critic, Carl Von Vechten, an avid supporter of the Harlem Renaissance and frequent visitor not only to clubs but to house parties as well, had betrayed them with the sexual portraits that made up his book about Harlem, *Nigger Heaven*.

In contrast, Nella Larsen's fiction explores the African-American middle class world and examines the constructs of race in *Passing*, and in *Quicksand* the Mulatto's place in society. Larsen's protagonist, Helga Crane, is divided in her feeling about Harlem, at first feeling it is home, then feeling later that Harlem is a world from which she must escape. She is not comfortable in either the black or the white world, and is destroyed as a result of her search for identity.

In Larsen's, McKay's, and Von Vechten's books, clubs, music and dancing are all important parts of Harlem life. It was, after all, primarily the music, musical artists, and new dance forms that attracted white audiences to the more "sexually free and primitive" Harlem. The influence of musical forms on literature may, however, be seen most clearly in the poetry of Sterling Brown and Langston Hughes. Brown celebrates Blues singer Ma Rainey as well as the Blues form from which jazz developed. Kathy J. Ogren, in her essay "Controversial Sounds: Jazz Performance as Theme and Language in the Harlem Renaissance" says "Hughes equates the effect of the performance atmosphere with that of the Garden of Eden and of ancient Africa" in "Jazzonia" (172). She says Hughes's 1920s poems are his "own blues and jazz performances" (174).

The clubs *were* music, and music more than any other expression survived the slave voyages form Africa, slavery, emancipation, segregation, and the Jim Crow laws. Transformations of musical forms and the interpretations given by musicians are perhaps the most outstanding heritage of the Harlem Renaissance. Music not only informed the other art productions of the time, but more than art, theatre, film or writing, music has been the transformative trope that created the most cultural and artistic appreciation for black artists.

Jazz, the musical drawing card of Harlem, was not unknown to the white population. World War I disseminated and popularized jazz. When James Reese Europe enlisted in the army and was asked to form a musical regiment, he presented concerts in the States before debarkation for Europe and left the trenches to play in Paris, taking France and Europe by storm with the innovative musical techniques that Europe described as innately black. Europe said:

> I have come back from France more firmly convinced than ever that negroes should write negro music. We have our own racial feeling and if we try to copy whites we will make bad copies.... Our musicians do their best work when using negro material. (Southern, 225)

In the jazz clubs of Harlem, the musician ruled. The world of Harlem, that pre-taste of paradise, was greatest for the musician. As Doctor Clayton wrote in "Angels in Harlem," Harlem was the place where brown-skinned angels in the form of blues singers, worldly angels, helped to find a way for an exchange of culture in an increasingly changing and transformative world. He wrote:

> I know Harlem can't be Heaven 'cause New York is right down here on earth,
> But it's headquarters for brownskin angels from everywhere else in this world....
> I know blues singers don't go to Heaven 'cause Gabriel bawls 'em out,
> But all the good ones go to Harlem and help them angles beat it out. (Oliver, 77)

Those angels of the blues and jazz musicians helped to carry the poetry, writing, music and art of Harlem far beyond its geographic boundaries as well as beyond the relational boundaries of time, leaving us not only with a memory of a nostalgic past, but with a tradition that continues to grow and change, and transform.

BIBLIOGRAPHY

Baker, Houston A. Jr. *Modernism and the Harlem Renaissance*. Chicago: University of Chicago, 1987.

Bakhtin, Mikhail M. "From the Prehistory of Novelistic Discourse." *The Dialogic Imagination: Four Essays by M. M. Bakhtin*. Ed. by Michael Holquist. Trans. by Caryl Emerson and Michael Holquist. Austin: University of Texas, 1981.

Brown, Sterling. "Ma Rainey." Houston A. Baker, Jr. *Modernism and the Harlem Renaissance*. Chicago: University of Chicago, 1987.

Campbell, Mary Schmidt. "Introduction." *Harlem Renaissance: Art of Black America*. Charles Meirs, ed. New York: Abrams, 1987.

Clayton, Doctor. "Angels in Harlem." Paul Oliver. *Aspects of the Blues Tradition*. New York: Oak, 1970.

Davis, Ossie. "Forward." Langston Hughes and Milton Meltzer. *Black Magic: A Pictorial History of the African American in the Performing Arts*. New York: DeCapo, 1990.

Driskell, David C. "The Flowering of the Harlem Renaissance: The Art of Aaron Douglas, Meta Warwick Fuller, Palmer Hayden, and William H. Johnson." *Harlem Renaissance: Art of Black America*. Ed. by Charles Meirs. New York: Abrams, 1987.

Fabre, Genevieve. *Drumbeats Masks and Metaphor: Contemporary Afro-American Theatre*. Trans. by Melvin Dixon. Cambridge: Harvard, 1983.

Green, Stanley. *Broadway Musicals, Show by Show*. Milwaukee: Leonard, 1990.

Hughes, Langston and Milton Meltzer. *Black Magic: A Pictorial History of the African-American in the Performing Arts*. New York: DeCapo, 1990.

Larsen, Nella. *Quicksand* and *Passing*. New Brunswick: Rutgers, 1986.

Lewis, David Levering. "Harlem My Home." *Harlem Renaissance: Art of Black America*. Ed. by Charles Meirs. New York: Abrams, 1987.

_____. *When Harlem Was in Vogue*. New York: Knopf, 1981.

McKay, Claude. *Home to Harlem*. Boston: Northeastern University, 1987.

Mitchell, Loften. *Black Drama: The Story of the American Negro in the Theatre*. New York: Hawthorn, 1967.

Molette, Carlton W. and Barbara J. Molette. *Black Theatre: Premise and Presentation*. Bristol: Wyndham Hall, 1986.

Ogren, Kathy J. "Controversial Sounds: Jazz Performance as Theme and Language in the Harlem Renaissance." *The Harlem Renaissance: revaluations*. Eds. Amritjit Singh, William S. Shiver, and Stanley Brodwin. Hofstra: Garland, 1989.

Oliver, Paul. *Aspects of the Blues Tradition*. New York: Oak, 1970.

Southern, Eileen. *Readings in Black American Music*. New York: Norton, 1971.

Stowe, Harriet Beecher. *Uncle Tom's Cabin or, Life Among the Lowly*. New York: Penguin, 1981.

GENEVIÈVE FABRE

Toomer's *Cane*
and the Harlem Renaissance

It seems ironical that, at a time when minds were set on ideas of rebirth and awakening, Toomer called *Cane*—a work that opened a new innovative and modernist era—his "swan song," ironical also that Toomer, who was considered one of the new and most promising stars, disappeared so quickly from the Harlem literary scene.[1] When the book came out, it was hailed mostly by whites who had read parts of *Cane* in *Broom*, *The Double Dealer*, or *The Little Review*. Waldo Frank, who had traveled with him to Georgia and wrote the foreword to this first edition, Gorham Munson, Alfred Kreymborg, Robert Littell, Paul Rosenfeld, who wrote enthusiastic reviews, and Sherwood Anderson, who had been corresponding with Toomer, all thought highly of Toomer's exceptional gifts as a writer. Among black critics the book received milder praise, and few were those who tried to assess its originality beyond cursory and impressionistic remarks.[2] W.E.B. Du Bois and William Stanley Braithwaite however hailed him in their reviews in *Crisis*. Years later, Alain Locke was to stress Toomer's ability to soar "above the plane of propaganda and apologetics to a self-sufficient presentation of Negro life in its own idiom," giving it "a proud and self-revealing evaluation."[3] Most critics were just eager to present the book as an example of the idealistic and assertive affirmation of race that was to characterize the renaissance. Claude Barnett, the editor of the Associated Negro Press, had a brief exchange of letters with Toomer, who seems not to have appreciated the

From *Jean Toomer and the Harlem Renaissance*, edited by Geneviève and Michel Feith. © 2001 by Rutgers, The State University.

terms in which he assessed his work: "My style, my esthetic, is nothing more or less than my attempt to fashion my substance into a work of art."

Cane eludes description and categories and can be seen as both a part of and apart from, the renaissance. Published before the guidelines for New Negro writing were set in Locke's seminal anthology, it is more of a forerunner than a direct emanation of the movement. In tune with certain concerns—social, moral and esthetic, or philosophical—of the time, it developed in directions that were dictated less by tradition, prescription, or fashion than by Toomer's inner convictions and exigencies, and these often went against the grain of the spirit of the era or were inspired by experiences—personal, literary, and professional—that took Toomer away from Harlem.

The book was born of two major experiences: Toomer's encounters with literature and with the South and "the souls of black folk."[4] After having experimented with a variety of trainings and activities, Toomer, following his paternal uncle's inclination for reading, discovered a new passion for books: Dostoevski, Baudelaire, Freud, Frost and the imagists, Hart Crane, Waldo Frank (the author of *Our America*), and Sherwood Anderson were among his favorite authors and awakened his vocation. After giving most of his time to writing, he suddenly felt that "he had in his hands the tools for his creation" (Turner, *Wayward*, 53–58). The attention he received from magazines like the *Double Dealer* and *Broom* confirmed him in his determination to become a writer. A visit to the South with Waldo Frank, who later published *Holiday*,[5] and a stay in Georgia where he had a position in a school further inspired him to write *Cane:* "There was a valley, the valley of cane, with smoke wreaths during the day and mist at night. The folk spirit was walking to die on the modern desert; that spirit was so beautiful, its death was so tragic. This was the feeling that I put in *Cane*" (Turner, *Wayward*, 58).

Toomer always connected his artistic growth with his Georgia experience; he spoke lyrically and metaphorically about it as a springing to life and repeatedly paid tribute to the folk spirit. The creation of *Cane*, he wrote, "is like a leaf that will unfold, fade, die, fall, decay and nourish me." In the same metaphorical mood, a mood that is to be found in many pages of *Cane*, he wrote to Anderson: "My seed was planted in the cane-and-cotton fields and in the souls of black and white people in the small southern town. My seed was planted in myself down there"(Turner, *Cane*, 148). Reversing the path that many took, seeking the "city of refuge" and embracing the future they saw opening on the horizon, Toomer returned to the land of his ancestors, to the land and soil, and embraced its fading culture.

"There is nothing about these pieces of the buoyant expression of a new race," he said about some pages that came nearest to the "Old Negro" (Turner, *Cane*, 151). In spite of his optimistic statements when he described his artistic involvement in the writing of *Cane*, a close reading of the work suggests that the experience must have been rather excruciating and perplexing; the work revealed greater complexities and contradictions than he was willing to admit in his enthusiastic reports to his friends. The book speaks insistently, through its images and metaphors, of the gap between what was sought and longed for and what had actually been reached and achieved. Toomer's communion with the South and his Negro heritage was fraught with ambivalent feelings, with uncertainty about the future of the race, about what literature or art could do, with a sense of unfulfilled hopes and ambitions and of partial failure. It is perhaps these tensions, to which he managed to give controlled artistic expression, that make for the unique character of *Cane*.

Two pieces may best illustrate the diversity of moods and modes, strains and voices to be found in *Cane* and the careful composition that pits them against one another or weaves them together: "Harvest Song" and "Kabnis."

In his description of the movement that informed *Cane* in his December 1922 letter to Waldo Frank, Toomer said that "from the point of view of the spiritual entity behind the work," after an awakening the curve plunges into "Kabnis" ... ends in "Harvest Song" (Turner, *Cane*, 152).

"Harvest Song"—an antithesis to the more hopeful "Song of the Son"—can be read as a prelude to "Kabnis" and an artistically pertinent ending to Toomer's swan song. Blending fear and anger, aspirations, and a sense of lack of accomplishment, it gives the lie to what one might read into its title. The time of the day—sundown and dusk—and of the year—the end of the harvest season—is conducive to reflection; after a day's work, the "reaper," in an implicit analogy with Toomer's own harvesting during his traveling season in the South, looks back on what he has accomplished and onward to what the future has in store for him. The voice that is heard through the poem is different from the new black voices one would expect to hear at the onset of the renaissance. Although the word "hunger," used as a verb and substantive and in many variations as a sort of inner rhyme and burden in this poem, may express desire, expectation, and anticipation, it also means deprivation, dearth, exhaustion, and weariness. The reaper-poet is shown here as having partly lost the acuity of his senses ("blades are dulled"), on which so much of the perception of the living world depends. "Chilled," "fatigued," "dry," "dulled," "blind," and "deaf": all these words seem to spell his fate and seal it in dusk and caking dust. The season is over, and yet the harvest has not been up to the reaper's expectations; his longing for knowledge—the grain—and for companionship is unfulfilled. Unfulfilled too is the promise expressed in "Cotton Song." The song will not be the work song and the call-and-response that could help sustain energy during the harvest between distant reapers. This is an unfinished song, and, more dramatically, the "singer" seems unable to respond to any call or offering from his fellow workers: "I fear I could not taste it."

The positive and poetic quality of dusk, so strikingly present at certain moments in *Cane*, seems lost here, even if some sweetness or softness still endures. But this unborn song is nevertheless a song, a blues from a solitary reaper, and the chant of all the other harvesters who, unseen, unheard, brothers or strangers, all share his condition and predicament.

If the harvest-reaper motif could serve as a metaphor for what the New Negro movement hungered to be, this song certainly did not fit the mood that prevailed when parties were organized in New York to celebrate the new era. Toomer's reaper is a poor prototype for the New Negro. Although the hunger for knowledge was vividly expressed in the poem, the fear of that hunger and the fear of sterility were never so clearly voiced. Yet the blues-song-poem, with all its tensions and uncertainties, is not only Toomer's parting song—when his own harvest is perhaps left unfinished and he realizes that "you can't go home again"—it also epitomizes the situation of any poet, whose mission is never totally accomplished. While experimenting with that particular musical form, the work song, Toomer also paid tribute to that part of the rural and folk heritage that did not receive much attention from the poets of Harlem and to the workers of the soil who nurtured tradition and were only left with the stubble since, as the popular song goes, "the white folks get the corn, the niggers get the stalk."

"And Kabnis is me," wrote Toomer when he spoke enthusiastically of his writing to his friend and travel companion, Waldo Frank, to whom he dedicated this third section of *Cane*. "Kabnis sprang up almost in a day, now it seems to me.... There [in Georgia] for the first time I saw the Negro, not a pseudo-urbanized and vulgarized, a semi-americanized product, but the Negro peasant, strong with the tang of fields and soil. It was there that I first heard the folk-songs rolling up the valley at twilight, heard them as spontaneous and narrative utterances. They filled me with gold, and tints of an eternal purple. Love? Man, they gave birth to a whole new life.... I am certain I would get more inner satisfaction from a free narrative form....

When I say 'Kabnis,' nothing inside me says 'complete, finished'" (Turner, *Cane*, 151).

Toomer's reports on his writing contain many clues for our reading of his text: the meaning folk songs had to him, the importance of their integration in the narrative structure, the emphasis on a free narrative form and on visual as well as aural images, the symbolic scheme of colors, and the opposition between the urban and rural Negro. One is struck also by the way the experience is described as a rebirth, in a mood that is in keeping with the renaissance discourse. Yet this text makes no reference to the strains and tangles that are very much present in "Kabnis"—a text that does not have the clarity of purpose, the illuminating simplicity that parts of the letter seem to suggest. In the little town of Sempter, the true peasant is seen only fleetingly; "Kabnis" offers a gallery of portraits that represent a whole range of characters in a setting that is already spoiled by the assault of "civilization" and where the effects of semiurbanization and Americanization can be felt. There is no mention in the letter of the critical gaze Toomer fixed on Northerners and Southerners and on their failure to communicate, on the inadequacies and inefficiencies of his central character, the would-be educator, poet, and singer. We have no indication either of why he chose to give to the title figure a puzzling mixture of poetic and burlesque traits.[6] The letter makes no mention of the mock-epic, grotesque, comic, and fantastic elements so frequent in "Kabnis" or of the use of irony and parody. Finally, the mood that dominates the text is more ambiguous and disquieting and poetically complex than what we would anticipate from Toomer's statements to Frank.

The following remarks will focus on two aspects in "Kabnis": dramatic form and songs.[7] Like other writers of the renaissance, Toomer was attracted to the theater and played with the idea of creating, not a folk drama as Hughes and Hurston did with *Mule Bone* and other productions, but a new idiom that would introduce a greater diversity of perspective and voices and those elements that his lyrical narrative and his poetical or realistic descriptions could not accommodate. The potentialities that the dramatic mode offered and that are explored in *Balo* or *Natalie Mann* and in many pages of *Cane* interested him both as a frame for this longer piece and as a metaphor to represent more fully a situation, a dilemma, or contradictory emotions, feelings, and ideas.[8] The mode also allowed for a greater distance—both critical and ironic—to his subject, the "Kabnis is me," and to the description of his own divided self and ambiguous response to the whole experience, to race and violence in the South, and to the dialectical tension between the beauty and the ugliness he encountered. Conflicts and contradictory impulses could thus be dramatized, and the tragedy of it all could be relieved by comic interludes.

Like Hurston, Toomer was fascinated with the language of the "folk" who lived in these rural communities, the way they dealt with the slave heritage of indirectness, double dealing, and disguise, with the whole range of expressive modes he found in the vernacular—jokes that Hurston called "lies," maxims, proverbs and sayings, witticisms, and the propensity for metaphor.[9] Toomer could experiment more freely with all these forms in his dialogue, integrate them in the new idiom he was striving to create, in homage to the richness and diversity of folk culture. Contrasting them with the more polished, intellectual language of the aspiring Southern elite or the Northern literati, he was able to dramatize the gap, the lack of understanding and communication when Kabnis is unable to take a joke or when his companions make fun of his lyrical flights or of his philosophical-metaphysical divagations. Toomer's talent for satire—which shows his closeness to other writers of the renaissance: George Schuyler (*Black No More*), Wallace Thurman (*The Blacker the Berry*), or Jessie Fauset (*Comedy, American Style* and *Plum Bun*)—could expose pretentiousness, pomposity, and inflation; it could even offer a sort of self-parody of his own poetic lyricism by introducing sudden antitheses or ironic comments by the narrator or one of the characters. Toomer could more freely express his objection to the religious language of some preachers, to the self-righteousness of moralists and "sin bogies of respectable southern colored folk," or to the rhetoric of his times, blending in a grotesque fashion the message of a Booker T. Washington with that of the New Negro. He did this in a masterly way by taking as a target Kabnis's worst enemy, Hanby, and turning him into a burlesque figure. Hanby's tirade in section three can be read as a brilliant parody of the prevailing discourse on the progress of the race.

In "Kabnis," more than in other pieces, Toomer was eager to find a way of discussing certain serious issues and ideas that he took very much to heart. These found expression in the dialogues with Lewis and with the representative figures of the small Georgia town and in Kabnis's conversation with himself, but the narrator treats them in a playful or grotesque mode that illuminates them in an unusual fashion. Toomer exposed them to more critical appraisal by having them discussed in the most preposterous moments or situations or by having them uttered as absolute truths or dangerous truisms or jokes by ludicrous or mock-heroic characters. His later writings which treated these matters more directly and seriously, were not as successful aesthetically. Although the grotesque has been carefully studied by some critics, like Fritz Gysin, the satiric and humorous veins have not always received the attention they deserve.

It is also interesting to look at Toomer's use of descriptions as stage directions or the use of stage directions as descriptions: given with precision and objectivity, in a neutral tone, in terse, short sentences, they offer a wealth of realistic details and notations that immediately assume symbolic or metaphoric dimensions. Objects, lights and colors, the moment of the day, the position of the characters in space or in relation to one another, their motions and gestures are meticulously described and suggest feelings or inner thoughts. One is struck also by their cinematic quality, and perhaps as directions they would be more appropriate in a film script than in a play. The descriptive passages alternate with poetic phrasing and more enigmatic statements that create a mysterious and elusive atmosphere and are often offered in sharp contrast to the dialogue that follows. Whether they portray interior scenes, faces, or the landscape, these "directions" are elaborate compositions, vividly visualized, musically treated, evoking Toomer's close connection in his writing with the pictorial arts and music of his time.

The rich and creative way in which Toomer plays with the idea and concept of theater/drama could be further developed by looking at his use of performance, theatricality, and role playing and shifting, not only in "Kabnis" but throughout *Cane*. A close look at two moments in "Kabnis" may illustrate Toomer's use of vocabulary, motifs, and imagery in order to enhance the dramatic irony.

In the opening scene, Kabnis, in a sort of monologue akin to, yet different from, the stream of consciousness method, has a long dialogue with an invisible companion, whose identity remains mysterious. This "sweetheart" could be one of the women whose presence he longs for, or he may have used the term ironically to designate a whole array of possible interlocutors with whom he will be confronted in his fits of anger and madness: the undesirable creatures that haunt his cabin—a hen, a stray dog— or himself, the "other" Kabnis, his double, or some deaf and mute irresponsible god in a Godforsaken country, or perhaps some incarnations of his fears and fantasies. This imaginary dialogue, staging Kabnis's divided self and inner tensions is tragicomic; Kabnis's solitary confinement in the "mud hole" is real, and so are his confusion and his hunger for companionship and communication; the scene anticipates other moments when desperate calls for attention will only meet sarcasm, silence, or indifference. Not really heard by his fellow companions, even in hours of joyful conviviality, Kabnis himself often will not listen or not hear what the others have to say, rejecting them or fearing to be rejected. The calls get no response. This opening also presents Kabnis as a rather comical and ludicrous figure, who fears harmless and familiar animals that are part of the daily lives of Southern rural blacks; it prepares us for all the inadequacies and deficiencies that other episodes will reveal. This rather trivial drama and comic interlude, which ends with Kabnis's wringing off the chicken's head because its insolent cackling is driving him mad, foreshadows other instances of insanity that will demand more tragic sacrificial victims.

The gruesome lynching stories that will be told to Kabnis to kill his excessive innocence and force him to face the real "face" of the South later throw a different light on the initial scene. The killing of the hen seems like a parody of lynching, performed with the same casualness—in the South the life of a "nigger" does not count more than that of a hen—with the same determination and destructive violence, the same self-righteousness and insanity. Ironically Kabnis is animated with the same anger and fear as the lynchers. Unconsciously, he reenacts a ritual of violence that is being perpetuated on his people (a people whom, in another moment of insanity, he will reject as his ancestors). The scene that in a more prosaic vein reminds us that blacks often vented their anger and frustrations on animals closest to them, has other, more tragic or ironic, implications. On one level, the overly soft Kabnis playfully trains himself to become a "square face" to confront the world, "and the body of the world is bullnecked" (153). His mock fight with the hen is part of his initiation into a violent and "ugly" world. His grotesque cursing of the hen heralds the curses to come, directed at all those who irritate him, shouters and preachers, and ultimately at God himself, his maker. On another level, the sacrifice of the hen introduces him as actor and accomplice into a world of violence and designates him as one of its next possible victims. Not only will a fear-ridden Kabnis imagine that he is the next prey of men hunters, but he will, in a self-destructive, suicidal impulse, wish to lynch his own soul: "I want t feed th soul ... wish t God some lynchin white man ud stick his knife through it an pin it to a tree. An pin it to a tree. You hear me?"(224–225). The lynching image becomes a fit metaphor for his love and hatred of the "nigger" soul, and the language of violence is perhaps the only possible response to the pain he could read in the eyes of his people and to the hell that is evoked in their songs: "You know what hell is cause youve been there. Its a feelin an its ragin in my soul in a way that'll pop out of me an run you through, an scorch y, an burn an rip your soul" (232). In many ways, Toomer anticipates the violence to be found in the theater of the 1960s, most notably in LeRoi Jones's Revolutionary Theater. One of Kabnis's major confrontations as a teacher educated in the North and a poet whose ambition is to "become the face of the South" ("How my lips would sing for it, my songs being the lips of its soul"; 158) is perhaps his grappling with words, the silent words on the lips of a muted people, the words on the lips of white folks, black or yellow niggers. "Been shapin words t fit my soul"—this phrase is repeated like a burden in a song, with many variations: "I've been shapin words after a design that branded here. Those words I was tellin y about, they won't fit int th mold thats branded on m soul." Part of the growth of Kabnis will be the recognition that the "beautiful an golden" words that he looked for to translate the beauty "his eyes had seen" in the Georgia landscape—to paraphrase a well-known spiritual—would not suffice to embrace the whole experience: "Th form thats burned int my soul is some twisted awful thing that crept in from a dream, a godam nightmare, an wont stay still unless I feed it. And it lives on words. Not beautiful words. Misshapen, split-gut, tortured, twisted words" (223–224), as twisted as the mind and soul of the one who utters them.

Toomer's choice of the dramatic form enabled him to stage all these confrontations, between the dream and the nightmare, the beauty and the ugliness, the excitement and the pain. In his word-shaping activity, Kabnis is also confronted with other artists, like Halsey, who has been carving things out of blocks of wood or with the liquor maker who is doing with a still what Kabnis tries to do with words (184). It is significant that Kabnis, at the end of the play in Halsey's workshop, resorts to a craft he "was good at th day he ducked from the cradle" (223). The descendant of a family of orators, who likes rhetorical outbursts, inflation, and exaggerations, has to learn his trade more modestly.

Kabnis's coming to grips with words is also effectively conveyed through the staging of his encounters with the various characters who, in some way, impersonate the discourse to be found in the South or force him to find an appropriate response through his own use of language to the enigma or challenge they offer.

Whether the dramatis personae are friends or foes, models or foils, doubles or antagonists—and most are both at the same time—they force Kabnis to dialogue with a part of himself that he has been unwilling to acknowledge or to see some aspect of the world he would rather be blind to. Kabnis's drama and the stages of his consciousness are illuminated through a multiplicity of scenes and settings that deserve careful attention. One of the most theatrical moments is perhaps when Toomer turns Kabnis into a real actor and stage director to perform a mock-heroic piece that is both a self-parody and a pastiche of a theater form (an implicit allusion to the minstrel tradition?) and seems best suited to Kabnis's personality and propensity for inflation and exaggeration. The theater serves also as metaphor for all the role-playing and shifting, for the masquerading, masking, and unmasking and disguise that are important motifs in *Cane:* it enabled Toomer to deal in both a playful and serious way with autobiographical material he treated very differently in his more straightforward autobiographical writings.

The staging of the last scenes of *Cane* contributes to enhance the mystery of the ending as it plays on sharp contrasts between settings: dusk and dawn, physical movements or words and moods, attitudes and emotions. The long delayed confrontation between Kabnis and the Old Man, the father image that the "bastard son" longed to find and was repeatedly denied, takes place in the Hole, another hole where Kabnis fears to be entrapped: it is suddenly transformed from a convivial merrymaking space where Halsey and his friends try to forget the frustrations of their lives into a dark and gloomy underground retreat where a solitary old figure seems to be awaiting death. The scene, highly visualized, can be read as the climax of "Kabnis" and as the son's parting song to a declining era.

To Kabnis's more dramatically inclined disposition, the immobility and apparent resignation of the mute, deaf, and blind old man is too remote from the "theatrics" he has imagined for the death of a parting soul (he would rather see it pinned to a tree). Just as the serenity of a Georgia landscape is too oppressing for him, so is the silence that surrounds the Old Man, and Kabnis tries to break it through his own gullibility, sarcasms, and curses. His verbal assault on Father John is like another (parodic) reenactment of the lynching ritual and accumulates all the terms used to insult "no count niggers." Kabnis's harangue is another way of rejecting what the Old Man represents—another denial—yet somehow they both share the same concern for the soul and the same insight: "The only sin is whats done against the soul. Th whole world is a conspiracy t sin" (236); and "O th sin th white folks 'mitted when they made the Bible lie" (237). The mock solemnity with which Kabnis acts, his exaggerated ceremonious gestures, his grotesque costuming in a gaudy robe he trips over help to play down the gravity of the situation. Because of his excessive physical, verbal, and emotional behavior, Kabnis cannot be taken any more seriously than the "old black fakir," "mumbling sin and death." Yet both characters, under whatever mask or disguise they appear, proffer part of that knowledge and truth that they hunger for. It is, significantly, Carrie K., the silent witness to the scene, who will gently soothe Kabnis and stop his masquerade. But, deprived of his rhetorical tools and of his robe, Kabnis, called back from his sleepless night or from his dream, must resume his new role as an apprentice to Halsey.

His ascent from the hole is not any more glorious than his descent. As he stumbles over a "bucket" of dead coals (an ironic allusion to Booker T.

Washington's famous metaphor?) and "trudges upstairs," with "eyes downcast and swollen" (238), he seems again like a "scarecrow replica" of himself and is excluded from the final scene.

The ending of "Kabnis" is deliberately problematic. Toomer often stated that he had no solution or resolution to offer, and he probably rightly sensed that the ambiguities that pervade *Cane* should not be dispelled. Lewis's questions about Father John, "Black Vulcan? ... A mute John the Baptist of a new religion—or a tongue-tied shadow of an old," are left unanswered. Kabnis's future as he goes back to the blacksmith's shop is uncertain, just as the accomplishment of his ambitious mission is deferred and his ability to embody the face of the South or the dream of a new age is questioned. This arrogant descendant of a family of orators, the butt of many jokes, still has to learn a lesson in language and has not learned to carve new words. His Northern education and concern for esthetics have "twisted" his mind and leave him unable to cope with the reality of the South. Yet we are made to think that his poetic sensibility may redeem and save him, and that the birth song that takes shape at the end of the play may anticipate his rebirth. The irony with which Toomer treated this "portrait of the artist"— Kabnis drawn as antihero or would-be poet—enabled him to deal more lightheartedly and with humorous distance with earnest matters: his sense of incompleteness when he finished *Cane*, his dissatisfaction with language, his irritation with constricting racial categories, and his hope in a new emerging identity (an identity that he tried to define through aesthetic and ethical interrogations) in an essay he may have proposed for publication in the *New Negro*; the piece was later titled "The Negro Emergent" (Jones, *Selected Essays*, 47–54).

The message, if any, is conveyed poetically in the ending, in a few lines where the narrator allows himself to use the golden words he temporarily denied Kabnis and through two picture images that are vividly visualized in two short, ambiguous paragraphs, still shrouded in mystery. One has often been described as a Nativity scene. The other is both sunrise and birth song and contains echoes of some of the most lyrical passages in *Cane*. Yet both combine effectively images of tomb and womb, of death and rebirth, imprisonment and escape, dream and reality, less to emphasize their opposition than perhaps to suggest a transitional age and a new composition that might be aptly called "dusk of dawn."

The dramatic form in "Kabnis" is further enhanced by the musical structure and the use of songs. Antiphonal in function and structure, the songs interspersed through the play interrupt or prolong the narrative and the dialogue; they serve as counterpoint, climax or anticlimax, or comment on the action and its dramatis personae; they themselves offer variations of rhyme and rhythm, of burden and chorus lines and stanzas, of moods and tones that reappear insistently and become part of the texture of the play. They often introduce, through the call-and-response pattern and the alternation of solo voice and chorus, a dramatic dialogue between the "singer"—the narrator or the central character—and the community of listeners whom he seems to summon, addressing them with an urgent request. Imperative or injunctive, the song also frames a statement or a question about a situation presented in a few phrases as a picture and an enigma, as a challenge to both mind and senses. Providing elements to frame some answer that may be expressed rhetorically as new unanswerable questions, it demands an immediate response.

Because in "Kabnis" the songs appear at crucial dramatic moments, the call is extended to the characters, who are summoned to respond, or it is a response and a comment on their situation. The songs relieve or reenforce the dramatic tension, illuminate the situation or enhance its confusion or mystery; they also encode complementary information or instructions and suggest communal relationship and spirit. They often have a narrative function: they present in a few concise terms a story or a significant, often intensely dramatic, moment in a person's life; these stories are more like vignettes in the structure of *Cane* and provide contrasts or echoes to the main story. They create a sudden irruption, a break in the narrative sequence, and at the same time serve as transitions and expansions. This interplay between songs and text is rendered even more complex by the repetition within "Kabnis" of the same song. In each reiteration, the song assumes a different meaning and intensity and in turn gives new meaning and intensity to Kabnis's "drama." Thus repeated, the song becomes irritating or haunting and cannot be dispelled. It insistently offers more images for Kabnis to deal with, and its semantic ambiguity increases the confusion. Yet as it creates an emotion and shapes an idea, it suggests keys to a deeper understanding of the "face of the South," for the rhythmical and spiritual exploration of its "soul." Repetitions within the song—phonetic and semantic—provide poetic continuities and reenforce the meaning. They also create a spell, a form of incantation, and function musically. Each song, at the same time unique and part of a collective utterance, is a call and response to other songs and echoes other calls and responses in the text. It acts as a burden whose musicality heightens the drama and challenges the imagination.

The songs, with their troubling simplicity and subtlety, play an important role in *Cane*, perhaps because Toomer sensed that this expressive form, so pervasive in the area he was visiting, was the very core of the folk culture he was suddenly confronted with. In many passages of his correspondence or his autobiographical writings, he has described his encounter with the music of black folk, which he saw as an expression of their feelings, an effort to control their emotions, a response to their experience in an attempt to transcend it. Poetically compelling, the songs were also rooted in the soil and in the community. Sensually, physically, and vibrantly present in the daily lives of the people, and with their ramifications in the past, they were solidly anchored in structures and institutions, in work and church activities; they were the mold in which the souls were shaped, offering both frame and patterns that could channel and discipline their outpourings. They resorted to devices borrowed from a diversity of traditions—of indirectness, double dealing, mask and disguise, imagery and metaphoric phrasing combined with intricate rhythmic, melodic, and harmonic variations. Improvisational, they were innovative and bore testimony to the intense creativity and dynamism of the culture. At the same time as he was overwhelmed by the music he heard in the fields, the shacks and the churches, Toomer saw it as a tragic and desperate effort to sustain a mood and tone that seemed about to disappear—an expression that was ridiculed and disparage 1 by some and might not be able to sustain the energy it so powerfully displayed: "A family of back country Negroes had only recently moved into a shack not too far away. They sang. And this was the first time I'd ever heard the folk-songs and spirituals. They were rich and sad, and joyous and beautiful. But I learned that Negroes of the town objected to them. They called them "shouting." They had victrolas and player-pianos. So, I realized with deep regret that the spirituals, meeting ridicule, would be certain to die out.... The folk spirit was walking to die on the modern desert" (Turner, *Wayward*, 123).

Like many of his contemporaries in the 1910s and 1920s, after Du Bois and Rosamond and James Weldon Johnson, before Locke, who theorized his view of the music, and like Hughes and Hurston, among many others, Toomer was fascinated with the music. His concerns were different from Locke, who wanted both to preserve the folk spirit and give it loftier forms,[10] and he was alarmed by the distortions and displacements he perceived in the new music he was beginning to hear in the small towns and cities (the second section of *Cane*, which significantly has only one song and in which the call seems unsuccessful in getting a response, is full of victrola records and sounds that are replacing the human voice). *Cane* is both celebration and dirge: it captures the vivid poignancy and beauty of the singing and, as a "parting song," it registers the signs of its dying away, and the tension between the two intensifies the drama. As a writer and poet, and very much like Hughes and other later writers like Ellison, Toomer was convinced that literature had much to learn from music, and he set out to explore all these potentialities. The whole text is full of references, explicit or implicit, to the musical culture and infused with musical motives, themes, ideas, and imagery. The songs in "Kabnis" are experiments in the poetics of music and the implications it may have for the creation of a new idiom. Toomer also delved into a deeper meaning of the songs, their capacity to convey and encapsulate the reality of experience, what he called "actuality" as opposed to vision.

It is interesting to look at the way the songs are inserted in "Kabnis," at what moment in the sequence of events, what time of day, for which listeners; at the purpose they serve, the resonance they give or receive from other parts of the text, the echoes they contain from other sections of *Cane*, their connection or sharp contrast with other poetic or dramatic utterances; at the extent to which the evocation of behavior or landscape alters them or how, conversely, they may introduce some sudden or progressive change in mood and tone, in sayings, behavior, emotions, or landscape.

We shall limit our remarks to the way these songs reverberate in Kabnis's consciousness. If we consider Kabnis's many contradictory roles—as protagonist in the drama but also as an outsider and spectatorial presence, as a "reaper" who has come from the North and shares some of the prejudices of city-bred people, as a poet who wishes to become the "lips of the south" but can be blind and deaf, as a person gifted with real insight, yet unable to deal with the whole of experience—we are made to feel that he will not be an active and creative participant in the drama. "Harvest Song" aptly describes the ambivalence of the reaper as someone who hungers for knowledge and wishes to frame a song and who fears that hunger. It anticipates Kabnis's failures as a spectatorial conscience—he is less receptive and perceptive than his double and fellow Northerner, Lewis—and as an unwilling and reluctant listener and a potential singer (the song will never come through his dry throat, and his confused utterings and his too intellectualized pronouncements will not meet with a response from indifferent listeners).

The first song occurs at dusk, in the opening scene, after a brief description of Kabnis's cabin and, like many songs, is introduced by a realistic and lyrical evocation of setting and mood. Whispered by night winds—

vagrant poets, a mirror to Kabnis's own ramblings—through black cracks in yellow walls, the weird song seems like an ironic response to the fantastic setting of the cabin and to Kabnis's attempt at settling down to a solitary and studious evening. The song is an intrusion, breaking the delusive quietness of the scene, and foreshadows many other disturbances to come. Kabnis is as unwilling to listen as he is to admit that there is more to learn from the songs than from books.

The song introduces him bluntly to the stark realities of the rural South. Verbs are at the same time injunctions—from God or from a white voice?—and statements about how things are. The "poor" rivers contrast sharply with the deep rivers of the spirituals and of Hughes's famous poem "I Have Known Rivers." There is also not much to reap from the red dust "of slave fields, dried, scattered." The enigmatic line "Burn, bear black children" anticipates at the same time images and horrid tales of violent destruction by fire and images of nurturing and fertility associated with the black (earth) mother of the later poems. In "white man's land" the only solace and escape offered to poor niggers will be the promise of "rest and sweet glory in Camp Ground." The irony of the last two lines, Toomer's incisive comment on the missionary work among Southern Negroes, will be further expanded through images of unnatural death and afterlife rest. The portentous ambiguities and silences of the song are more than Kabnis can bear to hear and he promptly dismisses the message, seeking release in a semicomic dialogue with his "sweetheart."

The second song, introduced by a lyrical passage that emphasizes the contrast between Kabnis's ludicrous but violent fight with the hen and the deceptive serenity of the Georgia night, encodes another complex message. It alternates lyrics from a lullaby with a description of a tableau: a black mother and a white child. This new scene from which black children are absent is loaded with historical memories of intimate connections between the two races and of the black mother's many functions and sacred power. It is also one of Toomer's numerous comments on the arbitrariness of the color line, the "chalk line" of clear divisions between black and white, that are offered throughout *Cane* as other elaborations on the same theme (the dramatized variation—white woman/black child presented in "Becky" or, in Layman's words: "An only two dividins. An even they aint permanent categories. They sometimes mixes um up when it comes to lynching" (172). Kabnis can identify with both the black and white children of the song: like the "half-moon" he is "half" and "neither black or white, yet both." The brown mulatto, who likes to think of himself as part of a Southern and Northern elite, is confronted with his "nigger soul" and becomes a bastardized son of the South. Kabnis is a symphony of colors and, like a chameleon, shifts from one to the other—brown or yellow or white, he can become as black as any "nigger."

The humming of the black mother in the song is ominous: "cradle will fall and down will come baby" may be nonsensical words in a croon song; they may also be prophetic of other falls to come, literally and figuratively— falls from treetops, from dreams and expectations; prophetic also of the power the Black Mother, who can kill or heal, can have over the fate of both white and black children. The cradle image contrasts with the nightmarish setting that the cabin is for Kabnis: in his mudhole, he finds neither protection nor serenity. As irritated by the song as he is by the cackling of the hen, he goes back to his mock fight and completes his mission as a "hen-neck-wringer." Yet the words, images, and sounds seem to penetrate into his consciousness, forcing him to acknowledge fragments of his identity—as both white and black, as a motherless child in search of a cradle, as an "earth child," before he sees himself as the bastard son of his maker: "God is a profligate red-nosed man about town. Bastardy; me. A bastard son has a right to curse his maker. God ... " (161). The grotesque figure of God is offered as an antithesis to the swaying black mother of the song. The lyric also announces Kabnis's encounters with several impersonations of the black mother, Stella or Carrie K., and his confrontations with her disfiguration and violent destruction.

Ironically, it not the lullaby that soothes him but the song of the chilling night winds. The repetition of the first song at the end of the second section in "Kabnis" is like a burden; enigmatic, it contains all the contradictions and tensions between white man's land and "nigger" life and the intimations of an uncertain future and certain death in an existence ruled by white will and law.

The hearing of the next song is prepared by a series of scenes that elaborate on the Camp Ground image: the gathering of Negroes around the church puts into action "the path that leads into Christian land," while another gathering in Halsey's shop unexpectedly becomes the setting for a storytelling session in which gruesome stories of cruel death and violent lynching will be told. The spiral of a buzzard above the church tower becomes as ominous as the court tower where "white minds, with indolent assumption, juggle justice and a nigger"(163) or as the moon in "Blood-Burning Moon": overshadowing Halsey's convivial meeting, it brings a "gathering heaviness" into the house. When Layman starts his tales of lynching, suddenly breaking the silence that follows such barbarous acts ("Thems things you neither does a thing or talks about if you want to stay around this away, Professor"; 173), he does so in a neutral and low-keyed voice, not unlike the soft whispering winds when they sing weirdly through the ceiling cracks (210), and is accompanied by the insistent, chanting monotone from the church. His stories are stark comments on some truths Negroes have learned to live by, illustrating sayings, maxims, or truisms: "Ain't supposed to die a natural death" or "A nigger's baby ain't supposed to live." Reminiscent of the blood-burning madness, they describe ways of going up "to rest and glory." In view of these stories, the spiritual "One More Sinner Is Acoming Home" assumes a different meaning when one knows who defines the "sin" and what kind of chastisement awaits the sinner.

If the dramatic tension is controlled in the telling, it bursts out with sudden violence in the yelling from a shouter, to recede again when the choir sings an old spiritual. While the woman's frantic cries are the immediate response to the climax in each story and an encouragement for the teller to become more daring in recalling his memories, the singing from the congregation—the chorus responding to her solo voice—is more subdued. Kabnis's reaction, his strong identification with the shouter ("Her voice is almost perfectly attuned to the nervous key of Kabnis"), his own physical response ("Fear flows inside him; it fills him up. He bloats"; 179) are as excessive as the sister's, yet he is unable to transmute the flow of emotions into song. His "I hate this yelling"—his more intellectualized reaction— exemplifies the objection many Negroes had against high-pitched notes in church singing. The parallel Toomer so artfully establishes between the drama in the church and the crescendo of the storytelling session in Halsey's home enables him to reach a deeper layer in his exploration of folk culture. This parallel is all the more effective as Kabnis's inability to cope with the face of the South is contrasted with the way the community manages to control its pain and anger. Everything in the singing in the church and in the telling in the home is carefully orchestrated, here by the preacher, there by the teller. The community, represented by both the congregation of churchgoers and by the "laymen" in two highly symbolic places, is demonstrating its capacity to find ways of dealing collectively with the experience and to create expressive forms, verbal or musical, that, in a sort of ritualistic reenactment, can help break the silence and salvage the memory.

Church choir and chorus from valley, treetops, and fields alternate in a call-and-response pattern, each set in different keys, and occasionally a solo voice rises. The music is described in vivid visual terms as it invades land and sky in a symphony of colors, sounds, and smells: "Like tallow flames, songs jet up" (192); and "An old woman fetches out her song, an th winds seem like th Lord made them fer t fetch an carry the smell o pine an cane" (220).

Images of "tongues" of flame and blood burning cannot be dispelled, just as images from "Portrait in Georgia" are conjured up here: the pervading whiteness in house walls, winds, and moonlit nights, the "ashen and still countryside" (180) evoke the image of the earlier song poem, "white as the ash of black flesh after flame" (50). The music, heard intermittently in between long silences and an unearthly hush, is insistent and overpowering, more gripping than Kabnis's solitary verbal explosions. Human voices and whispers from the wind merge in a common chant. Nature and people join to create a song that is first like a dirge, then becomes a birth song.

As the drama unfolds after several crescendos and the play proceeds to its ending, a gradual transformation from womb/night song to birth/day song takes place, and it is perhaps in this metamorphosis that the musical message of *Cane* lies, adding another enigma to Kabnis's consciousness, enjoining him to participate in the general chorus ("nigger, sing") or to create his own solo song.

When the first song is repeated in section 5, it is less grim, and the emphasis seems to be less on the destruction of body and soul than on fertility and the possibility of life's triumph over death. The few lines that open the section and introduce the "womb-song" effect this shift in meaning. The highly visualized incantatory and haunting picture of the pregnant Negress("Night, soft belly of a pregnant Negress, throbs evenly against the torso of the South"; 208), the impersonations of the night and the South, the powerful serenity of the woman—the picture evokes African sculpture and finds echoes in the "African princesses" or in the descriptions of Carrie K., "lovely in the fresh energy; in the calm and confidence and nascent maternity which rise from the purpose of her present mission" (233)—all set the scene for the womb song that in turn heralds the "birth-song" on which the play and the book end.

Songs in "Kabnis" as in the other parts of *Cane* perform many functions: poetic, lyrical, and musical, dramatic and narrative. They weave a complex web of images that combine pictures, smells, and sounds and, in their multilayered dimensions, blend literalness and metaphor, memory and prophecy, ugliness and beauty. On one level, they tell ruthless stories, harsh, unrelenting facts that create the "actuality" that Toomer encountered when he visited the South; he insisted, in one of his accounts, that what Waldo Frank called a "vision" that would have protected him was, in fact, an actuality strongly related to reality (Turner, *Cane*, 143). The facts are offered as fragments of that reality, "the face of the South," to nurture the reaper's hunger for, and fear of, knowledge. On another level, the songs, "carolling softly souls of slavery," are also "petals of dusk" (153) that the poet-reapers in *Cane*—personae like Paul and Kabnis—set out to gather; yet ironically none seems to be able to complete the harvest. If we return to "Harvest Song" as a kind of metaphor of Kabnis's unsung song and incomplete harvest, we read "Kabnis" as precisely an attempt at collecting scattered fragments that could compose the unborn song, a song that a more mature, "new" Kabnis might one day create, at last realizing an ardent wish and long deferred dreams and promises.

NOTES

This is a shorter and revised version of an essay on "Kabnis" published in Françoise Clary and Claude Julien, eds., *Jean Toomer's Cane* (Paris: Ellipses, 1997).

1. References are to Jean Toomer, *Cane* (New York: Harper and Row, 1979). References to Toomer's autobiographical writings are, unless indicated otherwise, to Darwin T. Turner, ed., *The Wayward and the Seeking: A Collection of Writings by Jean Toomer* (Washington, D.C.: Howard University Press, 1980), or to Darwin T. Turner, ed., *"Cane": The Authoritative Text, Background, Criticism* (New York: Norton, 1988). References to Toomer's essays are in Robert B. Jones, ed., *Jean Toomer: Selected Essays in Literary Criticism* (Knoxville: University of Tennessee Press, 1996). The most comprehensive bibliography is Robert Jones, "Jean Toomer: An Annotated Checklist of Criticism," *Resources for American Literary Studies* 12 (November 1995): 68–121. It provides a fairly complete list of books and articles on *Cane* published until 1995.

2. For a more detailed study of the response of contemporary writers to *Cane*, see Turner, *Cane*, 147–57; Toomer's correspondence with Sherwood Anderson, Waldo Frank, and his publisher, Liveright; and "Toomer's Art," 157–162.

3. Alain Locke, "From *Native Son* to *Invisible Man*: A Review of the Literature for 1952," *Phylon* 14:1 (March 1953): 34–44.

4. Toomer has written at some length about the genesis of *Cane*, his trip to Georgia, and his spiritual growth, both in his letters and such autobiographical writings as "Earth Being," "Incredible Journey," "Outline of an Autobiography," and "On Being an American" (see Turner, *Wayward*, section 1, 116–127, and Turner, *Cane*, 140–148).

5. Toomer wrote several critical pieces on Waldo Frank's books (see note 6). He mentions the fact that he wrote *Cane* before Frank completed *Holiday* (Turner, *Wayward*, 25). One should also note that, on several occasions, Toomer spelled *Cane* as "Cain" (Turner, *Cane*, 127).

6. One is tempted to see in both Kabnis and Lewis an ironic self-portrait in disguise. This essay does not deal with the intricate, mirrorlike relationship between Lewis and Kabnis as competing and complementary characters.

7. In "On Being an American," Toomer also mentions that his grandfather, who was an important figure in his life, "died on the day after [he] had finished the first draft of 'Kabnis,'" the long, semidramatic closing piece of Cane. Did this death lead

to significant changes in "Kabnis"? "Kabnis" is dedicated to Waldo Frank, whose complex relationship with Toomer has been analyzed by Toomer's biographers. Also see Toomer's "The Critic of Waldo Frank: Criticism, an Art Form" (Jones, *Selected Essays*, 24–31) and his "Waldo Frank's Holiday," *Dial* 75 (October 1923): 383–386.

8. On Toomer's drama, see Turner, *Wayward*, section 4, 243–410, which includes *Natalie Mann* (completed in 1922) and *The Sacred Factory: A Religious Drama of Today*. "Karintha" was written as part of *Natalie Mann*. This shows how the writing of pieces to be included in *Cane* was interwoven with Toomer's experiments in drama. Of all his plays, only *Balo* was produced, by the Howard University Dramatic Society. One should note that *Natalie Mann* and "Kabnis" were written shortly after the success of *Three Plays for a Negro Theater* by Ridgely Torrence (1917) and of *Shuffle Along* (1921). In the early 1920s, Toomer's ambition was to create a theater that would focus on the black culture and condition—an ambition later shared by Langston Hughes and Zora Neale Hurston, who, however, were more concerned with creating a dramatic Negro folk idiom.

9. Hurston treated the Negro folk idiom very differently in her anthropological works, as well as in her fiction and plays.

10. Although the importance of music in black life was recognized, many folk forms were seen as a threat to higher culture, and professional concert training and productions were encouraged. Alain Locke, who was proud to recall the folk origins of the very tradition that was then considered classic in European music, argued for a more systematic exploration of the resources of Negro music but insisted upon a broader concept and a more serious appreciation of its distinctiveness. The music after the heart of the Harlem Renaissance was to be produced much later in symphony form and concert halls with compositions like *Creole Rhapsody* (1931) and *Symphony in Black* (1934).

MICHEL FEITH

The Syncopated African: Constructions of Origins in the Harlem Renaissance (Literature, Music, Visual Arts)

The unity of the Harlem Renaissance as a historical moment and aesthetic movement has sometimes been questioned. Bundling together, under a single name tag, the extraordinary variety of the production of the time—which bridges at least two generations of African-American intellectuals and artists and several means of expression—might seem at best a convenient simplification. But trying to envisage the New Negro movement as a project rather than as a specific achievement could be a way to find a common purpose behind the widely different outlooks on the meaning of the Renaissance, as well as of African-American identity and culture. This chapter attempts to find such a unifying factor in a desire to control the image of black Americans by themselves, as opposed to the hitherto prevalent other-definition of stereotypes. The postwar era, characterized by the increased urbanization of African-Americans, seems to have been the first period in history when a project of this type had any chance of success. Even the precedent of the 1890s, which now appears as a rehearsal of the Harlem Renaissance, did not reach the same proportions and fame. It is also clear that by adopting the broad viewpoint of the image of the "race," one can encompass different artistic media, such as literature, music, and the visual arts.

We will still need a good deal of modesty before proceeding: systematic views are always flawed. What is more, because the material is so diverse and abundant, our study will have only a restricted basis. Owing to its double

From *Temples for Tomorrow: Looking Back at the Harlem Renaissance*, edited by Geneviève Fabre and Michel Feith. © 2001 by Indiana University Press.

nature as an overview of achievement and as a manifesto, we will take as our starting point the seminal *New Negro* anthology of 1925.[1] One could hardly wish for a better introduction to the politics of image.

In the first part of this chapter, I will attempt to examine a few definitions of identity, in the context of American cultural nationalism, following some of George Hutchinson's analyses. A crucial aspect of any artistic construction of African-American identity is the representation of Africa emerging from the aesthetic production: this representation will form the subject of the second part of this essay. We will finally try to ascertain the passage from black image to black vision, from African-America as subject matter to the voluntarist elaboration of an aesthetic mode of perception originating in a cross between Modernism and a specific folk culture. The lingering question in this chapter will therefore be that of heritage: what claims to authenticity can a definition of identity have when it is based on an invention of origins?

DEFINITIONS OF IDENTITY

In his *The Harlem Renaissance in Black and White*,[2] George Hutchinson contends that the Harlem Renaissance was the product of what he calls "interracial cooperation"—which could be better defined as "inter-ethnic" cooperation, given that "race," in spite of its overdetermined social currency, is an invalid concept in anthropology. More surprisingly, Hutchinson argues that for many intellectuals of the twenties, who were looking for a "usable past" as a support for American cultural nationalism, the only truly American culture was African-American. Writers and critics such as Van Wyck Brooks and Waldo Frank, in their rejection of the materialism of the United States, found few native traditions on which to build a real culture:

> The America [Brooks] saw lacked the peasantry and folk traditions of European cultures, from which great cultures are supposed ordinarily to develop.... Black writers, on the other hand, would point out that the United States *did* have a native folk culture, born of suffering and intimate contact with the soil, emotionally expressive, and above all rich in spirit as only the culture of an oppressed people could be.[3]

This passage reminds the reader of some of the developments in DuBois's *The Souls of Black Folk* (1903), both coming quite close to a literal rephrasing of European romantic nationalism, as first exposed by Herder. According to this concept, a national culture evolves from the contact between a specific soil and a specific folk, giving birth to a language and folklore, which in turn produce a particular type of high art and social institutions. The national *Kultur* is an emanation of the *Volksgeist* (spirit of the people), which it reflects at a "higher" level. This concept, which originated in Germany, soon became the dominant ideology in the Western world; it was the leading spiritual force behind the movements of German and Italian unification at the end of the 19th century and also provided a rationale for such cultural emancipation attempts as the Irish Renaissance, which Locke refers to as a model of the New Negro movement (NN 50).

George Hutchinson states that both Locke and DuBois developed a philosophy of cultural pluralism, according to which culture is a social product rather than a racial output. It may be so; but at the same time, the phraseology of a certain romantic nationalism cannot be made light of. One more example will suffice at this stage. It is another pronouncement by Locke on spirituals, in which the conjunction between a "race genius" and a "soil" is unmistakably put forward:

> The spirituals are really the most characteristic product of the race genius as yet in America. But the very elements which make them uniquely expressive of the Negro make them at the same time deeply representative of the soil that produced them. (NN 199)

If "the Negro was in vogue," according to Langston Hughes's formula, it may well be because the African-American idiom participated in this attempt at defining a "usable" folk culture in the United States. Between the extremes of excessive closeness to the European anti-model (the genteel culture of the Northeast or the pioneer world of the West) and excessive difference (Native American civilizations), African-American culture, because of its mixed nature, could provide a workable example of a purely American folk tradition. We might therefore venture the hypothesis that those intellectuals, black and white, who saw black culture as the true folk culture of the United States, as well as an image of its future evolution, did so not because they perceived it as a separate entity, but as a consequence of its plural heritage.

Yet, in a romantic cultural nationalist view, black culture had a double folk identification, which stemmed from the two "soils" of its origins: the

American South and Africa. "The Dixie Pike has grown from a goat path in Africa," Jean Toomer states in *Cane*.[4] But, in silencing the trauma of the "middle passage" and the deculturation of slavery, the poetic phrase begs the question of how to articulate, in an identity-building process, the dialectics of cultural continuity and disjunction, a process which is crucial to any consideration of the politics of image. The artistic treatment of African origins during the Harlem Renaissance might shed some light on these heterogeneous "soils of black folks."

LOOKING BACK: THE IMAGE OF AFRICA IN THE WORKS OF HARLEM RENAISSANCE ARTISTS

The central project of the Harlem Renaissance can be defined as that of controlling the image of black people, of refusing categorizations imposed from the outside. This is at least what can be inferred from Locke's statement in his preface to the *New Negro* anthology: he bestowed on African-American art the aim of "rehabilitating the race in world esteem ... a revaluation by white and black alike of the Negro in terms of his artistic endowments and cultural contributions, past and prospective" (NN 14–15). This declaration can help us assess the importance of a politics of image: because stereotypes both reflect and reinforce oppression, the act of counteracting them has symbolic efficacy. What emerges from this manifesto is the project of creating an artistic identity for African-Americans as worthy objects and as gifted subjects of art. This is very close to DuBois's notion of art as propaganda[5] or, in Nathan Huggins's ironic formulation, "The vogue of the New Negro, then, had all the character of a public relations promotion."[6]

Africa is a particularly sensitive bone of contention in this respect: the stereotype of the African as a savage has been used to justify oppression, racial inferiority having as its logical counterpart social inferiority. Hence the elaboration by several Renaissance artists of a "counter-stereotype," which is necessarily also a type, a synthetic figure, symbolizing heritage. This hypothesis seems to contradict Hutchinson's theory of the strong influence on New Negro intellectuals of Josiah Royce's philosophy of "wholesome provincialism" and cultural pluralism, according to which regional or ethnic identities are based on consent rather than descent, on identification rather than birth (Hutchinson 79).

Such a process of identification might nevertheless have recourse to a few role-models, which are little more than idealized abstractions. This reminds us of Werner Sollors's criticism of Royce, the latter apparently proposing a falsely pluralistic model, because the province is presented in terms as monolithic as the national entity it is supposed to contradict. Furthermore, in Royce's acceptation, the province and its individual denizen can be seen as mutual metaphors, which leads to the slippery notion of representativeness and, in aesthetic terms, to the type.[7] After all, the collective singulars "the Negro" and "the New Negro" are just such allegories.[8] It goes without saying that the representations of African-American life by Renaissance writers and artists were varied and complex and far exceeded any synthetic type or types. Yet, in the absence of direct knowledge of Africa, the images of the inhabitants of that continent were bound to be more symbolic than actual and therefore subject to revealing simplifications.

A Pan-African Image

The first characteristic of the type is its Pan-African nature. Two mainvisions are proposed and very often fused: the Egyptian and the West African.

The Egyptian theme is omnipresent in the visual arts of the time, one of the early examples being Meta Vaux Warrick Fuller's *The Awakening of Ethiopia* (1914) (fig. 2.1). The sculpture represents an erect woman in Egyptian garb, wrapped in mummy-like funeral bands, yet waking up from death or slumber. This signifies the awakening of black people to a new consciousness after the sleep of oppression or historical forgetfulness. It might, of course, also embody the hope for emancipation of African-American women—the artist included—at the beginning of the century.

Lois Mailou Jones's *Ascent of Ethiopia* (1932) features the same representative figure, but within a wider narrative context. The picture is actually a rendering of African-American history, which follows the displacement of African figures from the old continent who are following a star to the modern United States, where they find symbols of the cultural activities of black Americans: art, drama, music. The painting seems to answer Locke's and DuBois's programs perfectly: it gives an account of history and tradition in a euphemized way—the middle passage being toned down to a providential call and ascent. This painting serves as a tribute to the achievements of the race in artistic matters; it can therefore be deemed a work of propaganda in support of African-American pride. The influence of DuBois's *Star of Ethiopia* seems probable. The huge pharaoh-like figure on the right-hand side represents the transhistorical spirit of the "race," a tutelary soul pointing at heritage and permanence. This face, a profile in the ancient Egyptian style, is truly Pan-African because it unites a black skin with pharaonic regalia.

The same type of quasi-transcendent figure is to be found in the sphinx-like profile dominating Aaron Douglas's *Building More Stately Mansions* (1944). Its origin is signified by a pyramid next to it and a silhouette with an Egyptian hairdo in the opposite, lower-right corner. The painting seems to equate the architectural feats of ancient Egypt with the task of anonymous black workers building skyscrapers and bridges in modern cities. The epic dimension is enhanced by the technique of representation, the most celebrated influence on Douglas, borrowed from pharaonic funerary murals and in which the human body is represented facing the viewer, while the head is turned sideways. A burning house in the lower-left corner might allude to the war, or to racial tension, the dark past which a voluntary action of reconstruction and improvement might help overcome.

The poetry of the Harlem Renaissance also featured Egyptian references prominently: for example, in Gwendolyn Bennett's "Heritage" (1923—*Norton Anthology* 1,227), or Sterling Brown's striking superposition of Egyptian history and American geography in "Memphis Blues" (1931—*Norton Anthology* 1,217).

In "The Negro Speaks of Rivers" (1921, NN 141) Langston Hughes also includes Egypt in the black man's streams of heritage: "I looked upon the Nile and raised the pyramids above it." Once again the collective, allegorical "I" signifies pride, the enduring, transhistorical strength of the community's spirit, comparable to a river, whose eternal form is composed of myriad individual droplets of water: "My soul has grown deep like the rivers." It is of no little interest to notice that in Hughes's poem and in Douglas's painting, the conception of origins is hardly limitative. *More Stately Mansions* features more than African and Egyptian architecture; there are also a Buddhist pagoda and a Roman portico; the rivers mentioned by Hughes comprise the Nile, the Congo, and the Mississippi, but also the Euphrates, Besides reappropriating Egyptian references into a Pan-African concept of beginnings, these two artists enlarge their vision to the common patrimony of mankind.

Such a claim of ancient Egypt as part of the heritage of African-Americans is especially interesting. The origins of the Egyptian people and their civilization have been the subject of fierce debate. The population and language are usually referred to as Hamito-Semitic, indicating a mixture of Mediterranean and African influences, and the form of government seems to have been derived from the first city-states of Mesopotamia. Relationships with the interior of the continent are attested by the complex rivalries between the Egyptian empire and the kingdoms of Nubia or the Sudan. In spite of the short period of Meroe's domination, which DuBois makes much of ("The Negro Mind Reaches Out," NN 406), the direction of cultural influences is difficult to asses.

Whatever the case might be, Egypt and Ethiopia both belong to East Africa, whereas the overwhelming majority of the slaves imported to the United States came from West Africa.[9] The reappropriation of these two empires by the Harlem Renaissance appears therefore as a product of contemporary Pan-Africanism; a common colonial situation offsets the large geographical and cultural differences between black and white, as well as between the eastern and western parts of the continent. Another important motivation for this abrogation of distances lies in the impetus toward a politics of pride. At a time when very little was known about such West African empires as that of Mali, Egypt and Ethiopia were the only two African civilizations comparable to that of the United States, as far as power, influence, and architectural grandeur are concerned. Their annexation to a composite image of African heritage was therefore a key component in the fashioning of ethnic pride.

But, as Sterling Brown's "Memphis Blues" can remind us, Egypt had long had another meaning in African-American culture. The Negro spirituals allegorically identified black folks with the Hebrew slaves of *Exodus* and identified the subjects of "Ole Pharaoh" with the white planters and their overseers. There is therefore an ambivalent image of Egypt in the works of the Harlem Renaissance; one being a support for positive identification and race pride, the other picturing the white oppressors in Egyptian garb. The use of this reference can therefore be defined as syncretic, unifying two parallel traditions, a cultured one and a popular one. In the spirituals and the biblical tradition, God punished the Egyptians for their mistreatment of the slaves. Historically, on the contrary, the Hebrew slaves were at the origin of the religion of the white masters; an identification with the pharaoh's subjects might have meant symbolic dominance over the white world.

Whatever the psychological complications of this use of the past, the image of Egyptian heritage at work in the Harlem Renaissance—and later— is clearly a fabrication; it participates in the creation of a New Negro ethos. Like a myth, this complex and ambivalent icon is able to unite symbolically unsolvable oppositions and contradictory identifications.

West Africa: The Double-Edged Sword of Primitivism

The elements that represent Africa in Renaissance art and literature can be reduced to a limited number. Because, at the time, New Negro creators had very few opportunities to visit the continent, they selected emblematic symbols, in a quasi-metonymic way. These symbols were first the signifiers of the African landscape: the jungle, with its exuberant vegetation characteristic of a tropical climate, and a few animals such as the lion and elephant. This luscious nature connotes the maternal image of "Mother Africa," a picture of origins. Music and dancing, tom-toms and rhythm are associated with the people, whose body is depicted as a locus of power and sensuous beauty. Uniting the physical and the spiritual stand the masks and statues of African art.

All these ingredients can be found in the dancing figure of Richmond Barthé's *Feral Benga* (1937) or in the *Copper Masks* series (1935) by Sargent Claude Johnson, but even more in the celebrated mural by Aaron Douglas titled *The Negro in an African Setting* (1934), a panel in the historical series *Aspects of Negro Life* (fig. 2.2). The subject matter is a war dance, in which two figures perform in front of a fetish and a choruslike audience wearing Egyptian-inspired headdresses. The setting and subject are unified in the picture plane, suggesting the deep communion between man and nature, soil and folk in Africa. The striking organization of the planes of light is a complex interaction of circles and lines. Such an interplay between concentric, angular, and undulating shapes stresses the (poly)rhythmic unity of the picture, drawing its inspiration from African music.

The elements we have spelled out are also present in the poetry about Africa. They are used by Countée Cullen in his "Heritage" of 1925 to dramatize the conflict between the restraints of American life, which are seen as consequences of the Christian religion's denial of the senses, and the call of the blood, the rhythmic and instinctual truth that is the core of African heritage.

> What is Africa to me:
> Copper sun or scarlet sea,
> Jungle star or jungle track,
> Strong bronzed men, or regal black
> Women from whose loins I sprang
> When the birds of Eden sang?
> (*Norton Anthology* 1,314)

True, Africa is here seen through clichés, not through experience. The idealized quality of the picture becomes obvious when expressed in terms of the Christian myth of Eden. Still, it is more than "a book one thumbs / Listlessly, till slumber comes" (lines 31–32); even though the intellectual filiation is scant and artificial, the body has kept a sense of rhythm, either as a racial characteristic or as a means of cultural survival. The inheritance of suffering is also a support for identity, which leads to a questioning of white civilization: "Lord, I fashion dark gods, too.... Not yet has my heart or head / In the least way realized / They and I are civilized" (lines 126–28).

The same themes are to be found in Claude McKay's early poems such as "Outcast" (1922—*Norton Anthology* 987), and again in Gwendolyn Bennett's "Heritage" (*Norton Anthology* 1,227). Some of Langston Hughes's early poems, such as "Afro-American Fragment" or "Danse Africaine," can be added to our list, as can the short story "Sahdji," by Bruce Nugent (NN 113–14).

Whatever the more or less implicit criticism of stereotypes visible in the works we have mentioned, they still seem dangerously close to these stereotypes, in their depiction of a synthetic, idealized Africa. A tropical nature; sensuous, physical natives bent on dancing and playing music; a hint or more of savagery—all these ingredients of primitivism might explain the success enjoyed by Harlem Renaissance artists as a sort of co-optation by white people. This is the interpretation of the movement given by Nathan Huggins and David Levering Lewis.[10] It may nevertheless be possible to give a less dismissive interpretation of these primitivistic traits; they might be seen as an integral part of the New Negro project without questioning the integrity of this project.

Primitivism is first of all a vitalism. As such, it partakes of the general questioning, taking place at the end of the 19th and the beginning of the 20th centuries, of the respective positions of "life" and "civilization." Life became identified with the spontaneous, instinctual, sexual parts of human existence; whereas civilization and culture were increasingly seen as restraints and frustrations. This revaluation of the body and the instincts over intellect and social conformity found expression in the works of such writers and thinkers as Friedrich Nietzsche, D. H. Lawrence, Virginia Woolf, and, of course, Sigmund Freud and the psychoanalytic school.

As a consequence, the qualities often negatively associated with Africans and African-Americans—such as spontaneity, emotionalism, and sensuality—were suddenly endowed with positivity. From the point of view of the American cultural nationalism we mentioned earlier, a position of vantage was thus created for blacks in the modernist *épistème;* no wonder that some artists and writers were eager to fill it, thereby converting shame into ethnic pride. The primitivism of the New Negro movement appears to have obeyed a logic of *overdetermination*—a process of sharing a common intellectual field with the mainstream, but at the same time having specific motivations and strategies within this common *Weltanshauung*. This does not mean that it was innocuous or that it was not co-opted, at an early or later stage, by the dominant culture. But at least it does not deserve to be dismissed or demonized, as has sometimes been the case.

Like its Egyptian counterpart, the West African heritage of black Americans is not the rediscovery of some atavistic identity; rather, it is the creation of an identity and of a few types adapted to the needs of the times. Paradoxically this claiming or reclaiming of origins is a proof of integration in American and in global intellectual trends.

Except for DuBois, few African-American intellectuals and artists of the twenties had had the opportunity to visit Africa; their rediscovery of African arts was by way of white anthropologists and European modernists. Heritage, then, must not be seen as a given, but as a creation, a look backward which shapes its object in the process. This delving into the African past (added to, but not exclusive of, a consideration of African-American history or the complexities of the present) may have been the choice of those artists who were most influenced by late romantic definitions of nationalism and culture, by the notion of *Volksgeist;* in a word those who were closest to the ideas of the European and American mainstreams of the time. It is actually the paradox of nationalism to have been the most internationally widespread idea at the turn of the century, and possibly even today.[11]

SYNCOPATED VISION: A DEFINITION OF BLACK FORM

To fully restate the presence of African-Americans in the arts, their treatment as subject matter should be complemented by the evolution of formal qualities defining a black vision, a whole array of strategies of representation articulating a difference in perception from the mainstream. In the words of Locke, this shift in emphasis is defined as an "increasing tendency to evolve from the racial substance something technically distinctive, something that as an idiom of style may become a contribution to the general resources of art" (NN 51); or, in other terms, "Our poets have now stopped speaking for the Negro—they speak as Negroes" (NN 48). As readers and critics of the end of the 20th century, we do not believe in "racial substances," or in artistic forms organically evolved from them, whatever the expression might mean. This terminology we have analyzed as a scion of romantic nationalism and its essentialist assumptions. However invalid its epistemological phrasing, the project did exist and was one of the important impetuses behind some of the most innovative work of the Harlem Renaissance. We shall examine it, not as sprouting from a defined collective self, but as a construction of this collective self in the specific field of artistic production, through the privileging of certain *over-determined* formal qualities of the work. Once again, we shall find syncretism in operation, between the African-American folk tradition, on the one hand, and the experiments of European modernism, on the other, especially in its interest in African art and sculpture. The latter brings an emphasis on abstract, hieratic formal qualities; the folk tradition contributes its participatory, lyrical aspect (NN 254).

Imitation with a Vengeance

In painting, the most obvious of these strategies of formal appropriation is working "in the style of" Matisse or other European modernists. Palmer Hayden's *Fétiche et Fleurs* (1933) or Malvin Gray Johnson's *Self-Portrait* (1934) (fig. 2.3) are cases in point. The latter, for example, is a portrait of the artist with African masks. It seems to justify Romare Bearden's criticism that the Renaissance was purely imitative of white masters. But this is imitation with a vengeance, a form of signifyin(g) on influence. Whereas for the French avantgarde, African masks were meant as a shock to the viewer, a declaration of savagery, a questioning of "civilization," for the African-American painter they might bear associations with such notions as heritage, origins, pride. Instead of radical otherness, there is a feeling of continuity, of tradition. This informing presence of the past might be represented in Johnson's painting by the fact that one of the masks gives the shape and the other the color of the artist's face. Here, the visual evidence of juxtaposition begs the question of the rediscovery of African art through Europe and of the ambiguities of heritage. It amounts to a deeply ideological displacement of the accent of modernism, for the purposes of identity-definition.

From Folk Art to "High Art"

Many of the most widely hailed experiments of the Harlem Renaissance are those that take as their basis various types of folk expression and that convey their formal structure into better-recognized art forms, such as concert music, poetry, or the novel. Whether or not the artists themselves shared Locke's elitist philosophy, they did follow the pattern of romantic cultural nationalism advocated by the editor of *The New Negro*. In this trajectory from soil to folk to high culture, music seems to have had a preponderant role during the Renaissance as the model and origin of most attempts at defining specific "Characteristics of Negro Expression" in the arts.[12]

Because of its centrality in the culture, music was the most likely candidate to serve as a model and inspiration for other African-American arts. One of the striking characteristics of black cultures in protestant America is the prevalence of "motor memory" over "image memory" because the iconoclastic nature of Protestantism did not permit the kind of syncretism, which developed in Catholic colonies, between African deities and rites and the worship of the saints. Therefore, music and rhythm became the main vectors/supports of African cultural survival in the United States.[13] On the other hand, African-American music was the most widely recognized form of folk culture, popular among both blacks and whites, and therefore the clearest marker of identity and belonging. No wonder then that jazz, the blues, or the spirituals influenced many authors who wanted to signify their debt to the folk. Musicality was also one of the main traits of several modes of oral performance such as ballads or sermons, which helped bridge the gaps between music and literature.

Let us now examine the three main characteristics of African and African American music to determine how they influenced other forms of expression. First and foremost, African music and its various offspring favor rhythm over melody and harmony; this predominance often goes as far as a polyrhythmic interweaving of *tempi*. This leads us to the second characteristic: syncopation, which can be defined briefly as a displacement of accents in a given rhythmic structure, such as the carrying-on of a note of the melody onto a weak beat or the stressing of weak beats. Call-and-response, or antiphony, is the third important aspect, pointing at the communal nature of African and African-American performance, be it music-playing or storytelling. Audience participation implies a dialogue between the soloist and the community, making for both individual expression and general solidarity and interdependence. If we add the vestigial presence of the African pentatonic scale in the famous "blue notes," we now have a number of traits, not necessarily peculiar to black folk music but concentrated in it, which might serve as an approximative alphabet of style for Harlem Renaissance experiments in defining an African-American artistic identity.[14]

Many critics have already shown how folk poetry was integrated into Renaissance poetry. *God's Trombones* (1920) by James Weldon Johnson is a variation on the spiritual sermon; Langston Hughes's use of the blues has become famous; African-American ballads, such as that of John Henry, inspired poets and even a series of paintings by Palmer Hayden. Sterling Brown and Hughes added work songs to that variegated repertoire. These poets tried to convey the mood of the folk forms they recycled and to pay tribute to the genius for striking metaphor and word coinage that they exemplified, and which Zora Neale Hurston called the "will to adorn."[15]

> And God stepped out on space,
> And he looked around and said:
> I'm lonely—
> I'll make me a world.
> (*Norton Anthology* 775)

These opening lines from James Weldon Johnson's "The Creation," a poem from *God's Trombones*, render the qualities of humor and metaphysical concreteness of the folk sermon, which appealed to one Harlem Renaissance intellectual. What really anchors the poem in the black tradition, and distinguishes it from an attempt at rendering local color from outside, is the musical quality of the verse, carried over from the spiritual sermon itself. The variable length of the lines echoes the rhythm of the performance, in which a regular beat, corresponding to the orator's pauses for breath, encompasses a different number of syllables, pronounced at an elastic tempo, according to the amount of information or the emphasis which is conveyed. This variation within a single beat is called the syncopation of lines. In this sense, we can say there is a clear connection, in Renaissance poetry, between the African-American tradition and modernist experimentations in free verse, leading to an idiom which is at the same time identifiable as avant-garde and folk expression.

The call-and-response pattern, which is another of the characteristics African-American music shares with other types of oral performance, was often inscribed in poetry in the repetition of lines, whole or in part. It reminded the reader of the antiphonal dialogue between soloist and audience in the spirituals and work songs or of the performer's answering himself, as it were, in the blues. The blues pattern is to be found in "Tin Roof Blues" (1931) by Sterling Brown, one of the Harlem Renaissance poets who incorporated the widest spectrum of folk forms in his work:

I'm got the tin roof blues, got dese sidewalks on my mind,
De tin roof blues, dese lonesome sidewalks on my mind,
I'm goin' where de shingles covers people mo' my kind.
(*Norton Anthology* 1,220)

In prose narratives, call-and-response was dissociated from a purely musical context through the rendition of oral storytelling situations, which also involve give-and-take between the narrator and a group of narratees present in the story, thereby signifying (on) the reading public. This is what Henry Louis Gates, in reference to Hurston, calls "the speakerly text."[16] It is exemplified in *The New Negro* by this author's short story "Spunk," in which the chorus of loungers in the village store not only witness and comment on the events, but actually make them happen by influencing the protagonists. In Hurston's *Their Eyes Were Watching God* (1937), the neutral narrative voice gets caught in the heroine's act of recounting her life to her friend, while the presence of a curious porch audience looms large in the background. Thus the story becomes a "play of voices," answering one of Hurston's own "characteristics of Negro expression": drama (*Norton Anthology* 1,020).

A Syncopated Renaissance?

Rhythm and antiphony appear as crucial formal qualities belonging to the African-American tradition and as traits which were widely used at the time of the Harlem Renaissance to define a specific black aesthetic within the context of American modernism. But the concept of syncopation could be a more encompassing notion, which might give a fuller account of the common project of both formal innovation and ethnic appropriation.[17] Syncopation might be seen as a shared trope unifying the creative impetus behind the music, the visual arts, and the literature of the renaissance, and intimately connected with the will to control the image of African-Americans. It could be paralleled with Henry Gates's master trope of black expression, signifyin(g), or "repetition with a difference."

Gates defines signifyin(g) as an awareness that language never means only one thing at a time, as a subversion of the language of the masters and its pretense at being univocal. Such an awareness is seen as a necessity for African-American survival in an oppressive society; such a subversion is a space of freedom when freedom is denied. This dialectic between imitation and invention is also what constitutes an African-American literary tradition, one that signifies not only on white influence, but on itself as well.[18] Our suggestion to use syncopation as a defining trope of the Harlem Renaissance is aimed at supplementing Gates's analysis with a recognition that music was the wedge through which black culture gained recognition and evolved its most innovative attempts at defining an artistic identity.

Our understanding of the term syncopation will encompass its formal and metaphoric meanings. Syncopation was the main trope for the Africanization of Euro-American music. It gave birth to the spirituals and jazz, among other musical genres. It consists in a displacement of accent, in a sort of "creative distortion" of rhythm. By stressing weak beats, it can be said to reveal and valorize the "shadow" or "background" of the dominant beat. It can therefore represent an apt metaphor for the situation of a minority, especially as it tries to assert pride and identity through artistic means—one may be reminded of the title of Ralph Ellison's collection of essays, *Shadow and Act* (1964).

Syncopation can also be paralleled to the project of the most innovative avant-garde movement of the time, namely cubism. As a matter of fact, cubist aesthetics was based on a fragmentation of the representation of the object, which was reconstructed rhythmically on the picture plane. Such rhythmic distortion can be easily compared to syncopation; in the same way, the juxtaposition of multiple perspectives and points of view on the object can remind us of antiphony, as for example in *Cane*, whose construction oscillates between modernist collage, cubist perspectivism, and the tradition of call-and-response. After all, the last corresponds to a sort of harmonized, auditory collage of different subjective contributions to a central theme.

Cubism itself is indissolubly connected to African art. For Picasso and Braque, African sculpture was a means of questioning the Western visual canon based on the centrality of human proportions. "What Picasso cared about was the formal vitality of African art, which was for him inseparably involved with its apparent freedom to distort."[19] The modernist era was marked by a de-centering of the subject through the exploration of the unconscious; a de-centering of Western values through an interest in other cultures, a cultural relativism paradoxically fostered by the extension of imperialism through colonialism; and, in the arts, the abolition of the centrality of the human figure and Cartesian perception. Cubism was one of the most radical of these questionings, one that is often deemed as metonymic of the whole; its attempt at fractioning the object and reconstructing it in a rhythmic composition integrating time and multiple points of view even reflects the scientific revolution of the time: Einstein's theory of relativity.

It is in this coherent use of "creative distortion" and defamiliarization that we can find a real collusion between the modernist project and that of the African-American group. In this de-centering of the center—representational and ethnic—the relevance of the syncopating or syncopated African acquires its full significance. The Harlem Renaissance could claim as its own special locus a meeting point between modernist experimentation and a minority culture or situation; this amounted to a questioning of the Western tradition from a (rediscovered) African diasporic standpoint.

No wonder then, given this common ground, that many African-Americans participated in the avant-garde movements of the twenties. Still, their integration in the general cultural renewal of their time should not hide the fact that it was an avant-garde with an added dimension; even if it could not be limited to it, it had a largely ethnic character. In its attempts at defining a specific identity against a larger civilizational entity, it duplicated the situation of the American cultural nationalism of the beginning of the century, which tried to detach itself from European influence. This, of course, should help us relativize the accusations of provincialism sometimes leveled at the Harlem Renaissance (Huggins 308); there is a chance such accusations do not apply to black artists of the movement more than to their white contemporaries.

We could even qualify the Harlem Renaissance of "syncopated modernism," in the sense that it does displace the accent of modernism from a questioning of Western values and modes of representation to a celebration of African-derived cultures, in the name of the very tenets of the new Western avant-gardes: innovation and creative distortion. This would be a formal counterpart to the overdetermined uses of primitivism in the depiction of African heritage.

A pictorial example might clarify our analysis. Aaron Douglas's *Song of the Towers* (1934) (fig. 2.4) is another part of the *Aspects of Negro Life* series at the Schomburg Center of the New York Public Library. In the central presence of music and some of its structural features, it echoes the already mentioned *The Negro in an African Setting*. The scene is transported to the United States, making of the painting a comment on contemporary America rather than on the past, the link with the former picture showing the persistence of tradition. Formally speaking, the work stages the confluence of synthetic cubism and the African heritage in the angularity and rhythmic interaction of the color planes. Music itself is figured through the saxophone at the center—the position of the fetish in the earlier painting—which embodies the African-American spirit and a form of freedom. From the point of view of contents, we therefore have a "song under towers." It is the distortion of the perspective of the towers and smokestacks which gives the work its full title, by exemplifying the "music of the towers," possibly to show how the quintessential African-American artistic expression can transform a potentially oppressive and alienating environment.

Music, and more specifically jazz, is therefore both a thematic component and the organizing principle of the picture. The syncopated quality is to be found in the rhythmic displacement of accent occurring in the interaction between the diagonal and concentric lines—or between towers and sound waves—and especially visible in the shifts in hues resulting from the super-position of the different color planes they delimit. Background and foreground, weak and strong elements, are blurred and contaminate each other. The painting can then be termed a spiritual equivalent of the African-American ethos embodied in music.

Douglas's consistent use of black silhouettes can also strike a chord in this syncopated concert. Their poses, harking back to Egyptian funeral art, become symbols of heritage and dignity. The fact that only the contours are visible can be interpreted as an ingenious solution to the problems of surface and depth inherent in cubism and after. The very flatness of a silhouette on the picture plane participates in an exploration of the painterly nature of representation and amounts to a Matisse-like rejection of classical perspective. But they are also shadows, general and unidentified; signifyin(g) on the "invisible" status of minorities in the United States, they also paradoxically represent everyman in an African garb. It seems the perfect visual equivalent to our concept of syncopation: a rhythmic, musical stress on the weak beat, which comes to proud prominence against a background of suppression.

This epic project, which Douglas shared with many other artists of the period, might explain the fact that Harlem Renaissance painters and sculptors hardly ever ventured beyond the figurative dimension of their art. Their production was, as a rule, less iconoclastic than some cubist portraits, in which the human figure is so distorted as to become unrecognizable. If the New Negro project really *was* control of image and identity-building, figuration was of the essence. How to use image as a support for pride and self-assertion in the face of mainstream stereotypes, while radically questioning the very nature and validity of all representation? The special brand of modernism, which we have called syncopated, of the Harlem Renaissance was at the same time central and specific, bold and innovative, but within self-imposed limits; it laid the groundwork for other, later experiments that could transcend these restrictions.

In the general, cross-genre artistic project of control of image, embodied in an aesthetic philosophy inspired by a cultural nationalist *épistème*, the representation of the syncopated African as a type, or collection of types, is one crucial thematic element in a reappropriation of heritage. It is at the same time a way of integrating—and often signifyin(g) on—the modernist uses of Africa. The same overdetermination of traits can be witnessed, on the formal plane, in the general trope of syncopation, or creative, rhythmic distortion. The innovations of modernism are here rephrased as characteristics of African-derived cultures, and especially as African-American, whereas, paradoxically, the rediscovery of these traits, or their uses in "elevated" art, were initiated by the evolution in mainstream aesthetics.

But if syncopation, sometimes also called "stop-time" due to its rhythmic variations, can be compared to cubist experiments in variations of points of view, one can ultimately connect the project of the Harlem Renaissance to a syncopated picture. One can easily feel the common impetus, the intention of making a portrait of African America, past and present and possibly future; but this portrait remains elusive because of the multiplicity of sometimes contradictory perspectives adopted by the actors themselves. The heated debate between George Schuyler's "The Negro-Art Hokum" and Langston Hughes's "The Negro Artist and the Racial Mountain" (both 1926) is relevant here: both try to inscribe black culture and artistic expression within the general context of America and modernism; but they are at variance about the respective emphasis to be given the two terms. Whether race is incidental (Schuyler) or a social-spiritual unit (Hughes), the problem is the tension between integration and specificity in the new image to be presented to the world.

The New Negro, which as an anthology reflects these various trends, can possibly be read as an apt snapshot of the Harlem Renaissance: it renders its vitality, its character of collaborative work between black and white, older and younger generations, cultural nationalists and integrationists, as well as different artistic fields. In a word, once again, the unity of the project is felt, but it is impossible to reduce it to a single formula, a unified figure or type. We might then again see syncopation as a unifying trope of the project and achievement of the movement, with the twist that our critical evaluation, like any other, is subjected to the perspectivist relativism which reveals the influence of the observer on the object; we might then never be able to go beyond the vision of a "syncopated Renaissance."

Notes

1. Alain Locke, ed., *The New Negro: Voices of the Harlem Renaissance* (New York: Atheneum, [1925] 1992). Abbreviated as NN.

2. George Hutchinson, *The Harlem Renaissance in Black and White* (Cambridge, Mass.: Harvard University Press, 1995).

3. Hutchinson 101–102. According to the latter, all white intellectuals did not recognize in the same way the importance of the African-American contribution to the culture of the United States. "Authors such as Brooks, Randolph Bourne, Lewis Mumford, and even Waldo Frank repeatedly failed to appreciate the significance of African-American culture" (98). Still, some evolutions were noticeable: Bourne enthusiastically reviewed Ridgely Torrence's *Three Plays for a Negro Theatre* (1917), which to him was "reminiscent of Synge, represent[ing] the sort of direction that Bourne felt the United States should be exploiting" (Hutchinson 104). Waldo Frank's increasing closeness to black culture, under the influence of Toomer, led him to plan "a new edition [of *Our America*] including a section on black America" (108). While many of these artists and thinkers saw the African-American contribution as only one among many, in a "transnational America" (Bourne), some envisaged it as a model for other developments; others, such as Alfred Barnes, viewed it as the only successful example of truly American culture ("America's only great music—the spirituals" [NN 21]).

4. Jean Toomer, *Cane* (1923) (New York: Norton, 1988), 12.

5. W.E.B. DuBois, "Criteria of Negro Art" (1926), *The Norton Anthology of African-American Literature*, H.L. Gates and N. McKay, eds. (New York: Norton, 1997), 752–59.

6. Nathan Huggins, *Harlem Renaissance* (New York: Oxford University Press, 1971), 64.

7. Werner Sollors, *Beyond Ethnicity: Consent and Descent in American Culture* (New York: Oxford University Press, 1986), 193–94.

8. Alain Locke himself, looking back on the Harlem Renaissance from the vantage point of the fifties, seems to have deplored such recourse to counter-stereotypes and the oversimplification of African-American life they entailed. But he admitted his own use of such "defensive, promotive propaganda" as necessary at the time ("Frontiers of Culture," Leonard Harris, ed., *The Philosophy of Alain Locke: Harlem Renaissance and Beyond* [Philadelphia: Temple University Press, 1989], 193).

For a discussion of the tension in Locke's thought between philosophical pragmatism and racial idealism, see Jeffrey Stuart's introduction to Locke's *Race Contacts and Interracial Relations: Lectures on the Theory and Practice of Race* (Washington, D.C.: Howard University Press, 1992, xxv–xxvi) and the introduction to this volume.

9. This does not mean that cultural contacts did not exist between East and West Africa. Actually, black Africa can be seen as an inheritor of certain aspects of Egyptian and Mediterranean civilizations, which were mixed with local traditions. Jean Laude argues that these influences followed the path of the diffusion of metallurgy, from Libya or Nubia or both *(Les Arts de l'Afrique Noire* [Paris: Librairie

Générale Française, 1966), 128). Because Frobenius had already discovered this filiation, the concept was available to Renaissance thinkers. Yet the double remoteness of these origins—Egyptian influences on West African civilization and African survivals in America—makes the process of identification somewhat arbitrary and therefore designates it as an ideological construct. This is especially visible in the fact that it was used in a nationalistic way, rather than as a means to assert the common heritage of all Atlantic civilizations, and to question European claims to cultural supremacy in a clearly inclusive manner. Once more, history and tales of origins have to be read backwards, with a view on their present use.

10. Huggins, *Harlem Renaissance*, 301. David Levering Lewis, *When Harlem Was in Vogue* (New York: Random House, 1979).

11. Hutchinson, 9. This author makes another crucial remark on the paradoxical convergence of integration and particularism, about Locke's 1924 essay "The Concept of Race as Applied to Social Culture": "Indeed, Locke makes a point later developed by George Devereux and Fredrik Barth: that ethnicization and assimilation often go on simultaneously. That is, a group with a weak sense of racial or ethnic identity becomes increasingly race-conscious as its contacts with another group increase. Contacts lead to heightened boundary construction and racial stress, even as acculturation goes on" (91).

12. The purpose of the essay by that title, by writer and anthropologist Zora Neale Hurston (1934), is to define characteristics of African-American folk expression; however, it can also be very usefully applied to a study of Hurston's own creative artistry and that of some of her contemporaries.

13. Melville Herskovits, *The Myth of the Negro Past* (1941) (Boston: Beacon Press, 1958), 221.

14. Guy-Claude Balmir, *Du chant au poème* (Paris: Payot, 1982), 27–36 and 49–68.

15. "Characteristics of Negro Expression," *Norton Anthology*, 1,021.

16. Henry Louis Gates, "Their Eyes Were Watching God: Hurston and the Speakerly Text," H.L. Gates and K.A. Appiah, eds. *Zora Neale Hurston: Critical Perspectives Past and Present* (New York: Amistad, 1993), 154–203.

17. For an earlier discussion of the trope of syncopation, in a wider context, see Paul Gilroy, *The Black Atlantic: Modernity and Double Consciousness* (Cambridge, Mass.: Harvard University Press, 1993), 202–203.

18. H.L. Gates, "The Blackness of Blackness: A Critique of the Sign and the Signifying Monkey." H.L. Gates, ed. *Black Literature and Literary Theory* (New York: Methuen, 1984), 286–91.

19. Robert Hughes, *The Shock of the New: Art and the Century of Change* (London: Thames and Hudson, 1993), 21.

Chronology

1871	James Weldon Johnson is born in Jacksonville, Florida on June 17.
1890	Claude McKay is born in Sunny Ville, Jamaica on September 15.
1891	On January 7, Zora Neale Hurston is born in Eatonville, Florida.
1894	Jean Toomer is born in Washington, D.C. on December 26.
1902	On February 1, James Mercer Langston Hughes is born in Joplin, Missouri.
1903	Countee Porter Cullen is born in Louisville, Kentucky on May 30.
1914	Archduke Ferdinand is assassinated in Sarajevo on June 28; Austria-Hungary declares war on Russia on July 28 marking the beginning of World War I.
1915	Carter G. Woodson founds the Association for the Study of Negro Life and History; Jack Johnson, the first black heavyweight champion of the world, loses the title to Jess Willard, the "Great White Hope." Rumors claim he loses to avoid legal difficulties.
1916	Debut of the journal, *Challenge* under the editorial direction of William Bridge.
1917	United States declares war on Germany on April 6; Black men who volunteer for the United States armed services are rejected; The Selective Service Act is passed on May 18,

providing for the enlistment of all able-bodied American men between the ages of 21 and 31. Before the end of the war, more than two million black men have registered; *Three Plays for a Negro Theatre*, written by a white playwright, opens on Broadway.

1918   World War I ends on November 11; James Van Der Zee and his wife open the Guarantee Photo Studio in Harlem; *The Heart of a Woman* by Georgia D. Johnson and Natalie Curtis's *Negro Folksongs* are published.

1919   On February 17, the 369th Regiment, the first all-black United States armed troops, returns from France and marches from Manhattan to Harlem. The "Harlem Hell Fighters" marching band leads the troops; Claude McKay publishes *If We Must Die*; Benjamin Brawley publishes *The Negro in Literature and Art in the United States*; W.E.B. DuBois organizes the First Pan African Congress; Race riots occur in Washington, D.C., Chicago, Charleston, Knoxville, Omaha, and elsewhere. Marcus Garvey founds the Black Star Shipping Line; NAACP holds a conference on lynchings and publishes *Thirty Years of Lynching* in the United States 1889–1919.

1920   Prohibition goes into effect in the United States on January 16; Production of Eugene O'Neil's *The Emperor Jones*, starring Charles Gilpin, opens at the Provincetown Playhouse; The Theatrical Owners and Bookers Association (TOBA) for performers on the black circuit is founded; Marcus Garvey founds Negro World, an arts and literature journal supported by the United Negro Improvement Association (UNIA); W.E.B. DuBois publishes *Darkwater* and Claude McKay publishes *Spring in New Hampshire*.

1921   Marcus Garvey delivers an address at Liberty Hall on "DuBois and his Escapades" on January 2; Oscar Charleston leads his league in doubles, triples, and home runs, batting .434 for the year; Universal Negro Improvement Association (UNIA) Convention is held at Madison Square Garden in August; James Weldon Johnson is appointed first black officer (secretary) of NAACP; *Shuffle Along* by Noble Sissle and Eubie opens at Broadway's David Belasco Theater on May 22; Paul Robeson debuts in *Taboo*, by Mary Hoyt Wilborg; Marcus Garvey founds African Orthodox Church in September; Second Pan African Congress is held in London, Paris, and

Brussels; Colored Players Guild of New York is founded; *Social History of the American Negro* by Benjamin Brawley is published; Internal Revenue Service investigates Garvey and the Universal Negro Improvement Association.

1922   Garvey is arrested for fraudulent use of mails and is held on a $2,500 bond pending presentation of his case to a federal grand jury on January 12; Louis Armstrong plays second trumpet in King Oliver's Creole Jazz Band;

House of Representatives approves first Anti-Lynching legislation; Publications of *The Book of American Negro Poetry* edited by James Weldon Johnson, Claude McKay, *Harlem Shadows*, and T.S. Stribling's novel, *Birthright*.

1923   Blues singer Bessie Smith records "Downhearted Blues" and "Gulf Coast Blues"; Jean Toomer's *Cane* is published; *Opportunity: A Journal of Negro Life* is founded by the National Urban League;

The Cotton Club opens in Harlem; The *Conjure-Man Dies* by Rudolph Fisher is published; Marcus Garvey is arrested for mail fraud and sentenced to five years in prison; Third Pan African Congress is held in London and Lisbon.

1924   Ida Cox records "Wild Women Don't Have the Blues"; Countee Cullen wins the Witter Bynner Poetry Competition; Publication of Du Bois, *The Gift of Black Folk*, Jessie Fauset, *There is Confusion*, Marcus Garvey's, *Aims and Objects for a Solution of the Negro Problem Outlined*, and Walter White's *The Fire in the Flint*; Marcus Garvey addresses the First Annual Convention of UNIA.

1925   50,000 unmasked Ku Klux Klan members march in Washington, D.C.;

Bessie Smith records "St. Louis Blues"; Brotherhood of Sleeping Car Porters is founded and becomes the first successful black trade union;

Survey Graphic publishes a special issue entitled, "Harlem: Mecca of the New Negro"; First literary awards ceremony banquet held by *Opportunity* in May; Langston Hughes wins first place in poetry with *The Weary Blues*;

Zora Neale Hurston becomes editor of *The Spokesman*; American Negro Labor Congress held in Chicago. Publication of Countee Cullen's *Color*, Du Bose Heyward, *Porgy*, James Weldon Johnson and J. Rosamond Johnson, editors, *The Book of American Negro Spirituals*, Alain Locke's,

The New Negro, and Sherwood Anderson's, *Dark Laughter*.

1926   Jelly Roll Morton records "Black Bottom Stomp" and "Dead Man Blues";

Countee Cullen becomes Assistant Editor of *Opportunity*; begins to write a regular column called "The Dark Tower"; Savoy Ballroom opens in Harlem; The Universal Negro Improvement Association office building is sold for nonpayment of taxes; Publication of Wallace Thurman, *Fire!!*, Langston Hughes's, *The Weary Blues*; Carl Van Vechten's, *Tropic Death*, W. C. Handy, *Blues: An Anthology*, Carl Van Vechten's *Nigger Heaven* (novel's advertisements designed by Aaron Douglas), and Walter White's, *Flight*. W.E.B. DuBois's editorial "The Negro in Art: How Shall He Be Portrayed?" appears in *The Crisis*; Carter G. Woodson founds Negro History Week.

1927   Painter Henry Ossawa Tanner is the first black American to be granted full membership in to the National Academy of Design; *In Abraham's Bosom* by Paul Green wins the Pulitzer Prize; Marcus Garvey is deported to Jamaica; Louis Armstrong in Chicago and Duke Ellington in New York begin their musical careers; Harlem Globetrotters is established. Publication of Miguel Covarrubias, *Negro Drawings*, Countee Cullen's, *Ballad of the Brown Girl, Copper Sun and Caroling Dusk*, Arthur Fauset's, *For Freedom: A Biographical Story of the American Negro*, Langston Hughes', *Fine Clothes to the Jew*, James Weldon Johnson's, *God's Trombones: Seven Negro Sermons in Verse and The Autobiography of an Ex-Colored Man* (reprint of the 1912 edition). Aaron Douglas creates murals for Club Ebony in Harlem.

1928   Claude McKay publishes *Home to Harlem*, it becomes the first fictional work by an African-American to reach best-seller lists; Ethel Waters records "West End Blues."

1929   The Negro Experimental Theatre is founded in February, the Negro Art Theatre is founded in June, and the National Colored Players founded in September; Wallace Thurman's play *Harlem* opens at the Apollo Theater on Broadway; New York Stock Exchange crashes on October 24; Publication of Countee Cullen, *The Black Christ and Other Poems*, Claude McKay's, *Banjo*, Nella Larsen's, *Passing*.

1930	Publication of Langston Hughes's *Not Without Laughter*; Marc Connelly's drama *The Green Pastures* opens on Broadway; James VanDerZee's photography displayed in Harlem.
1931	Publication of George Shuyler's *Black No More*, Jean Toomer's *Essentials: Definitions and Aphorisms*, Alain Locke's "The American Negro as Artist." Arna Bontemp's novel *God Sends Sunday*, *The Chinaberry Tree*, by Jessie Fauset, *The Negro Mother* by Langston Hughes, and James Weldon Johnson's *Black Manhattan* are published; Duke Ellington records "Mood Indigo."
1932	Publication of Wallace Thurman's *Infants of the Spring*, Sterling Brown's *Southern Road*, *The Conjure-Man Dies* by Rudolph Fisher, and Countee Cullen's *One Way to Heaven*.
1933	Aaron Douglas's murals are exhibited at Caz-Delbos Gallery in New York; Claude McKay's novel, *Banana Bottom*, Jessie Fauset's *Comedy: American Style*, and James Weldon Johnson's *Along This Way* are published.
1934	Publication of Zora Neale Hurston's first novel, *Jonah's Gourd Vine* and Langston Hughes's story collection, *The Ways of White Folks*.
1935	Aaron Douglas is elected president of the Harlem Artist's Guild. George Gershwin's *Porgy and Bess* opens at the Alvin Theatre in New York.
1936	*Black Thunder* by Arna Bontemps is published.
1938	James Weldon Johnson dies on June 26 in Wiscasset, Maine.
1946	On January 9, Countee Cullen dies in New York.
1948,	On May 22, Claude McKay dies in Chicago, Illinois.
1960	Zora Neale Hurston dies in Fort Pierce, Florida on January 28.
1967	On March 30, Jean Toomer dies; Langston Hughes dies two months later in New York City on May 22.

Contributors

HAROLD BLOOM is Sterling Professor of the Humanities at Yale University and Henry W. and Albert A. Berg Professor of English at the New York University Graduate School. He is the author of over 20 books, including *Shelley's Mythmaking* (1959), *The Visionary Company* (1961), *Blake's Apocalypse* (1963), *Yeats* (1970), *A Map of Misreading* (1975), *Kabbalah and Criticism* (1975), *Agon: Toward a Theory of Revisionism* (1982), *The American Religion* (1992), *The Western Canon* (1994), and *Omens of Millennium: The Gnosis of Angels, Dreams, and Resurrection* (1996). *The Anxiety of Influence* (1973) sets forth Professor Bloom's provocative theory of the literary relationships between the great writers and their predecessors. His most recent books include *Shakespeare: The Invention of the Human* (1998), a 1998 National Book Award finalist, *How to Read and Why* (2000), *Genius: A Mosaic of One Hundred Exemplary Creative Minds* (2002), and *Hamlet: Poem Unlimited* (2003). In 1999, Professor Bloom received the prestigious American Academy of Arts and Letters Gold Medal for Criticism, and in 2002 he received the Catalonia International Prize.

WARRINGTON HUDLIN is an African American writer whose work challenges the idea that Harlem artists arrived in New York not because it was a cultural center, but because of the plethora of publishing houses. He introduced the possibility that the Harlem Renaissance was not a literary gathering in the traditional sense.

MARGARET PERRY earned her A.B. degree from Western Michigan University and her M.S.L.S. from Catholic University. Her first book *A Bio-*

Bibliography of Countee P. Cullen, 1903–146, was published by Greenwood Press in 1971.

AMRITJIT SINGH is an international lecturer on literary criticism and history, as well as translations. He is also author of *The Novels of the Harlem Renaissance*.

RAYMOND SMITH received an honorary D.D. from Transylvania College, Culver-Stockton College. He wrote *Toward Understanding Jesus, On Being Christian*, and *Front Sunset to Dawn*.

BRUCE KELLNER works in literary criticism, history, and biography. He has written several books, the most recent of which include *The Harlem Renaissance: A Historical Dictionary for the Era, Letters of Carl Van Vechten*, and *Donald Windham: A Bio-Bibliography*.

AKASHA GLORIA HULL is a poet and black studies scholar focusing on feminist issues. She is the author and editor of various books including *All the Women Are White, All the Blacks are Men, but Some of Us Are Brave: Black Women's Studies, Give Us Each Day: The Diary of Alice Dunbar-Nelson*, and *Healing Heart, Poems 1973–1988*.

RICHARD K. BARKSDALE, Professor Emeritus of English and former associate dean of the Graduate College at the University of Illinois at Urbana-Champaign has published widely in scholarly journals such as *Phylon, Western Humanities Review*, and *Black American Literature Forums*. He is the author of *Langston Hughes: The Poet and His Critics*.

EVA LENNOX BIRCH works as a Senior Lecturer in English at the Metropolitan University at Manchester. Her primary classes focus on American literature and women's studies.

DAVID LEVERING LEWIS has received a National Book Award nomination, and the Pulitzer Prize for *W.E.B. DuBois: Biography of a Race, 1868–1919*. His other books include *When Harlem Was in Vogue: The Politics of the Arts in the Twenties, W.E.B. DuBois: The Fight for Equality and the American Century*. He is best known for his works on the twentieth-century African-American experience.

JAMES WELDON JOHNSON is one of the most versatile writers and participants in the Harlem Renaissance. He is best known for *The*

Autobiography of an Ex-Colored Man, *God's Trombones: Seven Negro Sermons in Verse*, and *Black Manhattan*.

ALAIN LOCKE, a formative contributor to the Harlem Renaissance and the development and support of a new Negro culture through the arts, is the author of *The New Negro: An Interpretation*. His other works include *The Negro in America*, *The Negro and His Music*, and *Negro Art: Past and Present*.

CHARLES S. JOHNSON is the author of *The Negro in Chicago: A Study of Race Relations and a Race Riot*. He also was the editor for *Opportunity: A Journal of Negro Life*, a magazine which helped to support many young black writers and artists during the Harlem Renaissance.

AMY HELENE KIRSCHKE teaches at Vanderbilt University. Her primary teaching interests include African-American art and African art.

STERLING A. BROWN is a prolific writer and contributor to the development of folk literature. Known as a poet, critic, and teacher, he taught at Howard University for over forty years. He wrote several poetry and nonfiction books, including *Southern Road*, *The Last Ride of Wild Bill*, *and Eleven Narrative Poems*, *The Negro in American Fiction*, *The Integration of the Negro into American Society*, among others.

CHERYL A. WALL teaches English at Rutgers University. She has written for numerous literary journals such as *American Women Writers*, *Notable American Women*, and *Phylon*.

MAUREEN HONEY is a Professor of English at the University of Nebraska, Lincoln. She is the author of *Creating Rosie the Riveter*, *Shadowed Dreams: Women's Poetry of the Harlem Renaissance*, *Breaking the Ties that Bind*, and *Bitter Fruit: African American Women in World War II*.

PATTI CAPEL SWARTZ earned her PhD at Claremont Graduate University, Claremont, CA and currently is an Assistant Professor of English at Kent State University.

GENEVIÈVE FABRE has taught French and American studies at the University of Wisconsin, Tufts University, and the University of Paris VII, Paris. She is the author of *Drumbeats, Masks and Plays: Afro American Theatre* and has been a frequent editor on collections such as *Celebrating Ethnicity and Nation: American Festive Culture from the Revolution to the Early Twentieth Century*.

MICHAEL FEITH is an Assistant Professor at the University of Nantes, France. His publications include articles on Maxine Hong Kingston, John Edgar Weidman and the Harlem Renaissance.

Bibliography

"Afro-American Writers before the Harlem Renaissance." *Dictionary of Literary Biography*. Detroit: Gale, 1986.

"Afro-American Writers from the Harlem Renaissance to 1940." *Dictionary of Literary Biography*. Detroit: Gale, 1987.

Adoff, Arnold. *I Am the Darker Brother: An Anthology of Modern Poems by Negro Americans*. New York: MacMillan, 1968.

American Writers: A Collection of Literary Biographies. New York: Scribner, 1974.

Anderson, Jervis. *A. Phillip Randolph: A Biographical Portrait*. New York: Harcourt, 1972.

Anderson, Jervis. *This Was Harlem*. New York: Farrar, Straus, Giroux, 1982.

Andrews, William L. *Classic Fiction of the Harlem Renaissance*. New York: Oxford UP, 1994.

Baker, Houston A. Jr. *Afro-American Poetics: Revisions of Harlem and the Black Aesthetic*. Madison: U of Wisconsin P, 1988.

———. *Modernism and the Harlem Renaissance*. Chicago: U of Chicago Press, 1987.

Basset, John Earl. *Harlem in Review: Critical Reactions to Black American Writers*. Selinsgrove: Susquehanna UP, 1992.

Black History Month 1992 / [National Humanities Center]. Research Triangle Park, NC: The Center, 1992. 2 sound cassettes 120 min.

Black Literature Criticism: Excerpts from Criticism of the Most Significant Works of Black Authors over the Past 200 Years. Detroit: Gale, 1992.

Bloom, Harold, ed. *American Fiction 1914–1945*. New York: Chelsea House, 1987.

———, ed. *American Poetry 1915 to 1945*. New York: Chelsea House, 1987.

———, ed. *James Baldwin*. New York: Chelsea House, 1986.

———, ed. *Langston Hughes*. New York: Chelsea House, 1989.

Bodenheim, Maxwell. *Naked on Roller Skates*. New York: Horace Liveright, 1930.

Bone, Robert A. *Down Home: A History of Afro-American Short Fiction from its Beginnings to the End of the Harlem Renaissance*. NY: Putnam, 1975.

———. *The Negro Novel in America*. New Haven: Yale UP, 1965.

Bontemps, Arna W., ed. *The Harlem Renaissance Remembered: Essays*. New York, Dodd, Mead, 1972.

Bronz, Stephen H. *Roots of Negro Racial Consciousness; the 1920's: Three Harlem Renaissance Authors: Johnson, James Weldon; Cullen, Countee; McKay, Claude*. NY: Libra, 1964.

Brown, Claude. *Manchild in the Promised Land*. NY: Macmillan, 1965.

Brown, Sterling Allen. *The Collected Poems*. New York: Harper & Row, 1980.

Campbell, Mary S. *Harlem Renaissance: Art of Black America*. New York: Abrams, 1987.

Carby, Hazel. *Reconstructing Womanhood: The Emergence of the Afro-American Woman Novelist*. NY: Oxford UP, 1987.

Chapman, Abraham. "The Harlem Renaissance in Literary History." *CLA Journal* 11 (1967): 38–58.

Clarke, John H. "The Neglected Dimensions of the Harlem Renaissance." *Black World* 20 (Nov 1970): 118–29.

Coleman, Leon. "Carl Van Vechten Presents the New Negro." *Studies in the Literary Imagination* 7 (Fall 1974): 85–104.

Cooney, Terry. *The Rise of the New York Intellectuals: Partisan Review and Its Circle, 1934–1945*. Madison: U of Wisconsin P, 1986.

Cooper, Wayne F. *Claude McKay: Rebel Sojourner in the Harlem Renaissance: A Biography*. NY: Schocken Books, 1990.

Cruse, Harold. *The Crisis of the Negro Intellectual*. New York: Morrow, 1967.

Cullen, Countee. *Caroling Dusk: An Anthology of Verse by Negro Poets*. New York: Harper & Row, 1955.

———. *Color*. New York: Harper & Brothers, 1925.

———. *My Soul's High Song*. New York: Doubleday, 1991.

Curley, Dorothy Nyren, ed. *A Library of Literary Criticism: Modern American Literature*. New York: F. Ungar, 1960.

Dallas Museum of Art. *Black Art, Ancestral Legacy: The African Impulse in African-American Art*. NY: Abrams, 1989.

Dance Theater of Harlem. Video. 117 min. 1989. # 9S865. Insight Media, NY. 212–721–6316.

Davis, Arthur P. *From the Dark Tower: African-American Writers 1900–1960*. Washington, D.C.: Howard UP, 1974.

———. "Growing Up in the New Negro Renaissance, 1920–1935." *Negro American Literature Forum* (*NALF*) 2 (Fall 1968): 53–59.

Davis, Frank Marshall. *Livin' the Blues: Memoirs of a Black Jounalist and Poet*. Madison, WI: U of Wisconsin Press, 1992.

De Jongh, James. *Vicious Modernism: Black Harlem and the Literary Imagination*. NY: Cambridge UP, 1990.

Dickinson, Donald. *A Bio-Bibliography of Langston Hughes, 1902–1967*. Hamden, Conn: Archon, 1972.

Douglas, Ann. *Terrible Honesty: Mongrel Manhattan in the 1920s*. NY: Farrar, Straus & Giroux, 1995.

Driskell, David C., and others. *Harlem Renaissance: Art of Black America*. NY: Abrams, 1987.

Du Bois, W.E.B. *The Souls of Black Folk*. 1903. NY: Dodd, 1979.

Duberman, Martin, ed. *Hidden from History: Reclaiming the Gay and Lesbian Past*. New York: New American Library, 1989.

Dunbar-Nelson. "Negro Literature for Negro Pupils." *Southern Workman* 51.2 (1922): 59–63.

Early, Gerald, ed. *My Soul's High Song: The Collected Writings of Countee Cullen*. New York: Anchor, 1991.

Early, Gerald, ed. *Speech and Power: the African-American Essay and its Cultural Content from Polemics to Pulpit*. New York: Ecco Press, 1992.

Emanuel, James A. "Renaissance Sonneteers." *Black World* 24 (Sep 1975): 32–45, 92–97.

———. *Langston Hughes*. Boston: Twayne Publishers, 1967.

Fabre, Michel. *From Harlem to Paris: Black American Writers in France, 1840–1980*. Urbana: U of Illinois P, 1991.

Farrison, W. Edward. "Langston Hughes: Poet of the Negro Renaissance." *CLA Journal* 15 Sep 1977: 401–10.

Fauset, Jessie Redmon. *Plum Bun: A Novel without a Moral*. Boston: Beacon Press, 1990.

———. *There Is Confusion*. Boston: Northeastern UP, 1989.

Fisher, Rudolph. *Walls of Jericho*. Ann Arbor, MI: U of Michigan Press, 1994.

Fleming, Robert E. *James Weldon Johnson*. Boston: Twayne, 1987.

Floyd, Samuel A. ed. *Black Music in the Harlem Renaissance: A Collection Of Essays*. NY: Greenwood P, 1990.

Foner, Philip S., and James S. Allen, eds. *American Communism and Black Americans: A Documented History, 1919–1929*. Philadelphia: Temple UP, 1987.

Franklin, V. P. *Living Our Stories, Telling Our Truths: Autobiography and the Making of the African-American Intellectual Tradition*. NY: Oxford UP, 1995.

From These Roots: A Review of the Harlem Renaissance. Schromburg Center for Research and Black Culture. New York, NY: William Greaves Productions, Inc., 1988. 1 videocassette 29 min.: sd., b&w. ; 1/2 in.

Gates, Henry Louis. Jr. *The Signifying Monkey: A Theory of African-American Literary Criticism*. NY: Oxford UP, 1988.

Gayle, Addison. "The Harlem Renaissance: Towards a Black Aesthetic." *Mid-continent American Studies Journal* (Fall 1970): 78–87.

Genizi, Haim. "V.F. Calverton: A Radical Magazinist for Black Intellectuals, 1920–1940." *Journal of Negro History* 57.3 (1972): 241–53.

Gerghard, Ann. "The Emerging Self: Young-Adult and Classic Novels of the Black Experience." *English Journal* 82.5 (Sep 1993): 50–.

Gilbert, James. *Writers and Partisans: A History of Literary Radicalism in America*. 1968. New York: Columbia UP, 1992.

Goellnicht, Donald C. "Passing as Autobiography: James Weldon Johnson's *The Autobiography of an Ex-Coloured Man*." *African American Review* 30.1 (Spring 1996): 17–35.

Gold, Michael. *The Nation* 123 (14 July 1926): 37.

Green, J. Lee. *Time's Unfading Garden: Anne Spencer's Life and Poetry*. Baton Rouge: Louisiana State UP, 1977.

Greenberg, Cheryl. *"Or Does It Explode?": Black Harlem in the Great Depression*. NY: Oxford UP, 1991.

Hamalian, Leo, and James V. Hatch. *The Roots of African American Drama: An Anthology of Early Plays, 1858–1938*. Detroit: Wayne State UP, 1991.

Harlem Renaissance and Beyond. Video. 31 min. 1989. # 9S541. Insight Media, NY. 212–721–6316.

Harlem Renaissance: Art of Black America. New York: Studio Museum in Harlem, 1987.

Harris, Trudier. *Afro-American Writers from the Harlem Renaissance to 1940. Dictionary of Literary Biography. Volume Fifty-one*. Detroit: Gale, 1986.

Hart, Robert. "Black-White Literary Relations in The Harlem Renaissance." *American Literature* 44 (Jan 1973): 612–28.

Hatch, James V., and Ted Shine. eds. *Black Theatre U.S.A.: Plays by African Americans 1847 to Today*. NY: Free P, 1996.

Helbling, Mark. "Carl Van Vechten and the Harlem Renaissance." *Negro American Literature Form* 10 (Summer 1976): 39–47.

Hemenway, Robert E. *Zora Neale Hurston: A Literary Biography*. Urbana: U of Illinois P, 1977.

Henderson, Mae Gwendolyn. "Portrait of Wallace Thurman." In Bontemps, 145–168.

Henry, Katherine. "Angelina Grimke's Rhetoric of Exposure." *American Quarterly* 49.2 (Jun 1997): 328–356.

Hoffman, Frederick. *The Little Magazine*. Princeton: Princeton UP, 1946.

Holmes, Eugene C. "Alain Locke and the New Negro Movement." *Negro American Literature Form* 2 (Fall 1968): 60–68.

Honey, Maureen. *Shadowed Dreams: Women's Poetry of the Harlem Renaissance*. New Brunswick: Rutgers UP, 1989.

Howe, Irving and Lewis Coser. *The American Communist Party, a critical history*. New York: Praeger, 1962.

Hudson-Weems, Clenora. "The Tripartite Plight of African-American Women as Reflected in the Novels of Hurston and Walker." *Journal of Black Studies* 20.2 (Dec 1989): 192.

Huggins, Nathan I. *Harlem Renaissance*. NY: Oxford UP, 1971.

Huggins, Nathan, ed. *Voices from the Harlem Renaissance*. New York: Oxford UP, 1976.

Hughes, Langston, ed. *A Pictoral History of the Negro in America*. New York: Crown Publishers, 1983.

Hughes, Langston. *Selected Poems*. New York: Vintage Books, 1987.

———. *The Big Sea*. 1940. Rpt. New York: Hill and Wang, 1963.

———. *The Weary Blues*. New York: Knopf, 1926.

Hull, Akasha Gloria T. *Color, Sex, and Poetry: Three Women Writers of the Harlem Renaissance*. Bloomington: Indiana UP, 1987.

Hutchinson, Earl Ofari. *Blacks and Reds: Race and Class in Conflict, 1919–1990*. East Lansing: Michigan State UP, 1995.

Hutchinson, George. "Mediating 'Race' and 'Nation': The Cultural Politics of *The Messenger*." *African American Review* 28.4 (1994): 531–48.

Johnson, Abby A. "Literary Midwife: Jessie Redmon Fauset and the Harlem Renaissance." *Phylon* 39 (Summer 1978): 143–53.

Johnson, Abby A., and Ronald M. Johnson. *Propaganda and Aesthetics: The Literary Politics of African-American Magazines in the Twentieth Century.* Amherst: U of Massachusetts P, 1991.

Johnson, James Weldon. *God's Trombones: Seven Negro Sermons in Verse.* New York: Viking Press, 1980.

Johnson, James Weldon. *Saint Peter Relates an Incident.* New York: Penguin Books, 1993.

———. *The Autobiography of an Ex-Coloured Man.* New York: Vintage Books, 1989.

———. *The Book of American Negro Poetry.* San Diego: Harcourt Brace Jovanovich, 1983.

Jones, Gayl. *Liberating Voices: Oral Tradition in African American Literature.* Cambridge: Harvard UP, 1991.

Kellner, Bruce, ed. *The Harlem Renaissance: A Historical Dictionary for the Era.* Westport, CN: Greenwood Press, 1984.

Kent, George E. "Patterns of the Harlem Renaissance." *Black World* 21 (Jun 1972): 13–24, 76–80.

Knopf, Marcy, ed. *The Sleeper Wakes: Harlem Renaissance Stories by Women.* New Bruswick, NJ: Rutgers UP, 1993.

Kornweibel, Theodore. *No Crystal Stair: Black Life and The Messenger, 1917–1928.* Westport: Greenwood, 1975.

Kramer, Victor A., ed. *The Harlem Renaissance Re-Examined.* New York: AMS P, 1987.

Kuenz, Jane. "American Racial Discourse, 1900–1930: Schuyler's *Black No More.*" *Novel* 30.2 (Winter 1997): 170–193.

Larsen, Nella. *Quicksand; and Passing.* New Brunswick, NJ: Rutgers UP, 1986.

Lauter, Paul, ed. *The Heath Anthology of American Literature.* Lexington, MA: D.C. Heath, 1990.

LeSeur, Geta. "Mothers and Sons: Androgynous Relationships in Afro-West Indian and Afro-American Novels of Youth." *Western Journal of Black Studies* 16.1 (Sprg 1992): 21–.

Lewis, David. *The Portable Harlem Renaissance Reader.* New York: Viking, 1994.

Lewis, David L. *When Harlem was in Vogue.* NY: Knopf, 1981.

Lewis, Samella S. *Art: African American.* New York: Harcourt, Brace, Jovanovich, 1994.

Locke, Alain. *The New Negro.* 1925. Rpt. New York: Arno, 1968.

Lomax, Michael L. "Fantasies of Affirmation: The 1920's Novel of Negro Life." *CLA Journal* 22 (Dec 1972): 232–46.

Marable, Manning. "A. Philip Randolph and the Foundations of Black American Socialism." *Radical America* 14.2 (1980): 7–29.

Martin, Tony. *African Fundamentalism: A Literary and Cultural Anthology of Garvey's Harlem Renaissance*. Dover, Mass.: Majority P, 1991.

McKay, Claude. *A Long Way From Home*. New York: Arno Press, 1969.

———. *Harlem Shadows*. New York: Harcourt, Brace & Co., 1992.

———. *Home to Harlem*. Chatham, NJ: Chatham Bookseller, 1973.

Miller, Nina. "Femininity, Publicity, and the Class Division of Cultural Labor: Jessie Redmon Fauset's *There is Confusion*." *African American Review* 30.2 (Summer 1996): 205–221.

Mitchell, Angelyn. ed. *Within the Circle: An Anthology of African American Literary Criticism from the Harlem Renaissance to the Present*. Durham, NC : Duke UP, 1994.

Morgan, Stacy "'The Strange and Wonderful Workings of Science': Race Science and Essentialism in George Schuyler's Black No More." *CLA Journal* 42.3 (Mar 1999): 331–53.

Morris, Lloyd. "The Negro 'Renaissance.'" *Southern Workman* 59.2 (Feb 1930): 82–86.

Morrison, Toni. *Jazz*. New York: Knopf, 1992.

Murphy, James F. *The Proletarian Moment: The Controversy Over Leftism in Literature*. Urbana: U of Illinois P, 1991.

Musser, Judith. "African American Women's Short Stories in the Harlem Renaissance: Bridging a Tradition." *Melus* 23.2 (Summer 1998): 27–49.

Nelson, Cary. *Repression and Recovery: Modern American Poetry and the Politics of Cultural Memory, 1910–1945*. Madison: U of Wisconsin P, 1989.

North, Michael. *The Dialect of Modernism: Race, Language, and Twentieth-Century Literature*. NY: Oxford UP, 1994.

O'Neill, Eugene. *Plays*. New York: Horace Liveright, 1925.

Osofsky, Gilbert. *Harlem: The Making of A Ghetto*. NY: Harper, 1966.

Perry, Margaret. *The Harlem Renaissance: An Annotated Bibliography and Commentary*. NY: Garland Pub., 1982.

Pfeiffer, Kathleen. "Individualism, Success, and American Identity in *The Autobiography of an Ex-Colored Man*." *African American Review* 30.3 (Fall 1996): 403–421.

Podesta, Guido A. "An Ethnographic Reproach to the Theory of the Avant-Garde: Modernity and Modernism in Latin America and the Harlem Renaissance." *Modern Language Notes* 106.2 (Mar 1991): p395 (28).

Reed, Ishmael. *Mumbo Jumbo*. New York: Atheneum, 1989.

Reference Library of Black America. New York: Bellwether Publishing Co., 1971.

Reuben, Paul P. "Chapter 9: Harlem Renaissance—Selected Bibliography." *PAL: Perspectives in American Literature—A Research and Reference Guide.*

Roses, Lorraine E. *Harlem Renaissance and Beyond: Literary Biographies of 100 Black Women Writers, 1900–1945.* Boston: G.K. Hall, 1990.

Russ, Robert A. *The Harlem Renaissance: A Selected Bibliography.* New York: AMS, 1987.

———. *The Harlem Renaissance: A Selected Bibliography.* NY: AMS, 1987.

Schoener, Allon. *Harlem on My Mind: Cultural Capital of Black America, 1900–1968.* New York: Random House, 1969.

Schuyler, George S. "The Negro-Art Hokum." *Nation* 122 6/16/1926: 662–63.

———. *Black No More: Being an Account of the Strange and Wonderful Workings of Science in the Land of the Free, A.D. 1933–1940.* Boston: Northeastern UP, 1989.

Scruggs, Charles W. "Alain Locke and Walter White: Their Struggle for Control of the Harlem Renaissance." *Black American Literature Forum (BALF)*14 (Fall 1980): 91–99.

———. *The Sage in Harlem: H.L. Mencken and the Black Writers of the 1920s.* Baltimore: Johns Hopkins UP, 1984.

Singh, Amritjit, et al, ed. *The Harlem Renaissance: Revaluations.* NY: Garland, 1989.

Singh, Amritjit. "Black-White Symbiosis: Another Look at the Literary History of the 1920s." In Kramer, Victor A. *The Harlem Renaissance Re-Examined.* New York: AMS P, 1987, 31–42.

Spencer, Jon Michael. "The Black Church and the Harlem Renaissance." *African American Review* 30.3 (Fall 1996): 453–.

———. *The New Negroes and Their Music: The Success of the Harlem Renaissance.* Knoxville: U of Tennessee P, 1997.

Studio Museum in Harlem. *Harlem Renaissance: Art of Black America.* NY: Abrams, 1987.

Sudhalter, Richard M. *Lost Chords: White Musicians and Their Contribution to Jazz 1915–1945.* NY: Oxford UP, 1999.

Sundquist, Eric J. *To Wake the Nations: Race in the Making of American Literature.* Cambridge: Harvard UP, 1993.

Teres, Harvey. "'Their Negro Problem': The New York Intellectuals and African American Culture." Course Reader, 1995.

Thurman, Wallace. "Negro Artists and the Negro." *New Republic* 31 August (1927): 37–39

Toomer, Jean. *Cane*. New York: Liveright, 1993.

Turner, Darwin T. "Past and Present in Negro American Drama." *NALF* 2 (Sumr 1968): 26–27.

———. "W.E.B. Du Bois and the Theory of a Black Aesthetic." In Kramer, Victor A. *The Harlem Renaissance Re-Examined*. New York: AMS P, 1987, 9–30.

Tyler, Bruce M. *From Harlem to Hollywood: The Struggle for Racial and Cultural Democracy, 1920–1943*. New York: Garland, 1992.

Valenti, Suzanne. "The Black Diaspora: Negritude in the Poetry of West Africans and Black Americans." *Phylon* 34 (Dec 1973): 390–98.

Van Vechten, Carl. *Nigger Heaven*. New York: A.A. Knopf, 1926.

Vincent, Theodore G. *Voices of a Black Nation: Political Journalism in the Harlem Renaissance*. San Francisco: Ramparts P, 1973.

Wagner, Jean. *Black Poets of the United States*. Urbana-Champaigne: U of Illinois P, 1989.

Waldron, Edward E. *Walter White and the Harlem Renaissance*. Port Washington: Kennikat P, 1978.

Walker, Margaret. *How I wrote Jubilee and Other Essays on Life and Literature*. New York: Feminist Press at the City University of New York, 1990.

Wall, Cheryl A. *Women of the Harlem Renaissance*. Bloomington : Indiana UP, 1995.

Walrond, Eric. *Tropic Death*. New York: Collier Books, 1972.

Washington, Mary H. *Invented Lives: Narratives of Black Women, 1860–1960*. Garden City: Anchor P, 1987.

Watson, Steven. *The Harlem Renaissance: Hub of African-American Culture, 1920–1930*. NY: Pantheon Books, 1995.

Weixlmann, Joe, and Houston A. Baker, Jr., ed. *Studies in Black American Literature*. Greenwood, Fl: Penkeville, 1988.

Whatley-Smith, Virginia. "The Harlem Renaissance and its Blues-Jazz Traditions: Harlem and its places of Entertainment." *Obsidian II* 11.1/2 (Fall 1996): 21–.

Williams, John A. "The Harlem Renaissance: Its Artists, Its Impact, Its Meaning." *Black World* 20. Nov 1970: 17–18.

Wintz, Cary D. *Black Culture and the Harlem Renaissance*. Houston: Rice UP, 1988.

Woodson, Carter G. "Some Things Negroes Need To Do." *Southern Workman* 51.1 (Jan 1922): 82–86.

Wright, John S. A *Stronger Soul Within a Finer Frame: Portraying African-Americans in the Black Renaissance*. Minneapolis: U Art Museum, U of Minnesota, 1990.

Wright, Richard. *Black Boy, a Record of Childhood and Youth*. New York: Harper & Brothers, 1945.

Young, James O. *Black Writers of the Thirties*. Baton Rouge: Louisiana State UP, 1973.

Young, Mary E. "Anita Scott Coleman: A Neglected Harlem Renaissance Writer." *CLA Journal* 40.3 (MAR 1997): 271–288.

Acknowledgments

"The Renaissance Re-examined" by Warrington Hudlin. From *The Harlem Renaissance Remembered*, edited by Arna Bontemps. © 1972 by Warrington Hudlin. Reprinted by permission.

"The Shape and Shapers of the Movement" by Margaret Perry. From *Silence to the Drums: A Survey of the Literature of the Harlem Renaissance.* ©1976 by Margaret Perry.
Reproduced by permission of Greenwood Publishing Group, Inc., Westport, CT.

"Langston Hughes: Evolution of the Poetic Persona" by Raymond Smith. From *The Harlem Renaissance Re-examined*, edited by Victor A. Kramer. © 1987 by AMS Press, Inc. Reprinted by permission.

"Black-White Symbiosis: Another Look at the Literary History of the 1920s" by Amritjit Singh. From *The Harlem Renaissance Re-examined*, edited by Victor A. Kramer. © 1987 by AMS Press, Inc. Reprinted by permission.

"Black Autobiography and the Comic Vision" by Richard K. Barksdale. From *Praisesong of Survival: Lectures and Essays*, 1957–89. ©1992 by The Board of Trustees of the University of Illinois. Reprinted by permission.

"Toomer's Cane and the Harlem Renaissance" by Genevieve Fabre. From *Jean Toomer and the Harlem Renaissance*, edited by Geneviève and Michel Feith. © 2001 by Rutgers, The State University. Reprinted by permission of Rutgers University Press.

"The Syncopated African: Constructions of Origins in the Harlem Renaissance (Literature, Music, Visual Arts)" by Michel Feith. From *Temples for Tomorrow: Looking Back at the Harlem Renaissance*, edited by Geneviève Fabre and Michel Feith. © 2001 by Indiana University Press. Reprinted by permission.

"The Negro Author and His Publisher" by Sterling A. Brown. From *Remembering the Harlem Renaissance*. © 1996 by Cary D. Wintz. Reprinted by Permission.

"Survival and song: Women poets of the Harlem Renaissance" by Maureen Honey. From *Women's Studies* 16 (1989): 293–315. © 1989 by Maureen Honey. Reprinted by permission of Maureen Honey.

"Masks and Masquerade: The Iconography of the Harlem Renaissance" by Patti Capel. Swartz. From *Analysis and Assessment*, 1980–1994. © 1996 by Cary D. Wintz. Reprinted by permission.

Index

Characters in novels and poems are indexed by first name followed by the name of the work in parentheses.

Abraham Lincoln (play), 152–53
Abrahams, Peter, 178
Adam Negro's Tyrall (Saffin), 99
Adler, Elmer, 196
African Blood Brotherhood, 129
African heritage. *See also* New Negro movement as project
  Barnes Foundation and, 54, 56, 187–88
  creation of, 282–84
  fused with Modernism, 285
  influence of, 278–79
"Afro-American Fragment" (Hughes), 283
Afro-American women writers. *See* Women writers
"Afterglow" (Johnson, G.), 234
"Age of Washington," 5–6
"Aliens" (Johnson, G.), 82
All God's Chillin Got Wings (O'Neill), 156–58
All God's Dangers (Rosengarten), 99–100, 102, 110
Allen, Frederick, 175
Along This Way (Johnson), 145–46
Amenia Conferences, 61, 142
Amenia Times, 61

American Mercury, 54, 156
American Now (Stern), 31
Anderson, Marian, 70
Anderson, Regina, 69, 133
Anderson, Sherwood, 25, 30, 128–29, 197
Anita Bush Players, 153
Anne Grey *(Quicksand)*, 211
Anthology of American Negro Literature (Calverton, ed.), 30
"April Is on the Way" (Dunbar-Nelson), 67, 86
"As I Grew Older" (Hughes), 40, 49
Ascent of Ethiopia (Jones), 279
Asian-African Conference in Bandung, 172
ASK YOUR MAMA (Hughes), 43, 49
Aspects of Negro Life series (Douglas), 247, 282
Assimilationist-separatist dichotomy, 7
"At the Carnival" (Spencer), 77
Audrey Denney *(Quicksand)*, 211
"Aunt Sue's Stories" (Hughes), 43
Authors and publishers
  economic woes of writers, 199–200
  making a living by writing, 196–99
  Negro and his publisher, 205–6
  special problems of Negro writer, 200–202
  what publishers want, 202–5
Autobiography, black

comic distancing and, 102–3, 104–5
comments on, 111
rich heritage of, 100–101
The Autobiography of an Ex-Colored Man
(Johnson), 125, 140, 185
The Autobiography of Malcolm X, 100
The Awakening of Ethiopia (Fuller), 279
Awards by *Crisis* and *Opportunity*
magazines, 133–37, 173–77. *See also*
Civic Club gathering
Axel Olsen (*Quicksand*), 212–13

Baker, George Pierce, 24
Baker, Houston A., 118, 246
Baker, Jake, 107
Baker, Josephine, 25
Baker, Ray Stannard, 134
Baldwin, James Arthur, 100
Baltimore Afro-American Newspaper, 105
Banana Bottom (McKay), 146
Banjo (McKay), 142–43, 146
Barksdale, Richard K.
biographical sketch, 302
"Black Autobiography and the Comic
Vision," 99–112
Barnes, Albert C., 53–56, 126
Barnes Foundation , 54, 56, 187–88
Barthé, Richard, 25, 56, 69, 282
Bearden, Romare, 285
"beautiful black woman holding a child"
(Hayden), 247
"Before the Feast of Shushan"
(Spencer), 77
Bennett, Gwendolyn
Civic Club gathering and, 69, 126
exotic themes of, 280, 283
poetry of, 77, 139, 223
race consciousness of, 224
on Saturday night salons, 67
Bethane, Mary McLeod, 36, 70
Betts, Ellen, 102–3
Biddle, George, 57

The Big Sea (Hughes). *See also* Hughes,
Langston
Alain Locke, 14
birthday celebrations, 73
lack of personal detail in, 105–6
on refusal to deny race, 47–48
relationship with father, 39
Southern blacks, 45–46
writing poetry, 49
Birch, Eva Lennox
biographical sketch, 302
"Harlem and the First Black
Resistance," 113–22
Birth of a Nation (Griffith), 61
Birthright (Stribling), 128, 131
Black and White (Soviet film), 145
Black Art Movement, 53
Black Bottom (dance), 155
Black Boy (Wright), 99
The Black Christ (Cullen), 142
Black Drama (Loften), 250
Black Magic (Davis, O.), 243–44, 250
"Black man wearing a beret" (Hayden),
247
Black Manhattan (Johnson), 17, 144
Black Manhattan. *See also* Folk culture;
Harlem; Music; *Shuffle Along*
buying property, 149–50
getting foothold in Harlem, 150–51,
184
jazz and, 251–52
theater in, 152–55, 249–52
Black No More (Schuyler), 143, 260
Black Theatre: Premise and Presentation
(Molettes), 248–49
Black women writers. *See* Women
writers
Blackbirds (revue), 124
Blackburn, R. P., 198–99
The Blacker the Berry (Thurman), 106,
142, 260
Blair, Mary, 156
Blake, Eubie, 154
Bledsoe, Jules, 250

Bloom, Harold
  biographical sketch, 301
  editor's note, vii
  introduction, 1–4
Blue Blood (Johnson, G.), 82
Blue Reiter almanac, 189
"Blueprint for Negro Writing"
  (Wright), 147
"Blues Fantasy" (Hughes), 48
Boas, Franz, 25, 117
Bogan, Louise, 197
Bonner, Marita, 13, 61
Bontemps, Arna
  being "exhibited," 120
  depicts Negro in unflattering light,
    118
  first prize at awards dinner, 136–37
  on Harlem, 243, 244
  major novelist, 29, 176
  matures after Renaissance, 13
  teacher, 197
Book of American Negro Poetry (Johnson),
  131, 185
Botkin, B. A., 102–3
Bourne, Randolph, 127
A Boy Scout (Reiss), 190
Bradford, Roark, 143. *See also The Green
  Pastures*
Braithwaite, William Stanley, 169, 196
Braque, George, 24
"Brass Spitoons" (Hughes), 43
Brawley, Benjamin, 130–31, 196
Breaking Into Print (Adler), 196, 200
Br'er Rabbit stories (Harris), 246
Brignano, Robert, 100
Bronze: A Book of Verse (Johnson, G.), 83,
  91
Brooks, Van Wyck, 276
Brown, Sterling A.
  biographical sketch, 303
  comic distancing and, 104–5
  Egyptian themes of, 280
  on *The Green Pastures*, 143
  influence of, 223

  poetry of, 251–52, 287–88
  prizewinner at *Opportunity* dinner,
    135, 176
  "The Negro Author and his
    Publisher," 195–206
  on women writers, 223, 224–25
Brown, William Wells, 195
Bruce, Richard, 72
Brutus Jones (*Emperor Jones*), 250
Building More Stately Mansions
  (Douglas), 280
Butler Davenport's Bramhall Players,
  152

Calverton, Victor F., 25, 30–32
Campbell, Mary, 247
Cane (Toomer)
  background of, 256–57, 260
  "Cotton Song," 258
  critical acclaim, 4, 21, 255
  criticisms of, 260–61, 264
  dramatic form of "Kabnis," 261–65
  harvest-reaper motif, 257–58
  "Harvest Song," 257
  "Kabnis," 257, 258–59
  "Kabnis is me," 258, 259
  product of direct experience, 45
  publication at end of phase 1, 125,
    252
  songs of "Kabnis," 268–73
"Carma" Toomer, 45
Carolina Magazine, 25
Carolina Playmakers, 24–25
Caroling Dusk (Cullen), 2, 4, 67
Caution, Ethel, 231
cummings, e.e., 25, 128
Cellini, Benvenuto, 100
"Chalk-dust" (Spencer), 228
Chapin, Cornelia, 57
Chapin, Katherine Garrison, 56
Charles Chesnutt Honorarium, 8
Charleston (dance), 155
Chase, Harry Woodburn, 25

Chesnutt, Charles
　Charles Chesnutt Honorarium, 8
　The Colonel's Dream (Chesnutt), 125
　color-line fiction and, 83
　Conjure Woman (Chesnutt), 246
　The House Behind the Cedars
　　(Chesnutt), 73, 200
　on Negroes and publishers, 200–201
　silenced by low royalties, 125, 196
　The Wife of His Youth (Chesnutt), 83
The Chinaberry Tree (Fauset), 29
The Chip Woman's Fortune (Richardson),
　156
Chocolate Dandies (Sissle and Blake
　show), 156
Christian, Barbara, 88
Civic Club gathering (March 21, 1924),
　69, 125–27, 133
Civilization and Its Discontents (Freud), 24
Clifford, Carrie, 224
Cobb, Nate, 100, 102. *See also* Shaw,
　Nate
Cole, Bob, 16
Coleman, Anna Scott, 233
A College Lad (Reiss), 191
The Colonel's Dream (Chesnutt), 125
Color (McKay), 170
Color Struck (Hurston), 139
Comedy: American Style (Fauset), 145
The Comedy of Errors (Shakespeare), 156
"Confessions of a Lazy Woman"
　(Dunbar-Nelson), 90
The Congo (Lindsay), 25
Conjure Woman (Chesnutt), 246
Connelly, Marc, 143
"Contribution to the Study of Negro
　Art in America" (Barnes), 54, 55
"Controversial Sounds: Jazz
　Performance" (Ogden), 251
Cooper, Opal, 128
Copper Masks series (Johnson, S.), 282
Copper Sun (Cullen), 140
Corrothers, James D., 13
Cowdery, Mae V., 224, 228, 231, 234–35

CPUSA, 129
Crane, Hart, 3
"Creed" (Spencer), 77
The Crisis (magazine), 8, 10, 26, 68, 224
Crisis literary prizes, 140
Cubism and African art, 289, 292
Cullen, Countee
　1927 landmark collection, 67
　African heritage in poetry, 282
　classic beauty of poetry, 171
　criticisms of, 236
　identified with Keats, 3
　on poetry committee, 61
　as teacher, 196
　valued writer of movement, vii, 27,
　　170
　and the Yale collection, 19
"cultural compulsive" theory, 31
Cunard, Nancy, 147
Cuney, Waring, 29, 70

"Danse Afracaine" (Hughes), 283
Dark Laughter (Anderson), 129
"Dark Madonna" (Johnson, G.), 231
Dark Princess (Du Bois), 140
Davis, Allison, 224
Davis, Frank Marshall, 196–97
Davis, John P., 176
Davis, Ossie, 243–44
Dawn in Harlem (Reiss), 191
Delaney, Clarissa Scott, 71, 233–34
Dial, S4N, Brown (magazine), 127, 129
Dickinson, Blanche Taylor, 93, 232
Diez, Julius, 189
Dinah (Irving C. Miller show), 155
Dismond, Geraldyn, 67
Dixie to Broadway (show), 158–59
Door-to-door novels, 196
Douglas, Aaron
　Building More Stately Mansions, 280
　"father of Black American art,"
　　188–89
　in Harlem, 133, 181

Harmon foundation and, 143
patronage and, 56
primitive motifs in, 247, 282, 290–91
Reiss influence on, 191
Survey Graphic influence, 180
Douglass, Frederick, 102, 113, 152, 168,
    195
Dove, Rita, 4
Dover, Cedric, 82
Drama League, 153, 157
The Dream Keeper (Hughes), 36
The Dreamy Kid (O'Neill), 152
Dreiser, Theodore, 128
Driskell, David, 246–47
Drumbeats, Masks and Metaphor (Fabre),
    248
Du Bois, W.E.B.
    African visit, 284
    challenges Washington, 116
    criticisms of McKay novel, 250–51
    cultural pluralism and, 277
    as editor and teacher, 196
    espousal of Negritude, 118
    hailed Toomer in *Crisis*, 255
    Hughes and, 41–42
    NAACP and, 8, 60–61, 147
    at *Opportunity* dinner, 173, 179
    racial pride and, 19–20, 168–69, 179,
        251, 281
    radical views of, 6, 169
    symposium on arts, 140
    twoness and, 37, 100
Du Bois, W.E.B., works of
    Autobiography, 101
    Dark Princess, 140
    "Marxism and the Negro Problem,"
        147
    The Quest of the Silver Fleece, 125
    The Souls of Black Folk, 37, 127, 276
    "The Negro Mind Reaches Out," 281
    "The Song of the Smoke," 41, 81
"Dunbar" (Spencer), 77
Dunbar-Nelson, Alice. *See also* Women
    writers

color and, 81, 84
conflicted femininity of, 85–86
critical of Bontemps, 118
financial hardships of, 85
literary output, 78–81, 85–86, 90–91,
    91–92
marriages of, 84
Renaissance writer, 67, 69, 70
themes of, 83, 86–87, 92, 229–30
Dunbar, Paul Laurence, 2, 35, 70, 169,
    192, 196
Dunbar Theatre, 154
Dust Tracks on a Road (Hurston), 107–9

Eastman, Max, 127
Ebony and Topaz (anthology), 176
"Ecstacy" (Houston), 235
Egyptian "heritage," 279–81
"Elderly Race Leaders" (Hughes), 145
Elise Johnson McDougold (Reiss), 192
Ellington, Duke, 25, 245
Ellison, Ralph, 289
Ellison, Richard, 118
The Emperor Jones (O'Neill), 128, 152,
    153, 250
The Enormous Room (cummings), 128
"Escape" (Johnson, G.), 231
Ethiopian Art Players, 156
Europe, James Reese, 251–52
Exoticism, 10, 176

Fabre, Genevieve
    biographical sketch, 303
    Drumbeats, Masks and Metaphor, 248
    "Toomer's *Cane* and the Harlem
        Renaissance," 255–74
Fad, Negro, 24, 26, 130, 179, 210, 277,
    278
Father John (*Cane*), 265
Fauset, Arthur, 147
Fauset, Jessie
    love poems of, 77, 225, 231, 235

novels of, 29, 90, 142, 145, 260
short stories of, 133
smoking shocks Nance, 76
teacher, 197
Fauset, Jessie, works of
  The Chinaberry Tree, 29
  Comedy: American Style, 145
  Plum Bun, 142, 145, 260
  There Is Confusion, 126
Feith, Michel
  biographical sketch, 304
  "The Syncopated African," 275–94
Feral Benga (Barthé), 59, 282
Ferris, William H., 124
Fétiche et Fleurs (Hayden), 285
Fifty Years and After (Johnson), 185
Fighting Words (Hughes), 9–10, 201
Fine Clothes to a Jew (Hughes), 27, 35,
  36, 43, 48–49, 137, 171
Fire!! (Thurman, ed.), 119, 138, 139,
  141
The Fire in the Flint (White), 29, 126,
  131
Fisher, Rudolph
  death of, 106, 147
  Howard Medical School graduate,
  136
  successful doctor and satirist, 141, 196
  Van Vechten and, 17, 27
Fisher, Rudolph, works of
  "The South Lingers On," 136
  The Walls of Jericho, 56, 141
Fitzgerald, Robert, 198
Flight (White), 140
Folk culture. *See also* Exoticism; Music;
  Primitivism
  art, 282–84
  call-and-response pattern, 287, 289
  fused with Modernism, 284–85
  poetry, 287–88
  syncopation, 286, 288, 289, 291–92
  from two soils, 277–78
Four Harmony Kings, 154
Four Portraits of Negro Women (Reiss),
  192

Frank, Waldo, 25, 30, 70, 127, 129, 255,
  276
Franklin, Benjamin, 100, 101
Franklin, John Hope, 177
Frazier, E. Franklin, 135, 176, 178
"Free" (short story) (Johnson, G.), 85,
  91
Freud, Sigmund, 24, 283
Fuller, Meta Vaux Warrick, 237, 247,
  279

Gale, Zona, 19, 29, 126
Garden Street Theatre, 128
In the Garrett (Van Vechten), 27
Garvey, Marcus, 120, 132, 172
Garveyism, 68, 136, 172
Garvey's Universal Negro Improvement
  Association (UNIA), 129, 132, 147
Gates, Henry Louis, 288
Gayle, Addison, Jr., 236
Gee, Lottie, 154
"Georgia Dusk" (Toomer), 45
Gilpin, Charles, 25, 128, 152, 153
Girl in the White Blouse (Reiss), 190
God Sends Sunday (Bontemps), 29, 118
God's Trombones (Johnson), 67, 287
Goethe, 177
Goetz, George. *See* Calverton, Victor F.
"Golgotha Is a Mountain" (Bontemps),
  136–37
Gonzales, Barbara (Babs), 99
"Goodbye Christ" (Hughes), 145
Graham, Frank, 25
Granny Maumee (play) (Torrence), 128
Grant, Daniel T., 99
Grant, Robert Lee, 99
Great Black Migration, 68, 131, 182,
  183, 184
The Great Day (Hurston), 57
Green, Elizabeth Lay, 24
The Green Pastures (play) (Connelly,
  prod.), 143

Green, Paul, 24
Griffith, D. W., 61
Griggs, Sutton, 125, 196
Grimké, Angelina Weld. *See also*
    Women writers
  background, 81–82
  isolation of, 87
  lesbianism of, 84–85, 86
  literary output, 90, 230
  poetry and, 78–81, 86, 88, 94, 230–31
  Renaissance writer, 13, 67–68, 70
  themes of, 82, 86–87, 225, 235
Grimké, Angelina Weld, works of
  "A Mona Lisa," 235
  "Jettisoned," 82, 92
  Rachel, 79
  "Tenebris," 86, 230
  "The Black Finger," 94
Grimké, Charlotte Forten, 225
Guggenheim Fellowship for Creative
    Writing, 207
Guillaume, Paul, 187
Gysin, Fritz, 261

Haley, Alex, 100
Halsey (*Cane*), 263
Hanby (*Cane*), 260
Hapgood, Emily, 128
Harlem (magazine), 141, 142
Harlem. *See also* Black Manhattan;
    Iconography of Renaissance
  jazz and, 251–52
  nonviolent takeover of, 150–51, 181
  pan African movement and, 188
  as race capital, 182–85, 192, 243–44
  self-supporting community, 186–87
"Harlem: Mecca of the New Negro"
    (*Survey Graphic*), 135
Harlem Renaissance (Huggins), 23
Harlem Renaissance. *See* Renaissance
Harlem Renaissance Art of Black America
    (Campbell), 247
The Harlem Renaissance in Black and
    White (Hutchinson), 276

Harlem Shadows (McKay), 74, 125, 129,
    131
Harmon Foundation, 143
Harmon Traveling Exhibition of the
    Work of Negro Artists (1931), 144
Harper, Frances Watkins, 195
Harper's Magazine, 175
Harris, Joel Chandler, 246
Harrison, Richard, 143
"Hatred" (Bennett), 224
Hayden, Palmer, 246–47, 249, 285, 287
Hayden, Robert, 3, 4
Hayes, Roland, 14, 25, 70, 124, 188
Hayford, Gladys Mae
  born in Africa, 78
  "Nativity" (Hayford), 78
  "Rainy Season Love Song" (Hayford),
    78, 235
  "The Serving Girl" (Hayford), 78
The Heart of a Woman (Johnson, G.), 83,
    92
Heibling, Mark, 54
Helga Crane (*Quicksand*)
  becomes exotic female in Denmark,
    212
  confused about definitions of
    blackness, 208
  engaged to James, 209
  Harlem and, 210–11, 251
  refuses Axel's proposal of marriage,
    212–13
  returns to Harlem and marries Green,
    214
  trapped in need to express sexuality,
    209
Hemenway, Robert, 106, 107–8, 120
"Heritage" (Cullen), 282
"Heritage" (Bennett), 280, 283
Herskovits, Melville, 25, 186–87
Heyward, DuBose, 24
Himes, Chester, 27, 101
Holiday (Frank), 129
Holiday, Billie, 71
Hollywood stereotyping, 250–51

Holstein, Casper, 135, 136
Holt, Nora, 107
Home to Harlem (McKay)
    depicts Harlem as home to all, 17
    exoticism and, 10, 28–29, 146
    first best-seller, 140–41
    sexuality in, 250–51
    writing of, 74
Honey, Maureen
    biographical sketch, 303
    "Survival and Song: Women Poets of
        the Harlem Renaissance," 223–42
Horne, Frank, 134, 176
The House Behind the Cedars (Chesnutt),
    73, 83, 200
Houston, Virginia, 235
Howard Theatre, 154
Howard University, 104
Howells, William Dean, 169
Hudgins, Johnny, 156
Hudlin, Warrington
    biographical sketch, 301
    "The Renaissance Re-examined,"
        5–13
Huggins, Nathan Irvin, 23, 55, 62, 68,
    226, 278, 283
Hughes, Langston
    belief in American ideal, 46–47
    career of, 35–36, 176
    childhood, 42–43, 47
    comic distancing and, 102, 105–6
    detachment of, 46, 49, 105–6, 107,
        108
    Du Bois and, 41–42
    on his poetry, 49, 251
    Hurston and, 106, 107, 145
    on overpoliticising work, 119
    patronage and, 9, 30, 56–58, 119, 196
    philosophy of, 38–39, 140, 292
    as Poet Laureate of the Negro, 50
    poet's role, 38, 44, 50
    prejudice and the South, 44–46,
        47–48
    principal of Renaissance, 2, 5

    relationship with father, 39–40, 46, 49
    on Renaissance, 11
    Sandburg and, 3–4
    symbolizes emancipation of Negro,
        171
    themes of, 36, 37, 50, 137, 280, 283,
        287
    Van Vechten and, 27
Hughes, Langston, works of. *See also*
        The Big Sea (Hughes)
    "As I Grew Older," 40, 49
    ASK YOUR MAMA, 43, 49
    "Aunt Sue's Stories," 43
    "Blues Fantasy," 48
    "Brass Spitoons," 43
    The Dream Keeper, 36
    Fighting Words, 9–10
    Fine Clothes to a Jew, 27, 35, 36, 43,
        48–49, 137
    "Goodbye Christ" (Hughes), 145
    "I, Too, Sing America," 46, 48
    I Wonder as I Wander, 105–106
    "Negro Dancers" (Hughes), 48
    Not Without Laughter, 57, 59
    "Scottsboro, Limited" (Hughes), 145
    Shakespeare in Harlem, 48–49
    "The Cat and the Saxophone," 48, 49
    "The Negro Artist and the Racial
        Mountain" (Hughes), 10, 30, 138,
        139
    "The Negro Speaks of Rivers," 35,
        38, 39, 40, 49
    "The South," 45
    "The White Ones," 43–44
    The Ways of White Folks, 56
    The Weary Blues, 27, 35, 36, 37, 48,
        73, 131
Hull, Akasha Gloria
    biographical sketch, 302
    "Color, Sex, and Poetry in the
        Harlem Renaissance," 67–98
"Hunger" (Young), 235
Hurst, Fannie, 19

Hurston, Zora Neale, 288
    autobiography of, 107–9
    birthmate changed, 76–77
    comic distancing and, 102
    exoticism and, 10
    Hughes and, 106, 107, 145
    last novel of movement, 146
    matured after Renaissance, 13
    patronage and, 56–57, 59, 119
    personality of, 121–22
    power of, 1–2
    secretarial work and, 196
    "Sweat," vii, 1–2
    on word coinage, 287
Hurston, Zora Neale, works of
    Color Struck, 139
    Dust Tracks on a Road, 107–9
    The Great Day, 57
    Jonah's Gourd Vine, 146
    "Spunk," 288
    "Sweat," vii, 1–2, 139
    Their Eyes Were Watching God, 1–2,
        288
Hutchinson, George, 276–77, 277

I Paid My Dues (Gonzales), 99
"I Sit and Sew" (Dunbar-Nelson), 85
"I, Too, Sing America" (Hughes), 46, 48
"I Want to Die While You Love Me"
    (Johnson, G.), 87
I Wonder as I Wander (Hughes), 105–106
Iconography of Renaissance. See also
        Folk culture; Harlem; Music;
        Renaissance
    artistic control and, 243–45, 248–49
    carnival idea, 243–45
    masks and, 245–48
    musical revues, 249–52
    Signifying Monkey, 245–46
"If We Must Die" (McKay), 169
Infants of the Spring (Thurman), 146
"Insatiate" (Cowdery), 235

Irish Renaissance, 277
"Ivy" (Johnson, G.), 87

Jackman, Harold, 75
James Vayle (Quicksand), 209, 211
James Weldon Johnson Collection,
        36–37, 65
The Janitor Who Paints (Hayden), 247
Jannath, Heba, 229
Jazz, 251–52. See also Music
Jazz Age, 68, 247
"Jazz at Home" (Rogers), 191
The Jazz Singer (film), 249
Jenness, Mary, 233
"Jettisoned" (Grimké,), 82, 92
Jim Crow laws, 117, 244
John Drinkwater's Abraham Lincoln,
        152–53
John Henry, 287
Johnson, Charles S.
    Barnes and, 54–55
    biographical sketch, 302
    coming out party for artists, 9,
        125–27
    influence of, 20–21, 25, 93, 141
    "The Negro Renaissance and Its
        Significance," 167–78
Johnson, Fenton, 69
Johnson, Georgia Douglas. See also
        Women writers
    financial hardships of, 85
    literary output, 84, 90–91, 92, 93
    miscegenation and, 82
    personality of, 85
    poetry of, 78–81, 86–87, 223, 231
    race consciousness of, 225
    Richard Bruce and, 72
    salons of, 67–68, 70, 94
    as wife and mother, 84
Johnson, Georgia Douglas, works of
    "Afterglow," 234
    "Aliens," 82
    Blue Blood, 82

Bronze: A Book of Verse, 83, 91
"Dark Madonna," 231
"Escape," 231
"Free" (short story), 85, 91
The Heart of a Woman, 83, 92
"I Want to Die While You Love Me,"
　87
"Ivy," 87
"Old Black Men," 86
One and One Makes Three, 82
Plumes, 82
Popoplikabu, 82
A Sunday Morning in the South, 82
William and Ellen Craft, 82
Johnson, Hall, 56, 124
Johnson, Helene
　"Magalu," 232
　"Poem," 78
　pride of black woman, 232, 234
　race consciousness of, 77–78, 224
　"Sonnet to a Negro in Harlem," 77
　theme of romantic love, 88
Johnson, J. Rosamond, 16
Johnson, James Weldon
　autobiography of, 145–46
　background, 14–15
　biographical sketch, 302–3
　earning livelihood, 196
　Harlem and, 15–16
　influence of, 143, 147
　on inner turmoil of nation, 168
　poetry of, 169
　principal of Renaissance, 2, 15, 25, 27
　on reeducating whites, 117–18
　on Van Vechen, 62
Johnson, James Weldon, works of
　Along This Way, 145–46
　*The Autobiography of an Ex-Colored
　　Man*, 125, 140, 185
　Black Manhattan, 17, 144
　Book of American Negro Poetry, 131,
　　185
　Fifty Years and After, 185
　"From *Black Manhattan*," 149–60
　God's Trombones, 67

God's Trombones, 287
　"The Creation," 287
　"The Making of Harlem," 185
　tour d'horizon, 147
Johnson, Jimmie, 155
Johnson, Malvin Gray, 285
Johnson, Samuel W., 9
Johnson, Sargent, 69, 282
Jolson, Al, 249
Jonah's Gourd Vine (Hurston), 146
Jones, Lois Mailou, 279
Just, Ernest E., 61
Justice (Butler Davenport's Bramhall
　Players), 152

Kabnis (*Cane*)
　conversation with himself, 260
　dialogues with various characters, 263
　ending is problematic "dusk of dawn,"
　　265
　monologue with invisible companion,
　　261
　stories of lynchings bring fear, 262
　verbal assault on Father John, 264
Keats, John, 3
Keller, Helen, 127
Kellner, Bruce
　biographical sketch, 302
　"Refined Racism: White Patronage in
　　Harlem Renaissance," 53–66
Kellogg, Paul, 126, 131, 175, 179
Kerlin, Robert T., 137
Kirschike, Amy Helene
　biographical sketch, 303
　"Pulse of the Negro World," 179–94
Knopf, Alfred, 17, 73
Knopf, Blanche, 17, 106
Koch, Frederich, 24
Kreymborg, Alfred, 255
Ku Klux Klan, 113, 114, 132, 244

"Lady, Lady" (Spencer), 232–33
Lafayette Theatre, 155

Laluah, Aqua, 228–29
Langston, John, 102
Larsen, Nella
    accused of plagiarism, 120–21
    biography fictitious, 141–42
    excelled in novel, 71
    Guggenheim Fellowship for Creative
        Writing, 207
    misunderstood but appreciated, 90
    second novel printed, 143
    themes of, 207–8, 251
Lawrence, D. H., 1, 2, 283
Lay My Burden Down (Botkin), 102–3
"Legacy of the Ancestral Arts" (Locke),
    181
Lemming, George, 177
"Letter to My Sister" (Spencer), 77, 232
Lewis (*Cane*), 258, 260
Lewis, David L.
    biographical sketch, 303
    on Georgia Johnson's salons, 93–94
    on New Negro project, 283
    "Reading the Harlem Renaissance,"
        123–48
    on Van Vechen, 62
Liberator (magazine), 127, 129
The Librarian (Reiss), 192
Lindsay, Vachel, 25, 70, 199
"Lines to a Nasturtium" (Spencer), 77
Littell, Robert, 255
Liveright, Horace, 126
Liza, 155
Locke, Alain, 54, 181
    biographical sketch, 302
    cultural pluralism and, 277
    homosexuality of, 72
    host at first awards dinner, 177
    on Hughes, 35
    influence of, 25, 25–26, 54, 167,
        180–81
    misogyny of, 71–72
    on "Negro fad," 13
    on "New Negro," 14–15, 118, 181
    patronage and, 56

philosophy of, 286
    on race relationships, 7, 116–17, 182
    Survey Graphic editor, 135, 181
Logan, Rayford, 177
Loggins, Vernon, 99
"Luani of the Jungles" (Hughes), 141
"Lullaby" (Laluah), 228–29
Lyles, Aubrey, 25, 128, 154
Lyrical Left, 127, 129

"Magalu" (Johnson, H.), 232
Malcolm X, 100
Marshall, Marjorie, 227, 228, 231
"Marxism and the Negro Problem" (Du
    Bois), 147
Masks, 245–46, 247
Mason, Charlotte Osgood, 56–59, 72,
    74, 119, 143, 145
Masses (magazine), 127, 145
May, Henry, 235
McCardle, Carl, 54
McClendon, Rose, 152
McKay, Claude
    criticisms of, 236
    exoticism and, 10, 29–30, 283
    literary output, 3, 73–74, 146, 147,
        251
    patronage and, 56
    poetic defiance of, 132, 169–70
    Sinclair Lewis and, 74–75
    a transplanted African American,
        170–71
McKay, Claude, works of. *See also Home
    to Harlem* (McKay)
    Banana Bottom, 146
    Banjo, 142–43, 146
    Color, 170
    Harlem Shadows, 74, 125, 129, 131
    "If We Must Die," 169
    "Outcast," 283
    "Spring in New Hampshire," 170
    "The Tropics in New York," 136
"Melanctha" (Stein), 25

"Memphis Blues" (Brown), 280
Mencken, H. L., 29, 54, 126, 128
Messinger, 68
"Middle Passage" (Hayden), 3
Millay, Edna St. Vincent, 70
Miller, Flourney, 25, 128, 154
Miller, Irving C., 155
Miller, Kelly, 173
Miller, Mae, 70
Mills, Florence, 124, 155, 158–59, 245
Mitchell, Loften, 250
The Modern Quarterly (Calverton, ed.),
    30
Modernism, 3, 285, 291–92
Modernism and the Harlem Renaissance
    (Baker, H.), 246
Molette, Carlton and Barbara, 248–49
"A Mona Lisa" (Grimké), 235
The Moon of the Caribbees (O'Neill), 152
Moss, Thylias, 4
Mother Africa, 282–84
Mule Bone (play) (Hughes and
    Hurston), 106, 145
Munson, Gorham, 255
Music. *See also Shuffle Along*
    black musicians, 25
    characteristics of African, 286
    in Harlem clubs, 251–52
    musical revues, 249–52
    spirituals, 277, 282
My Bondage (Douglass), 195
My Freedom (Douglass), 195

NAACP (National Association for the
    Advancement of Colored People),
    8, 40, 59, 60, 61, 68, 124, 125,
    132–33
Nail, John E., 150
Nance, Ethel Ray, 76, 126, 133
"Nat Turner" (Hayden), 3
Nathan, Jean, 128
The Nation (magazine), 119
National Committee for Political
    Prisoners, 59

"Nativity" (Hayford), 78
Negritude, 118
Negro (Cunard), 147
The Negro Author (Loggins), 99
"Negro Dancers" (Hughes), 48
Negro housing report (1931), 144
The Negro in an African Setting
    (Douglas), 282, 290–91
Negro-owned property, 149–50
Negro Renaissance. *See* Renaissance
Negrotarians, 134–35, 141
"Neighbors" (Spencer), 77
"New Negro," 7–8, 10, 130, 132, 136,
    138, 180–81
The New Negro (Locke)
    African art key to expression, 55, 181
    constructive participation urged, 164
    legacy from Renaissance, 147–48
    new social identity, 15, 117, 162
    phenomenon of change, 10, 13,
        160, 162
    spiritual emancipation, 161, 165
New Negro Arts Movement, 123–24,
    133, 182, 183, 184, 278–79
New Negro movement as project
    authenticity of Renaissance, 275–76
    definition of black form, 284–85
    definitions of identity, 276–78
    folk art to high art, 285–88
    imitation with a vengeance, 285
    Pan-African image, 279–84
    syncopated Renaissance, 288–92
    West Africa and primitivism, 281–84
    works of Renaissance artists, 278–84
Newsome, Effie Lee, 77, 224
Niagra Movement, 116
Nigger (Wood), 128
Nigger Heaven (Van Vechten). *See also*
    Van Vechten, Carl
    exoticism and, 10
    influence of, 14, 26, 29
    plot, 27–28
    reactions to, 18, 63–64, 138, 139, 251
"Nigger Jeff" (Dreiser), 128

"Niggerati," 121, 125, 134–35
Niggerati Manor, 139–40, 146
"No Images" (Cuney), 29
Nobody Knows My Name (Baldwin), 100
"Nostalgia" (Marshall), 227
Not Without Laughter (Hughes), 57, 59, 143
Novels, door-to-door, 196
"November Cotton Flower" (Toomer), 4
Nugent, Richard Bruce, 139, 146, 283
    See also Bruce, Richard
NUL. *See* Urban League

Odum, Howard, 25
Ogden, Kathy J., 251
"Old Black Men" (Johnson, G.), 86
Old Man (*Cane*), 264
One and One Makes Three (Johnson, G.), 82
One Way in Heaven (Cullen), 145
O'Neil, Raymond, 156
O'Neill, Eugene, 25, 126, 128, 152, 250
O'Neill, Eugene, works of
    All God's Chillin Got Wings, 156–58
    The Dreamy Kid, 152
    The Emperor Jones, 128, 152, 153, 250
    The Moon of the Caribbees, 152
Opportunity: A Journal of Negro Life, 8, 10, 68, 125, 142, 147, 224
Opportunity magazine awards dinners.
    See Awards by *Crisis* and
    Opportunity magazines
Our America (Frank), 129
"Outcast" (McKay), 283

Page, Thomas Nelson, 201
Page, Walter Hines, 201
Pan-African image
    Egyptian heritage debunked, 279–81
    West Africa and primitivism, 281–84
Pan-African movement, 192. *See also*
    Garvey, Marcus

Passing (Larsen)
    critical reviews, 216–17, 219
    plot, 215–19
    race constructs explored, 251
    second Larsen novel, 143, 211
Patronage. *See also specific names of patrons*
    Barnes, Albert C., 54–56
    double-bind of artists, 9, 119
    Mason, Charlotte Osgood, 56–59
    Spingarn, Arthur and Joel, 59–62
    Van Vechten, Carl, 62–65
    WPA Writers Project, 147, 198
Patterson, William, 59
The People, Yes (Sandburg), 3–4
Perry, Bliss, 83
Perry, Margaret
    biographical sketch, 301–2
    "The Shape and Shapers of the
    Movement," 13–22
Peterkin, Julia, 24
Picasso, Pablo, 24, 289
Pig-Foot Mary (Harlem character), 149
Plum Bun (Fauset), 142, 145, 260
Plumes (Johnson, G.), 82
"Poem" (Johnson, H.), 78
Pointing the Way (Griggs), 125
Popel, Esther, 229
Popoplikabu (Johnson, G.), 82
Porter, Cole, 27
Portraits of Negro Women (Reiss), 192
Primitivism. *See also* Exoticism;
    Iconography of Renaissance;
    Signifying Monkey
    Hurston and, 57
    overdetermined uses of, 290–91
    problems with, 53
    return to roots, 245
    in vogue, 24, 28–29, 68–69
    West Africa and, 281–84
    women writers and, 226–27
prizes, literary, 8, 133–37, 140, 173–77
Publishers and authors. *See* Authors and
    publishers

The Quality of Hart (Himes), 101

Quarles, Benjamin, 25, 177

The Quest of the Silver Fleece (Du Bois), 125

Quick, Charlotte Louise Vandevere. *See* Mason, Charlotte Osgood

Quicksand (Larsen)

  highly praised first novel, 74, 141–42, 143, 215

  plot, 208–14

  themes of, 208

Quicksand (Larsen), characters in. *See also* Helga Crane (*Quicksand*)

  Anne Grey, 211

  Audrey Denney, 211

  Axel Olsen, 212–13

  James Vayle, 209, 211

  Reverend Pleasant Green, 213

  Robert Anderson, 209, 211

Rachel (Grimké), 79

"Rainy Season Love Song" (Hayford), 78, 235

Randolph, Philip, 117

Red (Van Vechen), 62

Red Summer of 1919, 132–33

Redding, Saunders, 32, 177, 236

Reiss, Fritz Winold, 188

Reiss, Winold, 14, 180, 188–92

Reiss, Winold, works of

  A College Lad, 191

  Dawn in Harlem, 191

  Elise Johnson McDougald, 192

  Four Portraits of Negro Women, 192

  The Librarian, 192

  Portraits of Negro Women, 192

  Two Public School Teachers, 192

  A Woman Lawyer (Reiss), 190

"Remembrance" (Hayden), 3

Renaissance, 177. *See also* Iconography of Renaissance; New Negro movement as project; Patronage; Women writers

African art in favor, 173

  criticisms of, 8–10, 11, 236–37, 244, 284, 285, 290

  defined by color, 80–81

  Depression and, 10, 26, 36, 144–48

  end of the, 144–48

  foundation of, 5–7, 67–68, 167–68, 181

  homosexuality and, 72–73

  legacy of, 13, 95, 120, 147–48, 177–78

  male dominance of, 74–75

  political philosophy of, 10–11, 119

  postwar effects, 172

  search for identity, 284–85

  symbolic character of, 69

  "talented tenth" and, 60, 119

  three phases, 125–26, 138, 142

Reverend Pleasant Green (*Quicksand*), 213

Richardson, Willis, 69, 156

The Rider of Dreams (play) (Torrence), 128

Rising Tide of Color (Stoddard), 172

Robert Anderson (*Quicksand*), 209, 211

Robeson, Paul, 25, 128, 133, 156, 158, 183

Robinson, Bill, 245

Rogers, J. A., 191, 196

Rolland, Romain, 127

Rosenfeld, Paul, 255

Rosengarten, Theodore, 100

Rosenwold fellowships, 143, 144

Roumain, Jacques, 35

Rowan, Carl, 177

"Runagate Runagate" (Hayden), 3

Runnin' Wild, 69, 155, 156

Saffin, John, 99

"Sahdji" (Nugent), 283

Salome (Wilde), 156

Sandburg, Carl, 3–4, 131, 199

Sanhedrin (Kelly Miller's), 173

Sardeau, Helene, 57

Saunders, Gertrude, 154–55
Savage, Augusta, 69
Schuyler, George, 139, 143, 176, 196–97, 260, 292
"Scottsboro, Limited" (Hughes), 145
Self-Portrait (Johnson, M. G.), 285
Senghor, Léopold, 35
Seven Arts (magazine), 127
Shadow and Art (Ellison), 289
Shakespeare in Harlem (Hughes), 48–49
Shaw, Nate, 100, 110–11
Sheeler, Charles, 191
Sheldon, Edward, 24
Sherman, Joan, 234
Shuffle Along (Miller and Lyles, prod.)
  appeal for both blacks and whites, 249–50
  black control of, 128
  overshadowed other shows, 155
  popularized the Charleston, 124
  song hits of, 153–54
  symbol of black New York, 25
  whites enthralled by, 68–69
Signifyin(g), defined, 288
Signifying Monkey, 245–46
Simmelkjaer, Harold, 152
Simon the Cyrenian (play) (Torrence), 128
Sinclair, Upton, 196
Singh, Amritjit
  biographical sketch, 302
  "Black-White Symbiosis: Another Look at the Literary History of the 1920s," 23–34
Sissle, Noble, 154, 154–55
Smith, Bessie, 25, 88–89, 124, 245
Smith, Raymond
  biographical sketch, 302
  "Langston Hughes: Evolution of the Poetic Persona," 35–52
Smith, Sidonie, 100
"Smoke, Lillies and Jade!" (Nugent), 139
Sollors, Werner, 278

Song of the Towers (Douglas), 290
"Sonnet to a Negro in Harlem" (Johnson, H.), 77
"A Son's Return: 'Oh, Didn't He Ramble'" (Brown), 104
The Souls of Black Folk (Du Bois), 37, 127, 276
Southern Renaissance writers, 24
Spencer, Anne
  avoidance of sorrow, 82–83
  compared with Emily Dickinson, 223
  poetry of, 77, 227–28, 232–33
  race consciousness of, 70, 225
Spingarn, Amy, 60–61, 134, 143
Spingarn, Arthur, 59–60
Spingarn, Joel, 60–62, 134
Spingarn Medal recipients, 61–62, 124, 153
Spirituals, 277, 282
"Spring in New Hampshire" (McKay), 170
"Spunk" (Hurston), 288
The Star Spangled Hustle (Grant, R. L.), 99
Stein, Gertrude, 25, 27
Stella, Joseph, 191
Stepin Fetchit, 250
Stereotyping, Hollywood, 249–51
Stern, Harold E., 31
Stetson, Erlene, 226
Stewart, Jeffrey, 190
Stoddard, Lothrop, 172
Stowe, Harriet Beecher, 246
Stribling, T. S., 24, 128, 131
Sugar Hill, 144
Sullivan, Noel, 73
A Sunday Morning in the South (Johnson, G.), 82
From Superman to Man (Rogers), 191
"Suppliant" (Johnson G.), 86
Survey Graphic, 14–15, 126, 131, 171–192, 175, 179–80
Swartz, Patti Capel
  biographical sketch, 303

"Masks and Masquerade: The
    Iconography of the Harlem
    Renaissance," 243–54
"Sweat" (Hurston), vii, 1–2, 139
Symbiosis, defined, 23
Syncopation, defined, 286, 288, 289,
    291–92. *See also* Folk culture; Music

"Talented tenth," 60, 119, 123, 129, 130,
    132–33, 136, 181
Tango (dance), 155
Tanner, Henry O., 25, 123, 183
Tate, Allen, 33
"Tenebris" (Grimké), 86, 230
"The Atlanta Compromise"
    (Washington speech), 114–15
"The Black Finger" (Grimké), 94
"The Cat and the Saxophone"
    (Hughes), 48, 49
"The Creation" (Johnson), 287
"The Criteria of Negro Art" (Du Bois
    symposium), 140
"The Dilemma of Social Pattern"
    (Herskovits), 186–87
"The Making of Harlem" (Johnson),
    185
"The Mask" (Delaney), 233–34
"The Negro-Art Hokum" (Schuyler),
    139, 292
"The Negro Artist and the Racial
    Mountain" (Hughes), 10, 30, 138,
    139, 147, 292
"The Negro in Literature and Art" (Du
    Bois), 41
"The Negro Laughs Back" (Jenness),
    233
"The Negro Mind Reaches Out" (Du
    Bois), 281
"The Negro Speaks of Rivers"
    (Hughes), 35, 38, 39, 40, 49, 280
"The Serving Girl" (Hayford), 78
"The Song of the Smoke" (Du Bois), 41,
    81

"The South" (Hughes), 45
"The South Lingers On" (Fisher), 136
"The Stones of the Village" (Dunbar-
    Nelson), 83
"The Tropics in New York" (McKay),
    136
"The White Ones" (Hughes), 43–44
"The Wife-Woman" (Spencer), 77
"Theft" (Popel), 229
Their Eyes Were Watching God (Hurston),
    1–2, 288
There Is Confusion (Fauset), 126
"This Lofty Oak" (Dunbar-Nelson), 90
Thompson, Era Belle, 177
Thompson, Louise, 56, 58–59, 145
Thornton, Hortense, 213
Thurman, Wallace
    alcoholism of, 106–7
    The Blacker the Berry, 106, 142, 260
    conflicted on color, 81
    criticisms of movement, 28
    death of, 146
    editor of *Fire!!*, 41, 119, 138, 139
    Infants of the Spring, 146
    Louise Thompson and, 145
"Tin Roof Blues" (Brown), 287–88
"To a Dark Girl" (Bennett), 224
"To Certain Critics" (Cullen), 3
Tolson, Melvin B., 3
Toomer, Jean
    on being stereotyped, 30
    denied African American roots, 121,
        147
    meteoric talent of, 170
    music and, 267–68
    poetry of, 4, 45
    proponent of new ideas, 33
    short stories of, 129
    style of, 261
    talent for satire, 260
Torrence, Ridgely, 128
Tradition, African American. *See* Folk
    culture
Travel studies, 177–78

Trilling, Lionel, 197–98
Tropic Death (Walrond), 137
tour d'horizon (Johnson), 147
Tucker, Louella, 133
Turner, Darwin, 108
Two Public School Teachers (Reiss), 192

Uncle Tom's Cabin (Stowe), 246
Up from Slavery (Washington), 101, 114
Urban League, 8, 54, 68, 125, 132–33, 134, 179
To Usward (Bennett), 126, 174–75

Van Doren, Carl, 126–27, 176
Van Vechten, Carl. *See also In the Garrett* (Van Vechten); *Nigger Heaven* (Van Vechten)
    controversial figure, 62–63, 65, 145, 251
    influence of, 16, 18–19, 21, 25, 27, 62–63, 135
    James Weldon Johnson and, 62, 63
    parties of, 17–18, 71, 73, 107, 138
Vanity Fair, 27, 55, 124
Versailles Peace Conference, 181
Villa Lewaro, 144
Villard, Oswold Garrison, 126
Von Stuck, Franz, 189
"Voodoo's Revenge" (Walrond), 135

Wagner, Jean, 237
Walker, A'Lelia, 53, 70–71, 75, 138, 144
Walker Manufacturing Company, 75
Wall, Cheryl
    on Bessie Smith, 88
    biographical sketch, 303
    "Passing for What? Aspects of Identity in Nella Larsen's Novels," 207–21
The Walls of Jericho (Fisher), 56, 141
Walrond, Eric, 5, 27, 70, 133, 135, 137

Washington, Booker T.
    Age of Washington, 5–6
    conciliation policy, 113–15, 168–69
    popular appeal of, 116
    Up from Slavery, 101
Waters, Ethel, 27
The Ways of White Folks (Hughes), 56, 140
The Weary Blues (Hughes), 27, 35, 36, 37, 48, 73, 131, 171
"Wedding Day" (Bennett), 139
West Africa and primitivism, 281–84
West, Rebecca, 70
Wheatley, Phillis, 195
When Harlem Was in Vogue (Lewis), 62, 93–94
When the Melon is Ripe (Grant, D. T.), 99
Where I'm Bound (Smith, S.), 100
White America
    abolition and, 113
    black artists and, 9, 10, 11
    black-white symbiosis, 23
    curiosity of, 179
    misconceptions of blacks, 233
    Washington and, 6
White Men's Children (Johnson, G), 82
"White Things" (Spencer), 228
White, Walter, 25, 27, 29, 54, 63, 70, 126, 131, 140
Whitman, Walt, 39
The Wife of His Youth (Chesnutt), 83
Wilde, Oscar, 156
William and Ellen Craft (Johnson, G.), 82
Williams, Lucy Ariel, 71
Wilson, Frank, 152
Wilson, Woodrow, 181
A Woman Lawyer (Reiss), 190
Women writers. *See also* Dunbar-Nelson, Alice; Grimké, Angelina Weld; Johnson, Georgia Douglas
    anger revealed in works, 233–34
    assets to Renaissance, 67–68, 70–71, 94–95, 237–38

compared with blueswomen, 88
criticisms of, 234–36, 236–37
European traditions and, 236–37
gender bias and, 71, 74–75, 87, 93,
 223–24, 236
genres other than poetry, 89–90
poetry and, 77–79, 223, 237
quest for identity, 237
race consciousness of, 224–25
restrained treatment of sex, 86, 88–89
self-publishing and, 91–92

socialization of, 75
 themes of, 226–32, 233
 youthfulness at premium, 76–77
Wood, Clement, 128, 135
Woodburn, Harry, 25
Woodruff, Hale, 25
WPA Writers Project, 102, 147, 198
Wright, Jay, 4
Wright, Richard, 99, 101, 147, 177, 200

Young, Kathleen Tannkersley, 235